STRATEGIC PLANNING FOR PUBLIC AND NONPROFIT ORGANIZATIONS

STRATEGIC PLANNING FOR PUBLIC AND NONPROFIT ORGANIZATIONS

A Guide to Strengthening and Sustaining Organizational Achievement

REVISED EDITION

John M. Bryson

Jossey-Bass Publishers
San Francisco

Substantial discounts on bulk quantities of Jossey-Bass books are available to corporations, professional associations, and other organizations. For details and discount information, contact the special sales department at Jossey-Bass Inc., Publishers. (415) 433–1740; Fax (800) 605–2665.

www.josseybass.com

Manufactured in the United States of America.

Credits are on p. 325.

Library of Congress Cataloging-in-Publication Data

Bryson, John M. (John Moore), 1947–
     Strategic planning for public and nonprofit organizations : a
guide to strengthening and sustaining organizational achievement /
John M. Bryson. — Rev. ed.
         p.   cm. — (A Joint publication in the Jossey-Bass public
administration series, and the Jossey-Bass nonprofit sector series)
     Includes bibliographical references (p.   ) and index.
     ISBN 0-7879-0141-5
     1. Strategic planning.   2. Nonprofit organizations—Management.
3. Public administration.   I. Title.   II. Series: Jossey-Bass
public administration series.   III. Series: Jossey-Bass nonprofit
sector series.
     HD30.28.B79   1995
     658.4′012—dc20   95-22313

REVISED EDITION
HB Printing   10 9 8 7 6

CONTENTS

PREFACE

How can the leaders and managers of public and nonprofit organizations cope with the challenges that confront them, now and in the years ahead? How should they respond to the increasingly uncertain and interconnected environments in which their organizations operate? How should these leaders respond to dwindling or unpredictable resources; new public expectations or formal mandates; demographic changes; deregulation or reregulation; upheavals in international, national, state, and local economies; and new roles for public, nonprofit, and business organizations? What should their organizations' mission be? How can they build on organizational strengths and take advantage of opportunities while minimizing organizational weaknesses and overcoming threats to their existence? How can they formulate desirable strategies and implement them effectively? These are the questions this book addresses.

Scope

Strategic Planning for Public and Nonprofit Organizations is based on the premise that leaders and managers of public and nonprofit organizations must be effective strategists if their organizations are to fulfill their missions, meet their mandates, and satisfy their constituents in the years ahead. These leaders and managers will need to exercise as much discretion as possible in the areas under their control. They need to develop effective strategies to cope with changed and changing circumstances, and they need to develop a coherent and defensible basis for their decisions.

Strategic planning is a set of concepts, procedures, and tools designed to assist leaders and managers with these tasks. Indeed, strategic planning may be defined as a disciplined effort to produce fundamental decisions and actions that shape and guide what an organization (or other entity) is, what it does, and why it does it. In the past thirty-five years, strategic planning has become a standard part of management thinking and practice in the business world. Only in the last ten to fifteen years, however, has strategic planning become the standard practice of large numbers of public and nonprofit organizations.

The first edition of this book played an important role in promoting the use of strategic planning by public and nonprofit organizations. The practice of strategic planning has since progressed substantially, and new areas of concern have emerged. Thus, while this revised and expanded edition covers the same topics as the first edition, it also focuses on additional areas requiring special attention. New chapters attend to implementation, reassessing strategies and the strategic planning process, and key leadership roles that must be played if strategic planning is to succeed. (Two chapters have been dropped. The first reviewed the variety of approaches to strategic planning—mostly developed in the private sector—that have influenced the development of strategic planning in the public and nonprofit sectors. This was dropped because it has become somewhat "old news" as experience with strategic planning in public and nonprofit organizations has grown. The second focused on various barriers to implementing strategic planning and strategies. These insights have been incorporated throughout the second edition, obviating the need for a separate chapter.)

The second edition thus reflects a major trend in the field by blending leadership, strategic planning, and management in a more explicit way. People realize that strategic planning is no substitute for leadership. Instead, strategic planning comprises a set of concepts, procedures, and tools that can help leaders and followers enhance organizational (and community) achievement. People also realize that it is not enough just to think—organizations must act as well. And it is not enough just to decide what to do and how to do it—the doing matters, too. Indeed, sometimes the acting and doing must come first, before people will know what they should think and choose. Of course, these points were all emphasized in the first edition, but they are stressed even more in this edition. The result is a book that is as much about strategic *management* as about strategic *planning*. I have kept the original title, however, because of the recognition and following the first edition achieved.

Said differently, in this edition there is a renewed emphasis on the fact that strategic planning is *not* the same as strategic thinking and acting. What matters most is strategic thinking and acting. Strategic planning is useful only if it improves strategic thought and action; it is not a substitute for them. The reader should keep in mind that the formation, or realization, of strategies in practice comes from a variety of sources (the vision of new leaders, intuition, group learning, innovation, what already works, chance) and that strategic planning is only one of them. Wise strategic thought and action takes all of these sources into account. As Mintzberg (1994b, p. 367) notes, "Strategy formation cannot be helped by people blind to the richness of its reality."

Specifically, this book

- Reviews the reasons public and nonprofit organizations (and communities) should embrace strategic planning as a way of improving their performance.
- Presents an effective strategic planning (and management) process that has been successfully used by a large number of public and nonprofit organizations. The approach, called the Strategy Change Cycle, enhances the process presented in the first edition with added attention to reviewing and adopting plans, implementing plans, and reassessing strategies and the strategic planning process.
- Offers detailed guidance on applying the process, including information on specific tools and techniques that might prove useful in various circumstances.
- Discusses the major roles that must be played by various individuals and groups for strategic planning to work and gives guidance on how to play those roles.
- Clarifies the various ways in which strategic planning may be institutionalized so that strategic thought and action are encouraged and embraced across an entire organization.
- Includes many new examples of successful and unsuccessful strategic planning practices.
- Relates the entire discussion to relevant research and literature.

Audience

This book is written for two main groups. The first consists of elected and appointed policy makers, managers, and planners in governments, public agencies, and nonprofit organizations who are responsible for and want to learn more about strategic planning. The book will help them understand what strategic planning is and how to apply it in their own organizations and, to a lesser extent, their communities. Thus, the book speaks to city council members, mayors, city managers, administrators, and planners; sheriffs, police, fire chiefs, and their staffs; school board members, administrators, and staff; county commissioners, administrators, and planners; governors, state cabinet secretaries, administrators, and planners; legislators; chief executive officers, chief administrative officers, and chief financial officers; executive directors, deputy directors, and unit directors; presidents and vice presidents; elected and appointed officials of governments and public agencies; and boards of directors of nonprofit organizations.

The second major audience consists of academics and students of strategic planning. Courses on strategic planning and management are now typically offered in schools of public affairs, public administration, planning, and public policy. This book offers participants in these courses a useful blend of theory and practice.

Others who will find the book interesting are businesspeople and citizens interested in increasing their understanding of how to improve the operations of governments, public agencies, and nonprofit organizations. To a lesser extent, the book is also intended to help these individuals understand and improve their communities.

Overview of the Contents

Part One introduces the reader to the dynamics of strategic planning. Chapter One introduces the concept of strategic planning and why such planning is important for governments, public agencies, nonprofit organizations, and communities. Attention is focused on strategic planning for (1) public agencies, departments, or major organizational divisions, (2) general-purpose governments, (3) nonprofit organizations, (4) services, such as transportation, health care, and education, that bridge organizational and governmental boundaries, (5) interorganizational networks, and (6) entire communities, urban or metropolitan areas, regions, or states seen as economic, social, and political entities.

Benefits of strategic planning are emphasized, as are the conditions under which strategic planning should *not* be undertaken. In this chapter, I also argue that public and nonprofit strategic planning is an innovation that is here to stay. The reason is that—at its best—strategic planning can accommodate both substantive *and* political rationality. That is, it can produce substantively desirable *and* politically acceptable changes. Finally, readers will be introduced to four organizations whose experience with strategic planning is used throughout this book to illustrate key points. The four include three public organizations (a school district, a public library, and a federal program) and one nonprofit organization (a church).

In Chapter Two, I present my preferred approach to strategic planning, which I call the Strategy Change Cycle. The approach has been used effectively by a large number of governments, public agencies, and nonprofit organizations in the United States, Canada, and the United Kingdom and, indeed, has been applied successfully on every continent. (Readers of the first edition will note that the Strategy Change Cycle in this revised edition differs from the process outlined previously. The new process combines the external and internal assessments into a single step and adds three new steps—7, 9, and 10.) Chapters Three through Ten, which make up Part Two, describe in detail how to apply the approach.

Chapter Three covers the initial agreement, or "plan for planning," phase of the strategic planning process. Chapter Four focuses on identification of mandates and the clarification of mission and values. Chapter Five addresses the assessment of an organization's external and internal environments. Chapter Six discusses strategic issues—what they are, how they can be identified, and how to critique them. Chapter Seven is devoted to the development of effective strategies and plans, along with their review and adoption. Chapter Eight covers the development of the organization's "vision of success," that is, what the organization should look like after it fulfills its mission and achieves its full potential. Chapter Nine attends to developing an effective implementation process. Chapter Ten covers reassessment of strategies and the strategic planning process as a prelude to a new round of strategic planning. Chapters Three through Seven thus emphasize the planning aspects of the Strategy Change Cycle, while Chapters Eight through Ten highlight the management aspects.

Part Three includes two chapters designed to help leaders understand what they will need to do to get started with strategic planning and to make it work. Chapter Eleven covers the many leadership roles and responsibilities necessary for the exercise of effective strategic leadership for public and nonprofit organizations. These roles include sponsoring, championing, and facilitating the strategic planning process in such a way that an organization's situation is clearly understood, wise decisions are made and implemented, residual conflicts are handled well, and the organization is prepared for the next round of strategy change. Chapter Twelve assesses the strategic planning experiences of the four organizations used as examples throughout the text. This chapter also provides guidance on how to begin strategic planning.

Five resource sections are included at the end of the text. Resource A presents a model external scanning process. Resource B provides a review of selected literature relevant to strategic issue identification. Resource C provides process guidelines for using "ovals" to develop "strategic issues maps" and advice on how they can be converted into "strategy maps." Other uses for the "oval mapping process" are covered as well. In Resource D, I review selected literature related to potential strategies for public and nonprofit organizations. And Resource E presents some useful concepts related to developing a vision of success.

Strategic Planning for Public and Nonprofit Organizations will provide most of the guidance that leaders, managers, and planners need to engage in a strategic planning process aimed at making their organizations (and communities) more effective and responsive to their environments. This book reveals a simple yet effective strategic planning process designed specifically for public and nonprofit organizations, detailed advice on how to apply the process, and examples of its application. The entire exposition is grounded in the relevant research and literature, so readers will know where the process fits in with prior research and practice and can gain added insight on how to apply the process.

Companion Workbook

Many readers of the first edition expressed a desire to have a companion workbook to help groups and organizations work through the nuts and bolts of the strategic planning process. I have teamed with Farnum Alston, a highly skilled and experienced consultant, to coauthor *Creating and Implementing Your Strategic Plan: A Workbook for Public and Nonprofit Organizations* (1995).

The workbook is designed primarily to help those who are relatively new to strategic planning guide themselves through the Strategy Change Cycle. In doing so, it expands considerably on the simple strategic planning worksheets included at the back of the first edition of *Strategic Planning for Public and Nonprofit Organizations* (not included in this edition). The workbook, however, is clearly not a substitute for this book. Effective strategic planning is an art that involves thoughtful tailoring to specific contexts. *Strategic Planning for Public and Nonprofit Organizations* provides considerable guidance on how to think about the tailoring process, including many process guidelines, caveats, and case examples. Thus, the book should be read before the workbook is used, and the book should be consulted on a regular basis throughout the course of a Strategy Change Cycle.

Minneapolis, Minnesota   John M. Bryson
July 1995

ACKNOWLEDGMENTS FOR
THE REVISED EDITION

Space limitations prevent me from rethanking by name all those who contributed to the first edition of this book. They should all rest assured, however, that I remain deeply grateful to them for their insights and thoughtfulness and for the help they gave me in gaining the experience and understanding necessary to write that book.

There is space, however, for me to thank the people who contributed their insights, advice, and support to the revised edition. My deepest thanks and appreciation must go to Colin Eden and Fran Ackermann, two colleagues at the University of Strathclyde in Glasgow, Scotland, and to Charles Finn, my close colleague at the Humphrey Institute. The four of us have been carrying on a dialogue about strategic public and nonprofit management for years, and this "continuing seminar" has been one of the most significant sources of my own learning. The fact that our discussions take place onboard Colin's sloop *Inshalla* in the Hebrides, on ski slopes in the Alps, in U.S. National Parks, while canoeing and camping in the Boundary Waters Canoe Area in northern Minnesota, and in other spectacular places only heightens the enjoyment, liveliness, and learning that occurs.

A number of academic colleagues (many of whom are also skilled consultants and practitioners) at various institutions in the United States and the United Kingdom have contributed to the revised edition through their writing and conversations with me. These include Stu Albert, Bob Backoff, Michael Barzelay, Kim Boal, Herman ("Buzz") Boschken, Barry Bozeman, Phil Bromiley, Andre Delbecq, Tim Delmont, Jane Dutton, Norman Flynn, John Forester, Lee Frost-Kumpf, Arie Halachmi, Patsy Healey, Chris Huxham, Judy Innes, Jerry Kaufman,

Paul Light, Jeff Luke, Seymour Mandelbaum, Brint Milward, Henry Mintzberg, Barry Nochs, Paul Nutt, Michael Patton, Ted Poister (who provided valuable commentary on the first draft of the second edition), Scott Poole, Hal Rainey, Sue Richards, Peter Ring, Nancy Roberts, Melissa Stone, Bernard Taylor, Andy Van de Ven, Bart Wechsler, and many others.

A number of practitioners have also provided immense help. I am reminded of the old adage, "A practitioner is a theorist who pays a price for being wrong." These thoughtful, public-spirited, good-hearted friends and colleagues have shared with me their hard-won insights and have provided invaluable knowledge and encouragement necessary to produce the revised edition. They include, of course, Bob Einsweiler, a friend for eighteen years and a former colleague at the Humphrey Institute (who also provided a very detailed commentary on the first draft of the second edition). I have learned more about strategic planning from Bob than from anyone else, and as far as I am concerned, he is simply the best in the business. He is now director of research at the Lincoln Institute of Land Policy in Cambridge, Massachusetts.

They also include Farnum Alston, a friend for twenty years and my coauthor for *Creating and Implementing Your Strategic Plan: A Workbook for Public and Nonprofit Organizations,* the companion piece to this book. Farnum has an incredible wealth of insights and experience gained as a political appointee to former governor Pat Lucey in Wisconsin (where we first met), as a high-ranking federal civil servant, and as head of Peat-Marwick's national consulting practice for strategic planning in the public sector. Farnum now heads The Resources Company, a strategic planning and management consulting firm located in Corte Madera, California.

Other practitioners who deserve special thanks for advancing my knowledge of strategic planning include Paul Armknecht, Bryan Barry, Ethel Bright, Doug Eadie (who also provided thoughtful, detailed commentary on the first draft), Phil Eckhert, Bill Gaslin, Vonnie Hagen, Lee Harness, Lonnie Helgeson, Kathy Huyens, Anne Spray Kinney, Jack Kurps, Dan McLaughlin, Tony Mounts, David O'Fallon, David Riemer, Jim Scheibel, Randy Schenkat, Julie Smendzuik-O'Brien, Kathy Stack, Gerry Steenberg, Bev Stein, Phyllis Sutton, Bob Terry (a former colleague at the Humphrey Institute), Marybeth Tschetter, and Carole Williams.

For many years, I have served as a strategic planning consultant to various health and social service organizations in Northern Ireland, and I would like to thank several people there who have been especially helpful. These include David Bingham, Richard Black, Tom Frawley, Pat Haines, Stephen Hodkinson, John Hunter, Janet Kells (now in England), Pat Kinder, Eric McCullough, Hilary McCullough, William McKee, Bob Moore, Joan O'Hagen, Gabriel Scalley and Rona Campbell (who have now moved to England), and Brian White. The opportunity to work over a long period of time on strategic planning projects in a different country, in a sector undergoing radical change, and in especially difficult political circumstances has immeasurably improved my understanding of both the limits and possibilities of strategic planning. Since most of my ancestors came from Ulster, it has also afforded me the opportunity to reconnect with important cultural roots and to meet warm and wonderful distant relatives I did not know I had. I also would like to thank the late Jim Maguire, Ronnie Mackrell, and Philip Anderson, who first brought me to Northern Ireland under the auspices of the Public Service Training Council. Other British colleagues who have been very helpful include Andrew Ironside and Tony Lavender of David Salomon's Centre in Tunbridge Wells, England.

Several people have helped me sharpen my ideas and presentations and offer them to a broad audience of practitioners. I would like to thank in particular Jeff Luke (already mentioned) and Joyce Ray of the Pacific Program for State and Local Government and Nonprofit Executives, sponsored by the University of Oregon; Karl Kurtz of the National Conference of State Legislatures and John Brandl of the Humphrey Institute, for their work in putting on the yearly Legislative Staff Management Institute; Tanis Salant of the Southwest County Executive Program, sponsored by the University of Arizona; Tim Delmont (already mentioned), head of the University of Minnesota's Administrative Development Program; Dick Grefe of the University of Minnesota's Department of Professional Development and Conferences; two people who made me a regular presenter at the British Civil Service College—Pat Carvel (now at the British Broadcasting Corporation) and Liz Mellon (now at the London Business School); and Norman Flynn (already mentioned), who heads the Public Sector Management Programme of the London School of Economics and Political Science.

At the Humphrey Institute, I would like to thank, in addition to those already mentioned, Dean Ed Schuh, Sharon Anderson of the Reflective Leadership Center, Dick Bolan, Barbara Lukermann, and my always helpful secretary, Donna Kern, for their help and support.

I must express deep gratitude to the many readers who gave me valuable feedback on the first edition. I am also grateful to William Least Heat-Moon (1982, p. 365) for pointing out that the correct source for the quote that begins Chapter Three was General John B. Stedman, a Rhode Island militia officer during the Dorr Rebellion of 1842. I mistakenly attributed the quote to Union general George Stedman in the book's first edition and had the wording somewhat wrong as well.

Most of the revised edition was written while I was on sabbatical leave in Oxford, England, for the 1993–94 academic year. While there, I was a visiting professor at three institutions. I would like to thank all the personnel in the Department of Management Science at the University of Strathclyde in Glasgow, Scotland, where I commuted regularly, for their hospitality. I would like to thank the faculty of the School of Planning at Oxford Brookes University for a most enjoyable stay. John Glasson, the school's head, and Basil Dimitrou, Chris Minay, Michael Thomas, and Riki Thorival were especially welcoming. And I would like to thank Sir David Cox, David Miller, Andy Hurrell, and especially Jim Sharpe and Byron Shafer for welcoming me at Nuffield College of Oxford University.

Sabbatical leaves are marvelous things, and I plan to take every one I can—hoping each will be as enjoyable as this last one was.

Some of the material in this book appeared elsewhere, and I would like to thank the editors and publishers of these earlier publications for allowing revised versions to be printed here. Parts of Chapter One appeared in the *Journal of the American Planning Association* (Bryson and Einsweiler, 1987; Bryson and Roering, 1987) and in a book I coedited with Bob Einsweiler (Bryson and Einsweiler, 1988). Parts of Chapter Seven appeared in *Public Money and Management* (Bryson, 1988a). Slightly different versions of Chapters Nine, Ten, and Eleven appeared in Bryson and Crosby (1992).

I would like to offer a special thanks to my father, Jim Bryson, for helping me understand from an early age what strategic thinking and acting are all about. Neither he nor I realized it at the time, but his taking me hunting and fishing, introducing me to canoeing (at which I would achieve major success as a young adult in whitewater competition), encouraging me to be adventurous, accepting that I often disagreed with him in fundamental ways, and especially, talking with me about how he addressed issues in his very successful business career all were seeds that in part grew into this book. In addition, he has taught me by example about the traditional virtues of wisdom, hard work, patience, courage, and a certain stoicism in the face of adversity. I seek these same virtues in colleagues when I begin any new strategy change effort.

Three people at Jossey-Bass have been particularly helpful with the revised edition: my editor, Alan Shrader, and Susan Williams and Noelle Graney. As a team, they have offered a superb blend of encouragement, insight, and editorial skill. Finally, I must thank my spouse, Barbara Crosby, and our two wonderful children, John Kee Crosby Bryson and Jessica Ah-Reum Crosby Bryson, for their love, support, understanding, intelligence, and good humor. Barbara is my best friend and closest advisor, and has also taught me a great deal about leadership and strategic planning. She is also a skilled editor whose deft hand can be seen throughout the pages of this book. Our sabbatical year in England was an especially good one for us as a family. Not only did I get to write most of this book, but we got to spend more time with one another in Oxford and elsewhere, including marvelous vacations in Shropshire, Wales, France, and Switzerland. If the book also helps make the world a better place, my efforts will have been more than repaid!

J. M. B.

THE AUTHOR

John M. Bryson is professor of planning and public affairs at the University of Minnesota's Hubert H. Humphrey Institute of Public Affairs. He also directs the Center for Information Technology and Group Decision Support, a research and service center established at the institute in 1991. From 1983 to 1989, he was associate director of the university's Strategic Management Research Center. He was a visiting professor at the London Business School for the 1986–87 academic year. During the 1993–94 academic year, he was a visiting professor in the Department of Management Science, University of Strathclyde; the School of Planning, Oxford Brookes University; and Nuffield College, Oxford University. He received his B.A. degree (1969) in economics from Cornell University and three degrees from the University of Wisconsin, Madison: an M.A. degree (1972) in public policy and administration, an M.S. degree (1974) in urban and regional planning (1974), and a Ph.D. degree (1978) in urban and regional planning.

Bryson's interests include public leadership and policy change, strategic planning, project planning, implementation, evaluation, and organizational design. His research explores ways to improve the theory and practice of policy change and planning, particularly through situationally sensitive approaches. He has received numerous awards for his work, including the 1978 General Electric Award for Outstanding Research in Strategic Planning from the Academy of Management, and awards for best articles in the *Journal of the American Planning Association* and the *Journal of Planning Education and Research*. He is the coauthor (with Barbara C. Crosby) of *Leadership for the Common Good* (Jossey-Bass, 1992), which received the Terry McAdam Award for "outstanding contribution to the advancement of the nonprofit sector" and was named Best Book of 1992–93 by the Public and

Nonprofit Sector Division of the Academy of Management. He is the editor of *Strategic Planning for Public Service and Nonprofit Organizations* (1993) and coeditor (with R. C. Einsweiler) of *Strategic Planning—Threats and Opportunities for Planners* (1988) and *Shared Power: What Is It? How Does It Work? How Can We Make It Work Better?* (1991).

Bryson has been a regular presenter in many practitioner-oriented training programs, including the Pacific Program for State and Local Government and Nonprofit Executives, sponsored by the University of Oregon; the Legislative Staff Management Institute, sponsored by the National Conference of State Legislatures and the Humphrey Institute; the Southwest County Leadership Program, sponsored by the University of Arizona; the Public Sector Management Programme of the London School of Economics and Political Science; and management programs of the British Civil Service College.

He has served as a strategic planning and leadership consultant to a wide variety of public, nonprofit, and for-profit organizations. He is president of Realizations, Inc., a Minneapolis-based leadership and strategic planning consulting firm.

STRATEGIC PLANNING FOR PUBLIC AND NONPROFIT ORGANIZATIONS

PART ONE

UNDERSTANDING THE DYNAMICS OF STRATEGIC PLANNING

The environments of public and non-profit organizations have become not only increasingly uncertain in recent years but also more tightly interconnected; thus, changes anywhere reverberate unpredictably—and often chaotically and dangerously—throughout the society. This increased uncertainty and interconnectedness requires a threefold response from public and nonprofit organizations (and from communities as well). First, organizations must think strategically as never before. Second, they must translate their insights into effective strategies to cope with their changed circumstances. Third, they must develop the rationales necessary to lay the groundwork for adopting and implementing their strategies.

Strategic planning can help leaders and managers of public and nonprofit organizations think and act strategically. Chapter One introduces strategic planning, its potential benefits, and some of its limitations. It also discusses what strategic

planning is not and in what circumstances it is probably not appropriate. It also presents my views on why strategic planning is an innovation that is here to stay in the public and nonprofit sectors—because of its capacity, at its best, to incorporate both substantive and political rationality. The chapter concludes by introducing four organizations that have used a strategic planning process to produce significant changes. Their experiences will be used throughout the book to illustrate the dynamics of strategic planning.

Part One concludes with an overview of my preferred strategic planning process (Chapter Two). The process was designed specifically to help public and nonprofit organizations (and communities) think and act strategically. The process, called the Strategy Change Cycle, is typically very fluid, iterative, and dynamic in practice, but it nonetheless allows for a reasonably orderly, participative, and effective approach to determining how to achieve what is best for an organization. Chapter Two also highlights several process design issues that will be addressed throughout the book.

A key point to be emphasized again and again is that it is strategic *thinking and* *acting* that are important, not strategic planning. Indeed, if any particular approach to strategic planning gets in the way of strategic thought and action, that planning approach should be scrapped! ◆

CHAPTER ONE

WHY STRATEGIC PLANNING IN PUBLIC AND NONPROFIT ORGANIZATIONS IS MORE IMPORTANT THAN EVER

Usually, the main problem with life conundrums is that we don't bring to them enough imagination.

THOMAS MOORE, *CARE OF THE SOUL*

Leaders and managers of governments, public agencies of all sorts, nonprofit organizations, and communities face difficult challenges in the years ahead. Upheaval and change surround them. Consider, for example, several events and trends of the past two decades: demographic changes, shifts in values, increased interest-group activism, the privatization of public services, tax levy limits, tax indexing, unfunded federal and state mandates, shifts in federal and state responsibilities and funding priorities, a volatile global economy, and the increased importance of the nonprofit sector. Organizations that want to survive and prosper must respond to these changes. Their response may be to do what they have always done, only better; it may also involve important shifts in organizational focus and action. While organizations typically experience long periods of relative stability, they also typically encounter periods of rapid change (Gersick, 1991; Land and Jarman, 1992; Mintzberg, 1994a, 1994b). These periods of organizational change can be exciting, but they can also be anxiety-producing—or even terrifying. As paleontologist Stephen Jay Gould notes, "Life seems to be characterized by long stretches of boredom punctuated by periods of intense terror."

These environmental and organizational changes are aggravated by the increased interconnectedness of the world. Changes anywhere typically result in changes elsewhere (Luke, 1989, 1991). This increased interconnectedness is perhaps most apparent in the blurring of three traditionally important distinctions—between domestic and international spheres; between policy areas; and between public, private, and nonprofit sectors (Cleveland, 1973, 1985; Nutt and Backoff, 1992; Osborne and Gaebler, 1992). These changes have become dramatically apparent since the mid seventies. During the 1973 and 1978 oil embargoes, it became obvious that the U.S. economy is part of a world economy and that events abroad have domestic repercussions. The completion of the General Agreement on Tariffs and Trade (GATT) in 1992 will eventually further integrate the U.S. economy with the rest of the world. And in a stunning about-face for those of us who grew up in the shadow of *Sputnik*, key elements of our current economic policy—reducing the national debt and converting the U.S. away from military production—have become tied not to *countering* Russia but to *cooperating* with her and other former communist states. If these nations fail in their attempts to convert to democracy and a free market economy, we may have no choice but to rebuild our arms budget and scale back our domestic ambitions.

Distinctions between policy areas are also hard to maintain. For example, educational reform is touted as a type of industrial policy, to help U.S. firms cope more effectively with foreign competition. Strengthening the economy will not eliminate government human service costs, but letting it falter will certainly increase them. The connections between national industrial or full employment policies and local economic development are obvious. Finally, the boundaries between public, private, and nonprofit sectors have eroded. Sovereignty, for example, is increasingly "farmed out." Taxes are not collected by government tax collectors but are withheld by private and nonprofit organizations from their employees and turned over to the government. The nation's health, education, and welfare are a public responsibility, yet increasingly, we rely on private and nonprofit organizations for the production of services in these areas. Weapons systems are not produced in government arsenals but by private industry. When such fundamental public functions as tax collection; health, education, and welfare services; and weapons production are handled by the private and nonprofit sectors, then surely the boundaries between public, private, and nonprofit sectors are irretrievably blurred.

The blurring of these boundaries means that we have moved to a world in which no one organization or institution is fully in charge, and yet many are involved or affected or have a partial responsibility to act (Bryson and Einsweiler, 1991; Bryson and Crosby, 1992). This increased jurisdictional ambiguity requires public and nonprofit organizations (and communities) to think and act strategically as never before. Strategic planning is designed to help them do so. The extensive experience of public, nonprofit, and private organizations with strategic planning in recent decades yields a rich storehouse of advice on how to apply strategic planning. We will draw on this storehouse throughout this book.

Purpose and Benefits of Strategic Planning

What is strategic planning? Drawing on Olsen and Eadie (1982), I define strategic planning as a disciplined effort to produce fundamental decisions and actions that shape and guide what an organization is, what it does, and why it does it. To deliver the best results, strategic planning requires broad yet effective information gathering, development and exploration of strategic alternatives, and an emphasis on future implications of present decisions. Strategic planning can help facilitate communication and participation, accommodate divergent interests and values, foster wise and reasonably analytic decision making, and promote successful implementation. In short, at its best strategic planning can prompt in organizations the kind of imagination—and commitment—that psychotherapist and theologian Thomas Moore thinks are necessary to deal with individuals' life conundrums.

Most work on strategic planning in this century has focused on for-profit organizations. Until the early 1980s, strategic planning in the public sector was applied primarily to military organizations and the practice of statecraft on a grand scale (Quinn, 1980; Bracker, 1980).

It can be applied, however, to a number of public and nonprofit organizations as well, as we shall see throughout this book. Specifically, strategic planning can be applied to

- Public agencies and their departments or other major organizational divisions
- General-purpose governments, such as city, county, state, or tribal governments
- Nonprofit organizations that provide what are essentially public services
- Organizations providing specific services—such as transportation, health, or education—which bridge organizational and governmental boundaries
- Interorganizational networks in the public and nonprofit sectors
- Entire communities, urban or metropolitan areas, or regions or states

This book concentrates on strategic planning for public and nonprofit organizations; its applications for communities and services that bridge organizational boundaries are considered as well, in lesser detail. (Please note that the term *community* is used throughout the book to refer to communities, urban or metropolitan areas, and regions or states.) While the process detailed in this book is applicable to all the entities listed above, we must keep in mind how the specifics of its implementation might differ for each one. When strategic planning is focused on an organization, it is likely that most of the key decision makers will be "insiders" (although considerable relevant information may be gathered from "outsiders"). Certainly this is true of public agencies, local governments, and nonprofit organizations that deliver "public" services. When most of the key decision makers are insiders, it will likely be easier to get people together to decide important matters, reconcile differences, and coordinate implementation activities. (Of course, whether or not an organization's governing body consists of insiders or outsiders may be an open question, particularly if they are publicly elected. For instance, are the members of a city council insiders, outsiders, or both? Regardless of the answer, it remains true that a major proportion of the key decision makers for the whole organization will be insiders.)

In contrast, when strategic planning is focused on a function—often crossing organizational or governmental boundaries—or on a community, almost all of the key decision makers will be outsiders. In these situations, the focus of attention will be on how to organize collective thought and action within an interorganizational network in which no one person, group, organization, or institution is fully in charge. It will likely be more difficult to organize an effective strategic planning process in such a "shared-power" context (Bryson and Einsweiler, 1991). More time will need to be spent organizing forums for discussion, involving diverse constituencies, negotiating agreements in existing or new arenas, and coordinating the activities and actions of numerous relatively independent people, groups, organizations, and institutions (Bryson and Crosby, 1992; Kemp, 1993).

Organizations engage in strategic planning for many reasons. Proponents of strategic planning typically try to persuade their colleagues with one or more of the following kinds of statements (Barry, 1986; Nutt and Backoff, 1992):

"We face so many conflicting demands, we need a process for figuring out our priorities."

"We need to clarify what we do well so that we can do it better, and we also need to figure out what we should be doing that is new."

"We have a total quality management program under way, and now we are being asked to 'reinvent' and 'reengineer' ourselves as well. How can we make sure all of this effort is headed in the right direction?"

"We can expect a severe budget deficit next year unless we drastically rethink the way we do business."

"A number of private-sector competitors are going after our clients; we have to figure out a way to meet the competition."

"Issue x is staring us in the face. We need some way to help us think about its resolution, or else we will be badly hurt."

"Our funders [or board of directors] have asked us to prepare a strategic plan."

"We need to integrate or coordinate better the services we provide with those of other organizations."

"We know a leadership change is coming, and we want to prepare for it."

"We want to use strategic planning to educate, involve, and revitalize our board and staff."

"Our organization has an embarrassment of riches, but we still need to figure out how we can have the biggest impact; we owe it to our stakeholders."

"Everyone is doing strategic planning these days; we'd better do it, too."

Regardless of why public and nonprofit organizations engage in strategic planning, similar benefits are likely to result. Many authors have argued that strategic planning can produce a number of different benefits for organizations (Steiner, 1979; Barry, 1986; Koteen, 1989; Mercer, 1991; Nutt and Backoff, 1992; Berry and Wechsler, 1995). The first and perhaps most obvious potential benefit is the promotion of strategic thought and action. This in turn leads to more systematic information gathering about the organization's external and internal environment and various actors' interests, heightened attention to organizational learning, clarification of the organization's future direction, and the establishment of organizational priorities for action.

The second benefit is improved decision making. Strategic planning focuses attention on the crucial issues and challenges an organization faces, and it helps key decision makers figure out what they should do about them. Strategic planning thus can help organizations formulate and clearly communicate their strategic intentions. It can help them make today's decisions in light of their future consequences. It can help them develop a coherent and defensible basis for decision making and then coordinate the resulting decisions across levels and functions. And finally, it can help them exercise maximum discretion in those areas under their organization's control.

The third benefit—enhanced organizational responsiveness and improved performance—flows from the first two. Organizations engaging in strategic planning are encouraged to clarify and address major organizational issues, respond wisely to internal and external demands and pressures, and deal effectively with rapidly changing circumstances. Strategic thinking *and* acting are what count, not just thinking alone.

Finally, strategic planning can directly benefit the organization's people. Policy makers and key decision makers can better fulfill their roles and meet their responsibilities, and teamwork and expertise are likely to be strengthened among organizational members.

Although strategic planning *can* provide all these benefits, there is no guarantee it will. Indeed, it is highly unlikely that any organization will experience all or even most of the benefits of strategic planning the first time through—or even after many cycles of strategic planning. For one thing, strategic planning is simply a set of concepts, procedures, and tools. Leaders, managers, and planners need to be very careful about how they engage in strategic planning because their success will depend at least in part on how they tailor the process to their specific situation. This book presents a generic strategic planning process, based on considerable research and experience. Advice is offered on how to apply the process in different circumstances. But the process will work only if enough key decision makers and planners support it and use it with common sense and a sensitivity to the particulars of their situation. And even then, success is never guaranteed, particularly when very difficult strategic issues are addressed.

Furthermore, strategic planning is not always advisable (Barry, 1986;

Mintzberg, 1994a, 1994b). There are two compelling reasons for some organizations to hold off on a formal strategic planning effort. First, as Mitroff and Pearson (1993) point out, strategic planning may not be the best first step for an organization whose roof has fallen (keeping in mind, of course, that every crisis should be *managed* strategically). For example, an organization may need to remedy a cash flow problem before undertaking strategic planning. Or it may need to postpone strategic planning until it fills a key leadership position. Second, if an organization lacks the skills, resources, or commitment by key decision makers to produce a good plan, strategic planning will be a waste of time. Such a situation embodies what Bill Roering and I have called "the paradox of strategic planning": it is most needed where it is least likely to work and least needed where it is most likely to work (Bryson and Roering, 1988, 1989). If strategic planning is undertaken in such a situation, it should probably be a focused, limited effort aimed at developing the necessary skills, resources, and commitment.

A number of other reasons can be offered for not engaging in strategic planning. Too often, however, these "reasons" are actually excuses, used to avoid doing what should be done. For example, one might argue that strategic planning will be of little use if its costs are likely to outweigh any benefits, or that the process takes time and money that might be better used elsewhere. These concerns may be justified, but recall that the purpose of strategic planning is to produce fundamental decisions and actions that define what an organization (or other entity) is, what it does, and why it does it. In Chapter Three, I argue that strategic planning probably should not take more than 10 percent of the regular work time of any key decision maker during a year. When is the cost of that time likely to outweigh the benefit of focusing it on the production of fundamental decisions and actions for the organization? In my experience, hardly ever.

Many organizations prefer to rely on the intuition and vision of extremely gifted leaders instead of on formal strategic planning processes. If these leaders are strategically minded and experienced, there may be no need for strategic planning for the purpose of developing strategies. It is rare, however, for any one leader to have all the information necessary to develop an effective strategy, and rarer still for any strategy developed by a single person to engender the kind of commitment that is necessary for effective implementation. A reasonably structured and formalized strategic planning process helps organizations gather the information necessary for effective strategy formulation. It also provides the discipline and commitment necessary to effectively implement strategies.

In addition, many organizations—particularly those that have enormous difficulty reaching decisions that cut across levels, functions, or programs—find that incremental decision making and mutual adjustments of various sorts among interested partisans is the only process that will work. "Muddling" of this sort, as Charles Lindblom (1959) describes it, legitimizes the existing distribution of power and resources in an organization and allows its separate parts to pursue opportunities as they arise. Interesting and useful innovations can result from muddling, enhancing learning, and promoting useful adaptations to changing circumstances. In fact, if the muddling occurs within the context of a general agreement on the organization's overall direction, everyone may be better off (Lindblom, 1959, 1965, 1977; Braybrook and Lindblom, 1963; Quinn, 1980). Unfortunately, muddling typically results in a chronic organizational underperformance, and therefore, key external and internal constituencies may be badly served.

Strategic planning also probably should not be undertaken if implementation is extremely unlikely. Engaging in strategic planning when effective implementation will not follow is the organizational equivalent of the average New Year's resolution. On the other hand, when armed with the knowledge that implementation will be difficult, key decision makers and planners can focus extra attention on ensuring implementation success.

Finally, organizations simply may not know where to start the process. The good news is that strategic planning can begin almost anywhere—the process is so interconnected that you end up covering most phases via conversation and dialogue, no matter where you start.

What Strategic Planning Is Not

Clearly, strategic planning is no panacea. As noted, strategic planning is simply a set of concepts, procedures, and tools designed to help leaders, managers, and planners think and act strategically. Used in wise and skillful ways by a "coalition of the willing" (Cleveland, 1993), strategic planning can help organizations focus on producing effective decisions and actions that further the organization's mission, meet its mandates, and satisfy key stakeholders. But strategic planning is not a substitute for strategic thinking and acting. Only caring and committed people can do that. And when used thoughtlessly, strategic planning can actually drive out precisely the kind of strategic thought and action it is supposed to promote.

Furthermore, strategic planning is not a substitute for leadership. In my experience there is simply *no* substitute for leadership when it comes to using strategic planning to enhance organizational performance. At least some key decision makers and process champions must be committed to the strategic planning process, or any attempts to use it are bound to fail.

In addition, strategic planning is not synonymous with creating an organizational strategy. Organizational strategies have numerous sources, both planned and unplanned. Strategic planning is likely to result in a statement of organizational *intentions*, but what is *realized* in practice will be some combination of what is intended and what emerges along the way (Mintzberg, 1987, 1994a, 1994b; Mintzberg and Waters, 1985; Mintzberg and Westley, 1992). Strategic planning can help organizations develop and implement effective strategies, but they should also remain open to unforeseen opportunities. Too much attention to strategic planning and excessive reverence for strategic plans can blind organizations to other unplanned and unexpected—yet incredibly useful—sources of information, insight, and action.

It should now be clear that the *discipline* necessary for strategic planning can be of two sorts. The first harkens back to the Latin root of the word *discipline*, emphasizing instruction, training, education, and learning. The second embodies later interpretations of the word, emphasizing order, control, and punishment. I personally prefer the emphasis on education and learning, although there clearly are occasions when imposing order, taking control, and enforcing appropriate sanctions are appropriate. However, I believe key leaders, managers, and planners can best use strategic planning as an educational and learning tool, to help them figure out what is really important and what should be done about it. Sometimes this means following a particular sequence of steps and preparing formal strategic plans, but not necessarily. The ultimate goal of strategic planning should not be a rigid adherence to a particular process or an insistence on the production of plans. Instead, strategic planning should promote wise strategic thought and action on behalf of an organization and its key stakeholders. What steps to follow, in what sequence, and whether or not to prepare formal plans are subsidiary concerns.

Why Strategic Planning Is Here to Stay

Many leaders and managers are likely to groan at the prospect of having yet another new management technique foisted upon them. They have seen cost-benefit analysis, planning-programming-budgeting systems, zero-based budgeting, management by objectives, Total Quality Management, reinvention, reengineering, and a host of other techniques trumpeted by a cadre of authors and management consultants. They have also, all too often, seen such techniques fall by the wayside after a burst of initial enthusiasm. Managers in particular frequently, and justifiably, feel like victims of some sort of perverse management hazing or "status degradation ritual" (Schein, 1987, pp. 84–86).

But strategic planning is not just a passing fad, at least not the sort of strategic planning proposed in this book. The reason is that the strategic planning process presented here builds on the nature of *political* decision making. So many other management techniques fail because they ignore, try to circumvent, or even try to *counter* the political nature of life in private, public, and nonprofit organizations. Too many planners and managers, at least in my experience, just do not understand that such a quest is almost guaranteed to be quixotic.

Most of these new management innovations have tried to improve government decision making and operations by imposing a formal rationality on systems that are not rational, at least in the conventional meaning of the word. Public and nonprofit organizations (and communities) are *politically rational*. Thus, any technique that is likely to work well in such organizations must accept and build on the nature of political rationality (Wildavsky, 1979; March and Olsen, 1989).

Let us pursue this point further by contrasting two different kinds of decision making: the "rational" planning model and political decision making. The rational planning model is presented in Figure 1.1. It represents a rational-deductive approach to decision making. It begins with goals; policies, programs, and actions are then deduced to achieve those goals. If there is such a thing as a traditional planning theology, this model is one of its icons. Indeed, if there had been a "Planning Moses," Figure 1.1 would have been etched on his tablets when he came down from the mount.

Let us now examine the fundamental assumption of the rational planning model—that in the fragmented, shared-power settings that characterize many public and nonprofit organizations, networks, and communities, there will either be a *consensus* on goals, policies, programs, and actions necessary to achieve organizational aims, or there will be someone with enough power and authority that consensus does not matter. This assumption just does not hold true in most circumstances. Only in fairly centralized, authoritarian, or quasimilitary bureaucracies will the assumption hold—maybe.

Let us now examine a model that contrasts sharply with the rational planning model—the political decision making model, presented in Figure 1.2. This model is inductive, not rational-deductive. It begins with issues, which by definition involve conflict, not consensus. The conflicts may be over ends, means, timing, location, political advantage, reasons for change, or philosophy, and the conflicts may be severe. As efforts proceed to resolve these issues, policies and programs emerge to address them that are politically rational; that is, they are politically acceptable to involved or affected parties. Over time, more general policies may be formulated to capture, frame, shape, guide, or interpret the policies and programs developed to deal with the issues. The various policies and programs are, in effect, treaties among the various stakeholder groups. And while they may not exactly record a consensus, at least they represent a reasonable level of agreement among stakeholders (Lindblom, 1965, 1980; Pfeffer and Salancik, 1978; March and Olsen, 1989).

Now, the heart of the strategic planning process discussed in Chapter Two is the identification and resolution of strategic—that is, very important—issues.

FIGURE 1.1. RATIONAL PLANNING MODEL.

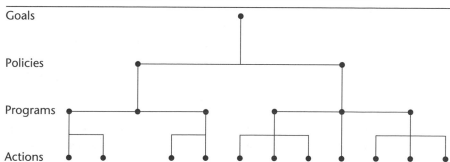

FIGURE 1.2. POLITICAL DECISION MAKING MODEL.

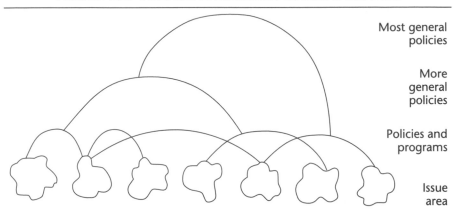

Most general
policies

More
general
policies

Policies and
programs

Issue
area

The process, in other words, accepts political decision making's emphasis on issues and seeks to inform the formulation and resolution of those issues. Effective
strategic planning, therefore, should make political decision makers more effective; and if it is practiced consistently, it might even make their professional lives
easier (Janis, 1989). Since every key decision maker in a large public or nonprofit
organization is, in effect, a political decision maker (Mintzberg, 1983; Pfeffer, 1992;
Fesler and Kettl, 1994; Herman, 1994; Peters, 1995), strategic planning can help
these organizations. Strategic planning, therefore, will last in government and nonprofit organizations because it accepts and builds on the nature of political decision
making. If done well, strategic planning can actually improve the political decisions made within these organizations, as well as their programs and policies.

Having drawn a sharp distinction between the rational planning model and
political decision making, I must now emphasize that the two models are not inherently antithetical. They simply need to be relied upon appropriately. This may
mean, for example, sequencing them properly. The political decision-making
model is thus necessary to work out consensual agreements on what programs and
policies will best resolve key issues. The rational planning model can then be used
to recast that consensus into the form of goals, policies, programs, and actions.
While the planning and decision making that goes into the formulation of a strategic plan may look fairly sloppy to an outsider, once a consensus is reached on what
to do, the resulting strategic plan can be rewritten in a form that is in fact quite
rational by ordinary definitions of the term. Furthermore, the rational planning
model may be used to sort out and address any minor (and perhaps major) in-
consistencies embedded in the political outcome.

To use another example, in many organizations and communities there already exists a broad-based consensus on basic purposes and values—and often on
many policies, programs, and actions as well. There may even be a consensus on
the organization's or community's "vision." This consensus can be recast using
the rational planning model. The political model can then be used to address re-

maining issues on which there is no agreement. In particular, these issues are likely to revolve around what needs to be done in order to achieve the agreed-upon goals or vision.

To summarize: a great advantage of the strategic planning process outlined in this book is that it does not presume consensus where consensus does not exist, but it can accommodate consensus where it does exist. Because there is no presumption of consensus, the process is more suitable for politicized circumstances than are purely "rational" approaches. An intense attention to stakeholders and their interests, external and internal environments, and strategic issues means that the actions that are ultimately agreed upon are more likely to be *politically* rational, and that organizational survival and prosperity are, therefore, more likely to be assured. Furthermore, by gathering relevant information, asking probing questions, and focusing on how best to raise issues, the process can be used to inform political decision making in such a way that virtuous public and nonprofit purposes are better served than they would be if only the rawest forms of political decision making prevailed. The process, in other words, provides a way of blending substantive *and* political rationality—content *and* process—in wise ways, to the betterment of the organizations and communities that use the process (see March and Simon, 1958; Lynn, 1987; Stone, 1988; Benveniste, 1989; March and Olsen, 1989; Bryson and Crosby, 1992).

Four Examples of Strategic Planning

Throughout this book the experiences of four organizations (three public and one nonprofit) are used to illustrate key points about strategic planning—including its capacity for accommodating substantive and political rationality. Each of these organizations used the strategic planning process outlined here, explicitly or implicitly adapting it for their own purposes. I was a strategic planning consultant for all four organizations, although the extent of my involvement varied from extensive to minimal.

The four organizations discussed here are a suburban school district, a public library, a federal program designed to measure change in prices (the Consumer Price Index program), and a large central city church (Mainline Church). The actual identities of three of the organizations and their members have been masked to preserve their anonymity. A number of other less detailed examples are used as well to clarify the discussion.

School District

The school district encompasses three suburban cities in a major Midwestern metropolitan area. During 1991 to 1992, the district had a population of approximately 61,000 people, of whom 9,700 attended the district's kindergarten through twelfth grade (K-12) and many thousands more participated in community education classes. The district had about 1,200 employees and an annual budget of approximately $44.4 million.

The district was interested in gaining all or most of the benefits of strategic planning. It was just emerging from a major series of difficulties, including a substantial operating debt. It also faced a number of important challenges. A new superintendent had been hired to get the district's finances in order and to help it successfully meet the organizational and educational challenges it faced. For example, major national reform movements were sweeping the field of education at the time because of the broad-based perception that public schools were failing to prepare students for an increasingly competitive world. Proposed reforms included outcome-based education, site-based management, diverse and inclusive classrooms and instruction, lifelong learning, and the inducement of improved school performance through competition by allowing parents and students greater choice in schools and programs. The district wanted to engage in strategic planning, in part to avoid past difficulties and in part to explore these reform ideas so that decisions might be made about how best to provide educational opportunities for its students.

The superintendent approached me in January 1991 about my availability to assist with a strategic planning effort. After several conversations involving me, Humphrey Institute colleague Charles Finn, the superintendent, his cabinet, and the school board, an agreement was reached on an overall process design and on Chuck's and my involvement in it. It was decided that the strategic planning process would attempt to address the major national reform initiatives in imaginative and constructive ways, deal with a developing space problem resulting from growth in the school-age population and out-of-date facilities, involve the community, and help the school board be a more effective policy-making body. The district's strategic plan was formally adopted in May 1993. A number of implementation efforts were under way prior to formal adoption, and additional ones have been under way since. But the process has not always been an easy one. Difficult negotiations with the teachers' union caused some delay—and resulted in defeat of the school board president in his reelection bid—but they were necessary to free up monies for many of the reform initiatives. In addition, two school bond referenda failed before the district finally passed one in August 1994; it will provide the money necessary to build new facilities and remodel old ones.

Public Library

At the beginning of its strategic planning process, the public library was a division of the community services department of a large Midwestern city. (At present the library reports directly to the mayor.) The library was founded over a century ago and has long been a valued resource for the city and the region. The library has a tradition of planning for the future, including improving each new planning endeavor based on what it has learned from prior efforts. In 1979, the library developed a mission statement and an annual goals and objectives program. A long-range five-year plan was developed in 1981, and the first strategic plan was developed in 1984 and revised in 1986. In 1987, the library's leadership initiated preparations for a major new round of strategic planning, which began in 1988. They were helped in their efforts by a well-established and well-connected nonprofit organization established to help the library with advice and financial support. (We will call this organization the "Friends of the Public Library.") They were also helped by a library staff training and development fund, administered by a local foundation and set up to acquire and dispense financial support not available elsewhere. Two colleagues and I served as external consultants to that process, which resulted in the library's 1989–91 strategic plan. The plan has been revised annually ever since, and at present the library's administrators are considering a major new community-based planning effort, to be integrated with the city's legally mandated comprehensive plan.

The key issues driving the need to revisit the 1986 plan involved finance and personnel. Since 1980, circulation had increased over 30 percent while the library's staff had increased by only one half-time position. The library ranked second in per capita circulation among U.S. cities with populations over two hundred thousand but only seventeenth in per capita budget. The result was a remarkably efficient public library, but also one in which the staff had reached the point of burnout. By 1988, for the first time, sick days for library employees exceeded the average for all city employees. Morale was declining, and there were few obvious prospects for new funding. The library's administrators recognized a potential crisis in the works. Besides the heavy workload and funding problems, other issues were apparent, including what the library's hours of service should be, how to take advantage of new technologies, how to manage the library's collection, and difficulties with the library's facilities. Clearly something needed to be done, and the administrators saw strategic planning as a way of helping them figure out what. At the time the process began, the library had the equivalent of approximately 164 full-time employees, a budget of $7.3 million, an annual circulation of approximately 2,285,000 items, and 646,000 reference transactions per year.

Consumer Price Index Program

The Consumer Price Index (CPI) program, housed in the Bureau of Labor Statistics of the U.S. Department of Labor, is charged with producing a timely, accurate, and objective measure of changes in consumer prices. The CPI program provides the primary measure of inflation in the United States, and it is a world leader in the measurement of pure price changes. In spite of its national and international preeminence, by the fall of 1992 the CPI program faced a number of serious issues, prompting its director, Paul Armknecht; a key staff member, Branch Chief Marybeth Tschetter; and its other senior management personnel to initiate strategic planning.

One important issue involved the huge federal deficit. In the past, the CPI program had not been targeted for drastic budget cuts, due to its importance to the operation of the federal government and to the economy as a whole. Literally billions of dollars of federal expenditures are tied to the index, including Social Security and federal pension payments. Private pension funds, labor contracts, and interest rates around the country are also tied directly or indirectly to the CPI. But with almost a third of the federal budget going to pay interest on the national debt, and with the Defense Department canceling weapons systems and closing bases across the country and around the world, it was clear that the CPI program's base budget of approximately $35 million and its staff of eight hundred would be increasingly hard to maintain. It was also clear that it would be extremely difficult to obtain a supplemental budget request totaling $61 million over six years to fund the decennial revision of the method used to compute the CPI based on the new census. The CPI program thus found itself requesting a budget increase in the midst of a wave of budget cuts across the federal bureaucracy, and no matter who won the 1992 presidential election, the cuts were not likely to disappear. Beyond the question of funding was the issue of how to integrate revision planning with the program's larger strategic planning efforts, which included possible wholesale redesign of the way the program generates its indices.

The Department of Labor had embraced Total Quality Management (TQM) as a philosophy and wanted all its component parts, including the CPI, to follow this direction. Another issue, therefore, was the need to develop a clear sense of the CPI program's strategic direction for pursuing continuous quality improvements. In other words, quality improvements in the *wrong* direction would be a waste of taxpayer money and employee time, providing a disservice to the CPI's users. The direction had to be right for quality improvements to make sense.

Yet another issue concerned the need to help the CPI management group perform better as a policy-making and coordinating body. The CPI program is essentially a kind of "matrix organization" (Davis and Lawrence, 1977) in which members of various functional divisions must coordinate their efforts across divisional lines in order to produce the index. The management group was thus a kind of "shared-power arrangement" (Bryson and Crosby, 1992; Radin, 1993) in which a variety of mixed motives were present. These needed to be reconciled in a reasonable way to allow the program to produce a high-quality, timely index and for its functional divisions to survive and prosper.

In the middle of the process, the CPI managers were informed that additional funding requested for the revision had not been approved. At best, it would be delayed a year; at worst, there would be no extra funding for the revision. The initial shock and continuing uncertainty could have had a paralyzing effect had the management group not already been engaged in strategic planning. As a result of their ongoing deliberations, however, the management group was able to see the delay or loss of additional funding as simply another strategic issue to be addressed, albeit a major one. The group's strategic plan was finalized in April 1994 and formally adopted the following June.

Mainline Church

Mainline Church is a Protestant congregation founded in 1857 in a small village in the upper Midwest. The village soon became a major city, and Mainline Church grew with it. The church has 2,700 members, a substantial complement of clergy, and an annual operating budget of approximately $1.5 million, which makes it larger than 95 percent of the other churches in the United States. The church is located on the edge of a thriving central city that also has a number of characteristic inner-city problems. The fact that the demographics of the central city and its metropolitan area are changing poses both threats and opportunities for the church's primarily white, middle-class membership.

The church has undertaken two strategic planning efforts in the past five years. The first, initiated in February 1988 and sponsored by the church's senior pastor and governing board, resulted in a strategic plan that was formally adopted in June 1989, designed to cover the years 1990–94. The planning process was initiated because of some very disturbing trends. In 1989, for the first time in memory, the church's pledge income had declined. In the past, programs were proposed and the church simply raised the necessary money from the congregation. That time-tested strategy was no longer working, and the fact that over half the congregation was over fifty-five meant that it might never work again. Unless more young and middle-aged people and families became members, the congregation was almost certain to shrink and perhaps even disappear.

Two other concerns prompted one of the primary initiators of the process— a retired executive with years of strategic planning experience and a respected church elder—to push ahead with strategic planning. One was the expected retirement of the church's senior pastor, a talented and charismatic preacher who had overseen a number of major accomplishments in his almost twenty years in office. The second was the initiator's clear sense that the church needed to learn how to do strategic planning if it was to survive and prosper into the next century. The church had rarely had to do much planning in the past, but the decline in pledge income, the decline in membership among mainline Protestant churches nationally, and the changing city and metropolitan scene meant that *not* planning was a luxury Mainline Church could ill afford.

The first strategic planning effort resulted in a number of major changes, including rescheduling Sunday services to better address the needs of adults interested in Christian education, to better include children and youth in the life of the church, and to generally make the church more attractive to younger people, especially those with children. But even though the effort was quite time consuming, a number of issues were incompletely addressed or not addressed at all. The next five-year plan would cover the period from 1995 to 2000, but the elder thought it unwise for the church not to address these remaining issues promptly. He thus convinced the church hierarchy to undertake a new series of planning initiatives, called "Vision for 2000," to address unresolved issues of facility needs, the membership base, the financial base, roles of clergy and program staff, and program needs. The *Vision for 2000* report was formally approved by the church's governing body in May 1992. Implementation efforts have been under way since then, and the document was relied on extensively in the search for the new senior pastor, who joined the church in early 1994.

Comparisons and Contrasts

These four organizations offer a number of comparisons and contrasts. They differ in size, staff, budgets, and legal status. One is a unit of local government. One is a single-function government agency initially located well down the organizational hierarchy. One is a major federal program housed in a major federal department. And one is an independent nonprofit organization.

The strategic planning effort for these organizations differed in the extent to which it focused directly on the organization and what it should do or on what should happen in the community of which the organization is a part. The school district and library focused on both organizational and community planning. The CPI program focused almost exclusively on itself and its key stakeholders. Mainline Church concentrated almost exclusively on organizational planning, but it remained aware that its status as a major community institution engaged in a host of social outreach projects has clear community consequences.

In addition, the four organizations engaged in strategic planning for different reasons. The school district was emerging from a number of serious difficulties, including the need to get its finances in order. The new superintendent and the board sought additional progress in these areas, but they also wished to take advantage of major national reform movements to improve the performance of the district and its students. The public library was facing serious financial and personnel issues. Demands on the staff had increased dramatically in the previous seven years, while staff size had hardly changed. A point of staff burnout had been reached, and a crisis loomed. Strategic planning was seen as a way to address the developing crisis. The CPI program's management knew they were about to face a serious financial crunch as a result of the federal deficit and competing demands on the public purse. They wished to use strategic planning to organize the program's work better, to help guide TQM efforts, and to help the management group perform better as a policy-making body. Finally, Mainline Church also faced continuing financial difficulties, in this case tied to a changing demographic profile. Growing "younger and bigger" rather than "older and smaller" would entail changes in the timing and nature of worship services and church education programs and perhaps changes in a host of other areas. Equally important for the church was to learn *how* to think and act strategically, in ways they never had to in the past. The first strategic planning exercise produced important substantive changes; it also set the stage for a second effort that dealt with other issues and was used to influence the hiring of a new senior pastor.

There are a number of similarities among these four cases as well. First, each organization succeeded because it had leaders willing to act as *process sponsors* to endorse and legitimize the effort. The sponsors were not always particularly active participants, but they did let it be known that they wanted important decision makers to give the effort a good try. Second, each organization had *process champions* committed to making the process work. The champions did not have preconceived ideas about what specific issues and answers would emerge from the process, although they may have had some good hunches. They simply believed that the process would result in positive answers, and they pushed until those answers emerged (see Kotler, 1976; Maidique, 1980; Kanter, 1983; Bryson and Roering, 1988, 1989).

Third, each organization began with a fairly clear understanding and agreement among key decision makers about what strategic planning was and what it expected from the process. Fourth, each followed a reasonably structured strategic thinking and acting process. Fifth, each established a decision-making or advisory body to oversee the process. Sixth, each designated a strategic planning team to manage the process, collect information and prepare for meetings, and draft a strategic plan. Seventh, each identified critical issues that required effective action if the organization were to avoid being victimized by serious threats, missed opportunities, or both. Eighth, each worked hard to develop strategies that were politically acceptable, technically workable, and ethically responsible. Ninth, each relied on outside assistance, including consultants, to help with the process. Tenth, each made a point of not getting so bogged down in the process that it lost sight of what was truly important: strategic thought and action. And finally, each gained many of the potential benefits of strategic planning outlined above.

Summary

This chapter has discussed what strategic planning is and why it is important. Its importance stems from its ability to help public and nonprofit organizations and communities respond effectively to the dramatically changed circumstances that now confront them.

Not only have the environments of public and nonprofit organizations and communities changed dramatically in the recent past, more upheaval is likely in the future. Those of us who grew up in the 1950s and 1960s came to think that continuous progress was the norm, that everything would always continue to get steadily better. How wrong we all were! The norm is not continuous progress, but periods of stability interrupted by significant change, uncertainty, and surprise. The period prior to the 1950s saw two world wars, big booms, big busts, and the development of major new roles for government. The period after the 1950s brought the civil rights movement, the women's movement, major student disruptions, the disastrous war in Vietnam, the environmental movement, dramatic shifts in the dominant political ideology in the United States, plus all of the other changes noted in the opening paragraphs of this chapter.

Strategic planning is one way to help organizations and communities deal with changed circumstances. Strategic planning is intended to enhance an organization's ability to think and act strategically. It can help organizations formulate and resolve the most important issues they face. It can help them build on their strengths and take advantage of major opportunities, while they overcome or minimize their weaknesses and serious threats to their existence. It can help them be much more effective in a hostile world. If it does not do that, it probably was not worth the effort, even though it may have satisfied certain legal mandates or symbolic needs.

Strategic planning is a leadership and management innovation that is likely to persist because, unlike many other recent innovations, it accepts and builds on the nature of *political* decision making. The raising and resolving of important issues is at the heart of political decision making, just as it is at the heart of strategic planning. Strategic planning seeks to improve on raw political decision making, however, by helping ensure that issues are raised and resolved in ways that benefit the organization, its key stakeholders, and society.

Chapter Two presents my preferred approach to strategic planning for governments, public agencies, nonprofit organizations, boundary-crossing services, and communities. Subsequent chapters will discuss how to apply the process. The process is offered in the hope that it will help public and nonprofit organizations, service networks, and communities fulfill their missions, meet their mandates, and serve their stakeholders effectively, efficiently, and responsibly.

CHAPTER TWO

THE STRATEGY CHANGE CYCLE: AN EFFECTIVE STRATEGIC PLANNING APPROACH FOR PUBLIC AND NONPROFIT ORGANIZATIONS

I skate to where I think the puck will be.

WAYNE GRETZKY

Boys, when you see the enemy, fire and then run. And as I am a little lame, I'll run now.

GENERAL JOHN B. STEDMAN, NINETEENTH-CENTURY RHODE ISLAND MILITIA OFFICER

This chapter presents my preferred approach to strategic planning for public and nonprofit organizations, boundary-crossing services, and communities. The process is called the Strategy Change Cycle. It includes the following activities:

- Setting the organization's direction
- Formulating broad policies
- Making internal and external assessments
- Paying attention to the needs of key stakeholders
- Identifying key issues
- Developing strategies to deal with each issue
- Planning review and adoption procedures
- Implementing planning
- Making fundamental decisions
- Taking action
- Continually monitoring and assessing the results

Thus, the Strategy Change Cycle is as much a strategic management process as it is a strategic planning process. It draws on a considerable body of research and practical experience, applying it specifically to public and nonprofit organizations (Bryson, Freeman, and Roering, 1986; Bryson and Roering, 1987, 1989, forthcoming; Bryson, 1994, forthcoming; Bryson and Finn, 1995; Bryson, Ackermann, Eden, and Finn, forthcoming). Subsequent chapters provide detailed guidance on moving through the cycle.

The epigraphs that begin this chapter help make the point that strategic thinking and acting are more important than any particular approach to strategic planning. Wayne Gretzky, one of the greatest ice hockey players of all time, is talking about strategic thinking and acting when he says, "I skate to where I think the puck will be." He does not skate around with a thick strategic plan in his back pocket (hockey uniforms do not always *have* back pockets). What he does instead is to think and act strategically (and tactically) throughout the game, in keeping with a typically simple game plan worked out with his coaches and teammates in advance.

But let us explore Gretzky's statement further. Think about what one must know and be able to do in order to make such a comment and deliver on its substance. One obviously would need to know the purpose and rules of the game, the strengths and weaknesses of one's own team, the opportunities and threats posed by the other team, the game plan, the arena, the officials, and so on. One would also need to be a well-equipped, well-conditioned, strong, and able hockey player. And, of course, it would not hurt to play for a very good team. In other words, those who can express confidently that they "skate to where they think the puck will be" know basically everything there is to know about strategic thinking and acting in hockey games.

Let us now consider the humorous statement of John Stedman, a nineteenth-century Rhode Island militia officer (quoted in Least Heat-Moon, 1982, p. 365). At one point during the Dorr Rebellion, he and his men were badly outnumbered by their opponents. A hasty retreat was in order, but it made sense to give the lame and wounded—including the general—a chance to put some distance between themselves and the enemy before a full-scale retreat was called. The men would then be in a position to fight another day. Stedman had no thick strategic plan in his back pocket, either (although we can assume that, unlike Gretzky, he did *have* a back pocket). At most he probably had a fairly general battle plan worked out with his fellow officers, recorded in pencil on a crude map. Again, strategic thinking and acting were what mattered, not any particular planning process.

A Ten-Step Strategic Planning Process

Now, with this caution in mind, let us proceed to a more detailed exploration of the ten-step Strategy Change Cycle. The process, presented in Figure 2.1, is more orderly, deliberative, and participative than the process followed by either Gretzky or Stedman. The ten steps are as follows:

1. Initiate and agree upon a strategic planning process.
2. Identify organizational mandates.
3. Clarify organizational mission and values.
4. Assess the organization's external and internal environments to identify strengths, weaknesses, opportunities, and threats.
5. Identify the strategic issues facing the organization.
6. Formulate strategies to manage these issues.
7. Review and adopt the strategic plan or plans.
8. Establish an effective organizational vision.
9. Develop an effective implementation process.
10. Reassess strategies and the strategic planning process.

These ten steps should lead to actions, results, and evaluation. It must be emphasized that action, results, and evaluative judgments should emerge at each step in the process. In other words, implementation and evaluation should not wait until the "end" of the process but should be an integral and ongoing part of it.

The process is applicable to public and nonprofit organizations, boundary-crossing services, interorganizational networks, and communities. The only general requirements are a "dominant coalition" (Thompson, 1967) that is willing to sponsor and follow the process and a process champion who is willing to push it. Many organizational strategic planning teams that are familiar with—and believe in the process will be able to complete most of the steps in a two- or three-day retreat, with an additional one-day meeting scheduled three to four weeks later to review the resulting strategic plan. Responsibility for preparing the plan can be delegated to a planner assigned to work with the team, or the organization's chief executive may choose to draft the plan personally. Additional time might be needed for further reviews and for sign-offs by key decision makers. Additional time might also be necessary to secure information or advice for specific parts of the plan, especially its recommended strategies. When applied to a network or community, however, the effort is likely to be considerably more time consuming due to the necessity of involving substantial numbers of leaders, organizations, or citizens.

Step 1: Initiating and Agreeing on a Strategic Planning Process

The purpose of the first step is to negotiate agreement among key internal (and perhaps external) decision makers or opinion leaders about the overall strategic planning effort and the key planning steps. The support and commitment of key decision makers within the organization are vital if strategic planning is to succeed (Olsen and Eadie, 1982; Bryson and Roering, 1988; Nutt and Backoff, 1992; Schein, 1992). Further, the involvement of key decision makers outside the organization is usually crucial to the success of public programs, if implementation will involve multiple parties and organizations (McGowan and Stevens, 1983; Goggin, Bowman, Lester, and O'Toole, 1990).

FIGURE 2.1. THE TEN-STEP STRATEGY CHANGE CYCLE.

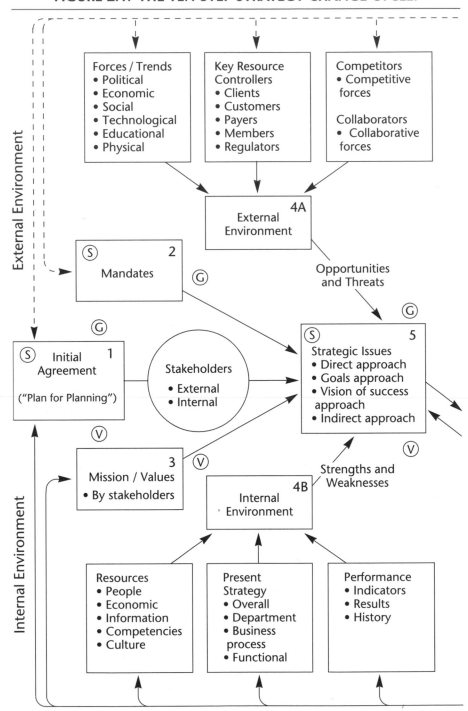

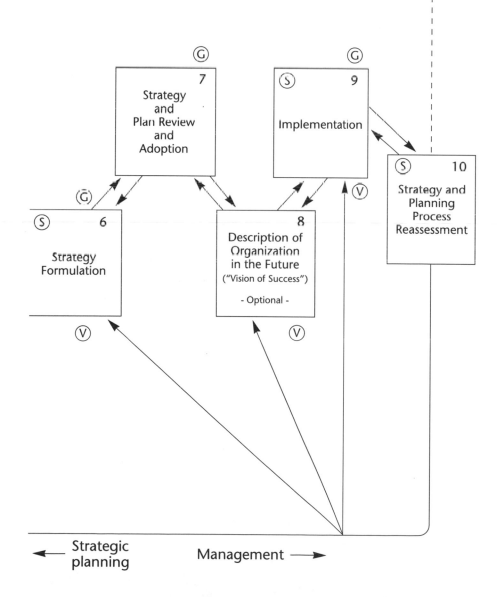

(S) = Places where the process typically starts

(G) = Places where the goal formulation may occur

(V) = Places where vision formulation may occur

(G)

7
Strategy
and
Plan Review
and
Adoption

(G)

(S) **9**

Implementation

(Ḡ)

(S) **6**

Strategy
Formulation

8
Description of
Organization
in the Future
("Vision of Success")

- Optional -

(S) **10**

Strategy and
Planning
Process
Reassessment

(V)

(V)

(V)

◄— Strategic
planning

Management —►

Obviously, some person or group must initiate the process. One of the initiators' first tasks is to identify exactly who the key decision makers are. The next task is to identify which persons, groups, units, or organizations should be involved in the effort. These two steps require some preliminary stakeholder analysis, which is discussed in more detail in Step 3. The initial agreement will be negotiated with at least some of these decision makers, groups, units, or organizations. In practice, a *series* of agreements typically must be struck among various parties as support for the process builds and key decision makers sign on. Strategic planning for a public or nonprofit organization is likely to work best if the organization has an effective policy-making body in place to oversee the effort.

The agreement itself should cover these points:

- The purpose of the effort
- Preferred steps in the process
- The form and timing of reports
- The role, functions, and membership of any group or committee empowered to oversee the effort, such as a strategic planning coordinating committee (SPCC)
- The role, functions, and membership of the strategic planning team
- The commitment of necessary resources to proceed with the effort

Any important limitations or boundaries on the effort should be made clear.

Step 2: Identifying Organizational Mandates

The formal and informal mandates placed on an organization consist of the various "musts" that it confronts. Actually, it is surprising how few organizations know precisely what they are (and are not) formally mandated to do. Typically, few members of any organization have ever read, for example, the relevant legislation, ordinances, charters, articles, and contracts that outline the organization's formal mandates. Many organizational members also do not clearly understand what informal mandates—typically political in the broadest sense—their organization faces. It may not be surprising, then, that most organizations make one or all of the following three fundamental mistakes. First, not knowing what they must do, they are unlikely to do it. Second, they may believe they are more tightly constrained in their actions than they actually are. Third, they may assume that if they are not explicitly told to do something, they are not allowed to do it.

Step 3: Clarifying Organizational Mission and Values

An organization's mission, in tandem with its mandates, provides its raison d'être, the social justification for its existence. For a government agency or nonprofit organization, this means there must be identifiable social or political needs that the organization seeks to fill. Viewed in this light, organizations must always be seen as a means to an end, not as an end in themselves. Communities, too, must justify their existence based on how well they address the values and meet the social and political needs of their various stakeholders—including the stakeholders' need for a "sense of community." Communities, however, are less likely to think they have "a mission"; they are more likely to talk about their purpose and values.

Identifying a mission, however, does more than merely justify an organization's existence. Clarifying the purpose can eliminate a great deal of unnecessary conflict in an organization and can help channel discussion and activity productively (Terry, 1993). An organization's purpose defines the arenas within which the organization will collaborate or compete, and it charts the future course of the organization (at least in a broad outline). Moreover, an important and socially justifiable mission is a source of inspiration to key stakeholders, particularly employees. Indeed, it is doubtful if any organization ever achieved greatness or excellence without a basic consensus among its key stakeholders on an inspiring mission.

Before developing a mission statement, an organization should complete at least the first few steps of a stakeholder analysis. A *stakeholder* is defined as any person, group, or organization that can place a claim on an organization's attention, resources, or output or is affected by that output. Examples of a government's stakeholders include citizens, taxpayers, service recipients, the governing body, employees, unions, interest groups, political parties, the financial community, businesses, and other governments. Examples of a nonprofit organization's stakeholders include clients or customers, third-party payers or funders, employees, the board of directors, volunteers, other nonprofit organizations that provide complementary services or are involved as coventurers in projects, banks holding the organization's mortgages or notes, and suppliers.

Attention to stakeholder concerns is crucial: *the key to success for public and nonprofit organizations (and for communities) is the satisfaction of key stakeholders.* A stakeholder analysis is a way for an organization's decision makers and planning team to immerse themselves in the politics surrounding the organization. An understanding of the political aspects of an organization's situation can provide invaluable clues to identifying strategic issues and developing effective strategies (Boschken, 1992, 1994). In addition, one might argue that performing a stakeholder analysis is an ethical necessity, since only by understanding stakeholder interests and concerns is an organization likely to take truly ethical action (Lewis, 1991).

Many public and nonprofit organizations assign the label of "customer" to their key stakeholder, particularly if the organization is trying to "reinvent" itself (Osborne and Gaebler, 1992; Barzelay, 1992; Gore, 1993; Thompson and Jones, 1994), "reengineer" its operations (Hammer and Champy, 1993), or employ Total Quality Management (Cohen and Brand, 1993; Schenkat, 1993). The danger in focusing on "customers" is that organizations may inadvertently ignore other important stakeholder groups. The public sector is not as simple as the private sector—there are typically many "bottom lines." Many community-based nonprofit organizations, as well as those that rely on government funding, have very diverse and complex constituencies.

The first few steps in a stakeholder analysis require the strategic planning team to identify who the organization's stakeholders are, what their criteria are for judging the organization's performance (that is, what their "stake" is in the organization or its output), and how well the organization performs according to those criteria *from the stakeholder point of view.* If there is time, additional steps should be considered, including attempting to understand how the stakeholders influence the organization, identifying what the organization needs from its various stakeholders (money, staff, political support), and determining in general how important the various stakeholders are. A stakeholder analysis will help clarify whether the organization needs to have different missions and perhaps different strategies for different stakeholders and whether it should seek to have its mandates changed.

After completing the stakeholder analysis, the strategic planning team can proceed to develop a mission statement. The mission statement itself might be very short, perhaps no more than a paragraph or even a slogan. But development of the mission statement should grow out of lengthy discussions about the organization's identity, its abiding purpose, its desired response to key stakeholders, its philosophy and core values, and its ethical standards. These discussions may also provide a basic outline for a description of the organization in the future, or its "vision of success," described in Step 8. Considerable intermediate work is necessary, however, before a complete vision of success can be articulated.

Step 4: Assessing the Organization's External and Internal Environments

The planning team should explore the environment outside the organization to identify both opportunities and threats (Step 4a). It should explore the environment inside the organization to identify both strengths and weaknesses (Step 4b). Basically, "outside" factors are those that are not under organizational control, while "inside" factors are controlled by the organization (Pfeffer and Salancik, 1978). Opportunities and threats are usually (though not necessarily) more about the future than the present, while strengths and weaknesses are about the present and not the future (Nutt and Backoff, 1992). Opportunities and threats can be discovered by monitoring a variety of political, economic, social, technological, educational, and physical environmental forces and trends. Unfortunately, all too often, organizations focus only on the negative or threatening aspects of these changes and not on the opportunities they present. Besides monitoring trends and events, the strategic planning team should also monitor particularly important external stakeholders, especially those that affect the organization's supply of resources (directly or indirectly). These groups include customers, clients, payers or funders, dues-paying members, regulators, and relevant policy bodies. The team should also attend to competitors, competitive forces, and possible sources of competitive advantage, as well as to collaborators, collaborative forces, and potential sources of collaborative advantage. The organization might construct various scenarios to explore alternative futures within a given external environment, a practice typical of private-sector strategic planning (Linneman and Klein, 1983; Schwartz, 1991).

Members of an organization's governing body (particularly if they are elected) are often better at identifying and assessing external threats and opportunities (particularly present ones) than are the organization's employees. This is partly due to a governing board's responsibility for relating an organization to its external environment and vice versa (Thompson, 1967). Unfortunately, neither governing boards nor employees usually do a systematic or effective job of external scanning. As a result, most organizations are like ships trying to navigate treacherous waters without the benefit of human lookouts, radar, or sonar.

Because of this, both employees and board members should rely on a somewhat formal process of external assessment to supplement their informal efforts. The technology of external assessment is fairly simple, and it allows organizations to cheaply, pragmatically, and effectively keep tabs on events in the larger world that are likely to affect the organization and its mission.

Attention to opportunities and threats along with a stakeholder analysis can be used to identify an organization's "key success factors" (Jenster, 1987; Leidecker and Bruno, 1984; Mintzberg, 1994b). Success factors are the things an organization must do or the criteria it must meet in order to be successful in relating to its external environment.

To identify internal strengths and weaknesses, the organization might monitor its resources (inputs), its present strategy (process), and its performance (outputs). Most organizations, in my experience, have volumes of information on inputs such as salaries, supplies, the physical plant, and full-time equivalent (FTE) personnel. Unfortunately, few organizations have a very clear idea of their philosophy, core values, distinctive competencies, and culture—a crucial set of inputs, both for ensuring stability and for managing change.

Organizations also tend to have an unclear idea of their present strategy, including both their overall strategy and their strategies for individual units or functions. And typically, they can say little, if anything, about their outputs, let alone the effect or outcome of those outputs on their clients, customers, or payers. For example, while schools may be able to say how many students they graduate—an output—most cannot say how well educated those students are. The recent movement toward standardized testing in many states is an attempt to specifically measure schools' output.

A lack of performance information presents problems both for organizations and for their stakeholders. Stakeholders judge an organization according to criteria *they* choose, which are not necessarily the same criteria the organization would choose. For external stakeholders in particular, these criteria typically relate to performance. If an organization cannot effectively meet its stakeholders' performance criteria, then regardless of its "inherent" worth, the stakeholders are likely to withdraw their support. The need to address this threat—particularly from key stakeholders, or "customers"—is one of the reasons organizations initiate reinvention, reengineering, and TQM efforts.

An absence of performance information may also create—or harden—major organizational conflicts. Without performance criteria and information, there is no way to evaluate the relative effectiveness of alternative strategies, resource allocations, organizational designs, and distributions of power. As a result, organizational conflicts are likely to occur more often than they should, to serve narrow partisan interests, and to be resolved in ways that do not further the organization's mission (Terry, 1993).

The difficulties of measuring performance are well known (Flynn, 1986, 1993; Jackson and Palmer, 1992). But regardless of these difficulties, organizations are continually challenged to demonstrate effective performance to their stakeholders. Employees of government agencies and nonprofit organizations dependent on government funds might see the public's desire to limit or even decrease taxation and funding as selfishness. Alternatively, one might interpret such limitations on public expenditures as an unwillingness to support organizations that cannot demonstrate unequivocally effective performance (Wholey and Hatry, 1992). The desire for demonstrable performance was clearly behind the Government Performance and Results Act (GPRA) of 1993 (Public Law 103-62), which requires all federal agencies to complete a strategic plan by 1996 that is based on outcomes rather than inputs or process measures. Each plan is to cover five years and must follow the annual performance plan framework mandated by the GPRA. Several states have initiated performance-oriented planning systems as well (National Governors Association, 1993).

A consideration of an organization's strengths and weaknesses can also lead to an identification of its "distinctive competencies" (Selznick, 1957), more recently termed "core competencies" (Prahalad and Hamel, 1990) or "capabilities" (Stalk, Evans, and Shulman, 1992). These consist of an organization's strongest abilities and most effective actions and strategies, or the resources (broadly conceived) on which it can draw routinely to perform well.

Step 5: Identifying the Strategic Issues Facing the Organization

Together, the first four elements of the strategic planning process lead to the fifth, the identification of strategic issues. *Strategic issues* are fundamental policy questions or critical challenges that affect an organization's mandates, mission, and values; product or service level and mix; clients, users, or payers; or cost, financing, organization, or management (see Ansoff, 1980).

Strategic planning focuses on achieving the best fit between an organization and its environment. Attention to mandates and the external environment, therefore, can be thought of as planning from the outside in. Attention to mission and organizational values and the internal environment can be considered planning from the inside out. Usually, it is vital for strategic issues to be dealt with expeditiously and effectively if the organization is to survive and prosper. An organization that does not respond to a strategic issue can expect undesirable results from a threat, a missed opportunity, or both.

The iterative nature of the strategic planning process often becomes apparent in this step, when participants find that information created or discussed in earlier steps presents itself again as part of a strategic issue. For example, many strategic planning teams begin strategic planning with the belief that they know what their organization's mission is. They often find out in this step, however, that one of the key issues their organization faces is deciding exactly what its mission ought to be. In other words, the organization's present mission is found to be inappropriate given the team members' new understanding of the situation the organization faces, and a new mission must be created.

Strategic issues, virtually by definition, involve conflicts of one sort or another. The conflicts may involve ends (what), means (how), philosophy (why), location (where), timing (when), and persons favored or disadvantaged by different ways of resolving an issue (who). In order for strategic issues to be raised and effectively resolved, the organization must be prepared to deal with the almost inevitable conflicts that will occur.

A statement of a strategic issue should contain three elements. First, the issue should be described succinctly, preferably in a single paragraph. The issue should be framed as a question that the organization can do something positive to answer. If the organization cannot do anything about the issue, it is best not to think of it as an issue for that organization to address (Wildavsky, 1979; Ring, 1988). An organization's resources are limited enough without wasting them on issues it cannot address effectively.

Second, the factors that make the issue a fundamental challenge should be listed. In particular, what in terms of the organization's mandates, mission, values, internal strengths and weaknesses, and external opportunities and threats make this a strategic issue for the organization? Listing these factors will become useful in the next step, strategy development. Every effective strategy builds on strengths and takes advantage of opportunities while minimizing or overcoming weaknesses and threats. The framing of an organization's strategic issues is therefore very important because it will provide much of the basis for the issues' resolution (Dutton and Jackson, 1987; Bartunek and Moch, 1987; Bryson and Crosby, 1992; Dutton and Ashford, 1993).

Finally, the planning team should prepare a statement of the consequences of failing to address the issue. This will help organizational leaders decide just how strategic, or important, various issues are. If no consequences will ensue from failure to address a particular issue, then it is not a strategic issue. At the other extreme, if the organization will be destroyed or will miss a valuable opportunity by failing to address a particular issue, then the issue is clearly *very* strategic and is worth attending to immediately. Thus, the step of identifying strategic issues is aimed at focusing organizational attention on what is truly important for the survival, prosperity, and effectiveness of the organization.

Once statements of strategic issues are prepared, the organization will know what kinds of issues it faces and just how strategic they are. There are three kinds of strategic issues:

- Those for which no organizational action is required at present, but which must be continuously monitored.
- Those that are coming up on the horizon and are likely to require some action in the future and perhaps some action now. For the most part these issues can be handled as part of the organization's regular strategic planning cycle.
- Those that require an immediate response and therefore cannot be handled in a more routine way.

In Chapter Six, four basic approaches to the identification of strategic issues are discussed. The *direct* approach goes straight from a discussion of mandates, mission, and SWOTs (strengths, weaknesses, opportunities, and threats) to the identification of strategic issues. The *indirect* approach begins with brainstorming about several different options before identifying issues. The options include actions the organization could take to address stakeholder concerns, to build on strengths, to take advantage of opportunities and minimize or overcome weaknesses and threats, and to incorporate any important recommendations from background studies or reports on present circumstances. These options are then merged into a single set of potential actions and clustered into potential issue categories. The *goals* approach starts with goals and then identifies issues that must be addressed before the goals can be achieved. And the *"vision of success"* approach starts with at least a sketch of a vision of success in order to identify issues that must be dealt with before the vision can be realized.

By stating that there are four different approaches to the identification of strategic issues, I may raise the hackles of planning theorists and practitioners who believe you should *always* start with either issues, goals, or a vision for the organization. I argue that what will work best depends on the specific situation and that the wise planner should choose an approach accordingly.

Step 6: Formulating Strategies and Plans to Manage the Issues

A *strategy* is defined as a pattern of purposes, policies, programs, actions, decisions, or resource allocations that define what an organization is, what it does, and why it does it. Strategies can vary by level, by function, and by time frame. Strategies are developed to deal with the issues identified in the previous step.

This definition is purposely broad, in order to focus attention on creating consistency across people's *rhetoric* (what they say), their *choices* (what they decide on and are willing to pay for), and their *actions* (what they do), as well as the *consequences* of their actions. Effective strategy formulation and implementation processes link rhetoric, choices, actions, and consequences into reasonably coherent and consistent patterns across levels, functions, and time. They are also tailored to fit an organization's culture, even if the purpose of the strategy or strategies is to reconfigure that culture in some way. Draft strategies and perhaps drafts of formal strategic plans are formulated in this step to articulate desired patterns. They may also be reviewed and adopted at the end of this step if the strategic planning process is relatively simple, small-scale, and involves a single organization. (Such a process would merge this step with Step 7.)

A Five-Part Strategy Development Process. I favor either of two approaches to strategy development. The first is a five-part, fairly speedy process based on the work of the Institute of Cultural Affairs (Spencer, 1989). The second can be used if there is a desire or need to articulate more clearly the relationships among multiple options, to show how they fit together as part of a pattern.

The first part of the five-part process begins with the identification of practical alternatives and dreams or visions for resolving the strategic issues. Each option should be phrased in action terms; that is, it should begin with an imperative such as "do," "get," "buy," "achieve," and so forth. Phrasing options in action terms helps make the options more "real" to participants.

Next, the planning team should enumerate the barriers to achieving those alternatives, dreams, or visions. Focusing on barriers at this point is not typical of most strategic planning processes. But it is one way to ensure that any strategies that are developed deal with implementation difficulties directly rather than haphazardly.

Once the alternatives, dreams, and visions and the barriers to their realization are listed, the team develops major proposals for achieving the alternatives, dreams, or visions either directly or indirectly by overcoming the barriers. (Alternatively, the team might solicit proposals from key organizational units, various stakeholder groups, task forces, or selected individuals.) For example, a major Midwestern city government did not begin to work on strategies to achieve its major ambitions until it had overhauled its archaic civil service system. That system was clearly a barrier that had to be changed before the city government could have any hope of achieving its more important objectives.

After the major proposals are submitted, two final tasks remain in order to develop effective strategies. Actions that must be taken over the next two to three years to implement the major proposals must be identified. And finally, a detailed work program for the next six months to a year must be spelled out to implement these actions. These last two tasks spill over into the work of Step 9, but that is good, because strategies should always be developed with implementation in mind.

As Mintzberg (1994b, p. 25) explains, "Every failure of implementation is, by definition, also a failure of formulation." In some circumstances, Steps 6 and 9 may be merged—for example, when a single organization is planning for itself. In addition, in interorganizational or community settings, implementation details must often be worked out first by the various parties before they are willing to commit to shared strategic plans. In situations such as these, implementation planning may have to precede detailed strategy formulation or plan adoption.

Structuring Relationships Among Strategic Options to Develop Strategies. The second method is based on the Strategic Options Development and Analysis (SODA) method, developed by Colin Eden and his associates (Eden and Huxham, 1988; Eden, 1989; Eden, Ackermann, and Cropper, 1992; Bryson and Finn, 1995). The method involves listing multiple options, again phrased in imperative action terms, for addressing each strategic issue. The options are then linked by arrows indicating which options cause or influence the achievement of other options. An option can be a part of more than one chain. The result is a "map" of action-to-outcome (cause-and-effect, means-to-an-end) relationships; those options toward the end of a chain of arrows are essentially goals or perhaps even mission statements. Presumably, these goals can be achieved by accomplishing at least some of the actions leading up to them, although additional analysis and work on the arrow chains may be necessary to determine and clearly articulate reasonable action-to-outcome relationships. The option maps can be reviewed and revised and particular action-to-outcome chains selected as strategies. (See Resource C for more information on how to develop maps of this sort.)

An effective strategy must meet several criteria. It must be technically workable and politically acceptable to key stakeholders, and it must fit the organization's philosophy and core values. Further, it should be ethical, moral, and legal, and it should further the organization's pursuit of the common good. It must also deal with the strategic issue it was supposed to address. All too often, I have seen strategies that were technically, politically, morally, ethically, and legally impeccable but did not deal with the issues they were developed to address. Effective strategies thus must meet a rather severe set of tests. Careful, thoughtful dialogue—and often bargaining and negotiation—between key decision makers who have adequate information and are politically astute is typically necessary before strategies can be developed that meet these tests. Some of this work usually must occur in this step; some is likely to occur in the next step.

Step 7: Reviewing and Adopting the Strategies and Plan

Once strategies have been formulated, the planning team may need to obtain official approval to adopt them and proceed with their implementation. The same is true if a formal strategic plan has been prepared. When strategies and plans are developed for a single organization, particularly a small one, this step may merge with Step 6. But a separate step will likely be necessary when planning for a community or a network of organizations. The SPCC will need to approve the resulting strategies or plan, and other implementing groups and organizations are also likely to have to approve the strategies or plan, or at least parts of it, in order for implementation to proceed effectively.

In order to secure passage of any strategy or plan, it is necessary to continue to pay attention to the goals, concerns, and interests of all key internal and external stakeholders. Finding or creating inducements that can be traded for support can also be useful. But there are numerous ways to defeat any proposal in formal decision-making arenas, so it is important for the plan to be sponsored and championed by actors whose knowledge of how to negotiate the intricacies of the relevant arenas can help ensure the plan's passage (Bryson and Crosby, 1992).

Step 8: Establishing an Effective Organizational Vision

In this step, the organization develops a description of what it should look like once it has successfully implemented its strategies and achieved its full potential. This description is the organization's "vision of success" (Taylor, 1984; Nanus, 1992, pp. 189–224). Few organizations have such a description, yet the importance of developing one has long been recognized by well-managed companies (Ouchi, 1981; Peters and Waterman, 1982), organizational psychologists (Locke, Shaw, Saari, and Latham, 1981), and management theorists (Kouzes and Posner, 1987, 1993; Senge, 1990; Nanus, 1992; Kotter, 1995). Such descriptions typically include the organization's mission, its basic strategies, its performance criteria, some important decision rules, and the ethical standards expected of all employees.

The description, to the extent that it is widely circulated within the organization, allows organization members to know what is expected of them, without constant managerial oversight. Members are freed to act on their own initiative to an extent not otherwise possible. The result should be a mobilization of members' energy toward pursuing the organization's purposes, and a reduced need for direct supervision.

Some might question why developing a vision of success comes at this point in the process rather than much earlier. There are two basic answers to this question. First, it does not have to come here for all organizations. Some organizations are able to develop a fairly articulate, agreed-upon vision of success much earlier in the process. Communities, in fact, often start with "visioning" exercises in order to develop enough of a consensus on purposes and values to guide issue identification and strategy formulation. Figure 2.1 indicates the many different points at which participants may find it useful to develop some sort of guiding vision. Some processes may start with a visionary statement. Others may use visions to help them figure out what the strategic issues are or to help them develop strategies. And still others may use visions to convince key decision makers to adopt strategies or plans or to guide implementation efforts.

Second, most organizations typically will not be able to develop a detailed vision of success until they have gone through several iterations of strategic planning—if they are able to develop a vision at all. A challenging yet achievable vision embodies the tension between what an organization wants and what it can have (Senge, 1990). Often, several cycles of strategic planning are necessary before organization members know what they want, what they can have, and what the difference is between the two. A vision that motivates people will be challenging enough to spur action yet not so impossible to achieve that it demotivates and demoralizes people. Most organizations, in other words, will find that their visions of success are likely to serve more as a guide for strategy implementation than strategy formulation.

Further, for most organizations it is not necessary to develop a vision of success in order to achieve marked improvements in performance. In my experience, most organizations can demonstrate a substantial improvement in effectiveness if they simply identify and satisfactorily resolve a few strategic issues. Most organizations simply do not address often enough what is truly important; just gathering key decision makers to deal with a few important matters in a timely way can enhance organizational performance substantially. For these reasons this step is labeled optional in Figure 2.1.

Step 9: Developing an Effective Implementation Process

Just creating a strategic plan is not enough. The changes indicated by the adopted strategies must be incorporated throughout the system for them to be brought to life and for real value to be created for the organization and its stakeholders. Thinking strategically about implementation and developing an effective implementation plan are important tasks on the road to realizing the strategies developed in Step 6. For example, in some circumstances, direct implementation at all sites will be the wisest strategic choice, while in other situations, some form of staged implementation may be best.

Again, if strategies and an implementation plan have been developed for a single organization, particularly a small one, or for an interorganizational network or community, this step may have been incorporated into Step 6. However, in many multidepartmental or intergovernmental situations, a separate step is required to ensure that relevant groups and organizations do the action planning necessary for implementation success.

Action plans should detail the following:

- Implementation roles and responsibilities of oversight bodies, organizational teams, and individuals
- Specific objectives and expected results and milestones

- Specific action steps and relevant details
- Schedules
- Resource requirements and sources
- A communication process
- Review, monitoring, and midcourse correction procedures
- Accountability procedures

It is important to build into action plans enough sponsors, champions, and other personnel—along with enough time, money, attention, administrative and support services, and other resources—to ensure successful implementation. You must "budget the plan" wisely to ensure implementation goes well.

It is also important to work quickly to avoid unnecessary or undesirable competition with new priorities. Whenever important opportunities to implement strategies and achieve objectives arise, they should be taken. In other words, it is important to be opportunistic as well as deliberate. And it is important to remember that what actually happens in practice will always be some blend of what is intended and what emerges along the way (Mintzberg, 1994a, 1994b).

Successfully implemented and institutionalized strategies result in a new "regime," a "set of implicit or explicit principles, norms, rules, and decision-making procedures around which actors' expectations converge in a given area" (Krasner, 1983, p. 2; Bryson and Crosby, 1992). Regime building is necessary to preserve gains in the face of competing demands. Unfortunately, regimes can outlive their usefulness and must then be changed; this involves the final step in the process.

Step 10: Reassessing Strategies and the Strategic Planning Process

Once the implementation process has been under way for some time, it is important to review the strategies and the strategic planning process as a prelude to a new round of strategic planning. Much of the work of this phase may occur as part of the ongoing implementation process. However, if the organization has not engaged in strategic planning for a while, this should be a separate phase. Attention should be focused on successful strategies and whether they should be maintained, replaced by other strategies, or terminated for one reason or another. The strategic planning process should also be examined, its strengths and weaknesses noted, and modifications suggested to improve the next round of strategic planning.

Tailoring the Process to Specific Circumstances

The Strategy Change Cycle is a general approach to strategic planning and management. Like any planning and management process, it must be carefully tailored to specific situations if it is to be useful (Christensen, 1985; Sager, 1994; Roberts and Wargo, 1994). Therefore, a number of adaptations, or variations on the general theme, are discussed in this section.

Sequencing the Steps

Although the steps are laid out in a linear sequence, it must be emphasized that the Strategy Change Cycle, as its name suggests, is iterative in practice. Participants typically rethink what they have done several times before they reach final decisions. Moreover, the process does not always begin at the beginning. Organizations typically find themselves confronted with a new mandate (Step 2), a pressing strategic issue (Step 5), a failing strategy (Step 6 or 9), or the need to reassess what they have been doing (Step 10), and this leads them to engage in strategic planning. Once engaged, the organization is likely to go back and begin at the beginning, particularly with a reexamination of its mission. (Indeed, in my experience, it does not matter where you start, you always end up back at your mission.)

In addition, implementation usually begins before all of the planning is complete. As soon as useful actions are identified, they are taken, as long as they do not jeopardize future actions that might prove valuable. In other words, in a linear, sequential process, the first eight steps of the process would be followed by implementing the planned actions and evaluating the results. However, implementation typically does not, and should not, wait until the eight steps have been completed. For example, if the organization's mission needs to be redrafted, then it should be. If the SWOT analysis turns up weaknesses or threats that need to be addressed immediately, they should be. If aspects of a strategy can be implemented without awaiting further developments, they should be. And so on. As noted earlier, strategic thinking *and* acting are important, and all of the thinking does not have to occur before any actions are taken. Strategic planning's iterative, flexible, action-oriented nature is precisely what makes it so attractive to public and nonprofit leaders and managers.

Making Use of Vision, Goals, and Issues

In the discussion of Step 8, it was noted that different organizations and communities may wish to start their planning process with a vision statement. Such a statement may foster a consensus and provide important inspiration and guidance for the rest of the process, even though it is unlikely to be as detailed as a statement developed later in the process. And as indicated in Figure 2.1, there are other points at which it might be possible to develop a vision statement (or statements). Vision thus may be used to prompt the identification of strategic issues, to guide the development of strategies, to inspire the adoption of strategic plans, or to guide implementation efforts. Mainline Church, for example, used several different vision statements to guide strategy development in different areas (worship, Christian education, ministry of caring, and so on). The decision to develop a vision statement should hinge on whether one is needed to provide direction to subsequent efforts; whether people will be able to develop a vision that is meaningful enough, detailed enough, *and* broadly supported; and whether there will be enough energy left over after the visioning effort is complete to push ahead.

Similarly, as indicated in Figure 2.1, it is possible to develop goals at many different points in the process. Some strategic planning processes begin with the goals of a new board of directors, elected policy bodies, chief executive officers, or other top-level decision makers. These goals thus embody a reform agenda for the organization (or community). Other strategic planning processes may start with goals that reflect mandates. For example, as noted earlier, the Government Performance and Results Act of 1993 requires all federal agencies to produce a strategic plan based on outcomes. A *starting* goal for these agencies, therefore, is to decide the outcomes they want to be measured against. This goal thus helps these agencies identify an important *strategic issue*—namely, what their outcomes should be. Subsequent strategic planning efforts are then likely to start with the desired outcomes the organization thinks are important.

Still other strategic planning processes articulate goals in order to guide strategy formulation in response to specific issues or to guide implementation of specific strategies. Goals developed at these later stages of the process are likely to be more detailed and specific than those developed earlier in the process. Goals may be developed any time they will be useful to guide subsequent efforts in the process *and* when they will have sufficient support among key parties to produce the desired action.

In my experience, however, strategic planning processes generally start neither with vision nor with goals. In part, this is because strategic planning rarely starts with Step 1. Instead, people sense something is not right about their current situation—they face strategic issues of one sort or another, or they are pursuing a strategy that is failing or about to fail—and they want to know what to do. One of the crucial features of issue-driven planning (and political decision making in general) is that you do not have to agree on goals to agree on the next steps. You simply need to agree on a strategy that will address the issue and further the organization's (or community's) and its key stakeholders' interests. Goals will likely be developed once viable strategies have been developed to address the issue, and they typically will be strategy-specific goals.

Describing a vision may help provide a better feeling for where a strategy or interconnected set of strategies should lead. Vision and goals thus are more likely to come toward the end of the process than the beginning. But there are clear exceptions (including Mainline Church's planning process), and process designers should think carefully about when and how—if at all—to bring vision and goals into the process.

Applying the Process Across Organizational Subunits, Levels, and Functions on an Ongoing Basis

To return to Wayne Gretzky and John Stedman, one can easily imagine them, already on the move, whipping intuitively through the ten steps in a rapid series of discussions, decisions, and actions. The steps merely make the process of strategic thinking and acting more orderly and allow more people to participate in the process. When the process is applied to an organization as a whole on an ongoing basis (rather than as a one-shot deal), or at least to significant parts of it, it is usually necessary to construct a *strategic planning system*. The system allows the various parts of the process to be integrated in appropriate ways, and it engages the organization in strategic *management*, not just strategic planning (Bozeman and Straussman, 1990; Koteen, 1989).

The process might be applied across subunits, levels, and functions in an organization as outlined in Figure 2.2. The application is based on the "layered" or "stacked units of management" system used by the 3M Corporation (Tita and Allio, 1984). The system's first cycle consists of "bottom-up" development of strategic plans within a framework established at the top, followed by reviews and reconciliations at each succeeding level. In the second cycle, operating plans are developed to implement the strategic plans. Depending on the situation, decisions at the top of the organizational hierarchy may or may not require policy board approval (which is why the line depicting the process flow diverges at the top).

Strategic planning systems for public and nonprofit organizations are usually not as formalized and integrated as the one outlined in Figure 2.2. Far more typical is a "strategic issues management" system, which attempts to manage specific strategic issues without seeking integration of the resultant strategies across all subunits, levels, and functions (Kemp, 1993; Roberts and Wargo, 1994). Tight integration is not necessary, because most issues do not affect all parts of the organization, are subject to different politics, and are on their own time frame. Hennepin County, Minnesota, has used such a system successfully to address several areas of strategic concern (finance, employment and economic development, transportation, program fragmentation, and coordination). Their system consists of three cycles: strategic issue identification, strategy development, and strategy implementation (Eckhert, Haines, Delmont, and Pflaum, 1988). Other common public and nonprofit strategic planning systems include the "contract model," "goal model," and "portfolio model." These will be discussed in more detail in Chapter Ten.

If the organization is fairly large, then specific linkages will be necessary in order to join the planning process to different functions and levels in the organization so that it can proceed in a reasonably orderly and integrated manner. One effective way to achieve such a linkage is to appoint the heads of all major units to the strategic planning team. All unit heads can then be sure that their units' in-

FIGURE 2.2. STRATEGIC PLANNING SYSTEM FOR LAYERED OR STACKED UNITS OF MANAGEMENT.

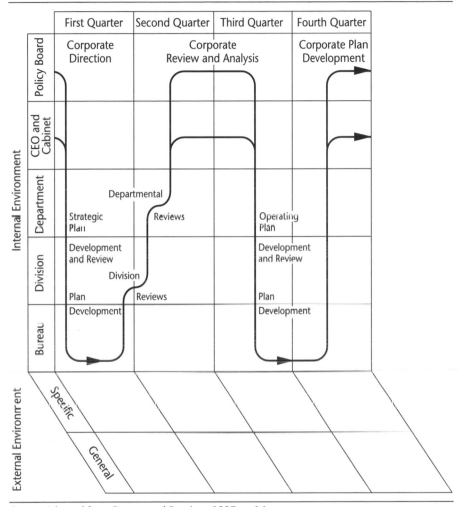

Source: Adapted from Bryson and Roering, 1987, p. 16.

formation and interests are represented in strategy formulation and can oversee strategy implementation within their units.

Indeed, key decision makers might wish to form a permanent strategic planning committee or cabinet. I certainly recommend this approach if it appears workable for the organization, as it emphasizes the role of line managers as strategic planners and the role of strategic planners as facilitators of the line managers' decision making. Pragmatic and effective strategies and plans are likely to result. Temporary task forces, strategic planning committees, or a permanent cabinet can work; but whatever the arrangement, there is no substitute for the direct involvement of key decision makers in the process.

Applying the Process to Interorganizational Networks, Communities, and Functions That Cross Organizational Boundaries

When applied to a function or network that crosses organizational boundaries or to a community, the process probably will need to be sponsored by a committee or task force of key decision makers, opinion leaders, "influentials," or "notables" representing important stakeholder groups. Additional working groups or task forces will probably need to be organized at various times to deal with specific strategic issues or to oversee the implementation of specific strategies. Because so many more people and groups need to be involved, and because implementation will have to rely more on consent than on authority, the process is likely to be much more time consuming and iterative than strategic planning within a single organization (Gray, 1989; Bryson and Crosby, 1992; Winer and Ray, 1994; Innes, 1994).

In addition, when a community is involved, special efforts are necessary to make sure that important connections are made—and incompatibilities are resolved—between strategic plans, the community's comprehensive plan, and the various devices used to implement the plan (such as a government's capital improvements programs, subdivision controls, zoning ordinances, and official maps). The fact that these connections need to be made should not unduly hamper the process, however. Strategic planning and comprehensive planning can be complementary; efforts should be made to ensure that they are in the community's best interests, and those of its various stakeholders, are to be advanced (Rider, 1983; King and Johnson, 1988; Kemp, 1993; Innes, 1994).

Roles for Planners, Decision Makers, Implementers, and Citizens

Planners can play many different roles in a strategic planning process. In many cases, the planners are not the people with the job title "planner," but are in fact policy makers or line managers. Planners often act primarily as facilitators of decision making by policy makers or line managers, as technical experts in substantive areas, or both. In other cases, planners operate in a variety of different roles. Sometimes the planner is an "expert on experts" (Bolan, 1971) who eases different people with different expertise in and out of the process for different purposes at different times. At other times, planners act as technicians, politicians, or hybrids (Howe and Kaufman, 1979; Howe, 1980). At still other times, they are "finders" of strategies, interpreting existing actions and recognizing important patterns in the organization and its environment; "analysts" of existing or potential strategies; "catalysts" for promoting strategic thought and action; or finally, "strategists" themselves (Mintzberg, 1994b, pp. 361–396).

Since the most important thing about strategic planning is the development of strategic thought and action, it may not matter much which person does what. However, it does seem that strategic planning done by policy makers, line managers, or both is most likely to be implemented. (Line managers in government are not usually charged with making important political trade-offs—politicians are. Therefore an effective strategic planning process in government entities probably needs the participation of both.) Exactly how those people formally designated as planners contribute to the development of strategic thought and action is unclear. In any particular situation, they should be involved in a way that promotes strategic thought and action and enhances commitment to agreed-upon strategies.

When a public organization is the principal focus of attention, there is often little citizen participation in the planning process beyond that of elected or appointed policy board members. One reason may be that the organization may already possess the necessary knowledge and expertise in-house, and therefore, citizen involvement would be redundant and excessively time consuming. In addition, insiders typically are the chief implementers of strategies, so their ownership of the process and the resultant decisions may be what is most crucial. Further, citizen participation may not be necessary to legitimize the process if an elected or appointed policy board is already directly involved (in keeping with the idea of representative, not direct, democracy). The absence of participation by ordinary outsiders parallels private-sector corporate planning practice.

Program-focused strategic planning appears to be much more likely to involve citizens, particularly in their capacity as "customers." Citizen involvement in program planning is thus roughly analogous to extensive consumer involvement in private-sector marketing and research and development projects. For example, the public library relied on extensive patron surveys and focus groups to figure out what services to emphasize. Planning for public transportation also typically involves a great deal of citizen participation. Citizens may provide information concerning their travel needs and desires, reactions to various vehicle designs, and advice on ways to resolve conflicts that arise during the process. Park planning also involves substantial citizen participation. Unfortunately, because the use of transportation systems or parks by citizens is generally broad based, users and "the citizen at large" are often equated. This is hardly ever justified, however, as it probably masks great variety in stakeholder concerns about the process and potential contributions to it. A stakeholder analysis, such as the one the public library used, can help keep various citizen interests and contributions analytically separate.

Finally, planning on behalf of a community almost always involves substantial citizen participation. Unfortunately, community-focused strategic plans also typically treat all citizens alike and assume that all citizens are interested in the community as a whole—two assumptions that are at odds with most studies of political participation (see Verba and Nie, 1972; Warren and Warren, 1977). Application of the stakeholder concept to community strategic planning can help avoid some of these errors—as it did in the case of the school district's efforts, where the interests of parents, businesses, taxpayers, and residents of particular neighborhoods were all explored.

Summary

This chapter has outlined a process called the Strategy Change Cycle for promoting strategic thinking and acting in governments, public agencies, nonprofit organizations, networks, communities, and other entities. While the process is presented in a linear, sequential fashion, it typically proceeds iteratively as groups continuously rethink connections among the various elements in the process on their way to formulating effective strategies. In addition, the process often does not start with Step 1 but instead starts somewhere else and then cycles back to Step 1.

As previously mentioned, my colleague Farnum Alston and I have prepared a strategic planning workbook designed to help individuals, teams, groups, and organizations work through this process (Bryson and Alston, 1995). The workbook should not be used without this book, however, since in practice the process typically requires careful tailoring to specific circumstances. Owing to space limitations, the workbook contains little advice on how to adapt the process to different situations. This book, however, offers a great deal of advice and guidance on designing and managing a successful process.

In Chapter Three, we will discuss how to negotiate an initial agreement between key internal (and perhaps external) decision makers and/or opinion leaders on the purpose and process of a strategic planning effort. The agreement will shape the nature and direction of discussions, decisions, and actions designed to deal with what is truly important to the organization or community.

PART TWO

KEY STEPS IN USING THE STRATEGY CHANGE CYCLE TO THINK AND ACT STRATEGICALLY

The ten-step strategic planning process is presented in detail in Part Two. It is a reasonably orderly, deliberative, and participative approach to facilitating strategic thought and action by key decision makers.

Chapter Three covers the initial agreement phase, the "plan for planning." Chapter Four focuses on clarifying organizational mandates and mission. Chapter Five describes how to assess an organization's strengths and weaknesses as well as the opportunities and threats it faces. Chapter Six discusses strategic issues—what they are, how they can be identified, and how to critique them. Chapter Seven is devoted to formulating and adopting effective strategies and plans.

The final three chapters in Part Two move from planning to management. Chapter Eight covers development of an organization's "vision of success," a description of what the organization should look like as it fulfills its mission and achieves its full potential. Chapter Nine focuses on implementing strategies and plans, and Chapter Ten on reassessing them.

An organization that completes this Strategy Change Cycle should be well on its way toward improving and maintaining its effectiveness, pursuing its mission, and meeting its mandates. It should be clearly focused on satisfying key stakeholders in ways that are politically acceptable, technically workable, and legally, morally, and ethically defensible. ◆

CHAPTER THREE

INITIATING AND AGREEING ON A STRATEGIC PLANNING PROCESS

The beginning is the most important part of the work.

PLATO, *THE REPUBLIC*

The purpose of the first step in the strategic planning process is to develop among key internal decision makers or opinion leaders (and, if their support is necessary for the success of the effort, key external leaders as well) an initial agreement about the overall strategic planning effort and main planning steps. This represents a kind of "plan to plan" (Steiner, 1979).

The support and commitment of key decision makers are vital if strategic planning and change are to succeed (Olsen and Eadie, 1982; Nutt and Backoff, 1992; Schein, 1992). But the importance of their early involvement goes beyond the need for their support and commitment. They supply information vital to the planning effort: who should be involved, when key decision points will occur, and what arguments are likely to be persuasive at various points in the process. They can also provide critical resources: legitimacy, staff assignments, a budget, and meeting space.

Every strategic planning effort is in effect a story or play that must have the correct setting; themes; plots and subplots; actors; scenes; beginning, middle, and conclusion; and interpretation (Mangham and Overington, 1987). Only key decision makers have access to enough information and resources to allow for the effective development and direction of such a story.

Planning Focus and Desired Outcomes

Ideally, this first step will produce agreement on several issues:

1. The purpose and worth of the strategic planning effort
2. The organizations, units, groups, or persons who should be involved or informed, and in what ways

3. The specific steps to be followed
4. The format and timing of reports

A strategic planning coordinating committee and a strategic planning team should probably be formed. Finally, the necessary resources to begin the endeavor must be committed.

As a general rule, the strategic planning effort should focus on that part of the organization (or function or community) that is controlled, overseen, or strongly influenced by the key decision makers interested in engaging in strategic planning. In other words, only under unusual circumstances would it make sense to develop strategic plans for organizations or parts of organizations over which the key decision makers involved in the effort have no control, or for which they have no responsibility.

The exception to this rule is externally initiated reform programs designed to demonstrate how an organization might conduct itself if it took the reformers' aims seriously. For example, candidates running for elective office often include in their campaign platforms proposed new strategies for the governments they wish to lead. Editorial and opinion pages of newspapers and public affairs magazines also often include what are in effect reformers' strategic plans for public or nonprofit organizations.

The agreement should also make clear what the "givens" are at the beginning of the process. In other words, what is it about the organization's history, arrangements, and practices that will be off-limits, at least for the time being, and what is open for revision? On one hand, if everything is a candidate for far-reaching change, potential participants may be scared off, and resistance to change within the organization may harden. On the other hand, if everything is sacred, then there is no reason for strategic planning. There should be enough tension to prompt change and make it worth the effort but not so much that it paralyzes potential participants with fear and anxiety (Dalton, 1970; Schein, 1987).

Benefits of the Process

The process of reaching an initial agreement is straightforward in concept but often rather circuitous in practice. It usually proceeds through the following stages:

1. Introducing the concept of strategic planning
2. Developing an understanding of what it can mean in practice
3. Thinking through some of its more important implications
4. Developing a commitment to strategic planning
5. Reaching an actual agreement

The more numerous the decision makers involved and the less they know about strategic planning, the more time consuming the process will be and the more indirect the route to agreement. Indeed, a series of agreements must usually be reached before the strategic planning process can begin in earnest.

A number of significant benefits flow from a good initial agreement (Delbecq, 1977; Benveniste, 1989; Janis, 1989). The first is simply that the purpose and worth of the strategic planning effort are likely to be widely recognized by the affected parties, leading to broad sponsorship and legitimacy. Broad sponsorship dispels any suspicion that the effort is a "power play" by a small group. And it ensures that the results of the planning efforts are likely to be seen as "objective" (that is, not manipulated to serve narrow partisan interests). Broad sponsorship is also a source of "psychological safety" that can help people address what otherwise might be highly threatening, anxiety- or guilt-provoking prospects for change (Schein, 1992).

Legitimacy justifies the content and timing of the discussions in the next stages of the planning process (Herson, 1984). Such discussions—particularly when they involve key decision makers across functions, levels, and organizational boundaries of various sorts—are unlikely to occur without prompting. And they are unlikely to be prompted without authorization.

Authorization for such discussions is an enormous resource for the planners who organize them because the planners gain considerable control over the forums in which the discussions occur, the agendas, the information provided, and how the issues to be discussed are framed. The planners gain control because the discussions are typically cross functional rather than under the control of any unit or department. As facilitators of such cross-functional discussions, planners gain leverage. Control of this sort is not manipulative in a partisan sense; instead, it ensures that the organization as a whole is looked at and discussed, rather than only the separate parts (Bryson and Crosby, 1989).

In the school district, for example, a group composed of the seven-member school board, the superintendent, the assistant superintendent, and the directors of finance, personnel, community education, and communications began the strategic planning process. They saw strategic planning as a way for them to engage each other in extended, reasonable, balanced, and holistic discussions about what was best for the district. Previously, each board member had tended to pursue his or her own agenda. Also, there had been inadequate coordination across district departments and levels, in part because the board had not provided clear policy guidelines, but also because of the previous superintendent's management style. The new superintendent (the "planner" who initiated the process) was interested in strategic planning precisely because he hoped it would engender this kind of changed, holistic thinking.

A well-articulated initial agreement also provides a clear definition of the network to be involved in strategic planning and the process by which it is to be maintained. The National Aeronautics and Space Administration (NASA), for example, tries to adhere to a "doctrine of no surprises" as it develops its networks and moves toward making major decisions. The doctrine specifies that major stakeholders must be kept informed of progress, events, and impending decisions. Nothing is dropped on them "out of the blue." When the need for cooperation and the risks of failure are high, such a doctrine appears to be quite valuable (Delbecq and Filley, 1974). NASA found out just how valuable when the doctrine produced information that conflicted with its famed "Can do!" ethic. The "ethic" led NASA to discount information it did not want to hear, and the *Challenger* space shuttle disaster of 1986 resulted. Engineers for Morton-Thiokol, the company responsible for the rocket, had warned of a possible disaster if the rocket were launched in cold weather, but senior NASA officials ignored the warning—and some of their own rules and precedents—and simply decided to go ahead. (See Janis, 1989, pp. 76–77; Maier, 1992.) The "no surprises" approach may be best in other situations as well—even when there seem to be good reasons for keeping certain stakeholders in the dark. In an era when a basic characteristic of information seems to be that it "leaks" (Cleveland, 1985), full and prompt disclosure may be advisable. As Ben Franklin used to say, "Three may keep a secret, if two of them are dead."

A good initial agreement will also include an outline of the general sequence of steps in the strategic planning effort. To be effective, the outline must ensure that the process is tied to key decision-making points in arenas such as budget decisions, elections, and the legislative cycle. Time in organizations is not linear; it is "junctural" (Bryson and Roering, 1988, 1989; Bromiley and Marcus, 1987; Albert, 1995), and the most important junctions are decision-making points.

To revert to our play metaphor, a good initial agreement will name the actors, outline the plot that is about to unfold, specify how it will be broken into acts and scenes, designate the stage on which it will be played, and describe the general character of the story and themes to be followed. Thus, the initial agreement step is extremely important because what follows depends significantly on the specifics of the beginning. The chapter epigraph captures the fatefulness embodied in this early work, particularly in systems prone to chaotic behavior (Cohen, March, and Olsen, 1972; Kingdon, 1995).

Moreover—and this will dramatically affect the story that develops—the agreement should specify exactly what in the organization's history is to be taken as a given, at least at the start. For example, an organization's existing legal commitments, mandates, personnel complements, organizational designs, mission statements, resource allocations, job descriptions, or culture may need to be taken as a given in order to gain agreement. It is very important to be clear from the start what is off-limits for the exercise; otherwise, several key decision makers are unlikely to participate. On the one hand, if too much is "up for grabs," the process will be too threatening or dangerous, will result in unconstructive or downright damaging conflict, or will produce a strategic plan that is useless because it lacks adequate support. On the other hand, the more history that is taken as a given, the less useful strategic planning is likely to be. It is important, therefore, to find the right balance between what is a given and what is possible (Mangham and Overington, 1987).

A good agreement also provides a mechanism such as a strategic planning task force or coordinating committee for buffering, consulting, negotiating, or problem solving among units, groups, or persons involved in or affected by the planning effort. Without these mechanisms, conflicts are likely to stymie or even destroy the effort (Fisher and Ury, 1981; Susskind and Cruikshank, 1987; Ury, Brett, and Goldberg, 1988; Gray, 1989).

In addition, these mechanisms allow errors to be detected as the process proceeds; a strategic planning task force or coordinating committee can then make needed midcourse corrections. A task force is also a valuable sounding board for ideas.

A good initial agreement guarantees the necessary resources. Money typically is not the most needed resource for strategic planning; the time and attention of key decision makers are more important. Staff time will also be needed to gather information and provide logistical and clerical support (probably one staff person part-time in a small organization, several people in a larger organization).

Finally, a good initial agreement signifies the political support of key decision makers or opinion leaders at several levels in the organization, and it helps maintain that support at different points in the process. For strategic planning to work, a coalition must develop that is large enough and strong enough to formulate and implement strategies that deal effectively with key strategic issues. Such coalitions do not develop quickly. Instead, they coalesce around the important strategic ideas that emerge from the discussions, consultations, mutual education efforts, and reconceptualizations that are at the heart of any strategic planning effort (Bryson, Van de Ven, and Roering, 1987; Mintzberg and Westley, 1992; Bryson and Crosby, 1992; Mintzberg, 1994a, 1994b).

Developing an Initial Agreement

So far we have covered the purpose, desired outcomes, and benefits of this first step in strategic planning. Now we can go into greater depth on specific aspects of developing an initial agreement.

Whose Process Is It and Who Should Be Involved?

Obviously, some individual or group must initiate and champion the process. This champion will need to make the initial decisions about what the process should focus on and who should be involved. If the strategic planning process is going to affect the entire organization, then the organization's key decision makers (and perhaps representatives of some of the external stakeholders) should be involved. For example, the school district chose a two-tiered system of involvement for its first strategic planning effort. The first tier included eight people: the seven school board members and the superintendent. The second tier included the superintendent and the five members of his cabinet. Those in the first tier were obviously the key decision makers, but they chose to involve the assistant superintendent and other senior district managers in a consultative role in order to get the necessary information, support, commitment, and resources to make the strategic planning effort work for the district as a whole. The group decided not to involve external stakeholders in major decision-making roles. (Outsiders did cochair and serve on advisory task forces, making recommendations on how to address the strategic issues identified by the board and superintendent. Outsiders were also involved in focus groups and community information-gathering meetings.) The group felt that it needed to learn how strategic planning worked before taking on potential complications from outsider involvement; in addition, as the official, legally responsible decision-making body for the district, they could not easily share decision-making responsibility.

If the strategic planning focus is on an organizational subunit, a function, or a community, then key decision makers (and possibly stakeholders) for those entities should be involved. For example, key decision makers or stakeholders in a community, such as the owners of major businesses, may not actually live in the community. The initial agreement for the public library's strategic planning effort was negotiated between the library's director and assistant director, the city's community services department (which the library was a part of at the time), the Friends of the Public Library, a nonprofit fundraising and support organization, the board of a foundation that had an endowment available to assist the library, all of the unit heads and key opinion leaders within the library, and strategic planning consultants hired to provide additional support.

For organizations, it may be advisable to involve insiders from three levels of the organization, as well as key outsiders. (Note that elected or appointed policy board members can be outsiders as well as insiders.) These include top policy and decision makers, middle-management personnel, and technical core or frontline personnel (Thompson, 1967; Crow and Bozeman, 1988; Nutt and Backoff, 1992). Top policy and decision makers should be involved for several reasons. First, they are formally charged with relating the organization to its domain. Second, because of their responsibilities, they are often highly effective "boundary spanners," providing links to many people and organizations—both inside and outside the organization (Whetten and Bozeman, 1991). Third, they are often among the first to perceive mismatches between the organization and its environment, and they are therefore the most responsive to external threats and opportunities affecting the organization (Hampden-Turner, 1990; Schein, 1992). Finally, they control the resources necessary to carry out the strategic planning effort and implement its recommendations. It is simply very difficult to plan without these people, so they should be included from the start if at all possible.

In governments and public agencies, the initial group is likely to include members of an elected or appointed board as well as high-level executives. In council-manager cities, for example, the initial agreement is typically negotiated between council members, the city manager, and key department heads. As noted earlier, the school district's initial agreement involved the elected school board, the appointed superintendent, and key managers. In nonprofit organizations, the key decision-making group is likely to include the senior managers and board of directors. The initial agreement for Mainline Church's effort was negotiated among the organization's elected trustees, elders, and deacons; the senior pastor and other clergy; and the elder and staff member—the champions—who initiated the process and provided most of the energy to keep it going.

Middle-management personnel should be included because of their vital role in translating policies and decisions into operations. Further, they are likely to bear the brunt of any managerial changes that result, and therefore they should be involved to reduce unnecessary resistance and to make implementation smoother (Kanter, 1983, 1989; Block, 1987).

There are several reasons to consider involving technical core or frontline personnel or their representatives (Benveniste, 1972, 1989; Normann, 1991; Cohen and Brand, 1993). First, they are in charge of the day-to-day use of the core technologies contributing to, or affected by, strategic change. As a result, they are likely to be the most knowledgeable about how the organization's basic technologies work, and they also are most likely to be immediately hurt or helped by change. Their early involvement may be necessary to ensure that needed changes are understood, wise changes are implemented, and resistance to change is minimized. Second, technical or frontline personnel are likely to be asked for their opinions by key decision makers anyway, so anything that can make them receptive to strategic change early on is a plus. Because the organization is highly dependent on their technical knowledge or their daily contact with customers, clients, or users, these personnel can severely hamper strategic changes they do not support. In extreme cases, they might undermine or even sabotage change efforts. Co-opting these groups early on can be an important key to strategic planning success.

An important caveat is in order. If it is clear from the start that strategic planning will result in the elimination of certain positions, work groups, or departments—as in major reengineering efforts, for example—then it may be both unnecessary and downright harmful to involve people in those positions. The most effective and humane approach may be to involve these people in planning for their transition to new jobs by obtaining their input on retraining, placement, and severance arrangements (Behn, 1983; Mercer, 1992).

How to Get Started

For an organization, often the best way to reach an initial agreement is to hold a retreat. Begin the retreat with an introduction to the nature, purpose, and process of strategic planning (Eadie and Kethley, 1994). Often key decision makers need such an introduction before they are fully willing to endorse a strategic planning effort. Orientation and training methods might include a lecture and discussion;

presentations by representatives of organizations that have used strategic planning, followed by group discussion; analysis by key decision makers of written case studies, followed by group discussion; circulation of reading materials; films; and so on.

A possible format for the first day of a strategic planning retreat is as follows:

Morning. Lecture and discussion about the nature, purpose, and process of strategic planning.

Lunch. Presentation from a representative of a similar organization that has engaged in strategic planning, highlighting the benefits and liabilities of the process.

Afternoon. Analysis and discussion of a written case study. Instruction in any special techniques necessary for successful strategic planning, such as brainstorming, the nominal group technique (Delbecq, Van de Ven, and Gustafson, 1975), the snow card technique (Greenblat and Duke, 1981; Spencer, 1989), or the oval mapping process (see Resource C).

By the end of the first day, it should be clear whether or not the key decision makers wish to proceed. If so, the second day might be organized as follows:

Morning. Stakeholder analysis, review of mandates, and development of a draft mission statement.

Lunch. A speaker presenting another case example.

Afternoon. SWOT analysis and identification of strategic issues.

Organizations already committed to strategic planning might skip the activities outlined for the afternoon of the first day. The retreat might end at the end of the second day, after the next steps have been consensually mapped out, or it might continue for a third day. The morning of the third day could be devoted to further identification and discussion of strategic issues, prioritizing among them and developing possible strategies for addressing them. The afternoon could carry this discussion further, outlining the possible next steps in the process. The retreat should not end until agreement is reached on what the next steps in the process will be and who will be responsible for what in each step.

If the group can quickly agree on each point, less than three days might be sufficient. If quick agreement is not possible, more time may be necessary to complete the various tasks, and sessions may have to be spread out over several weeks. Quick agreement is unlikely if the strategic issues imply the need for a major change. It takes a group time to cope with the anxiety, fear, anger, and denial that may accompany profound change, particularly if it senses that its culture and basic beliefs about the world are being threatened (Kubler-Ross, 1969; Mangham, 1986; Hampden-Turner, 1990; Schein, 1992).

A retreat might also be helpful for a community engaged in strategic planning, to help key decision makers reach agreement about the nature of the planning effort. Such a retreat, however, might be very difficult to organize. More groundwork will probably be necessary to gain agreement from decision makers on the purpose, timing, and length of the retreat. The retreat itself will probably have to be less than three days, and postretreat logistics, coordination, and follow-through will probably take more time and effort. Nonetheless, a retreat can provide an important sign that the community is about to address its most important issues and concerns, it can provoke desirable media attention and pressure to continue, and it can prompt stakeholders who are lukewarm about the process to participate (Winer and Ray, 1994).

How Many "Initial" Agreements?

Sometimes a series of agreements among successively larger groups of key decision makers may be necessary before everyone is on board. For example, the school district had several "initial" agreements. The superintendent saw that the district might benefit from strategic planning. That led to the first agreement, between the superintendent and the board, in a jointly negotiated 1990–91 work program that called for initiation of a strategic planning process. The board therefore expected strategic planning of some sort but was waiting for the superintendent to propose a process. A second agreement was reached after the superintendent spoke with the assistant superintendent, me, and my colleague Chuck Finn. This agreement included an outline of a proposed process, including specific steps, a time line, and likely consulting costs. This agreement was used to involve the rest of the cabinet, who signed on after they had had a chance to meet Chuck and me and to review, discuss, and modify the process. A final agreement was reached with the board after they, too, had had a chance to meet Chuck and me and to review, discuss, and modify the process informally. The "official" initial agreement was reached at a formal, televised, regular meeting of the board. This series of agreements was necessary to build understanding of what strategic planning would mean for the district, to tailor the process to the district and its needs, to establish trust in the consultants, and to develop the necessary commitment among key decision makers to move ahead (Bryson and Finn, 1995; Bryson, Ackermann, Eden, and Finn, forthcoming). The strategic planning efforts of the public library and Mainline Church also began with several "initial" agreements.

Indeed, it is worth keeping in mind that forging agreements of various sorts will go on throughout the Strategy Change Cycle. Coalitions are built incrementally, by agreement, and strategies and plans are typically adopted and implemented incrementally as well, through various agreements. These agreements may be signaled by various means, including handshakes, letters or memoranda of agreement, formal votes, and celebrations.

What Should the Initial Agreement Contain?

The initial agreement should cover the desired outcomes listed at the beginning of this chapter: the purpose of the effort (including what it will not achieve) and its worth; the organizations, units, groups, or persons who should be involved; a shared understanding about the nature and sequence of the steps in the process; and the form and timing of reports. Next, a committee should probably be established to oversee the strategic planning effort. The committee should be headed by someone with enough standing and credibility in the organization to ensure that the effort is given visibility and legitimacy. Ideally, this person will be trusted by all or most factions in the organization, so that the effort will not be seen as a narrow partisan affair. The committee can be an existing group, such as a board of directors or city council that adds strategic planning oversight to its responsibilities, or it can be a committee or task force established for this specific purpose. In the school district, the board and superintendent were the official overseers of the process, although the cabinet also shared responsibility for strategic planning (particularly since each cabinet member cochaired with a community leader a different task force set up to address some of the strategic issues). The public library established a very large strategic planning committee. The CPI program's management team added strategic planning to its responsibilities. And Mainline Church established a long-range planning committee to oversee its effort. The oversight committee will probably be the body that formulates the initial agreements, although it may be necessary to first work out agreements with various groups and factions who will then send representatives to sit on the oversight body.

Next, a team to carry out the staff work will probably be necessary. The team should include planners and change advocates, but it should also include helpful critics, to make sure that difficulties that arise over the course of the process are recognized and constructively addressed (Janis, 1989). For example, the school district's team was first composed of the superintendent, the assistant superintendent, and the two consultants. Later, specific tasks were assigned to the board and superintendent, to individuals supervised by the superintendent, and to task forces cochaired by members of the cabinet and community leaders.

Finally, the resources necessary to begin the endeavor must be committed. Obtaining needed financial resources may not be difficult, since they will be relatively minor in comparison with an organization's overall budget. The more important—and typically scarce—resources needed for a successful effort are the attention and involvement of key decision makers. Depending on the scale of the effort, strategic planning may demand from five to twenty-five days of attention from an organization's key decision makers over the course of a year—in other words, up to 10 percent of their ordinary work time. Is this too much? Not for what is truly important for the organization. If there is not enough time for everything, then something else—not strategic planning—should go.

The end of this first step typically signals the first major decision point in the process if the organization (or community) is large, if the situation is complex, or if many people are involved. (If the organization is small, few people are involved, or the situation is simple, the first major decision point comes later, although precisely when will depend on the situation.) If agreement is reached on the various content items, then it makes sense to go ahead with the process.

If agreement is not reached, then either the effort can go ahead anyway—with little likelihood of success—or else the initial step should be repeated until an effective agreement can be worked out. It usually makes sense to repeat the step or else to scale down the effort to focus on a smaller area in which agreement is possible. Part of a scaled-down effort might be to develop effective strategies to involve the other parts later.

Process Guidelines

The following process guidelines may be helpful in developing an initial agreement.

1. *Some person or group must initiate and champion the process.* Strategic planning does not just happen—involved, courageous, and committed people make it happen. In each of the examples in this book, the process worked largely because there were people involved—usually key decision makers and leaders—who acted as *process champions* (see Kotler, 1976, p. 200; Maidique, 1980; Kanter, 1983, p. 296; Bryson and Roering, 1988, 1989). These people believed in the process and were committed to it (and not to any preconceived solutions). They may have had good hunches about what might emerge, but their main belief was that following the process would produce good answers. Indeed, the champions were willing to be surprised by the answers that emerged. The champions were not necessarily the initiators, but they often were. For example, one of the main champions of the school district's process was the assistant superintendent, but she was not the initiator. The superintendent was the initiator as well as a champion of the process.

2. *It may be desirable for the initiators to do a quick assessment of the organization's readiness to engage in strategic planning.* The assessment should cover the organization's current mission; its budget, human resources, and communications systems; its leadership and management capabilities; the expected costs and benefits of a strategic planning process; how to overcome any expected barriers; and the ability of leadership and management to plan and execute strategic plans. Based on the assessment, the initiators may decide to push ahead, focus on improving the organization's readiness, or drop the effort. Readiness assessment worksheets can be found in Bryson and Alston (1995).

3. *Some person or group must sponsor the process to give it legitimacy.* Sponsoring a strategic planning process is different from championing it, even though sponsors and champions may be the same people. Sponsorship is necessary to provide legitimacy to the process, while championing provides the energy and commitment

to follow through. In the case of the school district, for example, the superintendent was the initial sponsor, but the board soon became sponsors as well. Two successive board presidents were especially strongly committed to the process. The
strategic planning coordinating committee or task force discussed below often
serves as the legitimizing, sponsoring body.

4. *Decide whether or not a detailed, jointly negotiated initial agreement is needed.* An informal understanding may suffice when the organization is small, few people need
to be involved in the process, and the situation faced is relatively straightforward. Conversely, a detailed, jointly negotiated initial agreement is likely to be
needed if the organization is large, many people need to be involved, the situation is complex, or a plan is being developed for a community.

A formal contract is probably unnecessary (except, of course, for contracts
with outside consultants), but someone should prepare a written memorandum
that outlines the content of the agreement, including statements on the following
items: the purpose and worth of the effort; organizations, units, groups, or persons who should be involved; steps to be followed; format and timing of reports;
the role and membership of a strategic planning coordinating committee; the role
and membership of the strategic planning team; and commitment of necessary
resources to begin the effort. The agreement might be summarized in a chart and
distributed to all planning team members. An example is shown in Exhibit 3.1,
which outlines the basics of an initial agreement for a nonprofit health center.

5. *Form a strategic planning task force or coordinating committee, if one is needed.* Again,
if the organization is small, if few people need to be involved, and if the situation
is easy to comprehend, then such a task force or committee probably will not be
needed. But if the organization is large, if many people need to be involved, and
if the situation is complex, then a task force or committee should probably be
appointed.

Such a group should not be formed too early, however. It is easier to include
someone later, after the committee is formed, than it is to drop a troublesome participant who is already a member. Consult with trusted advisers before inviting
people to participate.

Also keep in mind that there is a big difference between giving people a seat
on a committee and consulting with them as part of the process. People can supply a great deal of information and advice—and legitimacy for the process—without actually having a vote on a committee. Unless membership in the committee
is limited, it may balloon in size and become unmanageable and unproductive.

For an organization, the coordinating committee might include top-level
decision makers, midlevel managers, technical and professional opinion leaders,
outside resource persons, representatives of key stakeholder groups, process experts, and critics. Remember, however, that there may be a trade-off between having a broadly representative committee (which may be very large) and an effective
one (which probably should number no more than nine). Two groups may in fact
be necessary: a large representative legitimizing body and a small executive

EXHIBIT 3.1. STRATEGIC PLANNING PROCESS FOR A NONPROFIT HEALTH CENTER.

Steps	*Responsible Party*
1. Get agreement on planning steps.	Executive director Board chair Consultant
Meeting 1 *(5-hour meeting with board and key staff)*	
2. Orient board and staff to strategic planning.	Consultant
3. Do situation analysis: History and present situation Mission Opportunities and threats Strengths and weaknesses Critical issues for the future	Participants Consultant
4. Form board/staff team to complete the plan.	Board chair Executive director
5. Summarize situation analysis (between meetings).	Executive director Consultant
Meeting 2 *(2 hours)*	
6. Develop scenarios for the future (scenario approach). Develop scenarios (sketch of vision of success). Note areas of agreement and choices.	Planning team Consultant
7. Summarize scenarios and choices (between meetings).	Executive director Consultant
8. Gather information to test feasibility of scenarios (between meetings).	Executive director
Meeting 3 *(2 hours)*	
9. Evaluate scenarios (e.g., fit with mission, fit with needs, financial feasibility). Select the best scenario.	Planning team Consultant
10. Develop first draft of strategic plan. Include sections on mission, services, staffing, finances, facilities, and implementation (between meetings).	Executive director Consultant
Meeting 4 *(2 hours)*	
11. Review first draft. Note suggested improvements.	Planning team Consultant
12. Revise first draft (between meetings).	Executive director Consultant
Review, adopt, and implement plan:	
13. Review second draft with Board Staff 2–3 outsiders Note reactions and suggestions for improvement.	Board chair Executive director Executive director
14. Review reactions and make needed revisions; prepare final draft.	Planning team Consultant
15. Adopt plan.	Board
16. Implement plan. Review progress every 6 months. Update plan yearly.	Executive director Board

Total meeting time, including review sessions: 18–20 hours.
Time to develop plan: 3 months.

Source: Barry, 1986, p. 26.

committee that will engage in the most extensive discussions and make recommendations to the larger group. For a community, a large representative legitimizing body could coordinate the process while smaller representative bodies attend to specific issues.

6.   *If a coordinating committee is formed, use it as a mechanism for consultation, negotiation, problem solving, or buffering among organizations, units, groups, or persons involved.* The committee is likely to be the body that officially legitimizes the initial agreement and makes subsequent decisions, although it may also serve as an advisory body to "official" decision makers. For example, Mainline Church's strategic planning committee acted as an advisory body to the church's official boards of deacons, elders, and trustees as well as to the senior pastor and other clergy. The public library's strategic planning committee acted as an advisory body to the library director and his superior, the director of the Department of Community Services. Both directors served as advisers to the mayor and city council.

Committee decisions should be recorded in writing and probably should be circulated to key stakeholder groups. It is possible that the committee should include more than one representative from each key stakeholder group, so that a clearer picture of stakeholder preferences, interests, and concerns emerges. Also, if the group is to be a standing committee that oversees annual strategic planning efforts, it is probably wise to rotate membership to keep new ideas flowing and to widen involvement in the process.

You will not necessarily be asking for a major commitment of time from committee members, but they should expect to spend from five to twenty-five days on strategic planning over the course of a year. And that time must be quality time, typically away from the office and concentrated in one- to three-day blocks.

7.   *The process is likely to flow more smoothly and effectively if the coordinating committee and any other policy boards involved are effective policy-making bodies.* Recall that strategic planning has been defined as a disciplined effort to produce fundamental decisions and actions that shape and guide what an organization (or other entity) is, what it does, and why it does it. It is hard to produce those decisions unless the process is overseen by effective policy-making bodies. In other words, the work of strategic planning forums, no matter how good, will not be worth much unless it is linked to arenas in which effective policies can be adopted and decisions made.

Effective policy-making bodies

- Discipline themselves to focus most of their attention on their policy-making role.
- Have a mission statement that clearly states their purpose as a policy-making body.
- Establish a set of policy objectives for the organization, function, or community they oversee.
- Concentrate their resources to be more effective as policy makers.

- Control managers primarily through the questions they ask. The general form of these questions is, "How does this recommendation [whether a proposal, strategy, or budget] serve our purposes, values, or policies?"
- Have staff help them become better policy makers.
- Rely on various media (press releases, newsletters, television, and so forth) to transmit information to key stakeholders and the general public.
- Hold periodic retreats to develop strategic plans and work programs for subsequent years.
- Monitor appropriate performance data in appropriate ways (Houle, 1989; Carver, 1990; Eadie, 1994).

Not many public or nonprofit organizations, boundary-crossing services, or communities are governed by effective policy-making bodies. Thus, a strategic issue that often arises is how to make the governing bodies more effective policy-making bodies. The school district's elected board, for example, knew they should be a better policy-making body, and they wanted to make sure the strategic planning process would help them in this regard before they were willing to commit to it. Mainline Church also wanted to use the process to focus the attention of its policy-making bodies on what was truly important for the church.

8. *Form a strategic planning team if one is needed.* In theory, a strategic planning team would be assigned the task of facilitating decision making by the strategic planning committee. The team would gather information and advice and produce recommendations for committee action. The committee would legitimize the process, provide guidance to the team, and make decisions on team-produced recommendations. In practice, a team may or may not be formed and may or may not serve as a facilitator of decision making by the coordinating committee.

A team may not be needed if the organization or community is small, if few people need to be involved in the effort, or if the situation is relatively easy to handle. In these cases, a single planner, perhaps with the assistance of an outside consultant, will probably suffice.

However, if the organization or community is large, if many people need to be involved, and if the situation is complex, such a team will probably be necessary. Most of the team members probably will not need to work full-time on the effort except for brief periods. But formation of such a team will allow many different skills to be brought forward at important times. The team should be headed by an organizational diplomat and should include members skilled in boundary spanning, process facilitation, technical analysis, advocacy, and self-criticism. Such a team will almost certainly be needed for a large community effort.

Whether the team actually does much strategic planning itself or, instead, facilitates planning by key decision makers will depend on a number of factors. On the one hand, if team members actually possess most of the information needed to prepare the plan, and if they hold positions of substantial power, then they may go ahead and prepare the plan themselves. In this situation, the planners are themselves the key decision makers. On the other hand, if there are a number of key decision makers who already possess much of the necessary information, and if the planners are not themselves powerful by virtue of their position or person, then the planners will need to serve primarily as facilitators of the process.

In my experience, planners typically find that they can be of greatest service by serving as facilitators of cross-functional and cross-level planning, policy making, and decision making by key decision makers (Bryson and Crosby, 1989). Nevertheless, planners typically must have at least some substantive knowledge of the topic areas under discussion in order to be good facilitators. Thus, a blend of process skill and content knowledge is typically required of strategic planners and strategic planning teams. The specific proportions vary by situation, however.

Once you have decided that a strategic planning team is needed, you can turn your attention to procedures that will make the team more effective. First, to recruit skilled, committed team members, you may need to use special personnel hiring, transfer, and/or compensation procedures. If people cannot see how their careers could be helped by participating on the team, they are not likely to join voluntarily. If the assignment is to be temporary, people must be assured that they can return to their old jobs—or better ones—when the effort is completed. Second, clear (and positive) working relationships need to be negotiated among team members and supervisors. Third, the team should meet frequently and communicate effectively to foster information sharing and joint learning.

In the case of strategic planning for a community, the team or teams may have many volunteer members. Personnel hiring, transfer, and compensation procedures may not be an issue for volunteers, but clear, positive working relationships and effective communication are likely to be very important.

9. *Key decision makers may need orientation and training about the nature, purpose, and process of strategic planning before they can negotiate an initial agreement.*

10. *A sequence of "initial" agreements among a successively expanding group of key decision makers may be necessary before a full-scale strategic planning effort can proceed.*

11. *In complex situations, development of an initial agreement will culminate in the first big decision point.* If an effective agreement cannot be reached among key decision makers, then the effort should not proceed. The initiators may want to try again or they may want to focus on areas in which key decision makers can reach agreement. In relatively simple situations, the first major decision points are likely to be reached later in the process, although precisely when will depend on the particular situation.

Have Realistic Hopes for the Process

The initiation of strategic planning primarily involves a series of three simple activities for many organizations: (1) gathering key actors (preferably key decision makers), (2) working through a "strategic thinking and acting" process, and (3) focusing on what is truly important for the organization. While these activities may be conceptually simple, they are quite difficult to implement.

Organizations prefer to make things as routine and systematic as they can (Thompson, 1967; Van de Ven and Ferry, 1980). Strategic planning, however, is designed to question the current routines, along with the treaties that have been negotiated among stakeholders to form a coalition large enough and strong enough to govern the organization (Mintzberg, 1983; Pfeffer, 1992). Therefore, the process is inherently prone to fail because it is deliberately disruptive. Only strong sponsors and champions, a supportive coalition, and a clear view of the potential benefits can make it succeed. Even then, the best efforts can still be derailed by unexpected events, changes, or crises. Initiating strategic planning can be worth the effort, but the process will not necessarily be a smooth or successful one. Potential sponsors and champions should go into it with their eyes open (Bryson and Roering, 1988, 1989; Pettigrew, Ferlie, and McKee, 1992).

In part because of the disruption strategic planning can cause during strategy formulation (as opposed to implementation), Mintzberg (1994b, p. 333) argues that the *only* role for strategic planning is strategic *programming*. By this, he means the codification, articulation, and elaboration of strategies that are already in place. As he asserts, "planning works best when the broad outlines of a strategy are already in place, not when significant change is required from the process itself" (p. 176). I do not adopt this extreme a view although I can empathize with it. I obviously think strategic planning can play an important role in strategy formulation, but I also think no one should expect the process to succeed automatically.

One way to develop reasonable hopes for the process is to have the sponsoring group and planning team explicitly discuss, together or separately, their hopes, concerns, or fears for the process. The hopes can be a source of goals for the organization or community—or at least for the process—and the process can be designed in such a way that it deals effectively with the concerns.

Summary

The initial agreement is essentially an understanding among key internal (and perhaps external) decision makers or opinion leaders concerning the overall strategic planning effort. The agreement should cover the purpose and worth of the effort; the persons, units, groups, or organizations to be involved; the steps to be followed; the format and timing of reports; the role and membership of the strategic planning committee, if such a committee is formed; the role and membership of the strategic planning team, if one is formed; and the commitment of necessary resources to begin the effort.

The importance of an initial agreement is illustrated by viewing every strategic planning effort as a story or a play in which the most important questions an organization faces are raised and resolved. For the play to have a successful ending, the agreement needs to sketch out the setting, the themes, the plots and subplots, the actors, the scenes, the beginning, the climax, and the desired conclusion. As the tale itself unfolds, content and detail will be added to this sketch, along with surprise twists and turns, making it a rich, instructive, and emotional drama that is lived by the actors. In the absence of such an agreement, the story may never reach a climax or a conclusion.

An effective initial agreement helps leaders, managers, and planners raise and resolve key issues. Discussion of these issues helps effective political coalitions coalesce. Otherwise, issues and answers are likely to flow randomly through the organization, disconnected from the resources and decisions necessary for effective action (Cohen, March, and Olsen, 1972; Kingdon, 1995). Organizational survival, let alone effectiveness, will itself become random, and key decision makers will have abdicated their responsibility to focus on pursuing organizational purposes (Selznick, 1957; Burns, 1978; Terry, 1993).

In Chapter Four, we will move to Steps 2 and 3 in the Strategy Change Cycle: the identification of mandates and the clarification of mission and values. Together, these two steps stipulate which organizational purposes are to be strategically pursued.

CLARIFYING ORGANIZATIONAL MANDATES AND MISSION

Three outstanding attitudes—obliviousness to the growing disaffection of constituents, primacy of self-aggrandizement, and the illusion of invulnerable status—are persistent aspects of folly.

BARBARA TUCHMAN, *THE MARCH OF FOLLY*

This chapter covers Steps 2 and 3 of the Strategy Change Cycle, identifying mandates and clarifying mission and values. Together these things provide the social justification for an organization's existence.

Mandates

Although Step 3 is usually the more time consuming of the two, Step 2 is no less important. Before an organization can define its mission and values, it must know exactly what it is formally and informally *required* to do (and not do) by external authorities. Formal requirements are likely to be codified in laws, ordinances, articles of incorporation, charters, and so forth, and therefore they may be easier to uncover and clarify than an organization's mission. In addition, organizations typically must meet a variety of informal mandates, which may be embodied in the cultural norms or expectations of key stakeholders such as the electorate or their duly-elected representatives. These informal mandates may be no less binding. For example, newly elected officials often talk about the "mandate" they have received from the voters—and if the mandate is real and strong, woe be to those who ignore it. (Real clarity about these informal mandates may have to await the completion of a stakeholder analysis.)

Purpose and Outcomes

The purpose of Step 2 is to identify and clarify the nature and meaning of the externally imposed mandates, both formal and informal, affecting the organization. Three outcomes should be sought from this step:

1. Identification of the organization's formal and informal mandates
2. Interpretation of what is required as a result of these mandates (leading perhaps to explicit goals or performance indicators)
3. Clarification of what is not ruled out by these mandates (that is, the rough boundaries of the organization's unconstrained field of action)

Clarifying what is not ruled out is particularly important. Alerting organizational members to what they *might* do can lead to valuable discussions about what the organization's mission ought to be. Too many organizations think they are more constrained than they actually are. Indeed, many make the fundamental error of assuming that their mandates and mission are the same. They may be, but leaders and planners should not start out with that assumption.

The CPI program provides an interesting example. Previously, the program limited its mission to its formal mandate of producing measures of pure price change for the public. It has since expanded its mission to include (1) educating its stakeholders about the meaning of what it does and (2) providing data and other services to existing and new "customers." It has done so for two related reasons. One is the need to maintain political and budgetary support for its efforts. In an era of ballooning federal deficits and heightened competition for federal dollars, there is no substitute for strong stakeholder support. A second reason is the CPI program's desire to make itself even more useful to others. Doing so is likely to maintain and enhance stakeholder support; plus, it supports the Department of Labor's TQM efforts, and it certainly furthers the public interest. Indeed, had the CPI program continued to limit its mission to meeting its formal mandates, it might well have *jeopardized* its ability to meet those mandates.

Benefits and Guidelines

There are two potential benefits of Step 2. First, clarity about what is mandated will increase the likelihood that mandates will actually be met. Research on goal setting indicates that one of the most important determinants of goal achievement is the clarity of the goals themselves. The more specific the goal, the more likely it is to be achieved (Locke, Shaw, Saari, and Latham, 1981; Mazmanian and Sabatier, 1983; Boal and Bryson, 1987b). Second, the possibility of developing a mission that is not limited to mandates is enhanced. It helps people examine the *potential* purposes of organizational action if they know what is not explicitly forbidden.

The process guidelines for this step are straightforward:

1. *Have someone compile the organization's formal and informal mandates.*
2. *Review the mandates in order to clarify what is required and what is allowed.* This can provide a major clarification of organizational goals and/or performance in-

dicators. These goals can then be used, along with goals that might be derived from stakeholder analyses and the mission statement, to identify strategic issues.

3. *Regularly remind organizational members what the organization is required to do, as a way of ensuring conformity with the mandates.* In other words, institutionalize attention to the mandates. Certainly annual reports, staff retreats, and orientation sessions for new employees should include a section (perhaps a very brief one) on mandates. Other methods might prove useful as well.

Mission

Yogi Berra, the famous New York Yankees baseball player and manager, once said, "If you do not know where you're heading, you're likely to end up somewhere else." His maxim emphasizes that without a sense of purpose we are quite literally lost. Mission provides that sense of purpose. In addition, it can be very helpful (although not always necessary or possible) to expand an organization's mission into an early version of its vision of success, which may then guide subsequent efforts at issue identification and strategy development (see Figure 2.1). Without a vision of success, organizational members may not know enough about how to fulfill the mission. Communities, in particular, may find it useful to develop a guiding vision that embodies important purposes and values. They are unlikely to have a mission statement as such, but a guiding vision can provide the sense of purpose, values, and common ground that enables disparate and essentially independent groups and organizations to strive together for the common good.

Mission, in other words, clarifies an organization's purpose, or *why* it should be doing what it does; vision clarifies *what* the organization should look like and *how* it should behave as it fulfills its mission. Chapter Eight discusses constructing a vision of success; for now it is enough to note simply that the foundation of any good vision of success is an organization's mission statement or a community's statement of purpose and values.

The statement by Barbara Tuchman (1984) quoted at the head of the chapter makes a different point: any organization that becomes an end in itself is doomed to failure. The collapse of the former Eastern Bloc and Soviet Union illustrates how self-aggrandizement, illusions of invulnerability, and disregard for constituents' desires can lead to disaster. Indeed, most planning disasters probably meet Tuchman's criteria for folly (Hall, 1980; Bryson, Bromiley, and Jung, 1990; Bryson and Bromiley, 1993).

Purpose and Outcomes

Ultimately strategic planning is about purpose, meaning, values, and virtue. Nowhere is this more apparent than in the clarification of mission and the subsequent development of a vision of success. The aim of mission clarification is to specify the organization's purposes and the philosophy and values that guide it. Unless the purposes focus on socially useful and justifiable ends and the philosophy and values are virtuous, the organization cannot hope to indefinitely command the resources it needs to survive, including high-quality, loyal, committed employees (Selznick, 1957; Burns, 1978; Terry, 1993; Bartlett and Ghoshal, 1994).

Step 3 has two main desired outcomes: a stakeholder analysis and a mission statement. A stakeholder analysis provides useful information and valuable preparation for a mission statement. Agreement on the stakeholder analysis and mission statement by key decision makers should clarify the organization's arenas of action, many of the basic rules of the game within these arenas, the implicit if not explicit goals of the organization, and possible performance indicators. In addition, agreement on the organization's mission—particularly if it is consensual—will in itself be a source of power for the organization (Pfeffer, 1981, 1992). Finally, agreement on an organizational mission that embraces socially desirable and justified purposes should produce enthusiasm, even excitement, among organizational members (Kouzes and Posner, 1987, 1993; Nanus, 1992; Terry, 1993; Bartlett and Ghoshal, 1994).

Benefits

A number of benefits flow from clarifying and agreeing on an organization's mission. Perhaps the most important benefit is simply that it fosters a habit of focusing discussion on what is truly important. Too often, key decision makers in public or nonprofit organizations never come together to discuss cross-functional issues or, more importantly, the organization as a whole. The board of the school district was particularly concerned about finding the time to focus on what was important for the district, and board members used strategic planning specifically for this purpose.

Often, if key decision makers do gather—for example, at a staff meeting—most of their time is taken up with announcements or discussion of relatively trivial matters such as allocating parking spaces or scheduling floating holidays. While such discussions may serve to introduce key decision makers to one another and may provide some of the social glue necessary to hold any organization together, they are relatively useless and may in fact be a colossal waste of everyone's time.

A caveat: It is important to know *why* important issues are not addressed. Participants simply may not know how to do so, in which case targeted training might help. Or they may not be comfortable with one another and therefore may be fearful of the consequences of raising difficult issues. Team building might be used to build trust and to address these fears. Or avoiding discussions of real issues can be a way for senior decision makers to control the agenda and enhance their own power (see Benveniste, 1989). In this last case, senior personnel might possibly be persuaded of the benefits of more participatory decision making.

The second important benefit, of course, is the clarification of organizational (or community) purpose. Since defining the mission may be thought of as the central function of leadership, more effective leadership is another benefit (Selznick, 1957). Clarity of organizational purpose helps leaders in other ways as well. In particular, it helps clarify the purpose of organizational structures and systems, including the resource allocation system. In addition, leaders will be better able to control internal conflict so that it furthers organizational ends. Leaders are required to guide the "play of the game" within the structure of the rules, but they also need to change the rules on occasion. Clarity of purpose provides a valuable basis for understanding which rules help control conflict and which need to be changed (Ury, Brett, and Goldberg, 1988; Hampden-Turner, 1990; Schein, 1992; Terry, 1993).

A key point to be made here is that organizational conflicts are typically about something other than what is nominally in dispute, and for that reason, their resolution requires that the conflict be reframed at a higher level of abstraction (Watzlawick, Weakland, and Fisch, 1974). Terry (1993), for example, describes a hierarchy of human action. Fulfillment is at the top and is the embodiment of all that is underneath. Then comes meaning, or why people act; then mission, which guides one in a meaningful direction; then power, structures and systems, resources, and finally the "givens" of existence. He argues that disputes at any level in this hierarchy are usually really about what is at the next level up. Thus, power struggles in general are ultimately about the purposes the power is to serve. Arguments about organizational structures and systems are really about who is empowered or disempowered by different designs. Disputes over resources are typically about how the use of those resources should be regulated in structures and systems. A focus on the purpose and ultimate meaning of organizational efforts—to the extent that there is agreement on them—therefore can frame most of these conflicts in such a way that they facilitate the pursuit and fulfillment of organizational ends.

Agreement on purpose can also help the parties in a conflict disconnect ends from means and thus be clear about what goals are to be pursued, or problems addressed, prior to exploring solutions. The advantage of doing so is that most conflicts are about solutions; that is, there usually is no agreement about what problems the solutions are to meant to solve (Filley, 1975). Further, the organization cannot really know what problems it ought to address without some sense of the purpose it serves. Once an organization understands its purpose, it can define the problems it is meant to solve and can better understand how to choose among competing solutions. David Osborne and Ted Gaebler based their bestselling book *Reinventing Government* (1992) in part on this very point: if governments stick to *steering* (purpose and problem definition), then they are less likely to be a captive of any one approach to *rowing* (solutions).

Agreement on purpose therefore gets an organization to pursue the following (often preferable) sequence of conflict resolution activities: agree on purposes, identify problems, and then explore and agree on solutions. The likelihood that successful solutions will be found is increased because the sequence narrows the focus to fulfillment of the mission but broadens the search for acceptable solutions to include all that might possibly further the mission.

Agreement on purpose provides a very powerful means of social control. To the extent that purposes are socially justified and virtuous, agreement will invest organizational discussions and actions with a moral quality that can constrain self-serving and organizationally destructive behavior on the part of organizational members. Said differently, agreement on purpose can lead to a mobilization of organizational energies based on the pursuit of a morally justifiable mission that lies beyond self-interest (Lewis, 1991).

Another benefit of this step is the explicit attention given to philosophy, values, and culture. Organizations rarely discuss these matters directly. As a result, they are likely to misread their strengths and weaknesses and therefore make mistakes in the internal assessment step (to come). Also, without understanding their philosophy, values, and culture, organizations are likely to make serious errors in formulating strategy. They may choose strategies that are not consonant with their philosophy, values, and culture and are therefore doomed to fail (Hampden-Turner, 1990; Schein, 1992).

Finally, as a result of answering the six questions outlined below, the organization will be well on its way to developing a clear vision of success. Indeed, answers to these six questions may be necessary before organizational members can perceive success (Mitroff, 1978; May, 1969).

Stakeholder Analysis

A stakeholder analysis is a valuable prelude to a mission statement, a SWOT analysis, and the formulation of effective strategies. Indeed, I usually argue that if an organization has time to do only one thing when it comes to strategic planning, that one thing ought to be a stakeholder analysis. Stakeholder analyses are so critical because the key to success in the public and nonprofit sectors—and the private sector, too, for that matter—is the satisfaction of key stakeholders. If an organization does not know who its stakeholders are, what criteria they use to judge the organization, and how the organization is performing against those criteria, there is little likelihood that the organization (or community) will know what it should do to satisfy its key stakeholders (Boschken, 1994).

An example may prove instructive at this point. It comes from the Division of Fisheries and Wildlife of the Department of Natural Resources in a Midwestern state. The department (as the state's agent) is one of the major landowners in the United States. It manages a vast area, including water, forest, mineral resources, and a huge population of fish and wildlife. The fish and wildlife resources are important to in-state and out-of-state anglers and hunters and to the large recreational and tourist industry that depends on them. Something like a quarter of the state's people identify themselves as anglers and hunters, while an almost equal number enter the state each year to fish and hunt.

You would think that the Division of Fisheries and Wildlife would be one of the most protected and supported units of this state's government, that legions of interest groups—from the National Rifle Association to resort-industry groups and recreational equipment dealer associations—would be continually lobbying state legislators and the governor to maintain, if not increase, public financial support for the division. Until relatively recently, however, such was most definitely not the case. Indeed, quite the opposite was true. The division had been under frequent attack from some key stakeholders—hunters and anglers. They argued that the division saw itself primarily as a regulator and naysayer in relation to these stakeholders. They felt the organization was completely uninterested in their satisfaction.

The division decided to engage in strategic planning to turn around an increasingly bad situation. One of the first steps was a stakeholder analysis. The most important piece of information that emerged from that analysis was that the professionals in the division operated under the mistaken assumption that, in effect, their prime stakeholders were fish and deer! They felt their job was to regulate anglers and hunters, so that the state's fish and wildlife resources would be protected and managed over the long term.

There would have been little problem with this view if fish and deer could vote, spend money, and pay taxes. But they cannot. But anglers, hunters, and their families do, along with the owners of resorts and sporting goods establishments. While the division's maintenance of fish and wildlife resources was obviously one criterion anglers and hunters used to judge its performance, there were many more as well (such as its ability to provide enjoyable recreational opportunities), and the division was failing in many instances to provide these. The result was hostility on the part of these stakeholders and attempts by the legislature to cut the division's budget and curtail its powers. As a result of insights gained from its stakeholder analysis, the division is now pursuing several strategies to manage resources effectively over the long term while increasing the satisfaction of hunters and anglers (and not simultaneously alienating environmentalists). The division has, in fact, dramatically increased its support from the sports groups.

The first step in a stakeholder analysis is to identify exactly who the organization's stakeholders are. Figure 4.1 presents a typical stakeholder map for a government. The stakeholders are numerous (although many organizations have even more).

Three additional points should be made about this figure. First, the diagram makes it clear that any organization (and especially a government) is an arena in which individuals and groups contest for control of the organization's attention, resources, and output (Pfeffer and Salancik, 1978; Bryson and Crosby, 1992). A major purpose of a stakeholder analysis is to get a more precise picture of these contestants. Second, special attention should be paid to future generations. I

FIGURE 4.1. A STAKEHOLDER MAP FOR A GOVERNMENT.

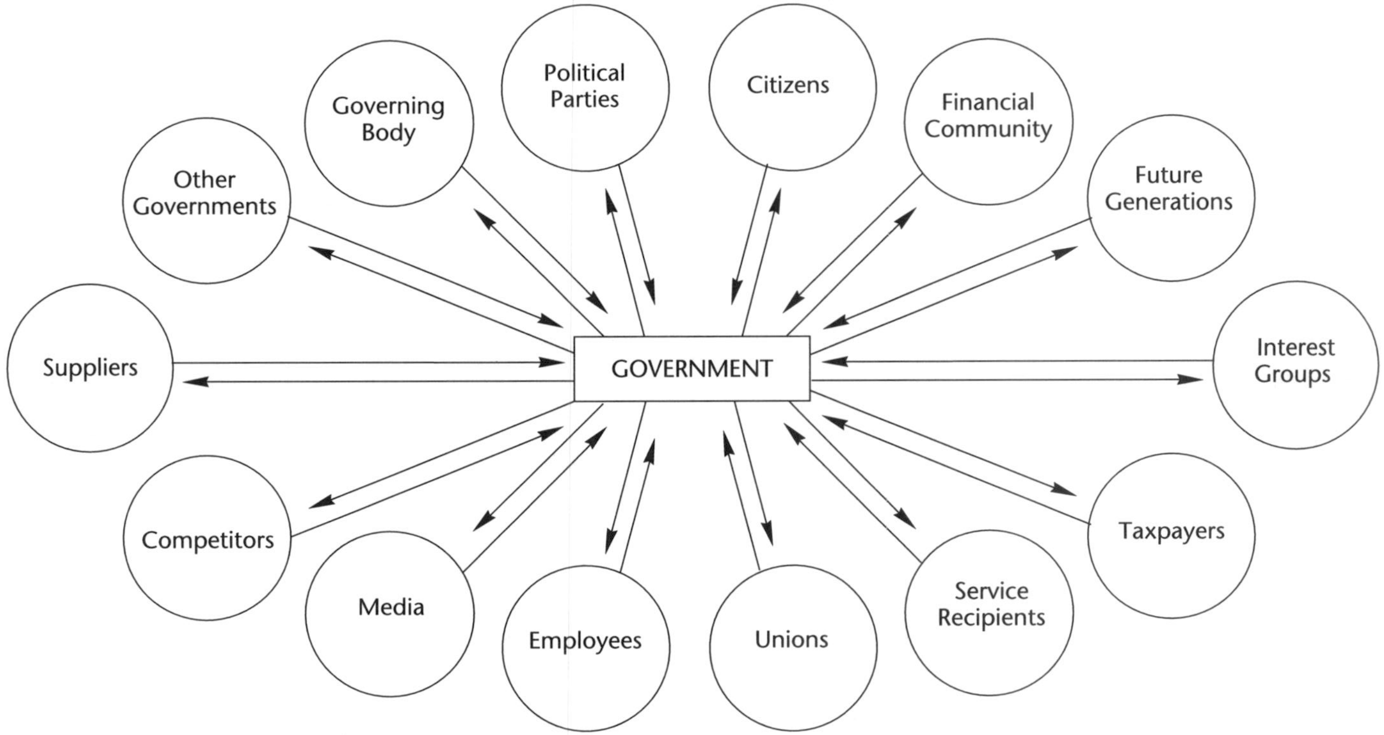

believe strongly that organizations (especially governments) have an obligation to leave the world in as good a shape as they found it, if not better. It is important in this era of special interest groups to keep this public trust in mind. As Theodore Roosevelt said, "We do not inherit the earth from our ancestors, we borrow it from our children."

Third, it is very important for key employee groups to be explicitly identified. Not all employees are the same. There are different groups with different roles to play who will use different criteria to judge organizational performance. Clarity about these groups is necessary to ensure organizational responses are sufficiently differentiated to satisfy each group. Fourth, key stakeholders for many organizations and communities are likely to be quite distant physically; nonetheless, they must all be considered carefully.

The public library presents an interesting example in this regard. It took considerable encouragement on my part to get the librarians to identify themselves as key stakeholders. Their self-effacing, altruistic view of themselves as public servants was admirable, but misplaced. By definition they are key stakeholders of the organization, and their own satisfaction is important to the success of their services. Indeed, one of the issues driving the strategic planning process for the library was the fact that the librarians were experiencing increased stress and burnout as a result of heightened job demands. Something had to be done to alleviate this stress. Furthermore, several of the key criteria they used to judge their organization's performance related to certain professional standards the library did or did not meet. In other words, it was the librarians themselves, not the other stakeholders, who held the organization to exacting professional standards of service.

The second step in the analysis is to specify the criteria the stakeholders use to assess the organization's performance. There are two approaches to this task. One is to guess what the criteria are; the second is ask the stakeholders themselves. The strategic planning team should always make its own guesses, but at some point it may prove instructive and politically useful to ask stakeholders (for example, through surveys, interviews, or group discussions) what their professed criteria are.

The compatibility of strategic planning with many newer governance and management approaches is directly related to its emphasis on addressing key stakeholder needs, particularly the needs of those that might be called "customers." For example, a hallmark of "reinvention" (Osborne and Gaebler, 1992), "reengineering" (Hammer and Champy, 1993; Linden, 1994), and TQM (Cohen and Brand, 1993) is their emphasis on meeting customer expectations. And nonprofit organizations are exhorted by the Peter F. Drucker Foundation (1993) to clearly identify their "primary" and "supporting" customer needs as part of their organizational assessment efforts.

Why should the team always make its own guesses? First, it is faster. Second, the stakeholders may not be completely honest. In the case of city council members, for example, city employees will usually say that one of the key criteria this important stakeholder group uses is whether the performance of city departments enhances their reelection prospects. Council members are unlikely to declare this criterion in public, even though it is important to them. Nevertheless, asking stakeholders what their criteria are can be instructive because the team's guesses can be wrong (Normann, 1991).

The third step in the process is to make a judgment about how well the organization performs against the stakeholders' criteria. The judgments need not be very sophisticated. Simply noting whether or not the organization does poorly, okay, or very well against the criteria is enough to prompt a very useful discussion. Topics of discussion should include areas of organizational strength and weakness; overlaps, gaps, conflicts, and contradictions among the criteria; and opportunities and threats posed the organization's current performance.

An amusing example is how such a discussion led the U.S. Forest Service to declare 1990 "The Year of the Sweet-Smelling Toilet." For decades the most common complaint received by rangers was smelly toilets. The Forest Service decided to do something about it. Following wind tunnel research by in-house scientist Briar Cook, vent stacks and roof lines were redesigned. Solar-powered fans were installed, improving the expulsion of odors. One can easily imagine the smiles—the "stakeholder satisfaction"—as the Forest Service retrofits its twelve thousand outdoor privies in 134 national forests and constructs an additional three hundred sweet-smelling potties each year (Bryson, 1990).

In a more serious vein, these three steps should help set the stage for a discussion of an organization's mission (or a community's purposes and values). In particular, a stakeholder analysis forces team members to place themselves in the shoes of others—especially outsiders—and to make a rather dispassionate assessment of the organization's performance from the outsiders' points of view. Such activity is one of the best possible ways to avoid the folly Tuchman describes. It is also likely to be a necessary precursor for ethical action (Lewis, 1991). In addition, the stakeholder analysis provides a valuable prelude to the SWOT analysis (Step 4), strategic issue identification (Step 5), and strategy development (Step 6).

If time permits, or circumstances demand it, three additional steps may be advisable. First, the strategic planning team may wish to discuss exactly how the various stakeholders influence the organization (Nutt and Backoff, 1992; Finn, 1995). Many members of the team may not know precisely how the organization is influenced. (Also, this discussion may help to highlight the really important stakeholders.)

Second, the strategic planning team may wish to discuss what the organization needs from each stakeholder group. I have emphasized the need for organizations to satisfy key stakeholder groups, but it may also be important to focus attention directly on what the organization needs to survive and prosper. The usual assumption is that if the organization satisfies key stakeholders, the organization can survive and prosper. But that may not be the case. A direct focus on what the organization needs to survive may reveal an important strategic issue: how can the organization secure the resources necessary to continue pursuing its mission if it does not already receive those resources from its key stakeholders?

Finally, the team may wish to rank stakeholders according to their importance to the organization. The order, of course, might vary with different issues, but a rough ordering will give the team an idea of which stakeholders demand the most attention.

The team will have to decide whether or not to circulate the stakeholder analysis outside the strategic planning team. It is primarily just an input to other steps in the process (especially mission statement and strategy development), so there may be no good reason for a more public discussion of it.

The Mission Statement

A mission statement is a declaration of organizational purpose. Mission statements vary in length, but they are typically short—no more than a page and often not more than a punchy slogan. They should also be inspiring.

The actual statement should grow out of discussions aimed at answering six questions (a process that is often highly informational, as Samuel Goldwyn may have been acknowledging when he said, "For your information, let me ask you a few questions"). The statement should at least touch on most answers, though for some purposes it may be distilled into a slogan. Answers to the six questions (outlined below) will provide the basis for developing a vision of success later in the process.

Developing answers to the questions is a valuable but very demanding process. Several hours (and in some cases days) of discussion by the strategic planning team may be required to reach consensus on the answers, and perhaps additional time for reflection may be necessary. Sometimes, as in the case of the CPI program, the organization may need to come back and revise its mission statement in light of later discoveries.

At times, the discussions may seem too philosophical or academic to be of much use. If discussions seem to get bogged down in grand abstractions or minutiae, by all means move ahead. Assign someone the task of writing up what has been discussed so far, including points of agreement and disagreement, and come back for further discussions when the time seems right or when decisions must be reached. Strategic planning should not be allowed to get in the way of useful action.

However, it is important to remember that strategic planning is ultimately about purpose, meaning, value, and virtue, and therefore, it is philosophical at its base. To paraphrase management guru Peter Drucker, strategic planning involves responding to a series of Socratic questions. The six questions that follow structure one of the most important parts of that Socratic process.

1. *Who are we?* If your organization were walking down the street and someone asked it who it was, what would its answer be? The question is one of identity, defined as what organizational members believe is distinct, central, and enduring about their organization (Dutton and Dukerich, 1991). The answer probably needs to be more than just what appears on the organization's letterhead. Clarity about identity is crucial because, as the late psychiatrist R. D. Laing argued, the most effective way to influence a person is not to tell them what to *do* but to communicate who they *are* (quoted in Dalton and Thompson, 1986, p. 147). So, too, with organizations. To say that we are the Internal Revenue Service or the United States Marine Corps or the CPI program or the Mainline Church carries an enormous amount of meaning and implies a great deal about what our organization can and ultimately will do.

It is also important to ask a question about identity in order to help the organization draw a distinction between what it is and what it does. Too many organizations make a fundamental mistake when they assume they are what they do (Osborne and Gaebler, 1992). As a result, important avenues of strategic response to environmental conditions are unwittingly sealed off. An example of this sort of error is often cited in business texts. Earlier in this century, companies that ran railroads thought of themselves as railroad companies rather than as transportation companies that happened to be in the railroad business. As a result, the railroads were caught off guard by the emerging automobile and trucking industries. If they had defined themselves as transportation companies, they might have avoided the serious decline they experienced in this century (Levitt, 1960).

2. *In general, what are the basic social or political needs we exist to meet, or what are the basic social or political problems we exist to address?* The answer to this question, along with the organization's mandates, provides the basic social justification for the organization's existence: the purpose of the organization is to meet these needs or address these problems. The organization can then be seen as a means to an end and not as an end in itself. The question may need to be asked stakeholder by stakeholder.

3. *In general, what do we do to recognize, anticipate, and respond to these needs or problems?* This question prompts the organization to actively stay in touch with the needs it is supposed to fill or the problems it is supposed to address. Left to their own devices, organizations will generally talk primarily to themselves and not to the outside world (March and Simon, 1958; March and Olsen, 1989). When we see individuals talk mainly to themselves, we often suspect mental illness; when we see organizations talking primarily to themselves, we should suspect some sort of pathology as well. In order to remain "healthy," organizations must be encouraged to stay in touch with the outside world that justifies their existence.

Furthermore, constant attention to external needs or problems is likely to prompt the necessary adjustments to the organization's mission, mandates, service or product level and mix, costs, financing, management, and structure that are necessary for it to remain effective. Successful innovations are typically a response to real needs or problems; mere technological feasibility is not enough (Zaltman, Duncan, and Holbek, 1973; Bryson, Bromiley, and Jung, 1990). Furthermore, most of the information that is critical for fostering innovation usually comes from outside the organization (Kanter, 1983, 1989). The more that the people in the organization as a whole attend to external needs and problems, the more likely it will be that a climate conducive to innovation will prevail, and the easier it will be to justify desirable innovations to internal audiences (Wilson, 1967, 1989; Rainey, 1991; Osborne and Gaebler, 1992).

Finally, people often need to be reassured that they will not be punished for returning from the outside world with bad news. We have all seen the messenger shot down because key decision makers did not like the message. An explicit endorsement of contact with the outside world is likely to make it safer for messengers to deliver bad news that should be heard.

4. *How should we respond to our key stakeholders?* This question forces the organization to decide what relations it wishes to establish with its key stakeholders and what values it seeks to promote through those relations. It also focuses attention on what the stakeholders value and what the organization does, or might do, to provide stakeholders with what they value. If the key to success in the public and nonprofit sectors is satisfying key stakeholders, what will the organization do to satisfy them? Obviously, a really detailed discussion may have to wait until Step 6, but discussions of this sort can be pursued usefully throughout the process.

5. *What are our philosophy, values, and culture?* The importance of reflecting upon and clarifying an organization's philosophy, core values, and culture becomes most apparent in the strategy development step. Only strategies that are consonant with the philosophy, core values, and culture are likely to succeed; strategies that are not are likely to fail (Hampden-Turner, 1990; Schein, 1992). Unfortunately, because organizations rarely discuss their philosophies, values, and culture, they often adopt strategies that are doomed to failure. Clarity about philosophy and values in advance of strategy development is one way to avoid this error.

Perhaps even more important, however, clarifying these points will help an organization maintain its integrity. If an organization is clear about its philosophy and core values, it will be able to more easily refuse proposals or actions that are likely to damage its integrity and to accept those that maintain or enhance its integrity. In a time when public confidence in most institutions is low, it is vital to maintain organizational integrity. Once this integrity is damaged, it is very difficult to reestablish public confidence. Therefore, an organization may choose to develop and publicize a values statement that is separate from its mission statement. This values statement sets out a desirable code of behavior to which the organization adheres or aspires.

A caution is in order at this point, however. It might be argued that a relatively open discussion of an organization's philosophy, values, and culture might actually damage its effectiveness in some cases. Because only the publicly acceptable aspects of its philosophy, values, and culture are likely to be discussed in public, an organization whose success depends in part on the pursuit of publicly unacceptable actions could suffer. For example, a government agency might in effect further the ends of wealthy land developers as part of a strategy of encouraging private development and investment to bolster the local economy. No matter how beneficial such a strategy is to the community in the end, it is probably unacceptable in most parts of the country for a government agency to say publicly that as a by-product of its successful pursuit of its mission, it helps the rich get richer. Therefore, public discussion of the agency's philosophy and values might require it to change its strategy and, as a result, become less effective. At the very least, the agency may need to engage in some public education about the virtues of private markets and the fact that there is no guarantee that private developers and investors will survive in those markets.

Key decision makers will have to decide whether to go public with a discussion of the organization's philosophy, values, and culture. Those persons interested in "reform" are likely to favor public discussion; those against it are not. The point to be made, of course, is that *any* discussion of philosophy, values, and culture, whether public or not, will have political consequences (Herson, 1984; Stone, 1988).

6. *What makes us distinctive or unique?* There was a time in the not-too-distant past when it seemed that public organizations were, as Herbert Kaufman (1976) put it, "immortal." Not anymore. "Cutback management" is now a term familiar to most public managers (Levine, 1979; Behn, 1983; Mercer, 1992), and many public organizations or parts of organizations have disappeared, their functions taken over by private or nonprofit organizations. Privatization is here to stay, and its domain may be expected to increase (Savas, 1982; Kolderie, 1986; Osborne and Gaebler, 1992; Flynn, 1993). Public organizations must be quite clear about what makes them or the functions they perform distinctive or unique, or they will be likely candidates for privatization. Indeed, if there is nothing distinctive or unique about a public organization, then perhaps it should be privatized.

Nonprofit organizations also need to be clear about what makes them distinctive or unique, or they, too, may find themselves at a competitive disadvantage. The world has become increasingly competitive, and those organizations that cannot point to some distinct contribution may lose out.

Some Examples

Some examples can help illustrate how the six mission questions might be answered or at least touched upon. The mission statements for the school district, the public library, and Mainline Church are presented in Exhibits 4.1, 4.2, and 4.3. (The CPI program's mission statement is included in Chapter Eight.) While all are fairly short, each grew out of extensive discussions, emphasizes important

EXHIBIT 4.1. SCHOOL DISTRICT'S MISSION STATEMENT.

The district's learners will acquire the knowledge, skills, values, attitudes, and habits necessary for living in and contributing to a peaceful, democratic, and pluralistic society.

EXHIBIT 4.2. PUBLIC LIBRARY'S MISSION STATEMENT.

The library's mission is to anticipate and respond to the community's need for information, to facilitate lifelong learning, to stimulate and nurture a desire to read in young people, to provide reading materials that meet the interests of all ages, and to enrich the qualitiy of life in the community.

EXHIBIT 4.3. MAINLINE CHURCH'S MISSION STATEMENT.

In response to the Grace of God through Jesus Christ, the mission of Mainline Church is

- To proclaim and celebrate the Good News of Jesus Christ
- To gather as a community to worship God with dignity, warmth, and beauty
- To nourish personal faith and commitment through study, prayer, and fellowship
- To work for love, peace, and justice
- To be a caring Christian community witnessing to God's love day by day
- To work locally and beyond with our denomination and the larger Christian church
- To be a telling presence in the city

purposes to be served, and articulates what many employees see as a calling worthy of their commitment.

Another example comes from the Amherst H. Wilder Foundation, a large nonprofit organization located in St. Paul, Minnesota. It provides a wide range of effective and often quite innovative social services and programs. Its mission statement, presented in Exhibit 4.4, clearly authorizes and prompts the foundation

EXHIBIT 4.4. THE AMHERST H. WILDER FOUNDATION MISSION STATEMENT.

The foundation's purpose is to promote the social welfare of persons resident or located in the greater Saint Paul metropolitan area by all appropriate means, including relief of the poor, care of the sick and aged, care and nurture of children, aid to the disadvantaged and otherwise needy, promotion of physical and mental health, support of rehabilitation and corrections, provision of needed housing and social services, operation of residences and facilities for the aged, the infirm and those requiring special care, and in general the conservation of human resources by the provision of human services responsive to the welfare needs of the community, all without regard to or discrimination on account of nationality, sex, color, religious scruples, or prejudices.

Amherst H. Wilder Foundation, 1993, p. 1.

to seek the biggest impact it can in its chosen domain (Amherst H. Wilder Foundation, 1993).

Process Guidelines

Several process guidelines should be kept in mind as a strategic planning group works at clarifying the mission and mandates:

1. *Someone should be put in charge of compiling the organization's formal and informal mandates.* The group should then review and discuss this list and make any modifications that seem appropriate.

2. *The group should complete a stakeholder analysis using the worksheets found in Bryson and Alston (1995).* Public and nonprofit organizations typically consist of shifting coalitions involving networks of internal and external stakeholders. The organizational purpose should be crafted at least in part out of a consideration of these stakeholders' interests. Otherwise, successful agreement on organizational purposes is unlikely (Fisher and Ury, 1981).

3. *After completing the stakeholder analysis, the group should fill out the mission statement worksheets, also found in Bryson and Alston (1995).* Group members should fill them out as individuals first, and then they should discuss their answers as a group. Extra time should be reserved for a "culture audit," if necessary, to identify organizational philosophy, values, and culture. (Guidelines for performing a culture audit are found in Schein, 1992, pp. 147–168; see also Hampden-Turner, 1990, pp. 185–207.)

4. *After the worksheets have been completed and discussed by the group, the task of developing a draft mission statement (and perhaps a separate values statement) should be turned over to an individual.* It is very important to allow sufficient time to discuss and debate the draft mission statement, particularly if the draft introduces any changes to the mission. Quick agreement may occur but should not be expected.

After an agreed-upon mission statement is developed, the group may also wish to brainstorm a slogan that captures the essence of the mission or run a contest among organizational members or stakeholders for an appropriate slogan. The public library, for example, came up with the wonderful slogan "Mind of the City," which emphasizes intelligence, information, community, and wholeness, rather than the older view of libraries as book warehouses.

5. *It is important not to get stalled in developing a mission statement.* If the group hits a snag, record areas of agreement and disagreement and move on to the next steps. Return later to discuss the mission, incorporating any additional information or solutions that turn up in future steps.

6. *Indeed, strategic planning teams should expect to have to reexamine their draft mission statement as they move through the process, either to reaffirm the statement or to redraft it in light of additional information or reflection.* Even if the organization has a satisfactory

mission statement, it still should expect to reexamine the statement periodically during the process. Steps 4 through 6 provide additional opportunities to discuss the mission. As the process proceeds, more detail may be added to the mission statement in terms of specific programs, products, services, or relationships that will be offered to stakeholders, particularly customers.

7. *Once agreement is reached on a mission statement, it should be kept before the strategic planning group as it moves through the planning process.* The group should refer to the statement as it seeks to formulate goals, identify strategic issues, develop effective strategies, prepare a vision of success, and in general resolve conflicts among the team. The organization's mission provides a basis for resolving conflicts based on purposes and interests, not positions (Fisher and Ury, 1981; Terry, 1993; Schwarz, 1994).

8. *Once general agreement is reached, the mission should be presented to all organizational members.* It should be referred to in preambles to official organizational actions and posted on walls and in offices—it should become a *physical* presence in the organization. Otherwise, it is likely to be forgotten at the very times it is most needed. Explicit reference to the mission should be the standard first step in resolving conflicts. The organization that forgets its mission will drift, and opportunism and loss of integrity are likely to spread and perhaps become rampant. Organizational survival itself—or at least the survival of its leadership—will then be in serious jeopardy (Selznick, 1957; Kouzes and Posner, 1993; Terry, 1993).

9. *Adoption of a mission should mark an important decision point.* Agreement may not occur at the end of this step, however, as the draft mission may be revised over the course of the strategic planning process. Formal agreement on the organization's mission definitely should be reached by the end of the strategy development step.

Summary

This chapter has discussed identifying the mandates an organization faces and clarifying the mission it wishes to pursue. Mandates are imposed from the outside; they may be considered the "musts" the organization is required to pursue (although it may want to pursue them as well). Mission is developed more from the inside; it identifies the organization's purpose. Mission may be considered what the organization "wants" to do. Rarely is an organization so boxed in by mandates that its mission is totally limited to meeting those mandates.

CHAPTER FIVE

ASSESSING THE ENVIRONMENT TO IDENTIFY STRENGTHS AND WEAKNESSES, OPPORTUNITIES AND THREATS

You wouldn't think something as complexly busy as life would be so easy to overlook.

DIANE ACKERMAN, *A NATURAL HISTORY OF THE SENSES*

So it is said that if you know others and know yourself, you will not be imperiled in a hundred battles; if you do not know others, but do know yourself, you win one and lose one; if you do not know others and do not know yourself, you will be imperiled in every single battle.

SUN TZU, *THE ART OF WAR*

To respond effectively to changes in their environments, public and nonprofit organizations (and communities) must understand their external and internal contexts so they can develop effective strategies to link the two. The word *context* comes from the Latin for "weave together," and that is exactly what well-done environmental assessments help organizations do: weave together their understandings and actions in such a way that organizational performance is enhanced.

The need for effective assessments is heightened by the sheer pace of change in the world at large. There are disputes about whether or not the pace of change is accelerating (Land and Jarman, 1992; Mintzberg, 1994b). Regardless of whether it is or not, there is enough change all around that wise organizational leaders feel compelled to pay attention. In part, this is because change so often occurs where, when, how, and in a form that is least expected.

Purpose

The purpose of Step 4 in the strategic planning process, therefore, is to provide information on the organization's strengths and weaknesses in relation to the opportunities and threats it faces. Strengths and weaknesses are usually internal and refer to the present state of the organization, while opportunities and threats are typically external and future oriented. The distinctions, however, between internal and external and present and future oriented are fluid, and people should not worry too much about whether they have made them properly.

In addition, communities may wish to focus not on strengths, weaknesses, opportunities, and threats, but on their hopes and concerns for the community. The distinction between internal and external ceases to be very meaningful when applied to communities, since what is internal and external for the groups and organizations who will be the key implementers of the strategic plan is not the same as what is internal and external for the jurisdiction. Also, attention to hopes and concerns is more likely to elicit value concerns, which are typically more central to community-oriented strategic planning than to strategic planning for organizations (R. C. Einsweiler, personal communication, 1995).

The approach to external and internal environmental assessments outlined in this chapter will set the stage for the identification of strategic issues in Step 5. It will also provide valuable information for use in the following step, strategy development. Strategic issues typically concern how the organization (what is inside) relates to the larger environment it inhabits (what is outside). Every effective strategy will take advantage of strengths and opportunities at the same time it minimizes or overcomes weaknesses and threats. In other words, it will link inside and outside in effective ways.

Chapter One highlighted several major trends and events that are currently forcing sometimes drastic changes on governments, public agencies, and nonprofit organizations. Unfortunately, for various reasons, organizations typically are not very savvy about perceiving such changes quickly enough to respond effectively. Instead, a crisis often has to develop before organizations respond (Wilson, 1967, 1989). This may open up significant "opportunity spaces"; but for the unprepared organization, many useful avenues of response will typically be closed off by the time a crisis emerges (Bryson, 1981; Mitroff and Pearson, 1993). Also, in crisis situations people typically stereotype, withdraw, project, rationalize, oversimplify, and otherwise make errors that are likely to produce unwise decisions (Janis, 1989). The result can be colossal errors (Tuchman, 1984). A major purpose of any strategic planning exercise, therefore, is to alert an organization to the various external or future-oriented threats and opportunities that may prompt or require an organizational response in the foreseeable future. In other words, a major purpose of strategic planning is to prepare an organization to respond effectively to the outside world—before a crisis emerges. Even in a crisis, however, organizations can use many of the concepts, procedures, and tools of strategic planning to help them think and act strategically (Mitroff and Pearson, 1993).

But any effective response to threats and opportunities must be based on an intimate knowledge of the organization's strengths and weaknesses. Effective responses build on strengths and minimize or overcome weaknesses in order to take advantage of opportunities and minimize or overcome threats. Strategic planning, in other words, is concerned with finding the best or most advantageous fit between an organization and its environment, based on an intimate understanding of both.

Desired Outcomes

Step 4 produces documented lists of external or future-oriented organizational opportunities and threats and internal or present organizational strengths and weaknesses. Ordered differently, these four lists comprise the classic SWOT analysis, a popular strategic planning tool. The team may also wish to go further (building on its previous stakeholder analysis) to identify what the organization's "key success factors" are (Jenster, 1987; Leidecker and Bruno, 1984; Mintzberg, 1994b). These are the things the organization must do, the criteria it must meet, or the performance indicators it must satisfy to survive and prosper in the external environment. In addition, the team may wish to clarify the organization's "distinctive competencies" (Selznick, 1957; Prahalad and Hamel, 1990; Stalk, Evans, and Shulman, 1992). These are the abilities, strategies, and actions the organization is particularly good at or the resources (broadly construed) on which it can draw easily to perform well. (Resource E discusses several methods for identifying key success factors and distinctive competencies.)

First, however, it may be necessary to prepare various background reports on external forces and trends; key resource controllers, such as clients, customers, payers, or dues-paying members; and competitors and collaborators. Additional reports may be needed on internal resources, present strategy, and performance. It also may be necessary to prepare various *scenarios,* or stories, that capture important elements of the organization's possible alternative futures; its strengths, weaknesses, opportunities, and threats are then assessed in relation to these possible futures (Schwartz, 1991). Further, once the lists of SWOTs is prepared (with or without the help of scenarios), it may be necessary to commission careful analyses of some listed items in relation to the overall strategic posture of the organization.

Another important outcome of these two steps may be the formulation of specific actions to deal with threats and weaknesses, build on strengths, and take advantage of opportunities. As soon as appropriate moves become apparent, key decision makers should consider taking action. A sharp temporal distinction between planning and implementation is not only unnecessary, it is probably un-

desirable. As long as the contemplated actions are based on reasonable information, have adequate support, and do not foreclose important strategic options, serious consideration should be given to taking them. The feedback arrows in Figure
2.1 try to capture this continuous blending and interplay of thinking and acting.

Completing Step 4 should also provide the impetus for establishing a formal
environmental scanning operation, if one does not exist already. It will need adequate staff—typically with an in-house coordinator and volunteer in-house scanners. Added staff may be needed for special studies. Scanning should result in a
newsletter or some other form of regular report that is distributed widely within
the organization. Special studies should produce detailed analyses, which also may
need to be distributed widely. Environmental scanning, however, should never
be allowed to become a bureaucratic, paper-pushing exercise. It should be kept
simple and relatively informal; otherwise, it will deaden strategic thought and
action, not promote it.

The most effective scanning operations involve a network of scanners from
several organizations who exchange information and mutually develop scanning
skills and insights. If this network does not exist, it may be possible to create it
through regular meetings and the use of electronic mail.

Completion of Step 4 should also prompt the development, if it does not already exist, of an effective management information system (MIS) that includes
input, process, and output categories. An effective MIS is usually expensive and
time consuming to develop, but without it, an organization is unable to assess
relatively objectively and unambiguously—its strengths, weaknesses, efficiency,
and effectiveness. Again, the MIS should not be allowed to become excessively
bureaucratic or cumbersome. And in no circumstances should it drive out attention to the kinds of qualitative information that are so vital to real understanding and so useful to effective managers (Mintzberg, 1973). As Mintzberg (1994b,
p. 266) notes, "While hard data may inform the intellect, it is largely soft data that
generates wisdom."

Thoughtful discussions among key decision makers and opinion leaders concerning strengths, weaknesses, opportunities, and threats are one of the most
important outcomes of this step. Such discussions, particularly when they cross
functional lines in the organization, provide important quantitative and qualitative insights into the organization and its environment. They also prepare the way
for the identification of strategic issues in the next step. Such discussions provide
a way to *not* "overlook" important information embedded in the "complexly busy"
life of an organization, to use Diane Ackerman's words.

Benefits

An effective external and internal environmental assessment should provide several benefits to the organization. Among the most important is that it will produce

information that is vital to the organization's survival and prosperity. It is difficult to imagine that an organization can be truly effective over the long haul unless it has an intimate knowledge of its strengths and weaknesses in relation to the opportunities and threats it faces (Luttwak, 1977; Quinn, 1980, pp. 155–162; Nutt and Backoff, 1992; Doig and Hargrove, 1987).

Said somewhat differently, Step 4 allows the strategic planning team to see the organization as a whole in relation to its environment. This is usually one of the singular accomplishments of strategic planning. An ability to see the organization as a whole in relation to its environment keeps the organization from being victimized by the present. Instead the organization has a basis for *reasoned* optimism in that difficulties may be seen as specific rather than pervasive, temporary rather than permanent, and the result of factors other than irremediable organizational incompetence (Seligman, 1991; Kouzes and Posner, 1993). The organization thus prepares itself to follow Hubert Humphrey's advice: "Instead of worrying about the future, let us labor to create it."

Step 4 clarifies for the organization the nature of the "tension fields" it inhabits. Backoff and his coauthors (Wechsler and Backoff, 1987; Nutt and Backoff, 1992) argue that every organization must manage the tension between its capacities and intentions in relation to the opportunities and threats it faces. A SWOT analysis clarifies the nature of these tensions by juxtaposing two fundamental dimensions of existence: good (strengths and opportunities) and bad (weaknesses and threats), as well as present (strengths and weaknesses) and future (opportunities and threats).

External and internal assessments also develop the boundary-spanning skills of key staff members, especially key decision makers and opinion leaders. Assessments draw attention to issues and information that cross internal and external organizational boundaries. In effect, key decision makers and opinion leaders are prompted to move beyond their job descriptions in their thinking and discussions, increasing the opportunities for them to produce creative and integrative insights that bridge functions and levels of the organization and link it to its environment.

If reasonably routine, formal environmental scanning and MIS operations are established, then the organization will routinely turn its attention to major and minor external trends, issues, events, and stakeholders and to internal inputs, processes, and outputs (Emmert, Crow, and Shangraw, 1993). The chances of encountering major surprises are reduced, and the possibilities for taking anticipatory actions enhanced.

But even if external scanning and MIS are not institutionalized, the organization will become more externally oriented if it engages in periodic assessments, and it will gain a better understanding of its internal strengths and weaknesses. In my experience, organizations tend to be extremely insular and parochial and must be forced to face outward. Unless they do this, they are virtually certain not to satisfy their key external stakeholders.

In addition, people should never assume that the existence of a formalized system of environmental assessment relieves them of the need to constantly pay attention to what is going on in the outside world and to talk about it. For one thing, systems are designed around categories—and the categories may be wrong. The categories may make it hard or impossible to see important new developments that do not fit the categories (Mintzberg, 1994b). So the best advice may come from Yogi Berra, who once aptly observed that "you can observe an awful lot just by watching." Beyond that, perhaps writer Salman Rushdie is right: most of what matters in our lives takes place in our absence (Rushdie, 1981, pp. 19, 236). But that does not mean that one has to be taken completely by surprise.

Another major benefit of this step is that timely actions may be taken to deal with threats and weaknesses. As appropriate actions become apparent at any point in the process, they should be taken, as long they are based on reasonable information, have adequate support, and do not prematurely close off important strategic avenues. The final benefit of this step is that it prepares the organization to focus on identifying key strategic issues stemming from the convergence of its mandates, mission, strengths, weaknesses, opportunities, and threats.

External Environmental Assessments

The purpose of the first part of Step 4 is to explore the environment outside the organization in order to identify the opportunities and threats the organization faces (and perhaps to identify key success factors). Figure 2.1 identifies three major categories that might be monitored in such an exploration: (1) forces and trends, (2) key resource controllers, and (3) actual or potential competitors or collaborators and important forces affecting competition and collaboration and the competitive and collaborative advantages available to the organization. These three categories represent the basic foci of any effective environmental scanning system.

Forces and trends are usually broken down into political, economic, social, and technological categories (sometimes designated PESTs). (Organizations may also choose to monitor additional categories. For example, the University of Minnesota has added education; see Pflaum and Delmont, 1987. And the Scottish Natural Heritage, an organization responsible for promoting environmental protection, conservation, enhancement, and enjoyment, has added the natural environment.) The acronym PEST aptly suggests the often painful changes forced on organizations by these forces and trends. Unfortunately, it does not suggest the potential opportunities presented by environmental changes. Strategic planners must be sure they attend to both threats and opportunities.

What are the recent issues and trends that affect public and nonprofit sector organizations? Innumerable reviews and forecasts are available, but it is hard to know what to make of them (see, for example, Schlesinger, 1986; Kennedy, 1987, 1993; Cornish, 1990; Naisbitt and Aburdene, 1990; Popcorn, 1992; Land and

Jarman, 1992). As W. S. Gilbert said in *H.M.S. Pinafore*, "Things are seldom what they seem;/Skim milk masquerades as cream." The trick is to figure out which is which. Emmert, Crow, and Shangraw (1993, pp. 347–352) offer a very useful review of much of this literature and have identified eight categories of particular importance to the public sector. These are listed below in slightly modified form, adapted to include the nonprofit sector as well:

1. *Social and organizational complexity.* Increased complexity is driven by a number of forces, including technological change, the globalization of information and economies, and the consequent interconnectedness of almost everything. Meanwhile, many of our most important institutions were designed for a world that was more stable and simpler.

2. *Privatization and increased interaction among public, private, and nonprofit sectors.* As outlined by Osborne and Gaebler (1992), government's principal role is to steer, not row. Governments of the future—and not just in the United States—will rely far more on the nonprofit and for-profit sectors to do much of the actual rowing. Opportunities for increased effectiveness will be opened to organizations in each sector, but numerous threats will arise as well, through heightened competitive pressures, uncertainty, and revenue instability.

3. *Continuation of technological change.* Many futurists see technological innovation as *the* major force driving change. Public and nonprofit organizations' personnel will need new skills to utilize new technologies, and their organizations will need to adapt their processes, structures, and resource allocation patterns. The nature of work itself may change, perhaps as a result of fundamental "business process reengineering" (Hammer and Champy, 1993). Information technologies, in particular, are driving major changes that are likely to have a dramatic impact on organizational performance, accountability, stakeholder empowerment, and issues related to data use and privacy (Cleveland, 1985).

4. *Limited public-sector resources and growth.* The size of government is not likely to increase in relation to gross domestic product (GDP) although the cost of public problems almost certainly will. Productivity-enhancing innovations in institutional designs and collaborative problem solving across public, private, and nonprofit sectors will be necessary if we are not to become overwhelmed by the magnitude of the problems that now spill beyond the boundaries of any single organization (Bryson and Crosby, 1992).

5. *Diversity of the workforce, customer base, and citizenry.* This diversity will take many forms, including racial, ethnic, gender, and cultural forms. United Way of America (1989) calls this the "mosaic society," the "demassified" version of the "mass society" of the 1950s and early 1960s. In the jargon of strategic planning, the number of stakeholders is increasing, each with its own ideas, interests, and needs. This differentiation will complicate governance, service design and delivery, and workforce recruitment, retention, training, and management.

6. *Individualism, personal responsibility, and civic republicanism.* Most futurists en-

vision a move away from reliance on large institutions, particularly governmental institutions, toward self-reliance and greater personal responsibility. Most recent welfare reform initiatives emphasize these values, as do tax code reforms favoring saving rather than spending. There also are signs that citizenship is being "reinvented" to emphasize active citizen involvement in public problem solving and governance—the kind of "civic republicanism" favored by Jefferson and the Anti-Federalists, the Jacksonian Democrats, the Populists, John Dewey and many of the Progressives, and present-day communitarians (Barber, 1984; Herson, 1984; Boyte, 1989; Etzioni, 1993).

7. *Quality of life and environmentalism.* Concern for the quality of life is likely to increase. The sources of this concern are numerous, including the emergence of an era in which time is more scarce than money for many people (Burns, 1993). There is also a search for meaning beyond work, fears about the long-term viability of the planet, and worry about people's health and physical safety. The increased numbers of women in the workforce are bringing demands for changes in the workplace. Flexibility and workplace improvements are likely to be demanded, health care reform will be necessary, crime prevention will be called for (yet difficult to provide), and "green" policies and practices will be preferred.

8. *Transitions with continuity, not revolution.* The American tradition emphasizes "disjointed incrementalism" involving "partisan mutual adjustment" among actors (Lindblom, 1959, 1965, 1980; Braybrooke and Lindblom, 1963; Herson, 1984). We had the American Revolution and many major convulsions such as the Civil War and the Great Depression; but generally, "muddling through" (Lindblom, 1959) has been our preferred strategy as a nation. The good news is that continuous improvement in institutions is possible; the bad news is that typically it is very difficult to stimulate major institutional change in the absence of a crisis (Land and Jarman, 1992).

In addition to the PESTs, public and nonprofit organizations might monitor important stakeholder groups, especially actual or potential clients, customers, payers, and members (for volunteer organizations), as well as competitors and collaborators and the forces driving competition or collaboration.

In my experience, members of a public or nonprofit organization's governing board, particularly if they are elected, are generally better at identifying and assessing external threats and opportunities than are the organization's employees. Partly this is a reflection of differing roles; unlike most employees, a governing board typically has formal responsibility for relating an organization to its external environment (Thompson, 1967; Carver, 1990). In the public sector, there is a further reason. Employees get their mandates from laws, rules, and policies. Elected officials and politicians get their mandates primarily from elections. There usually is a major difference between legal or quasilegal mandates and political mandates. Politicians mostly pay attention to political mandates, because they must. Indeed, they typically employ "external environmental assessors" (pollsters, that is) to keep them informed about likely new external mandates. So it may actually be easier to sell external scanning to elected officials than to planners and public administrators since politicians live or die by how well they scan.

Even though the board may be better than staff members at identifying external opportunities and threats, typically neither group does a systematic or effective job of external scanning. Thus, both groups should rely on a more or less formal and regular process of external assessment. The technology is fairly simple, and it allows organizations to cheaply, pragmatically, and effectively keep tabs on outside events that are likely to have an impact on the organization and its pursuit of its mission. A simple process for external assessment is outlined later in this chapter. A more complicated, yet still simple, process is outlined in Resource A.

In addition to performing external scanning, organizational members can construct scenarios to help them pinpoint possible opportunities and threats (as well as the organization's internal strengths and weaknesses). A simple method of scenario construction is outlined in Resource C. A more complicated, yet still relatively simple, method is found in Schwartz, 1991, pp. 226–234.

Internal Environmental Assessments

The purpose of the second part of Step 4 is to assess the organization's internal environment in order to identify its strengths and weaknesses (that is, those aspects of the organization that help or hinder the accomplishment of its mission and fulfillment of its mandates). This step may also lead to clarification of the organization's core competencies. The three major categories that should be assessed (see Figure 2.1) are the basic elements of a simple systems model: resources (inputs), present strategy (process), and performance (outputs). Not only are these categories basic to any internal organizational assessment, they are also the fundamental categories around which any effective MIS should be built (Wetherbe, 1984; Romzek and Dubnick, 1987; Wholey and Hatry, 1992). Indeed, organizations with effective MIS programs should be in a better position to assess their strengths and weaknesses than organizations without such systems (although no MIS can provide all the information an organization needs—especially qualitative information, which is absolutely crucial).

In my experience, most organizations have plenty of quantifiable information—salaries, supplies, physical plant, full-time equivalent (FTE) personnel, and so on—readily available. They typically have much less of a command of qualitative information, such as the nature of their culture (even though culture is typically crucial to their performance).

Also, organizations generally cannot succinctly say what their present strategy is, either overall, by function, or by business process. One of the most important things a strategic planning team can do is simply to articulate what the organization's current strategy-in-practice is. This role of "finding the strategy"—

codifying the organization's "logic in action"—is a very useful one for planners (Mintzberg, 1994a, 1994b). The pattern recognition involved, and the discovery of pockets of innovative strategies in various parts of the organization, can be immensely instructive and can provide a better-informed basis for assessing strengths and weaknesses. As psychiatrist Fritz Perls once observed, "Nothing changes until it becomes what it is."

Organizations also typically can say little, if anything, about their outputs, either historical or present, let alone about the effects those outputs have on clients, customers, or payers. For example, social welfare agencies can say a lot about their budgets, staff, physical facilities, and so on, but usually they can say very little about the effects they have on their clients.

This relative absence of performance information presents problems both for the organization and for its stakeholders. Stakeholders will judge the worth of the organization by how well it meets the criteria for success the stakeholders have chosen. For external stakeholders in particular, these criteria typically relate to performance. If the organization cannot demonstrate its effectiveness, then stakeholders are likely to withdraw their support.

The absence of performance information may also create or harden major organizational conflicts. Without performance criteria and information, there is no way to judge the relative effectiveness of different resource allocations, organizational designs, and distributions of power. Without such judgments, organizational conflicts are likely to occur unnecessarily, be more partisan, and be resolved in ways that undermine the organization's mission.

The difficulties of measuring performance in the public and nonprofit sectors are well known (Flynn, 1986; Jackson and Palmer, 1992). Nevertheless, stakeholders will continue to demand that organizations demonstrate effective performance to justify their existence. Indeed, the Government Performance and Results Act of 1993 requires each federal agency to submit a strategic plan for its program activities to the Office of Management and Budget (OMB) by September 30, 1997. Beginning with fiscal year 1999, the act requires federal agencies to prepare annual performance plans for each program activity. These annual plans will be derived from the strategic plan and will set performance goals for each fiscal year. In most cases, performance goals are meant to be "objective, quantifiable, and measurable" and to measure and assess the relevant service levels, outputs, and outcomes. Qualitative descriptive goals may be used if quantification is not possible. The individual agency performance plans will be incorporated into a federal government performance plan, and this overall plan will become a part of the annual budget of the U.S. government in fiscal year 1999. Agencies will then be required to submit annual reports to Congress on their actual performance compared to the goals in their performance plans. If performance goals are not met, the report must explain why and describe what will be done in the future to achieve the goal (Panetta, 1993). There are likely to be instances where this attempt to create a federal governmentwide strategic planning system will actually drive out strategic thought and action; nonetheless, the unmistakable message is that key agency stakeholders (Congress, OMB, and the president) are vitally interested in performance, and agencies must respond in a thoughtful way.

The Assessment Process

The "Organizational Highs, Lows, and Themes" Exercise

It is often helpful for organizations to look forward by first looking backward. Indeed, organizations will find it easier to look forward any period of time (five, ten, twenty years) if they first look backward for an equivalent period of time (Kouzes and Posner, 1987). An extremely useful technique for helping organizations assess strengths, weaknesses, opportunities, and threats in a historical context is the "Organizational Highs, Lows, and Themes" exercise. The exercise is patterned after one designed for individuals, outlined in Bryson and Crosby (1992, pp. 349–351). (That exercise is in turn based on a more elaborate charting exercise described by Kouzes and Posner, 1987.) The exercise consists of the following steps:

1. Reserve a room with a large wall. A room with a whiteboard that covers a whole wall is ideal. Alternatively, you might wish to cover a wall with sheets of flip chart paper taped together, so that the results of the exercise may be saved intact.

2. Divide the wall into top and bottom halves. This can be done by drawing a line on the whiteboard or flip chart sheets or by using a long strip of masking tape.

3. At the right-hand end of the line, write in the current year. At the left-hand end, write in a date that is as far *back* as you wish the strategic planning team to ultimately look *forward* (typically five or ten years).

4. Group members individually and silently brainstorm, on a sheet of scratch paper, all of the organizational "highs" and "lows" they can recall within the agreed time frame. These might include the organization's founding, arrival or departure of respected leaders, successful or unsuccessful management of crises, particularly useful or disastrous innovations, and so on. Participants date each item and label it as a high or a low.

5. Participants transcribe their highs and lows onto half sheets of paper, one high or low per sheet. Once this is done, a piece of tape rolled sticky side out or a small bit of adhesive putty is attached to the back of each sheet.

6. Participants then stick their cards to the wall at the appropriate place on the time line. The height of each card above or below the line indicates just how high the "high" was or how low the "low" was.

7. The group then identifies themes common to the highs, to the lows, and to both.
8. The group analyzes the data and themes by answering these questions:

> What opportunities have we had? Which have we taken advantage of, which were we unable to take advantage of, and which have we ignored?

> What threats have we had to deal with? Which have we handled successfully, which unsuccessfully, and which have we ignored?

> What strengths have we relied upon to deal with threats and to take advantage of opportunities? Which have we ignored?

> What weaknesses have we had in dealing with threats and opportunities? What have we done about them?

9. Identify patterns in the way strengths, weaknesses, opportunities, threats, and themes have interrelated over the relevant organizational history. In particular, identify what the organization's strategies have been *in practice*—what has actually happened as opposed to what might be voiced in official pronouncements.
10. The group moves the time line forward an equivalent distance and discusses what the previous analyses imply for the future. In particular, have the group speculate about future opportunities and threats and the strengths and weaknesses the organization might have in the future to address them. What themes, patterns, and strategies from the past would the group like to see projected into the future? Which would group members not like to see projected? What new themes would the group like to see?

One example of the usefulness of this exercise is provided by a generally quite successful nonprofit organization in the United Kingdom devoted to addressing the needs of children (the organization's patron is a member of the royal family). Its management team realized as a result of this exercise that the organization almost always performed better when the team did careful planning, attended to key stakeholder interests, and took advantage of opportunities. Conversely, the organization did less well when the team got caught in crisis management, failed to attend to key stakeholder interests, and failed to deal with important threats. The exercise thus renewed the team's commitment to strategic planning and helped it focus on some key strengths, weaknesses, opportunities, and threats related particularly to stakeholder concerns.

The "Snow Card" Technique

The "snow card" technique (Greenblat and Duke, 1981; Spencer, 1989) is a very simple yet effective group technique for developing a list of strengths, weaknesses, opportunities, and threats. Also referred to as the "snowball" technique (Nutt and Backoff, 1992), the method combines brainstorming—which produces a long list of possible answers to a specific question—with a synthesizing step in which the answers are grouped into categories according to common themes. Each of the individual answers is written on a white card called a "snow card" (for example, a half sheet of photocopy paper, a five-by-seven-inch card, or a large self-stick note); the individual cards are then stuck to a wall with tape or putty according to common themes, producing several "snowballs" of cards.

The technique is extremely simple, easy to use, speedy, and productive. The technique is particularly useful as part of a SWOT analysis and as part of the strategy development step. In a SWOT analysis the technique would be used four times, in order to focus on these four questions:

- What major external or future opportunities do we have?
- What major external or future threats do we face?
- What are our major internal or present strengths?
- What are our major internal or present weaknesses?

The strategic planning team then, very quickly, has four lists to discuss, compare, and contrast, both to determine actions that should be taken immediately and to prepare for the identification of strategic issues in the next step. The SWOT analysis also helps the team prepare effective strategies in response to the issues.

Guidelines for using the snow card technique are as follows:

1. Select a facilitator.
2. Form the group that will use the technique. The ideal size for the group is five to nine persons (Delbecq, Van de Ven, and Gustafson, 1975), but the technique can still be effective with as many as twelve. Even larger numbers of participants can be involved if subgroups are formed.
3. Have the members of the group seat themselves around a table near a wall onto which the snows cards can be attached.
4. Focus on a single question, problem, or issue. (Thus, the entire process will be repeated four times in a SWOT analysis, once each for strengths, weaknesses, opportunities, and threats.)
5. Have the participants silently brainstorm as many ideas as possible in response to the question and record them on their personal worksheets.
6. Have individuals pick out the five to seven "best" items on their worksheets and transcribe them onto separate snow cards. Make sure people write legibly enough and large enough for the cards to be readable once they are posted on the wall.
7. Collect the cards (shuffle them if anonymity is important) and attach them one at a time to the wall, clustering cards with similar themes together. A tentative

label for each cluster should be selected by the group. As an alternative, the group members may wish to tape all of the cards to the wall at once and then together rearrange them into thematic clusters.

8. Label each cluster with a separate card. These label cards should be differentiated in some way from the snow cards, perhaps by using a different color card stock or ink or by drawing a box around the cluster name.

9. Once all items are on the board and each one is included in a cluster, rearrange the items and tinker with the categories until the group thinks the results make the most sense. Categories might be arranged in logical, priority, or temporal order. New items may be added and old ones deleted as necessary. Subcategories should be added as needed. In addition, structuring within categories may be advisable to highlight any linkages among items (see Resource C).

10. When the group members are satisfied with the categories and their contents, have them discuss, compare, and contrast the results.

11. The group's collective opinion of the importance of the categories (or individual items) may be visually accented with colored stick-on dots. For SWOT analyses, I usually give each participant seven dots per list and ask them to place one dot on each of the seven most important categories or items in each list. The pattern of the dots graphically displays the pattern of group opinion.

12. When the session is over, collect the cards in order, have them typed up in outline or spreadsheet form, and distribute the results to the group. Having a notebook computer and secretary at the session will speed this process. It may also be advisable to take photographs of the display, both as a backup and to provide a pictorial record and reminder of the process.

SWOT Analyses: An Example

Simply creating lists of strengths, weaknesses, opportunities, and threats is not enough. The lists must be carefully discussed, analyzed, compared, and contrasted; that is, a "SWOT analysis" must be performed. Planners should note specific implications for the formulation of strategic issues and effective strategies, as well as actions that might be necessary (and could be taken) before the end of the strategic planning process.

One of the fascinating features of most SWOT analyses is that strengths and weaknesses are often highly similar to one another. That is, an organization's greatest strengths may also be its greatest weaknesses. Likewise, the opportunities and threats an organization faces are also often similar to one another. Strategic planning team members should not be surprised to see such relationships. Indeed, they should expect that every organization will carry the weaknesses of its strengths and face the threats of its opportunities (and vice versa). The trick is to take advantage of the strengths and opportunities without being disadvantaged by the related weaknesses and threats.

The team also should not be surprised to find internal opportunities and threats and external strengths and weaknesses. Figure 2.1 indicates that opportunities and threats are primarily external and strengths and weaknesses are internal; meanwhile Nutt and Backoff (1992) argue that strengths and weaknesses are primarily in the present and opportunities and threats are primarily in the future. As a result, SWOTs may arise either inside or outside the organization, in the present, or in the future.

The CPI program provides an interesting example of SWOT lists developed through the use of snow cards (see Exhibit 5.1). (The CPI program's strategic planning team did the Organizational Highs, Lows, and Themes exercise prior to de-

EXHIBIT 5.1. CPI PROGRAM SWOT LISTS.

Strengths
- Relatively secure budget.
- Staff.
- Public support.
- Program is meeting short-term goals and objectives.
- Total Quality Organization (TQO) efforts.
- CPI affects millions of people and billions of dollars.
- CPI recognized as high-quality statistical program.

Weaknesses
- Employee dissatisfaction.
- Bureaucratic roadblocks and delays.
- Lack of planning.
- Complacency.
- Some biases in measures.
- No measure of value added.

Opportunities
- Things that can be taken advantage of.
- Right conditions, including new commissioner.
- Production of products beyond current CPI.
- Educate users on CPI limitations.
- Boundary issues.
- Quality research and analysis.
- Conceptual framework.
- Unproven technology.

Threats
- Congressional demands.
- CPI budget revision.
- Negative image of government.
- Competition.
- Views of new commissioner not known.
- Top-staff turnover.
- Federal budget deficit.
- Complacency.
- Lack of response to price surveys.
- Loss of reputation.
- Staff dissatisfaction.
- New technology.

veloping the SWOT list.) Only the main category headings will be discussed here, but they are enough to illustrate some of the points made above.

The fact that the complete list of strengths, weaknesses, opportunities, and threats was in need of further elaboration is to be expected. The list was a first crack, to show the management group where more information was needed. The quick snow card exercise by the CPI program's ten top managers took only two to three hours, including an extremely valuable discussion. It helped shape the way strategic issues were identified, provided the basis for a number of decisions and actions to improve the performance of the CPI program and its management group, and in general moved the CPI program's strategic planning process forward.

A few observations about the CPI program's complete SWOT list are in order. First, there are somewhat more opportunities and threats than there are strengths and weaknesses. This may be because the CPI program involves a matrix structure in which most members of the CPI management group (the strategic planning team) report both to the head of the CPI program and to senior people in the Bureau of Labor Statistics, who are in charge of particular functions such as surveys, computing, and so forth. Therefore, the CPI program's management group members always find themselves straddling various boundaries; they are thus exposed both to the opportunities and the threats such a position entails. As a group, they must constantly deal with the fact that the program must cross internal organizational boundaries and must rely on many external data suppliers if it is to survive.

This is the reverse of what usually occurs when a group of senior managers get together. Typically, most managers are responsible for the day-to-day operations of their departments. Their jobs often virtually preclude paying careful attention to external trends and events. Furthermore, most organizations do not have well-established occasions and forums for operating managers, as a group, to discuss external trends and events and their likely impact. Most organizations are thus in danger of being blindsided by external developments, unless they have external scanning operations and organized forums for managers to discuss information developed through external scanning or an invited speakers program.

Second, the list of threats is by far the longest list. The most likely reason for this is that it accurately reflects the threatening nature of the CPI program's current environment. However, when I have seen similar results in other organizations I have wondered whether it reflects the highly stressful work climate many public servants and nonprofit employees currently face rather than an accurate assessment of the threats (or opportunities) that are actually present. In psychologically punishing circumstances, it may be quite natural to focus on what seems to have produced an all-too-familiar climate of fear, anxiety, shame, or guilt—that is, threats—rather than what might evoke more pleasant but somehow diffuse emotions such as satisfaction, happiness, joy, or even love—namely, opportunities

(Dutton and Jackson, 1987; Ortony, Clore, and Collins, 1990; Kaufman, 1992; Csikszentmihalyi, 1990).

The good news is that a shared perception of threats may induce both group cohesion and action. Indeed, as was noted in Chapter Two, most organizations get into strategic planning because they face strategic issues that they do not know how to handle or because they are pursuing strategies that are failing or likely to fail. In either case, it is the perception of threats that prompts strategic planning. The bad news is that without some sense of safety provided by credible leaders, inspiring missions, visions, goals, or skilled group facilitators, groups gripped by threats may become paralyzed and unable to think of or take advantage of opportunities (Bellman, 1990; Schein, 1992; Kouzes and Posner, 1993; Schwarz, 1994).

Third, the CPI program's lists of strengths and weaknesses seem to be about equal in length. This is good; it helped keep them from succumbing to the natural human tendency to become a captive of action inhibitors (weaknesses) rather than focusing on what facilitates action (strengths). It also protected them from the equally familiar human tendency to assign blame or find a scapegoat as a way of avoiding action. Whatever the reasons, it is important to turn weaknesses into challenges to be overcome (Seligman, 1991; Csikszentmihalyi, 1990).

A final point to be made about SWOT analyses is that if a government performs a SWOT analysis (in contrast to the CPI example), the results will involve both the government as an organization and its jurisdiction as a place or community. This blending should be expected of governments responsible both for themselves and for places. The same blending of results for both the organization and its jurisdiction occurred for the school district. This was expected, given the interdependence between the school district and its supporting community. It also was expected because the district invited representatives of key stakeholder groups to participate in its SWOT analysis. These representatives typically were at least as concerned with the community as a whole as they were with the district's role in it.

Strengths. The CPI program's strategic planning team identified a solid set of strengths. Team members can build on these strengths to enhance the program's ability to meet its mandates and fulfill its mission. Further, there are entries for all three broad kinds of features of the internal environment—resources, present strategy, and performance. The fact that some categories belong on more than one list is to be expected.

Unfortunately, the "relatively secure budget" turned out to be less secure six months later, under the new Clinton administration, than team members imagined it would be. Bureau of Labor Statistics (BLS) and Department of Labor requests for supplementary funds for the CPI's decennial revision were not initially approved. This event might have been totally demoralizing before the CPI program began its strategic planning process. Fortunately, by the time it occurred, the management group had thought through enough of the issues, including the threat of not getting supplemental funds for the revision, that it was able to take the blow in stride. Ultimately, funding for the revision was approved as BLS and CPI management were able to argue persuasively about the negative effects that not doing the revision would have on the federal deficit.

Weaknesses. The CPI program's management group identified a significant set of weaknesses, although none is unusual or insurmountable. As would be expected, most of them mirror strengths. For example, able, enthusiastic staff are a strength, but employee dissatisfaction still emerges as a weakness. The level of government pay is a problem; there are concerns about the frequency of symbolic rewards; data collection staff in some parts of the country have serious health and safety concerns; and staff may not be receiving enough information about program vision and direction. While the program is meeting its short-term goals and is recognized as a high-quality statistical program (strengths), there are corresponding weaknesses:

1. The program has to cope with various bureaucratic roadblocks and delays (difficulties in procurement, hiring, and promotion processes; a cumbersome yearly budgeting cycle).
2. Planning is focused on fire fighting and short-term goals.
3. There is a certain complacency or smugness about the CPI program as a result of its excellent reputation. The program certainly can take deep satisfaction in its accomplishments; at the same time, constant attention to improvement and stakeholder satisfaction are certainly merited (Recall the adage "Nothing fails like success.")
4. Finally, in spite of its sound theoretical base and methodology, the CPI has some built-in biases in its measurement process (quality changes are hard to measure). In addition, the program has no measures of value added (there is a lack of overall performance measures for the program as a whole and for its major subcomponents), which can make it difficult to persuade key stakeholders of the index's worth.

Fortunately, general solutions to many of these weaknesses are not difficult to find, and indeed the search is already under way. The TQM efforts of the CPI program, BLS, and Department of Labor are addressing many of the bureaucratic roadblocks and delays. The federal government as a whole is looking at many of the same difficulties as a consequence of its National Performance Review (see Gore, 1993). The CPI program's TQM effort and its plans for the decennial revision are both looking at how to address the biases in measures. The management group's strategic planning effort is designed to move the program beyond its short-term planning focus and complacency; it will also address the need for performance measures that are persuasive to key external stakeholders.

Opportunities. The list of opportunities is helpful, hopeful, and cause for optimism. It is also a bit vague and therefore in need of elaboration. The first category of opportunities—things that can be taken advantage of—includes many items, such as freedom to innovate, the availability of new technology, and the benefits of empowering employees. The category also includes what probably are strengths, such as dedicated staff and a management group committed to making positive changes. As it stands, the category is something of a catchall, and needs further analysis. Other opportunities on the list that appear to be strengths as well include quality research and analysis and the CPI program's conceptual framework.

At the time of the SWOT analysis, conditions were right for change. Because planning for the decennial revision was under way, people expected change. Also, the fact that a new BLS commissioner was to be appointed by President Clinton provided a significant opportunity for change.

There also are opportunities to create new products beyond the current CPI, including products produced by potential collaborators. The obvious aim would be to respond to users' needs to the greatest extent possible. What needs careful analysis is the CPI program's competitive and collaborative advantages in relation to these products.

The final set of opportunities involves educating the various users of the CPI about its limitations so there are no misunderstandings, resolving various boundary issues within the program, and making possible use of new, but unproven, technologies.

Threats. The list of threats is substantial, and in many respects, it is more specific than the list of opportunities. At the head of the list are the threats posed by Congress, the Office of Management and Budget, and the Office of Personnel Management. These are important stakeholders that can place demands on the CPI program that it must respond to, whether or not they are reasonable. Control over the CPI program's budget, personnel, and other matters is in important ways out of the management group's hands. Given the federal budget deficit and the prevailing negative image of government (additional threats), damaging and perhaps unwise actions by these stakeholders are always possible.

Another threat at the time of the analysis was the possibility that the decennial revision would not be funded by a supplemental budget allocation. The CPI was expecting $61 million to fund the revision. Previous revisions had always received supplemental funding, and it would be difficult to do a revision without it. But the federal budget deficit made it unlikely that the CPI program would get all it wanted when it wanted it. As noted earlier, the supplemental money was in fact not received when expected, so the threat came to pass. But as a result of the strategic planning process, the CPI management's team figured out ways to restage the revision to keep major objectives on schedule even though the funding was delayed.

As noted, the prevailing negative view of government could affect the program's budget, at least indirectly. It also could affect staff recruitment. In addition, specific criticism of the CPI program's work by outside technical experts might affect the program's budget.

Competition from the private sector and other government departments is a potential threat, particularly since the CPI is not always sure what is important to its users. Careful surveys of existing and potential users, along with the competitive and collaborative analyses mentioned above, are warranted.

The CPI program's management group also had to consider potential challenges that the new BLS commissioner might pose. As it turned out, the new commissioner, Katherine Abraham, became a strong supporter of the CPI program and its revision plans.

Some threats appear to be current weaknesses projected into the future. Included here would be the consequences of complacency (the feeling that everything is already okay), declining response rates from data sources, and staff dissatisfaction over issues of safety and health.

The threat of possible turnover among key staff members (and the difficulties of hiring qualified new staff), the possible loss of the CPI program's reputation in the future, and known and unknown new technologies round out the list.

In sum, the CPI program's strategic planning team identified a number of strengths, weaknesses, opportunities, and threats through use of the snow card technique. Specific actions were suggested based on the lists, and the identification of strategic issues was facilitated. The lists were not exhaustive, however, and a more extensive SWOT analysis, with more staff support, would be merited in the future.

Process Guidelines

One of the special features of strategic planning is the attention it accords external and internal environments. Coupled with attention to its mandates and mission, external and internal environmental assessments give an organization a clear sense of its present situation and lay the basis for identifying strategic issues and developing strategies in the next two steps. As the ancient Chinese military strategist Sun Tzu (1991) might have said, without this kind of in-depth understanding, an organization is likely to be continuously imperiled. The following process guidelines may be helpful as an organization looks at its external and internal environments.

1. *Keep in mind that simpler is likely to be better.* Highly elaborate, lengthy, sophisticated, and quantified procedures for external and internal assessment are likely to drive out strategic thinking, not promote it.

2. *The organization may wish to review its mission and mandates, stakeholder analyses, existing goal statements, results of the Organizational Highs, Lows, and Themes exercise (if it*

was used), cultural audits, relevant survey results, MIS reports, possible future scenarios, and other information related to the organization's internal and external environments prior to performing a SWOT analysis. Alternatively, a "quick and dirty" SWOT analysis may prompt strategic planning team members to pay attention to what they have previously ignored, or it may indicate where additional information is needed.

Because an organization's culture can place severe limits on its ability to perceive SWOTs as well as constrain possible strategic responses, an analysis of the culture may be particularly useful. If key decision makers and opinion leaders are willing, a serviceable cultural analysis can be performed in one and a half days, following guidelines provided by Schein (1992, pp. 147–168; see also Hampden-Turner, 1990, pp. 185–207).

3. *Consider using the snow card technique with the strategic planning team to develop a list of strengths, weaknesses, opportunities, and threats.*

4. *Always try, if possible, to get a strategic planning team to consider what is going on outside the organization before it considers what is going on inside.* Attending to the outside is crucial, because the social and political justification for virtually every organization's existence is what it does, or proposes to do, about external social or political problems. Organizations, therefore, should focus on those problems first and on themselves second.

5. *As part of the discussion of its SWOT list, the strategic planning team should look for patterns, important actions that might be taken immediately, and implications for the identification of strategic issues.*

6. *A follow-up analysis of the SWOT list developed by the strategic planning team is almost always a good idea.*

7. *The organization should take action as quickly as possible on those items for which it has enough information.* Doing so is desirable if it does not foreclose important strategic options for the future. It is important to show continuous progress and desirable results from strategic planning if people are to stay with it when the going gets tough.

8. *The organization should consider institutionalizing periodic SWOT analyses.* The simplest way to do this is to schedule periodic meetings of the strategic planning team, say, once or twice a year, to engage in a snow card exercise to develop a SWOT list as a basis for discussion. In more elaborate form, this would mean establishing a permanent environmental scanning function.

9. *The organization may wish to construct various scenarios in order to help it identify SWOTs.* There are advantages to doing so, in that the stories conjured up by scenarios can help many people better imagine the future. As poet Muriel Rukeyser said, "The world is made of stories, not atoms." The often abstract categories of a SWOT analysis may just be vague "atoms" to people when what they need is a tangible story with "real" scenes, events, and actors. The story can help them see the whole rather than just the parts. I have seen effective assessments done with and without scenarios. Not using scenarios can save time, but some of the possible richness of a good assessment exercise can be lost without them.

Summary

Step 4 explores the organization's external and internal environments in order to identify the strengths, weaknesses, opportunities, and threats the organization faces. When combined with a greater attention to mandates and mission, these steps lay the foundation for identifying strategic issues and developing effective strategies in the following two steps. Recall that every effective strategy will build on strengths and take advantage of opportunities while it minimizes or overcomes weaknesses and threats.

By far the most important strategic planning technique is group discussion. The Organizational Highs, Lows, and Themes exercise and the snow card technique can be used to provide the basic SWOT list that will be the focus of group discussion.

Organizations should consider institutionalizing their capability to perform periodic SWOT analyses. If they do, they will need to establish an external scanning operation, develop a good MIS system, and undertake regular strategic planning exercises.

As with every step in the strategic planning process, simpler is usually better. Strategic planning teams and organizations should not get bogged down in external and internal assessments. Important and necessary actions should be taken as soon as they are identified, as long as they do not prematurely seal off important strategic options.

CHAPTER SIX

IDENTIFYING STRATEGIC ISSUES FACING THE ORGANIZATION

When a man knows he is to be hanged in a fortnight, it concentrates his mind wonderfully.

SAMUEL JOHNSON

Identifying strategic issues is the heart of the strategic planning process. Recall that a strategic issue is defined as a fundamental policy question or challenge affecting an organization's mandates, mission, and values; product or service level and mix; clients, users, or payers; or costs, financing, structure, or management. The purpose of Step 5, therefore, is to identify the fundamental policy questions—the "strategic issue agenda" (Nutt and Backoff, 1992)—facing the organization. The way these questions are framed can have a profound effect on decisions that define what the organization is, what is does, and why it does it.

The organization's culture will affect which issues get on the agenda and how they are framed, and it will also affect which strategic options get serious consideration in the next step, strategy formulation and plan development (Herson, 1984; Hampden-Turner, 1990; Schein, 1992; Kingdon, 1995). The need to change the organization's culture thus may become a strategic issue itself if the culture blinds the organization to important issues and possibilities for action.

As noted in Chapter Two, strategic issues are important because they play a central role in political decision making. Political decision making begins with issues, but strategic planning can improve the process by affecting the way the issues are framed and addressed. With carefully framed issues, subsequent choices, decisions, and actions are more likely to be politically acceptable and technically workable, in accord with the organization's basic philosophy and values, and morally, ethically, and legally defensible.

Identifying strategic issues is typically one of the most riveting steps for participants in strategic planning (Ackermann, 1992). Virtually every strategic issue involves conflicts: what will be done, why it will be done, how it will be done, when it will be done, where it will be done, who will do it, and who will be favored or disadvantaged by it. These conflicts may draw people together or pull them apart. In any event, participants will feel heightened emotion and concern (Filley, 1975; Ortony, Clore, and Collins, 1990; Schein, 1992). If strategic planning is partly about the construction of a new social reality, then this step outlines the basic paths along which that drama might unfold (Mangham and Overington, 1987). As in any journey, fear, anxiety, and sometimes depression are as likely to be travel companions as excitement and adventure.

Desired Planning Outcomes and Benefits

This step should result in the creation of the organization's strategic issue agenda. The agenda is a product of two intermediate outcomes. The first is a list of the strategic issues faced by the organization. These issues may have their origins in many different places (see Resource B); the list, however, is likely to be a product of the strategic planning team's deliberations. The second is an arrangement of the issues on the list in some sort of order: priority, logical, or temporal. The listing and arrangement of issues should help people consider the nature, importance, and implications of each issue.

A number of benefits ensue from the identification of strategic issues. First, attention is focused on what is truly important. The importance of this benefit is not to be underestimated. Key decision makers in organizations are usually victimized by the "eighty-twenty rule." That is, key decision makers usually spend at least 80 percent of their time on the least important 20 percent of their jobs (Parkinson, 1957). When this is added to the fact that key decision makers in different functional areas rarely discuss important cross functional matters with one another, the stage is set for shabby organizational performance.

It also helps to remember that there are three different kinds of strategic issues: (1) issues where no action is required at present, but the issue must be continuously monitored; (2) issues that can be handled as part of the organization's regular strategic planning cycle; and (3) issues that require an immediate response and therefore cannot be handled in a more routine way.

A second benefit is that attention is focused on issues, not answers. All too often, serious conflicts arise over solutions to problems without any clarity about what the problems actually are (Filley, 1975; Eden and Sims, 1978; Fisher and Ury, 1981; Janis, 1989). Such conflicts typically result in power struggles, not problem-solving sessions. More importantly, they are unlikely to help the organization achieve its goals, be satisfied with its outcomes, or enhance its future problem-solving ability (Bryson, Bromiley, and Jung, 1990; Bryson and Bromiley, 1993).

Third, the identification of issues usually creates the kind of useful tension that is necessary to prompt organizational change. Organizations rarely change unless they feel some need to change, some pressure or tension—often fear, anxiety, or guilt—that requires change to relieve or release the stress (Schein, 1988,

1992; Nutt and Backoff, 1992). The tension must be great enough to prompt change, but not so great as to induce paralysis. Strategic issues that emerge from the juxtaposition of internal and external factors—and involve organizational survival, prosperity, and effectiveness—can provide just the right tension to focus the attention of key decision makers on the need for change. Key decision makers will be particularly attentive to strategic issues that threaten severe consequences if they are not addressed. As Samuel Johnson observed, albeit humorously, frightening situations quickly focus one's attention on what is important.

Fourth, strategic issue identification should provide useful clues about how to resolve the issues identified. By stating exactly what in relation to the organization's mission, mandates, and internal and external factors (or SWOTs) makes an issue strategic, one also gains some insight into possible ways the issue might be resolved. In particular, if one follows the dictum that any effective strategy must take advantage of strengths and opportunities and minimize or overcome weaknesses and threats, then one will gain insights into the nature and shape of effective answers to the issue (Mintzberg, 1994b, p. 277). Paying attention to strengths and opportunities is likely to promote action-enhancing optimism, as opposed to the depression and inaction associated with paying attention only to weaknesses and threats (Dutton and Jackson, 1987; Seligman, 1991).

Fifth, if the strategic planning process has not been "real" to participants up until this point, it will become real for them now. For something to be real for someone, there must be a correspondence between what the person thinks, how he or she behaves, and the consequences of that behavior (Brickman, 1978; Boal and Bryson, 1987a). As the organization's situation and the issues it faces become clear, as the consequences of failing to face those issues are discussed, and as the behavioral changes necessary to deal with the issues begin to emerge, the strategic planning process will begin to seem less academic and much more real. The more people realize that strategic planning can be quite real in its consequences, the more seriously they will take it. A qualitative change in the tone of discussions among members of the team often can be observed at this point, as the links between cognition, behavior, and consequences are established. Less joking and more serious discussion occur.

A typical result of this "real-ization" is that the group may wish to cycle through the process again. In particular, the group's initial framing of the strategic issues is likely to change as a result of further discussion among members who have come to more fully realize the consequences of addressing (and failing to address) the issues (Eden and Sims, 1978). Or, to go back to the theatrical metaphor, as the group "rehearses" the various decision-making and action sequences that might flow from a particular framing of an issue, they may wish to reframe it so that certain kinds of strategies are more likely to find favor.

A further consequence of the understanding that strategic planning may be all too real in its consequences is that key decision makers may wish to terminate the effort at this point. They may be afraid of addressing the conflicts embodied in the strategic issues. They may not wish to undergo the changes that may be necessary to resolve the issues. They may fall into "the pit," where they may experience stress, anger, depression, feelings of powerlessness, and grief (Spencer and Adams, 1990). Such feelings are quite common among individuals undergoing major changes until they let go of the past and move into the future with a new sense of direction and renewed confidence. A crisis of trust or a test of courage may occur, and it may lead to a turning point in the development of the organization's character. If after completing this step the organization's key decision makers decide to push on, a final very important benefit will be gained: the organization's character will be strengthened. Just as an individual's character is formed in part by the way he or she faces serious difficulties, so too is organizational character formed by the way the organization faces difficulties (Selznick, 1957; Schein, 1992). Strong character only emerges from confronting serious difficulties squarely and courageously (Terry, 1993).

Examples of Strategic Issues

It may help to present two examples of strategic issues. Both were prepared by the Hennepin County Office of Planning and Development as training aids to help key managers compile their list of strategic issues for the county's first strategic planning process (Hennepin County, 1983; Eckhert, Haines, Delmont, and Pflaum, 1988). The first, a historical example from the late 1960s and early 1970s, is an elaboration of the question, How should the county meet its long-term office space requirements? The second example, still current, poses the question, How should the solid waste the county produces be handled?

In these examples, strategic issues emerge from the conjunction of internal and external environmental factors, externally imposed mandates, and the county's own policy objectives. The county did not have a mission statement per se, but its policy objectives served the same purpose.

The issue of what to do about long-term office space requirements was presented to county staff graphically (see Figure 6.1). The issue arose in an environment characterized by significant overcrowding, significant projected program and staff growth, a shortage of downtown office space in Minneapolis, rising lease costs, and a dysfunctional scattering of county office locations. On top of this, the county was mandated to take over Minneapolis General Hospital (which became the Hennepin County Medical Center), to provide major administrative services as part of new Medicaid legislation, and to develop new management organizations to administer the various county responsibilities mandated by new federal programs. Given the changes in the environment and the new mandates, the county faced serious difficulties in achieving its relevant policy objectives—namely, to provide efficient and professional management of county operations; to provide convenient, high-quality public services; and to contain the cost of its facilities.

FIGURE 6.1. EXAMPLE OF A STRATEGIC ISSUE: LONG-TERM OFFICE SPACE REQUIREMENTS.

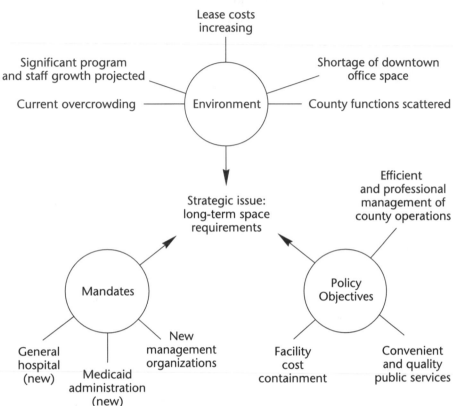

The issue of long-term office space requirements was resolved by the construction in downtown Minneapolis of a striking twin-tower skyscraper, a large underground parking garage, and a spacious surrounding urban park.

The second issue (what to do about solid waste) was also presented graphically to county staff (see Figure 6.2). In this case, the environmental factors were large volumes of waste, rapidly increasing disposal costs, the reduction of existing landfill space, public opposition to new landfills, and the emergence of a number of potentially economical and environmentally safe technologies such as recycling and incineration with concurrent generation of electricity. The pressure to find a solution was increased by two mandates from the state legislature: each county had to prepare a landfill abatement plan, and each county had to recommend new landfill sites. The county did not really have any policy objectives in this area, other than a desire to find a solution that would satisfy all its key stakeholders. The issue has not been resolved, although the county has constructed a huge incineration and power generation plant just north of downtown Minneapolis, and it has initiated ambitious recycling programs. But in spite of the

FIGURE 6.2. EXAMPLE OF A STRATEGIC ISSUE: SOLID WASTE MANAGEMENT.

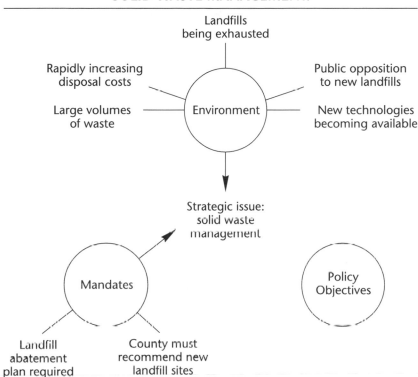

plant's large size and the county's sizable recycling efforts, they are not able to handle the solid waste that is now projected for the county.

How Should Strategic Issues Be Described?

An adequate strategic issue description (1) phrases the issue as a challenge that the organization can do something about and that has more than one solution, (2) discusses the confluence of factors (mission, mandates, and internal and external environmental aspects, or SWOTs) that make the issue strategic, and (3) articulates the consequences of not addressing the issue. A strategic issue description probably should be no longer than a page or two for it to attract the attention of and be useful to busy decision makers and opinion leaders.

The issue should be phrased as a challenge the organization can do something about for several reasons. First, if there is nothing the organization can do about a situation, then there is no strategic issue, at least not for that organization. That is, there is no strategic issue unless the organization is forced by circumstances into doing something—however symbolic or ineffective—about it (Edelman, 1964, 1971, 1977). Second, effective strategic planning has an action orientation. If strategic planning does not produce useful decisions and actions, then it probably is a waste of time. Third, focusing on what the organization can do helps it attend to what it controls, instead of worrying pointlessly about what it does not. Finally, organizations should focus their most precious resource—the attention of key decision makers—on issues they can do something about.

Articulating strategic issues as challenges the organization can do something about, particularly when done on a regular basis, should help the organization strongly influence the way issues get framed and what might be done about them. In the vernacular, this will help the organization "get out in front of" the issues. If the organization waits until a crisis develops, it may be very difficult to deal with it strategically and wisely. Thus, strategic issues typically are not *current* problems or crises—although obviously there are almost always strategic implications to the way current problems or crises are resolved, and equally obviously, decision makers *should* think strategically about how to address current problems and crises. In any event, strategic issues are typically complex and potentially destructive if they are not satisfactorily resolved (Hennepin County, 1983).

There are also several reasons why the issue should be phrased as a challenge that has more than one solution. If the question has only one answer, it is probably not really an issue, but a choice about whether or not to pursue a specific solution. In addition, if people are forced to frame issues in such a way that there might be more than one answer, the chances are increased that strategic issues will not be confused with strategies and that innovative or even radical answers to those issues might be considered (Nutt, 1984b). Innovative or radical answers may not be chosen, but they almost always should be considered, since dramatic performance gains or increases in key stakeholder satisfaction may result.

Attention to the factors that make an issue strategic is important both in order to clarify the issue and in order to establish outlines for potential strategies to resolve the issue (Freedman and Van Ham, 1982, pp. 184–186; Nutt and Backoff, 1992). Strategic issues arise in three kinds of situations. First, they can arise when events beyond the control of the organization make or will make it difficult or impossible to accomplish basic objectives acceptably and affordably. These situations would probably be called threats. Second, they can arise when technology, cost, financing, staffing, management, or political choices for achieving basic objectives change or soon will change. These situations might present either threats or opportunities. Lastly, they can arise when changes in mission, mandates, or internal or external factors suggest present or future opportunities to (1) make significant improvements in the quantity or quality of products or services delivered, (2) achieve significant reductions in the cost of providing products or services, (3) introduce new products or services, or (4) combine, reduce, or eliminate certain products or services (Hennepin County, 1983). Unless the context surrounding the issue is clearly understood, it is unlikely that key decision makers will be able to act wisely in that context, which they must do to improve the chances for successful issue resolution (see Bryson and Delbecq, 1979; Neustadt and May, 1986; Janis, 1989).

Finally, there should be a statement of the consequences of failing to address the issue. These consequences may be either exposure to serious threats or failure to capitalize on significant opportunities. If there are no positive or negative consequences, then the issue is not a strategic issue. The issue may be interesting in an academic sense, but it does not involve an important or fundamental choice for the organization. Again, the resource in shortest supply is the attention of key decision makers, so they should focus on the issues that are most consequential for the organization.

Once a list of strategic issues has been prepared, it is possible to figure out just how strategic each issue is. Two methods for doing this, a "litmus test" and a "directed graph," are covered later in the Process Guidelines section.

Four Approaches to Strategic Issue Identification

Four approaches to identifying strategic issues are possible: the direct approach, the indirect approach, the goals approach, and the "vision of success" approach (Barry, 1986; Bryson, 1994). Which approach is best depends on the organization's or community's characteristics. Guidelines for using these four approaches are presented in this section; guidelines for the whole strategic issue identification step are presented in the following section.

The direct approach (along with the related indirect approach) is probably the most useful to governments and nonprofit organizations. In it, planners go straight from a review of mandates, mission, and SWOT analyses to the identification of strategic issues. The direct approach is best if (1) there is no agreement on goals, or the goals on which there is agreement are too abstract to be useful; (2) there is no preexisting vision of success, and developing a consensually based vision will be difficult; (3) there is no hierarchical authority that can impose goals on the other stakeholders; or (4) the environment is so turbulent that development of goals or visions seems unwise, and partial action in response to immediate, important issues seems most appropriate. The direct approach, in other words, can work in the pluralistic, partisan, politicized, and relatively fragmented worlds of most public (and many nonprofit) organizations, as long as there is a "dominant coalition" (Thompson, 1967) that is strong enough and interested enough to make it work. That is, there must be a coalition that is fully committed to identifying and resolving at least some of the key strategic issues the organization faces, even if it is not committed to developing a comprehensive set of goals or a vision of success.

In the goals approach—which is more in keeping with traditional planning theory—an organization first establishes goals and objectives for itself and then goes on to identify issues that need to be addressed in order to achieve those goals and objectives (or else it goes straight to developing strategies). For the approach to work, a fairly broad and deep agreement on the organization's goals and objectives must be possible, and the goals and objectives themselves must be specific and detailed enough to provide useful guidance for developing issues and strategies (but not so specific and detailed that they filter out wise strategic thought and action). This approach is also more likely to work in organizations with hierarchical authority structures in which key decision makers can impose goals on others affected by the planning exercise. Finally, externally imposed mandates may embody goals that can drive the identification of strategic issues or the development of strategies.

The goals approach, in other words, is more likely to work in public or nonprofit organizations that are hierarchically organized, pursue narrowly defined missions, and have few powerful stakeholders. In contrast, organizations with broad agendas and numerous powerful stakeholders are less likely to achieve the kind of consensus ("forced" or otherwise) necessary to use the goals approach effectively—although they may achieve it in specific areas as a result of political appointments, elections, referenda, or other externally imposed goals or mandates. Similarly, the approach is likely to work for communities that are relatively homogeneous and have a basic consensus on values, but is unlikely to work well for heterogeneous communities or those without agreement on basic values unless extraordinary efforts are put into developing a real consensus on goals.

In the vision of success approach, the organization is asked to develop a "best" picture of itself in the future as it fulfills its mission and achieves success. The issues then involve how the organization should move from the way it is now to how it should look and behave, based on its vision of success. The vision of success developed in this step will be sketchier than the more elaborate version called for in Step 8. All that is needed here is a relatively short idealized scenario of the future.

The vision of success approach is most useful when it is particularly necessary to take a holistic approach to the organization and its strategies—that is, when integration across a variety of strategies is necessary. In other words, the approach can be used when sponsors, champions, and planning team members believe that simply identifying issues directly or indirectly or articulating goals is unlikely to promote the level of strategy integration that is perceived as necessary. It also is likely to be a preferred approach when a new policy board or chief executive takes office based on a vision espoused prior to election or appointment. The approach also can be particularly useful if drastic change is likely to be necessary. Since conception precedes perception (May, 1969; Schein, 1992), development of a vision of success can provide the concepts necessary in times of major change to enable organizational members to see what changes are necessary (Morgan, 1986; Mintzberg and Westley, 1992; Mintzberg, 1994a, 1994b). Finally, many people understand the utility of beginning with a sense of vision. When enough key actors think that way, it may be the best approach and may lead to truly integrated strategies, assuming the actors are able to agree on a vision.

This approach is more likely to apply to nonprofit organizations than to public organizations, as public organizations are usually more tightly constrained by mandates and the conflicting expectations of numerous stakeholders. Public organizations will find the approach particularly useful, however, when new leaders are elected or appointed because of their vision of the future. The approach may also work for communities if they are reasonably homogeneous or share an underlying value consensus.

Finally, there is the indirect approach, which, as its name implies, is a more indirect way to identify strategic issues than the direct approach. The indirect approach works in the same situations as the direct approach and is generally as useful. In addition, the indirect approach is particularly useful when major strategic redirection is necessary but members of the planning team and the organization have not yet grasped the need for it or cannot sense where such changes might lead. The method starts with participants' existing system of ideas, helps them elaborate on the action implications of those ideas, and then recombines the ideas in new ways so that they "socially construct" (Berger and Luckman, 1967) a new reality that allows them to convince themselves of the need for change (Kelly, 1963; Eden and Huxham, 1988; Eden, 1989; Bryson and Finn, 1995). In other words, the participants' own ideas, when recombined in new ways, help them see things differently and act accordingly (Kanter, 1983). Innovation is thus more a consequence of recombination than mutation (Kingdon, 1995).

When using this approach, the planning team develops several sets of options, merges them, and then sorts the combined sets into clusters of options with similar themes, using the snow card process (discussed in Chapter Five) or the oval mapping process (see Resource C). Each cluster's theme represents a potential strategic issue. The sets consist of options to (1) make or keep stakeholders happy according to their criteria for satisfaction; (2) build on strengths, take advantage of opportunities, and minimize or overcome weaknesses and threats; (3) fulfill the mission and mandates; (4) capture existing goals, strategic thrusts, and details; and (5) articulate stated or suggested actions embodied in other relevant background studies.

The Direct Approach

The following guidelines may prove helpful to organizations that wish to use the direct approach.

After a review of mandates, mission, and SWOTs, strategic planning team members should be asked to identify strategic issues on their own. For each issue, each member should answer these three questions on a single sheet of paper:

- What is the issue?
- What factors (mandates, mission, external and internal influences) make it a strategic issue?
- What are the consequences of failing to address the issue?

Sample worksheets can be found in Bryson and Alston (1995).

It may be best to give individuals at least a week to propose strategic issues. Identifying strategic issues is a real art, and it cannot be forced. Also, an individual's best insights often come unpredictably, at odd moments and outside the group setting (Isenberg, 1984; Agor, 1989; Mintzberg, 1994a, 1994b).

Each of the suggested strategic issues—phrased as a challenge the organization can do something about—should then be placed on a separate sheet of flip chart paper and posted on a wall, so the strategic planning team can consider and discuss them as a set. The sheets may be treated as giant snow cards, with similar issues grouped together or perhaps recast into a different form on blank sheets held in reserve for that purpose.

Alternatively, ask planning team members to individually brainstorm as many strategic issues as they can—answering only the first question—on individual worksheets. Have each participant place a check mark next to the five to seven most important issues on their individual lists. These items should be transferred to snow cards and then clustered into issue categories. For each cluster, the group (or subgroups) can then answer the three questions listed above.

Whichever method is used, it is usually helpful to clarify the group's opinion about which are the most important issues in the short term and the long term. I usually rely on the use of colored stick-on dots to indicate individuals' views. I ask each person to place an orange dot on each of the five issues he or she thinks are most important in the short term and a blue dot on each of the five issues he or she thinks are most important in the long term. (The same issue can be important in both the short and the long term.) The pattern of dots will indicate where the majority opinion lies, if any exists.

As with any judgmental exercise, it is usually best to have people make their individual judgments first and record them on a piece of scratch paper before they publicly express their views (by placing colored dots, for example). After individuals have expressed their views, a group discussion should ensue, followed by additional individual "voting" (using the dots) if it appears people have changed their minds. A more reasoned group judgment is likely to emerge via this procedure (Delbecq, Van de Ven, and Gustafson, 1975).

When at least tentative agreement has been reached on the list of strategic issues, prepare new single sheets of paper that present each issue and answer the three questions. These new sheets will provide the basis for further discussion, if necessary, or for the development of strategies to resolve the issues (in the next step).

The public library used the direct approach to identify seven strategic issues at a retreat. After considerable follow-up discussion, the list was refined to six issues:

- What should our mission be?
- How can we reduce or streamline our staff workload?
- How can we increase library funding?
- How can we improve our facilities?
- How can we utilize new technologies?
- How can we upgrade the library's services?

The first three issues are interconnected and were clearly the most important in the eyes of the planning team. As noted, the library's staff were experiencing sinking morale as a result of increased workloads and no new resources. The limits of productivity gains using existing strategies and structures had been reached. Because the library could not maintain customer service and satisfaction levels or staff morale in the face of staff and funding shortages, it had to do one or more of the following: (1) narrow its range of services, (2) find new ways to increase its productivity, or (3) generate additional financial and staff resources. In the view of the planning group, the other three issues were not nearly as important or pressing, though they still merited attention.

The fact that the library decided it had to rethink its mission and refine its strategic issues is not unusual. Indeed, it should have been expected. One bit of process wisdom I have learned is that it does not matter where you start in strategic planning, you always end up back at your mission—and you often rethink it as a result.

One other point to make about the library's effort is that during the strategic planning retreat, where the first tentative list of strategic issues was drawn up, planning team members clearly fell into "the pit"—or to use their language, "hit the wall." The wall consisted of a vicious circle that was a product of library culture (Senge, 1990; Hampden-Turner, 1990). The first part of this vicious circle was that existing strategies had begun to fail since the system was at its limit and staff stress and burnout were reaching crisis proportions. The second part was that the librarians could not yet see what to do about it. They were all deeply committed to giving library patrons what they wanted—almost no matter what it took—but they could not continue to do so without increased resources. The obvious need to narrow their role, set priorities among patrons, and adopt a more entrepreneurial and political mentality challenged the professional identities they had built up over many years. They felt they were surrounded by walls they did not know how to climb, skirt, tunnel under, or blow up. However, through lots of discussion, emotional venting, mutual support, and consideration of various options, they did eventually figure out how to knock down the walls.

The Goals Approach

The following guidelines are for organizations that choose to use the goals approach.

If the organization does not already have a set of goals, then after a review of mandates, mission, and SWOTs, members of the strategic planning team should be asked to propose goals for the organization as a basis for group discussion. Again, the snow card procedure is an effective way to develop and organize a set of possible goals quickly as a basis for further group discussion. More than one session may be necessary before the group can agree on a set of goals that are specific and detailed enough to guide the development of strategies for action.

It may not be necessary to identify strategic issues if this approach is used; rather, the team may move directly to the strategy development step. If strategic issues are identified, they are likely to pose questions such as "How do we gain the agreement of key decision makers on this set of goals?" "How do we establish priorities among these goals?" "What are the best strategies for achieving the goals?"

An alternative way to identify a set of goals for the organization is to assign one or more members of the team the task of reviewing past decisions and actions to uncover the organization's implicit goals. This approach can uncover an existing consensus about what the organization's goals are. It can also uncover any divergences between this consensus and the organization's mandates, mission, and SWOTs. Dealing with the divergences may itself represent strategic issues for the organization.

Hennepin County staff reviewed the previous decisions and actions of the county board and administrative branch to uncover the implicit goals (or "policy objectives," as they called them) of the county government. The countywide policy objectives developed in this way are presented in Exhibit 6.1. These objectives had the advantage of embodying an existing consensus on what the county should seek in the areas of service delivery, finance, and management. The potential robustness of this approach is demonstrated by the fact that the list is for all intents and purposes still current—over ten years after it was first formulated—even though there has been major turnover on the county board and some significant demographic changes in the county (Philip Eckhert, personal communication, 1994; Hennepin County, 1995). This stability in the county's goals was made possible partly by the existence of a significant consensus in the political culture of the county and partly because a single political party has generally dominated the county during this period. Obviously these conditions do not prevail everywhere, and they may change in Hennepin County as well.

Whichever approach to goals development is used, specific objectives will be developed in the next step (strategy development). Strategies are developed to achieve goals; objectives (as opposed to goals) should be thought of as specific milestones or targets to be reached during strategy implementation.

EXHIBIT 6.1. HENNEPIN COUNTY POLICY OBJECTIVES.

Service Delivery Objectives
One of Hennepin County's primary goals is to provide services that are cost-effective, timely, and responsive to the changing needs of the county's citizens. It is the objective of the county to:

- Furnish mandated and optional public services in the areas of assessment, elections, public records, licenses, tax administration, transportation and environmental concern as provided in Minnesota statutes and in a cost-effective and coordinated manner.
- Protect life and property, administer justice, protect the rights of citizens and rehabilitate offenders through effective and appropriate use of its law enforcement, prosecution, legal defense, civil and criminal courts, and corrections programs.
- Maintain and improve the physical well-being of county residents by reducing the number of illnesses and disabilities, or by lessening their severity.
- Provide effective citizen access to informational and outdoor recreational resources.
- Protect from abuse, exploitation, and neglect county residents who are unable to assure themselves of basic rights and opportunities.
- Assist in achieving and maintaining basic levels of economic, social, and personal independence for individuals.
- Provide a permanent and stable family setting for all dependent children.
- Maximize the economic self-sufficiency of individuals and families by effectively, efficiently, and humanely managing the federal and state aided economic assistance programs administered by the county.
- Provide legislative direction, administrative support, and general services for the efficient operation of county business and the effective management of county programs.

Financial Objectives
The operating and capital budgets of the county are to be prepared annually according to law and reviewed in public meetings which provide for citizen input. The budget shall contain programs and capital projects that are responsive to the needs of the citizenry and that meet the requirements of federal and state mandates.

In financing the budget, property taxes are the funding source of last resort for the county. The level of property taxes required by the county is primarily dependent on the amount of federal, state, and fee revenues available; and the level of property tax–related expenditures to be financed. It is the objective of the county to:

- Limit the rate of growth in the property tax levy to the rate of increase in the estimated market value of property in Hennepin County.
- Ensure that increases in county expenditures do not exceed the rate of inflation for the SMSA from May to May.
- Aggressively seek to ensure that state and federal program appropriations are sufficient to fully fund mandated services and statutory reimbursement formulas.
- Seek added federal and state support through general purpose revenue-sharing programs and local government aids.
- Aggressively seek grants and other private sources of funding for new and existing programs.
- Maximize fees for services based on the full cost of providing the service, or based on competitive market forces unless prohibited by law.
- Maintain a minimum cash position adequate to finance 60 days of operations for the county.

Management Objectives
The county considers management to have a progressive as opposed to a maintenance role. Improvements, innovation, and progress in administering the business of the county are to be encouraged, pursued, and achieved. It is the objective of the county to:

- Emphasize hiring practices that reflect the equal opportunity employment philosophy of the county.
- Maintain wage and benefit programs for employees that are competitive with the private sector and other units of government.
- Maintain a personnel policy that is designed and administered in a manner that provides adaptability and efficiency.
- Improve its productivity by 2 percent per annum.
- Actively consider alternative approaches for providing services whenever an alternative offers quality service at the levels needed in a more cost-effective manner.
- Foster the development of intergovernmental cooperation agreements and joint ventures in order to improve service, enhance efficiency or reduce costs, and improve intergovernmental relations.
- Develop program evaluation and performance measurement standards for existing and new county programs.

Source: Hennepin County, 1983, pp. 3-2–3-5.

The Vision of Success or Idealized Scenario Approach

New boards or appointed officials may arrive with a vision already worked out. Their main task often involves selling their vision and incorporating any useful modifications that are suggested. Other organizations wanting to develop a vision of success from scratch may wish to keep in mind the following guidelines.

After a review of mandates, mission, and SWOTs, each member of the strategic planning team should be asked to develop a picture or scenario of what the organization should look like after it successfully fulfills its mission and achieves its full potential. The visions should be no longer than a page in length; they might be developed in response to the following instructions: "Imagine that it is three to five years from now and your organization has been put together in a very exciting way. It is a recognized leader in its field. Imagine that you are a newspaper reporter assigned to do a story on the organization. You have thoroughly reviewed the organization's mandates, mission, services, personnel, financing, organization, management, etc. Describe in no more than a page what you see" (Barry, 1986, p. 41).

The members of the strategic planning team should then share their visions with one another. A facilitator can record the elements of each person's vision on large sheets. Either during or after the sharing process, similarities and differences among them should be noted and discussed. Basic alternative visions should then be formulated (perhaps by a staff member after the session) as a basis for further discussion.

At a subsequent session, planning team members should rate each alternative vision or scenario according to several criteria deemed to be of strategic importance (such as fit with mandates and mission, stakeholder support, SWOTs, and financial feasibility). They should then develop a list of the relative advantages and disadvantages of each vision. The team may also wish to consult internal and external advisers, critics, and possible partners to gain further insights and opinions. Discussion should follow to decide which vision is best for the organization.

An alternative approach involves asking team members to develop two lists: what the organization is moving *from* (both good and bad) and what it is moving *toward* (both good and bad) (Nutt and Backoff, 1992, pp. 168–177). This approach involves capturing the essence of the organization's past and present and then projecting it into a possible future. The good and bad aspects inherent in future possibilities can be used to formulate best- and worst-case scenarios. A subsequent sketch of an organizational vision of success would highlight the good points the organization wants to move toward and take account of the bad points the organization wants to avoid.

Once agreement is reached among key decision makers on the best vision, the strategic planning team may be able to move on to the next step: developing strategies to achieve the vision.

Mainline Church pursued the vision of success approach. Its strategic planning team constructed visions to guide subsequent strategy development in areas covered by its mission statement and in other areas where it was clear new strategies were needed. These included the following:

- Worship
- Nurturing (Christian education for member families and their children)
- Global outreach (education and action abroad)
- Local outreach (local social service and community action)
- Children and youth (bringing member youth more into the life of the church and doing more for nonmember youth)
- Ministry of caring (mutual support and comfort for those in need)
- Evangelism (faith sharing and development)
- Stewardship (resource development)
- Communication with the public (radio and television broadcasts of services, public forums on timely issues)
- Facilities (redoing the sanctuary and entrances to the building, enhancing educational and outreach facilities)

Goals, strategies, and action steps were then formulated within each of these vision areas.

Visions developed with this approach may actually form a "grand strategy" for the organization, an overall scheme or plan for how best to "fit" with its environment. The strategy development step could then concentrate on filling in the details for putting the grand strategy into operation.

The strategic planning team may decide to identify strategic issues first, however, before developing more detailed strategies for implementation. The strategic issues typically concern how to gain broad acceptance of the vision and how to bridge the gap between the vision and where the organization is at present.

The Indirect Approach

The following guidelines may help organizations identify strategic issues using the indirect approach.

Planning team members should review the organization's current mission, the summary statement of its mandates, the results of the stakeholder and SWOT analyses, statements of present goals and strategies, and any other pertinent background studies. The team should then systematically review these materials and brainstorm sets of possible options for organizational action. Each option should be phrased in action terms—that is, it should start with an imperative (get, acquire, create, develop, achieve, show, communicate, and so on). Each should then be placed on a separate snow card or oval (see Resource C). The following option sets should be created:

1. Create options that will keep stakeholders happy or make them happy. (Obviously, the organization may not wish to make some stakeholders happy. For example, police forces are not likely to pursue options that will make drug dealers happy by relaxing law enforcement efforts. However, police forces might collaborate with economic development agencies to find alternative employment for drug dealers.)
2. Develop options that enhance strengths, take advantage of opportunities, and minimize or overcome weaknesses and threats.
3. Identify options that are tied directly to fulfilling the organization's mission and meeting its mandates.
4. Create options that articulate the goals, thrust, and key details of current organizational strategies.
5. Create cards or ovals for options identified or suggested by any other pertinent background studies.

The source of each option (stakeholder or SWOT analysis, mission or mandates, existing goals and strategies, background reports) should be indicated in small print somewhere on the snow card or oval. Knowing the source can help participants assess the potential importance of an option.

Once the option sets have been assembled, they should be mixed and regrouped by team members into clusters sharing similar themes. The theme of each grouping represents a candidate strategic issue. The oval process can also be used to structure the clusters further by showing interrelationships among clusters and the various options comprised by the clusters (see Resource C).

When suitable categories have been identified and key interrelationships noted, the team should develop one-page descriptions of the strategic issues that answer the three questions discussed earlier. The process of noting the source of each option will help the team answer the second question (about relevant situational factors) and the third question (about the consequences of not addressing the issue).

The CPI program used the indirect approach to identify strategic issues. (Actually, I invented the technique specifically for them—at least, I think I am the technique's inventor!) Use of the technique helped them formulate two key strategic issues they might not otherwise have identified. The first was the need to develop an aggressive and effective communication program for a broad range of stakeholders. The CPI program had an ongoing communication program for employees; although they communicated well with superiors in the Bureau of Labor Statistics, their communication with other groups whose understanding and support they required was less effective than it needed to be. The need for an expanded communication program became obvious as a result of the large number of communication-related options tied to improving stakeholder satisfaction and overcoming weaknesses and threats.

The second issue was the need for the CPI to develop additional products to meet customer needs and to make it easier for potential collaborators and users of CPI data to do likewise. The option cluster made it clear that doing so was important to enhance stakeholder satisfaction, to build on existing program strengths, to take advantage of opportunities, and to avoid some serious threats.

Identification of these two issues, in particular, had a profound effect on the thinking of the CPI program's management group. Each implied a need for the program to modify its basic way of doing business, to include development of a broader set of relationships with stakeholders, and to create significant new added value for customers and users. The implied changes were so significant that it took several months for the management group to absorb them fully. One sign of their significance is that the programs's new mission statement highlighted the CPI program desire "to cooperate with customers and other key stakeholders to improve our products and their understanding of them."

It should be noted that the four approaches to identifying strategic issues are interrelated; it is a matter of where you choose to start. For example, an organization can frame strategic issues directly or indirectly in Step 5, and then, in Step 6, it can develop goals and objectives for the strategies developed there to deal with the issues. Mission, strategies, goals, and objectives can then be used to develop a vision of success in Step 8. Or an organization may go through several cycles of strategic planning using the direct or goals approaches before it decides to develop a vision of success. Or the organization may start with the idealized scenario approach in this step and then expand the scenario into a vision of success after it completes the strategy development step.

Finally, a planning team may use more than one approach as part of the same strategic planning effort. Differing conditions surrounding different issue areas can prompt the use of multiple approaches to identifying strategic issues. When useful goals or visions are already developed, they may be used to help formulate strategic issues or strategies. When they are not, efforts to develop them, or use of the direct or indirect approach, should be considered.

Process Guidelines

The following process guidelines should prove helpful as a strategic planning team identifies the strategic issues its organization faces.

1. *Review the organization's (or community's) mandates, mission, strengths, weaknesses, opportunities, and threats, including any key indicators the organization watches (or should watch).* (Participants may also find it helpful to review Resource B.)

2. *Select an approach to strategic issue identification that fits your situation: the direct approach, the indirect approach, the goals approach, or the vision of success approach.* Whichever approach is used, prepare one-page descriptions of the resulting strategic issues that (1) phrase the issue as a challenge the organization can do something about; (2) clarify what in terms of the mission, mandates, and internal and external fac-

tors makes it an issue; and (3) outline the consequences of failing to address the issue.

3. *Once strategic issues have been identified, they should be sequenced in either a priority, logical, or temporal order as a prelude to strategy development.* The attention of key decision makers is probably the resource that is in shortest supply in most organizations, so it is very important to focus that attention effectively and efficiently. Establishing a reasonable order, or agenda, among strategic issues allows key decision makers to focus on them one at a time. (It must be recognized, however, that the issues may be so interconnected that they have to be dealt with as a set.)

An effective tool for figuring out a useful issue order is the directed graph, or "digraph" (Nutt and Backoff, 1992; Bryson and Finn, 1995). A digraph consists of nodes (in this case issues) and arrows indicating the direction of influence relationships among them (see Resource C). Figure 6.3 presents a digraph of the strategic issues facing a Roman Catholic order. The order consists of priests and brothers who work with low-income people and communities. The order employs many laypeople to teach in its schools, work with target communities, produce publications, and assist with fundraising and management.

The digraph indicates that in order to achieve more effective ministries—an issue closely linked with the order's mission—four additional issues must be dealt with first: maintain or increase ministries, clarify vision of success, maintain and improve income in the long run, and have satisfied, productive employees. If the order is to maintain or increase ministries, more members will need to join it (increase vocations), and income will need to be maintained and improved in the long run. In general, arrows leading to an issue indicate issues that also must be addressed if the focal issue is to be resolved. Arrows leading from an issue indicate potential consequences of addressing the issue.

Preparing this digraph produced two crucial insights for the planning team. First, they were able to see that the key to the "increase vocations" issue was the sequence of issues flowing into it from "improve community life" (key strategy options are indicated by bullets), "improve interpersonal relations," "improve attention to individual needs," "promote healthy life-styles," and "improve governance and management processes and structures." It is this set of issues, in particular, that is most closely tied to the order's community life and that prompted members of the order to push for strategic planning in the first place. Second, the planning team was able to convince those members of the order who mainly cared about gaining more effective ministries and increasing vocations that the best way to achieve those goals was first to address the issues tied to improving community life. The digraph thus helped all the members of the order understand the logical, and probably temporal, relationships among the issues. It also helped key stakeholder groups understand how their individual agendas might be served by working together on each other's issues, and it helped the group decide what its priorities for action should be.

Of course, the strategic implications of the issue agenda should be considered carefully. For example, it may not be wise to have key decision makers focus first on the top-priority issue, especially if there has been little prior interaction among key decision makers and little experience with constructive conflict resolution. In such circumstances, it may be best to start the process of resolving strategic issues by focusing first on the *least* important issue, so decision makers can gain experience in dealing with one another and can defuse conflict when its consequences are least severe. Planning team members should talk through the likely implications of different agendas before deciding on the appropriate sequence for action in the next step.

4. *It may be helpful to use a "litmus test" to develop some measure of just how strategic an issue is.* For example, a litmus test that might be used to screen strategic issues is presented in Exhibit 6.2. (The test is based on one presented in Hennepin County, 1983.) A truly strategic issue is one that scores high on all the questions on the test. A strictly operational issue would score low.

5. *There is a real art to framing strategic issues.* Considerable discussion and revision of first drafts of strategic issues are likely to be necessary in order to frame issues in the most useful way. If the organization's mission is itself a strategic issue, the organization should expect to develop a second set of issues after the mission is reexamined. Once the new or revised mission is in place, the "real" strategic issues can be identified. The importance of Hubert Humphrey's advice, "When in doubt, talk," should be apparent.

It is important to critique strategic issues to be sure that they really do usefully frame the fundamental policy questions and challenges the organization faces. The strategic planning team should ask itself several questions about the issues it identifies before it settles on a set of issues to address. Some useful questions include the following:

- What is the issue, conflict, or dilemma?
- Why is it an issue? What in terms of the mission, mandates, or SWOTs makes it an issue?
- Who says it is an issue?
- What would be the consequences of not doing something about it?
- Can we do something about it?
- Is there a way to combine or eliminate issues?
- Should issues be broken down into two or more issues?
- What issues are missing from our list, including issues that our culture might have kept us from recognizing?

It is especially important to remember that strategic issues framed in single-function terms will be dealt with by single-function departments or agencies. Strategic issues that are framed in multifunctional terms will have to be addressed by more than one department. And strategic issues that are framed in multi-

FIGURE 6.3. STRATEGIC ISSUES FACING A ROMAN CATHOLIC RELIGIOUS ORDER.

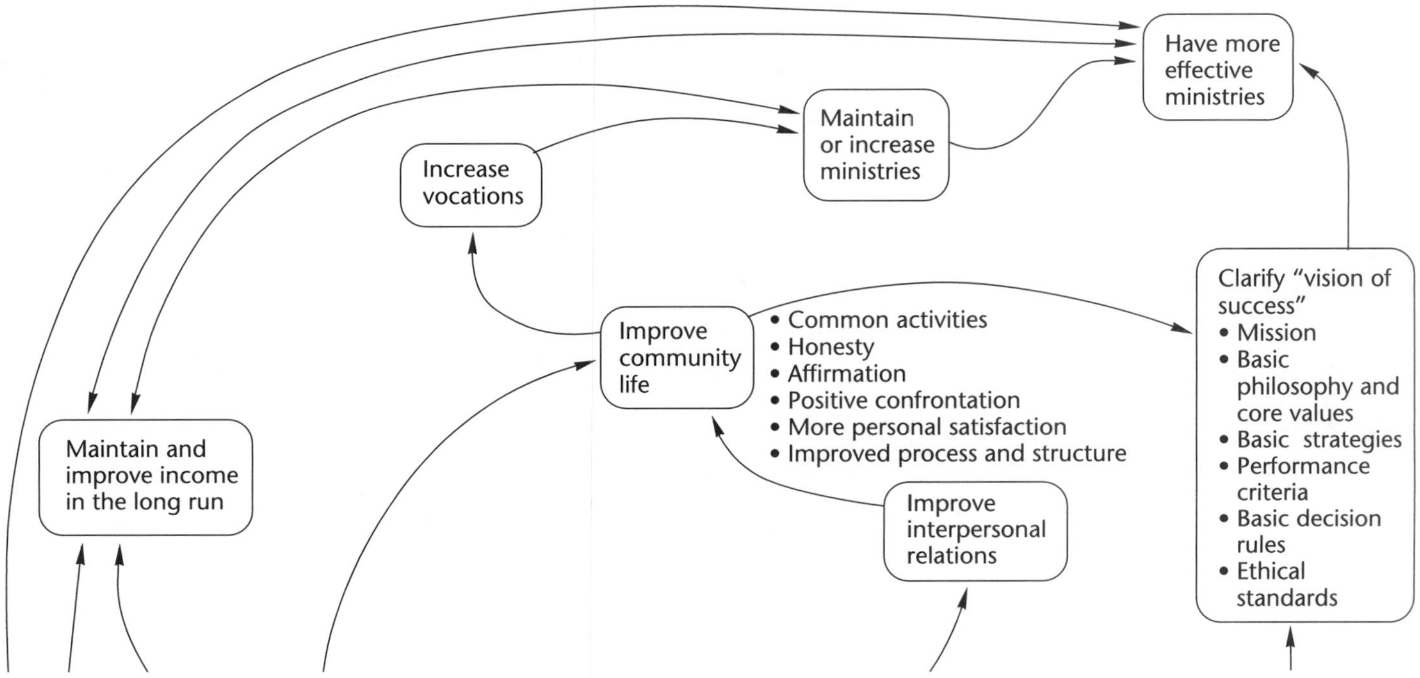

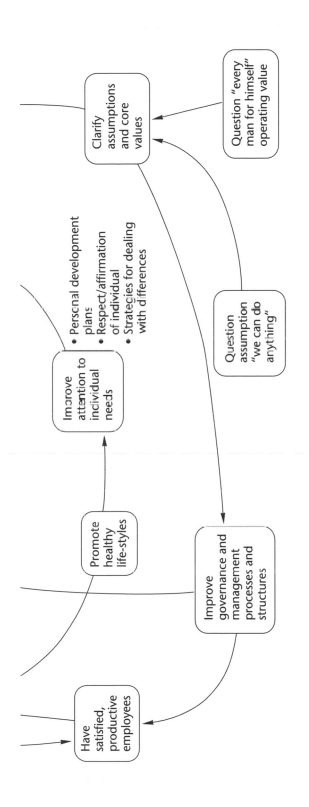

EXHIBIT 6.2. LITMUS TEST FOR STRATEGIC ISSUES.

Issue: _____   Issue is: ☐ Primarily operational   ☐ Primarily strategic

	Operational ⟵————————⟶		Strategic
1. Is the issue on the agenda of the organization's policy board (whether elected or appointed)?	No		Yes
2. Is the issue on the agenda of the organization's chief executive (whether elected or appointed)?	No		Yes
3. When will the strategic issues challenge or opportunity confront you?	Right now	Next year	Two or more years from now
4. How broad an impact will the issue have on your department?	Single unit or division		Entire organization
5. How large is your department's financial risk/financial opportunity	Minor (≤$250,000, or 10% of budget)	Moderate ($250,000–$1,000,000 or 10–15% of budget)	Major ($1,000,000-plus or ≥25% of budget)
6. Will strategies for issue resolution likely require			
a. Development of new service goals and programs?	No		Yes
b. Significant changes in tax sources or amounts?	No		Yes
c. Significant amendments in federal or state statutes or regulations?	No		Yes
d. Major facility additions or modifications?	No		Yes
e. Significant staff expansion	No		Yes
7. How apparent is the best approach for issue resolution?	Obvious, ready to implement	Broad parameters, few details	Wide open
8. What is the lowest level of management that can decide how to deal with this issue?	Line staff supervisor	Division head	Department head
9. What are the probable consequences of not addressing this issue?	Inconvenience, inefficiency	Significant service disruption, financial losses	Major long-term service disruption and large costs/ revenue setbacks
10. How many other departments are affected by this issue and must be involved in resolution?	None	1–3	4 or more
11. How sensitive or "charged" is the issue relative to community, social, political, religious, and cultural values?	Benign	Touchy	Dynamite

organizational, multi-institutional terms will have to be addressed by more than one organization or institution. If one seeks to wrest control of an issue from a single department, then the issue must be framed multifunctionally. If one seeks to wrest control of an issue from a single organization, then it must be framed multi-organizationally. Strategic planners can gain enormous influence over the strategic planning process and its outcomes if the issues are framed in such a way that decision makers must share power in order to resolve the issues (Bryson and Crosby, 1989, 1992).

The importance of this admonition is apparent when one examines organizations' efforts to use TQM, performance budgeting, or new information technologies (IT). In my experience, organizations often get into these ventures without carefully thinking through why they wish to do so. This may partly be the result of particular professionals' championing fashionable causes. TQM then gets assigned to a "quality czar" of some sort, performance budgeting to the budget director, and information technology improvement strategies to IT professionals. The reform agenda then becomes the captive of these particular units, and organizationwide perspectives and goals are subverted. The means substitute for the ends, and a kind of "goal displacement" occurs in which instrumental values become terminal values (Merton, 1940). While the power of the subunits may be enhanced, organizational performance is less than it should be. The TQM initiative ends up making continuous improvements in unwise strategies; budgets enhance performance in the wrong directions; and IT improvements are led by technology rather than by overarching organizational strategies. Convening forums in which an organizationwide perspective is developed is the best way to make sure the means serve the ends and not the other way around.

6. *Remember that there are likely to be at least three kinds of strategic issues, and each will need to be treated differently.* The three kinds are (1) those that require no action at present, but must be monitored, (2) those that can be handled as part of the organization's regular strategic planning cycle, and (3) those that require urgent attention and must be dealt with immediately.

7. *Focus on issues, not answers.* The answers will be developed in the next step, strategy formulation. Those answers will be helpful only if they are developed in response to the issues that actually confront the organization. Put differently, an answer without an issue is not an answer.

Keep in mind, however, that people can be counted on to put forward favored solutions, whether or not they have much to do with the real issues (Nutt, 1984b; Neustadt and May, 1986). Planners can utilize this tendency to their advantage by constantly getting team members to define what problems or issues their proposed solutions actually address. When this question is asked about several proposed solutions, a useful picture of what the real issues might be is likely to emerge (Eden and Sims, 1978; Bryson and Crosby, 1992). Issues developed in this fashion have the advantage of having emerged from what people can actually imagine themselves doing; thus, these issues may seem more "real" to people.

8. *Get key decision makers to agree that a major fraction of their time together will be devoted to identifying and resolving strategic issues.* Without an agreement of this sort, it will be too easy to forget when key decision makers get together that one of their most important tasks is to deal with what is most important to the organization. The decision-making bodies in all four organizations highlighted in this book made such a commitment.

9. *Keep it light.* As noted at the beginning of this chapter, this step in the strategic planning process can quickly become very serious and "heavy." Participants may fall into the pit or hit the wall as the librarians did. It is important for members of the strategic planning team to keep a sense of humor, acknowledge their emotions, and release their tensions with good-humored mutual solicitude. Otherwise, destructive conflicts or paralysis may set in, and the group may find it difficult to agree on a set of strategic issues or move on to developing effective strategies to deal with those issues. Emotions may run high—or low in the case of depression and grief. The group will have to acknowledge these emotions and deal with them constructively.

10. *Agreement on strategic issues is likely to mark an important organizational turning point.* Remember that identifying strategic issues is the heart of the planning process. Identifying the fundamental challenges the organization faces will have a profound effect on the actual choices it makes and ultimately on its viability and success.

11. *Managing the transition to the next step in the process—strategy development—is crucial.* Too often, organizations move quickly to the identification stage and then back off from resolving the issues they identify. The conflicts or choices embodied in the issues may seem too difficult or disruptive to address. Strong leadership and commitment to the strategic planning process must be exercised if the organization is to deal effectively with the basic issues it confronts.

Summary

The purpose of Step 5 is to identify the fundamental challenges facing the organization concerning its mandates; its mission; its product or service level and mix; its clients, customers, or users; its costs; its financing; its structure; and its management. At the end of this step, key decision makers should agree on a strategic issue agenda—the set of strategic issues to be addressed, arranged in priority, logical, or temporal order.

The four basic approaches to identifying issues are the direct approach, the indirect approach, the goals approach, and the vision of success approach. In general, governments and nonprofit agencies will find the direct and indirect approaches most useful.

To return to the play metaphor, Step 5 constitutes the framing of conflicts (issues). The climax will be reached in the next two steps, when these conflicts are resolved through the construction and adoption of effective strategies. Fear, anxiety, guilt, dread, or grief about how these issues might get resolved can cause people to flee from strategic planning. Faith, hope, courage, and reasoned optimism are needed to press forward.

The transition to the next step in the process will require careful management. It is one thing to talk about what is fundamental, quite another to take action based on those discussions. Strong leadership, high morale, and a reasonable sense of psychological safety and optimism will be required to keep moving ahead. Unless the team and organization push on, organizational effectiveness and stakeholder satisfaction are likely to suffer, and the organization will not fulfill its mission.

CHAPTER SEVEN

FORMULATING AND ADOPTING STRATEGIES AND PLANS TO MANAGE THE ISSUES

If you play with the fibers, they suggest possibilities.

ANNIE ALBERS, WEAVER

This chapter covers Steps 6 and 7, formulating and adopting strategies and plans. While the two are likely to be closely linked in practice, they should be kept separate in the planning team members' minds. This is because the dynamics that surround each may be dramatically different, especially when strategies must be adopted by elected or appointed policy boards. Strategy formulation often involves freewheeling creativity and the give-and-take of dialogue, while formal adoption of strategies and strategic plans can involve political intrigue, tough bargaining, public posturing, and high drama. Strategies should be formulated that can be adopted in a politically acceptable, technically workable, and legally and morally defensible form.

A strategy may be thought of as a pattern of purposes, policies, programs, actions, decisions, and/or resource allocations that defines what an organization is, what it does, and why it does it. A strategy, therefore, is the extension of an organization's (or community's) mission, forming a bridge between the organization and its environment. Strategies are typically developed to deal with strategic issues; that is, they outline an organization's response to the fundamental challenges it faces. (However, if the goal approach to formulating strategic issues is taken, strategies may be developed to achieve the goals; and if the vision of success approach is taken, strategies may be developed to achieve the vision.)

This definition of strategy is purposely very broad. It is important to recognize patterns that transcend organizational policies, decisions, resource allocations, and actions large and small. General strategies will fail if specific steps to implement them are absent. Further, strategies are prone to failure if there is no consistency between what an organization says, what it pays for, and what it does.

The definition of strategy offered here—a plan to achieve the mission and meet the mandates—calls attention to the importance of such consistency.

Effective strategies require an effective link with the organization's environment, even if their purpose is to change it. As noted in Chapter Five, the word *context* comes from the Latin for "to weave together." The arrows in the strategic planning process outlined in Figure 2.1 may be thought of as "threads" of communication about the organization's context and what might be done to respond effectively to it (Healey, 1992a, 1992b; Fischer and Forester, 1993; Innes, 1994). Various possibilities for useful patterns are suggested if you play with these threads or fibers, as weaver Annie Albers proposes. The *art* of creating an effective response is highlighted in this chapter—as it should be, since decision makers and strategic planning team members are often not creative enough in addressing strategic issues and crafting strategies to address them (see also Mintzberg, 1987).

The art, however, typically does not come without anguish. As the psychotherapist and theologian Thomas Moore observes, "Creative work can be exciting, inspiring, and godlike, but it is also quotidian, humdrum, and full of anxieties, frustrations, dead ends, mistakes, and failures" (1992, p. 199). Rosabeth Moss Kanter goes further, asserting that basically every innovation is a failure "in the middle" of the change process introducing it (Kanter, 1983, 1989). They are failures in the middle because they *must* be. By definition, innovations have never been tried before, at least not by the current organization, and success can only be determined after they have been implemented. Thus, *strategy* is defined in an intentionally broad way to help ensure that strategic changes (a kind of innovation), though they may be failures initially, are successes in the end.

Also, according to my definition, every organization (or community) already *has* a strategy (or strategies). That is, for every organization there is already some sort of pattern—or logic-in-action (Karpik, 1977)—that lies across its purposes, policies, programs, actions, decisions, and/or resource allocations. The pattern is there—it just may not be a very good one. It may need to be refined or sharpened or (less frequently) changed altogether for it to provide an effective bridge between the organization and its environment. The task of strategy formulation typically involves highlighting what is good about the existing pattern, reframing or downplaying what is bad about it, and adding whatever new bits are needed to complete the picture (Mangham, 1986; Mintzberg, 1987; Hampden-Turner, 1990; Schein, 1992; Nutt and Backoff, 1992). The organization's culture becomes very important during strategy formulation, because whatever patterns exist are typically manifestations of its culture. The culture affects how strategic issues are framed and placed on the agenda in the first place, and it subsequently affects which strategy options are given serious consideration (Hampden-Turner, 1990; Schein, 1992; Kingdon, 1995).

Put differently, every strategy is thus almost always both emergent *and* deliberate, although the balance can vary a good deal (Mintzberg, 1994b). The world of sports provides two useful examples of this emergent and deliberate quality. Jean-Claude Killy of France, triple gold medal winner in alpine skiing at the 1968 Winter Olympics, was asked why he drank wine for lunch. His reply: "What would you have me do—drink milk and ski like an American?" His unorthodox (some said wild) style of skiing revolutionized alpine ski racing. His style capitalized on his physique and psyche, and, he said, it was the only way he knew how to ski. In this sense, his strategy was at first emergent and then became deliberate. It also became deliberate for many other racers who tried to imitate him.

The other example comes from Francis Tarkenton, former quarterback of the Minnesota Vikings and New York Giants, member of the NFL Hall of Fame, and still the holder of several NFL records. Tarkenton was known as a "scrambling" quarterback; he drove defenses crazy by running around in the open field, buying time until he could run or pass for a big gain. In describing his strategy as it moved from deliberate to emergent, he said, "Whenever things break down completely, I don't hesitate to roam out of the pocket and do the boogaloo."

Recall also that most organizations' strategies remain fairly stable for long periods of time, and then they may abruptly change. Thus, strategic planning most of the time will focus on adapting and programming strategies whose outlines are already reasonably clear (Mintzberg, 1994a, 1994b). At other times, though, strategic planning will be called upon to assist with the formulation of new strategies to deal with quite new and different circumstances. Even in times of rather drastic change, however, an organization is unlikely to discontinue all of its existing strategies, so the task of blending the old with the new and the deliberate with the emergent still remains.

Strategies can also vary by level and by time frame. Four basic levels of strategies include the following:

- Grand strategies for the organization as a whole
- Subunit strategies. Subunits may be divisions, departments, or units of larger organizations (Montanari and Bracker, 1986)
- Program, service, or business process strategies (Hammer and Champy, 1993)
- Functional strategies (such as financial, staffing, facilities, information technology, and procurement strategies)

All these strategies may be either long term or short term.

Strategies are different from tactics. Tactics are short-term, adaptive actions and reactions used to accomplish limited objectives. Strategies provide the "continuing basis for ordering these adaptations toward more broadly conceived purposes" (Quinn, 1980, p. 9). One needs to be cautious, however, about drawing too sharp a distinction between the two, given the importance of changing environments and emergent strategies. As Mintzberg (1994b, p. 243) observes, "The trouble with the strategy-tactics distinction is that one can never be sure which is which until all the dust has settled."

Purpose

The purpose of the strategy formulation and plan development step (Step 6) is to create a set of strategies that will effectively link the organization (or community) to its environment. Typically these strategies are developed in response to strategic issues, but they may also be developed in order to achieve goals or a vision of success. The purpose of the strategy and plan adoption step (Step 7) is to gain authoritative decisions to move ahead with implementing the strategies and plans.

A good example of formulated and adopted strategies is provided by the Amherst H. Wilder Foundation of St. Paul, Minnesota, a large, well-managed, highly effective nonprofit organization active in health and welfare services and education. In 1993, the foundation had an endowment and assets worth over $209.4 million, spent over $10.5 million of its trust income plus millions from other sources, employed 1,400 people, and served over 62,000 people through its many programs. The foundation's thirteen-page 1993 strategic plan outlines the organization's grand strategy for the 1990s through a set of linked statements about mission, focus, vision, roles, goals and outcomes, program development, and challenges, along with supporting text.

The plan begins with the foundation's current mission statement, adopted in 1974 (see p. 79). The foundation's president and board of directors thought the statement needed further clarification regarding what the mission should mean for the 1990s. The result was the Strategic Focus Statement, which indicates *with whom* the foundation will primarily work (first bulleted point), *how* the foundation will serve the community (second bulleted point), and *where* it will work (third bulleted point). Text and examples are used to support and illustrate each point. The focus elements are reproduced in summary form in Exhibit 7.1.

The plan includes a vision statement (not reproduced) of what a successful community would look like, as a way of helping to articulate the foundation's roles and strategies to help it achieve its vision. Note that the vision is for the *community*, not for the organization. This is unusual in that visioning of this sort is more typical of governmental and community-based strategic planning. But it makes sense for a foundation that sees itself as a capacity builder and facilitator of change as well as a provider of direct services. The foundation realizes that the community's needs are so great that it cannot hope to meet them without the efforts of lots of other people and organizations, including the community as a whole and city, county, state, and federal governments. The foundation therefore finds that a vision of community success helps it figure out how it might best achieve desirable outcomes in concert with other actors. The vision is not "owned" by St. Paul's central urban communities, which might be a problem, although it is hard to imagine their objecting to the components of the vision.

The next major section in the plan outlines three basic roles for the foundation

EXHIBIT 7.1. AMHERST H. WILDER FOUNDATION STRATEGIC FOCUS STATEMENT.

During the 1990s, the Foundation will place emphasis on:

- **Working with individuals and families whose access to community resources is severely limited**
- **Strengthening the capacity of people to meet their own needs**
- **Serving the central urban communities of Saint Paul**

The Focus Statement challenges the Foundation to reach an ideal, acts as an internal "guidepost" for current programming efforts, and captures the spirit of the Wilder family wills and the Foundation's mission. The Statement indicates *"how"* the Foundation will serve the community, *"with whom"* it will work, and *"where"* it will conduct its major activities.

"Working with individuals and families whose access to community resources is severely limited"

The first part of the Focus Statement indicates with whom the Foundation, in general, will place service emphasis. These are the individuals and families whose access to community resources is severely limited for various reasons. These groups include, but are not necessarily limited to:

- Persons at or below poverty.
- The working poor.
- High-risk groups within communities of color.
- Low-income, single-parent families.
- Frail, vulnerable seniors.

"Strengthening the capacity of people to meet their own needs"

The second part of the Focus Statement indicates that the Foundation intends to build upon the inherent strengths of people. Referred to as *"capacity-building,"* Foundation services should bring the right resources to individuals, families, and organizations in a way that people can meet their own needs and improve their own lives.

This "capacity-building" focus suggests that the Foundation will continue to create programs that, through the interactive process between staff and service recipient, help individuals achieve personal growth and adjustment. Examples of current "capacity-building" service efforts within the Foundation are programs designed to improve family functioning, to facilitate the social adjustment of Southeast Asians, to enhance the lives of frail seniors living in their own homes, and to assist other nonprofit organizations with improving their own performance.

"Serving the central urban communities of Saint Paul"

The third part of the Focus Statement specifies where the Foundation will place its emphasis. *"Central urban communities"* are defined as those geographic areas or neighborhoods in close proximity to the Saint Paul downtown area, such as Thomas-Dale, Summit-University, Westside, West Seventh, Payne-Phalen, North End, and Dayton's Bluff, where there tends to be a concentration of individuals and families with limited access to the broader communities' resources.

The Foundation has selected a central-city geographic emphasis because:

- Central urban communities have the largest concentraiton of human service needs in the East Metropolitan area.

EXHIBIT 7.1. AMHERST H. WILDER FOUNDATION
STRATEGIC FOCUS STATEMENT, Cont'd.

- Saint Paul is confronted with an eroding tax base; it will be competing more and more for scarce resources; and it will have less money for central city services.
- The overall well-being of the East Metropolitan area is largely affected by the condition of the core communities of Saint Paul.
- It furthers the spirit and tradition of the Wilder family and the earliest activities of the Wilder Charity.

To effectively address the issues of the urban core, the Foundation will work directly with urban communities and also deploy strategies that will support the central city through East Metropolitan–wide efforts. For example, current wisdom suggests that urban regions will have a higher standard of living for all their residents if these regions have adequate housing opportunities within both their cities and their suburbs, thus not forcing low-income people to live in concentrated areas. Therefore, Wilder will likely serve persons with least access to resources, regardless of their location in the East Metropolitan region, as a way of enhancing central urban communities.

Some human service solutions will have to be addressed through a community-wide service delivery system. For example, good health care and housing options for at-risk, frail, urban elderly will be delivered through a large Wilder managed-care system that serves the entire community. Programs that provide culturally appropriate social support to urban Southeast Asians will need to be delivered through a larger mental health managed-care network that has at least an East Metro area presence.

Amherst H. Wilder Foundation, 1993, pp. 2–4.

in assisting communities to achieve their interpretation of the vision. The roles include direct service, capacity building, and system change, especially through development and demonstration of new approaches to social difficulties and through public policy changes. The mission, focus, vision, and role statements essentially compose the foundation's grand strategy.

Goals and outcomes follow, to be achieved via the roles. Programs designed to achieve the goals must address the criteria stated in that section. Finally, in pursuing its mission through its various efforts, the foundation cautions itself to maintain a broad scope and a long-term horizon, to be attentive and creative in its approach to funding, to emphasize cooperation, coordination, and collaboration, and to keep fresh and open to new opportunities and methods.

Unfortunately, very few governments, public agencies, or nonprofit organizations think as long and hard as this about what they want to do and for whom, why, and how. Nor do many condense their thinking into a grand strategy. As a result, there is usually little more than an odd assortment of policies or goals to guide decision making and action in pursuit of organizational purposes. In the absence of deliberate or emergent overall strategic direction, the sum of the organization's parts can be expected to add up to something less than a whole. Of course, in a period of transition from a deliberate strategy to an emergent one whose contours are not yet clear, perhaps this is acceptable—even good.

Alternatively, the organization may face powerful stakeholders whose expectations are conflicting or contradictory, making it unwise or impossible to develop a coherent grand strategy. In either case, the organization's key decision makers and planning team should be clear about legitimate reasons—as opposed to excuses—for why they do not have a grand strategy.

Desired Outcomes and Benefits

Several desired planning outcomes may come from these two steps. The organization might seek a grand strategy statement for itself. It might also want subunit; program, service, or business process; and functional strategy statements for its constituent parts. On the one hand, a complete set of these statements may be warranted if the organization has chosen the vision of success approach; the set would be necessary to clarify strategies for achieving the vision. On the other hand, the organization may have more limited aims. If it has chosen the direct or indirect approaches, it may simply want a statement of how it will deal with each issue. If it has chosen the goal approach, it may want statements that clarify how it will achieve each goal. Second, the organization may or may not wish to have a formal strategic plan at the end of this step, to be formally adopted in the next step. Possible contents of a strategic plan will be discussed later in this chapter.

Third, planners may seek a formal agreement to push ahead at the conclusion of Step 6. If a strategic plan has been prepared, and the organization is governed by an elected or appointed policy-making body, this agreement likely will mean proposing policy board adoption of the plan in Step 7. Policy board adoption would then be a fourth desired outcome. (Community-based strategic plans are likely to need adoption by several organizations if the plans are to be implemented.) If the unit doing the planning is the board itself or if the organization does not need the approval of its board (or does not have a board), then Steps 6 and 7 may be collapsed into a single step. Formal agreement by key decision makers may not be necessary, but it usually enhances the legitimacy of strategic actions and provides an occasion for widely communicating the intent and substance of such actions.

Finally, as is true throughout the process, actions should be taken as soon as they are identified and become useful or necessary. Otherwise, important opportunities may be lost or threats may not be countered in time. It is also important to ease the transition from an old reality, whatever that may have been, to the new reality embodied in the organization's emerging strategies. If the transition can be broken down into a small number of manageable steps, it will be easier to accomplish than if it requires a major leap.

Ten benefits of the strategy and plan development and adoption steps can be identified:

1.   A fairly clear picture will emerge—from grand conception to many implementation details—of how the organization can meet its mandates, fulfill its mission, and deal effectively with the situation it faces. This picture provides a measure of clarity about where an organization is going, how it will get there, and why; this is an important part of most successful change efforts (Dalton, 1970; Kanter, 1983, 1989; Mintzberg, 1994a, 1994b). A new reality cannot be fully realized until it is named and understood (May, 1969; Morgan, 1986, 1993).

2.   This new picture should have emerged from a consideration of a broad range of alternative strategies, which in itself should enhance organizational creativity and overcome the usual tendency of organizations to engage in simplistic, truncated, and narrow searches for solutions to their problems (Cyert and March, 1963; Nutt, 1984b).

3.   If actions are taken as they become identified and useful, a new reality will emerge in fact, not just in conception. If the strategic planning exercise has not become "real" for team members and key decision makers prior to this point, it certainly will become real now (Boal and Bryson, 1987a).

4.   Early implementation of at least parts of major strategies will facilitate organizational learning. The organization will be able to find out quickly whether its strategies are likely to be effective. Thus, strategies can be revised or corrected before being fully implemented. Learning of this sort will be facilitated if a "formative evaluation"   designed to help shape implementation as it "forms"—has been included in the strategic plans.

5.   Emotional bonding to the new reality can occur as it emerges gradually through early and ongoing implementation efforts. To return to the play metaphor, no drama can reach an effective and satisfying conclusion without a catharsis phase in which the audience is allowed time to break its emotional bonds with an old reality—and perhaps experience confusion, distress, depression, and despair—so that it can forge new emotional bonds with the new reality (Kubler-Ross, 1969; Spencer and Adams, 1990). This bonding process is likely to fail if the gap between old and new realities is too large and is not bridged in a series of "acts" and "scenes" (Mangham and Overington, 1987; Quinn, 1980).

6.   Organizational members will get help working their way through the "failure in the middle" syndrome identified by Kanter (1983). In many of the strategic planning efforts in which I have been involved, decision makers and planning team members all experience this sense of failure somewhere between identifying strategic issues and formulating strategies to deal with them. As noted in Chapter Six, the public library's planning team hit a wall when they articulated strategic issues for which they could not imagine acceptable strategies. The CPI program's management group fell in a pit of sorts when they found it hard to grapple with the new roles that their strategic issues seemed to imply for the CPI. The school district's board came close to falling into a pit when they had difficulty coming to grips with relocating a symbolically important high school. Finally, Mainline Church's planning team also had difficulties in finding ways to get church

traditionalists to accept an altered Sunday worship schedule and greater involvement of young people in the main worship services. Each of these organizations had to acknowledge its difficulties, engage in constructive (though not always easy) dialogue, offer support, and search for thoughtful responses to the issues before they could see their way through the difficulties and imagine a better and viable future. Thus, if you fall into a pit, recall philosopher Jean-Paul Sartre's observation that "Hope is on the other side of despair."

7. Heightened morale among strategic planning team members, key decision makers, and other organizational members should result from task accomplishment and early successes in the resolution of important issues. If the organization is pursuing an important mission and dealing with the fundamental questions it faces, it can expect involvement and excitement on the part of key organizational actors (Selznick, 1957; Kouzes and Posner, 1987, 1993).

8. Further planning team development (and indeed broader organizational development) should result from the continued discipline of addressing fundamental questions constructively (Eadie and Steinbacher, 1985). Improved communication and understanding among team (and organizational) members should occur. Strategic thinking and acting are likely to become a habit.

9. If key internal and external stakeholder interests have been addressed successfully as part of the strategic planning process, a coalition is likely to emerge that is large enough and strong enough to agree on organizational strategies and pursue their implementation. If a formal strategic plan is prepared, there is likely to be a coalition large enough and strong enough to adopt it, implement it, and use it as an ongoing basis for decision making.

10. Organizational members will have the permission they need to move ahead with the implementation of strategies. Those who wish to preserve the status quo will find themselves fighting a losing battle as the organization mobilizes to implement adopted strategies.

If all of these benefits are realized, the organization will have achieved progress in an effective and artful way. Following Alfred North Whitehead's observation about "the art of progress," the organization will have preserved "order amid change, and change amid order." It will have built new and more effective bridges from itself to its environment and from its past to its future. And people will be able to cross those bridges relatively easily and painlessly.

Two Approaches to Strategy Development

In this section, I present two approaches to strategy development that I have found to be particularly effective.

The Five-Step Process

One useful approach to strategy development involves a five-step process in which planners answer five questions about each strategic issue. (The approach is adapted from one developed by the Institute of Cultural Affairs; see Spencer, 1989.) The following questions should be adjusted depending on whether the direct or indirect, goals, or vision of success approach to strategy formulation is used.

1. What are the practical alternatives, dreams, or visions we might pursue to address this strategic issue, achieve this goal, or realize this scenario?
2. What are the barriers to the realization of these alternatives, dreams, or visions?
3. What major proposals might we pursue to achieve these alternatives, dreams, or visions directly or to overcome the barriers to their realization?
4. What major actions (with existing staff and within existing job descriptions) must be taken within the next year (or two) to implement the major proposals?
5. What specific steps must be taken within the next six months to implement the major proposals, and who is responsible?

The process begins conventionally, by asking planning team members to imagine grand alternatives for dealing with the specific issue. Then comes an unconventional step—enumerating the barriers to realizing the alternatives, instead of developing major proposals to achieve them directly. Listing barriers at this point helps ensure that implementation difficulties are dealt with directly rather than haphazardly.

The next step asks for major proposals to achieve the alternatives either directly or indirectly by overcoming the barriers. Many organizations find that they must spend considerable time overcoming barriers before they can get on with achieving an alternative. For example, the school district had to find a way to control personnel costs—the largest component of its budget—or it would never have had enough money to achieve its preferred alternatives for educational reform. The fact that the district's teachers already had the best pay and benefit package in the state made it possible for the district to gain some control over personnel costs without harming staff welfare. The fact that the teachers also wanted many of the educational reforms made it difficult for them to oppose efforts to cap their pay and benefits.

The answer to the fourth question will essentially consist of a one- to two-year work program designed to implement the major proposals. Note that the work will be done by existing staff within existing job descriptions. This question begins to elicit the specifics necessary for successful strategy implementation. The question also conveys the notion that any journey must begin where one is (Kahn, 1982). For example, if full-blown implementation of the strategy will require more staff and resources, this question will ask strategists to be clear about what can currently be done, using existing staff and resources, to procure them. The question also begins to force people to "put their money where their mouth is." As the precise shape and content of strategy implementation emerges, it will become quite clear who is willing to go ahead with it and who is not.

The final question asks strategists to be even more specific about what must be done and who must do it. The implications of strategy implementation for organizational members becomes quite real at the conclusion of this step. The specificity of actions and the assignment of responsibilities to particular individuals are requisites of successful strategy implementation (Dalton, 1970; Morrisey, Below, and Acomb, 1987; Frame, 1987; Randolph and Posner, 1988). In addition, such specificity will often determine *exactly* what people are willing to live with and what they are not. (Often such details prefigure the emerging future better than any grand vision. To paraphrase poet William Blake, the divine is in the details.)

The fourth and fifth questions involve the group in the work of Step 9 (implementation), but that is desirable because strategies should always be developed with implementation in mind. Actually, Steps 6 and 9 may be merged in some circumstances (for example, when implementation must be understood clearly before key decision makers or policy boards, within an organization or across organizations, are willing to act, or when a small single-purpose organization is involved).

A strategic planning team can use the snow card process to answer each question. This technique allows for great creativity, and it facilitates the development of organization-specific categories to hold the individual ideas. The public library, for example, developed many of its strategies for dealing with its strategic issues by using the five-step process and the snow card technique.

Using this five-step process together with the snow card technique has several other advantages. First, relatively large groups of people can be involved (at least if subgroups of five to twelve people are employed). Second, the process keeps people from jumping immediately to solutions, a typical failing of problem-solving groups (Janis, 1989; Johnson and Johnson, 1994). Third, it keeps people from overevaluating their ideas; it keeps idea creation and evaluation in a reasonable balance. Fourth, it forces people to build a bridge from where they are to where they would like to be. Fifth, it forces people to deal with implementation difficulties directly.

Finally, a particular advantage of the technique is that a great deal of unnecessary conflict is avoided simply because items proposed in answer to one question will drop out if no one suggests a way to handle them in the next step. For example, instead of struggling over the advantages and disadvantages of some major proposal to realize an alternative, the process simply asks the group what has to happen in the next year or two, with existing staff and within existing job descriptions, to implement the proposal. If no one can think of a reasonable response, then an unnecessary struggle never happens and strategy remains tied to what people can actually imagine themselves doing. Strategy formulation thus remains more realistic and grounded. Of course, the group needs to make sure that answers in previous steps are linked to answers in subsequent steps to keep proposals from being unintentionally dropped from sight.

But there is a caveat: the five-part process is very useful for developing the broad outlines of a strategy and for engaging fairly large groups of people, but it does not promote much understanding of the structure of relationships between ideas. Categories of ideas are created in response to the five questions, but the connections between them remain unclear. Care should be taken to ensure that important connections are made.

It may not be necessary to answer all five questions; some groups find they can collapse the last three questions into two questions or even a single question. The important point is that the specifics of implementation must be clarified as much as necessary to allow effective evaluation of options and to provide desired guidance for implementation. Recall that a strategy has been defined as a *pattern* of purposes, policies, decisions, actions, or resource allocations that effectively link the organization to its environment. The purpose of the questions, whether or not all five are used, is to get the organization to clarify exactly what the pattern has to be and who has to do what to make the link truly effective.

Some organizations (and communities), particularly larger ones, find it useful to have their strategic planning team answer the first two questions using the snow card technique and then delegate to task forces, committees, or individuals the task of developing answers to the last three questions. Those answers are then brought back for review and perhaps decisions by the team. Alternatively, the task of answering all five questions may be turned over to a division, department, task force, committee, or individual that then reports back to the appropriate review or decision-making body.

Yet another alternative is to use the two-cycle strategic planning process outlined in Chapter Two (or Hennepin County's three-cycle process, discussed in the same chapter). In the first cycle, divisions, departments, or smaller units are asked to identify strategic issues (or goals or scenarios) and to prepare strategies, using the five-part process (or the process discussed below), within a framework established at the top. The strategies are then reviewed by cross-divisional or cross-departmental strategic planning coordinating committees, perhaps including a cabinet. Once this committee agrees to specific strategies, detailed operating plans may be developed. These plans would include detailed answers to the last two questions.

Once answers have been developed to deal with a specific strategic issue, the strategic planning team is in a position to make judgments about what strategies should actually be pursued. (The team may rely on one or more of the concepts presented in Resource D to inform its judgments.) In particular, the team needs to ask the following:

1. What is really reasonable?
2. Where can we combine proposals, actions, and specific steps?
3. Do any proposals, actions, or specific steps contradict each other, and if so what should we do about them?
4. What would we or key implementers really be willing to commit to, including the necessary resources, over the next year?
5. What specific actions have to occur in the next six months to make this strategy work?

This process also helps with ongoing strategy implementation efforts. Once specific strategies have been adopted and are being implemented, the organization should work its way back up the original set of five questions on a regular basis. Every six months, the last question should be addressed again. Every year or two, the fourth question should be asked again. Every two or three years, the third question should be asked. And every three to five years, the first two questions should be addressed again as well.

The Oval Mapping Process

The oval mapping process is a second helpful approach to formulating effective strategies. The approach is based on the Strategic Options Development and Analysis (SODA) method developed by Eden and associates over the past twenty years (Eden, 1989). The method involves creating options (phrased as actions) to address each issue. (This will already have been done if the indirect approach to strategic issue identification has been used.) The planning team should be as practical *and* as creative as possible when brainstorming options. Specific options can be triggered by any number of considerations relevant to the issue at hand, including mission and mandates, stakeholder analyses, SWOTs, existing strategies, applicable reports and background studies, and knowledge of what other organizations are doing. Each option is written on a separate oval-shaped sheet of paper, seven and one-half inches long by four and one-half inches wide. (Experience indicates that this is the best size for capturing one idea per card and allowing cards to be grouped and moved around easily; see Resource C for a pattern for ovals and for more detailed instructions in the use of oval mapping.)

Once a set of ovals is in hand, they are stuck on a wall covered with flip chart sheets or on a whiteboard by means of adhesive putty or tape. The options are then arranged by a facilitator or by the team and linked with arrows indicating which options cause or influence the achievement of other options. An option can be part of more than one influence chain. The result is a "map" of action-to-outcome (cause-to-effect, means-to-end) relationships between the options intended to address the issue at hand. The team is then asked to develop options that outline the consequences (desired or otherwise) of effectively addressing the issue. These options are used to extend the action-to-outcome chains to develop goals for the organization in each issue area. Options toward the end of a chain of arrows (usually placed near the top of the map) are likely to be goals and are likely to be closely related to the organization's mission.

Once a draft map has been prepared, it can be discussed further, reviewed, and revised until the full range of options for addressing each issue has been articulated and the full range of possible goals for each issue area is understood. Particular action-to-outcome sets can then be selected as strategies for addressing each issue. As with the five-step process, this method also shades over into the work of Step 9.

Maps can get quite large, and therefore computer support may be needed to understand, analyze, and manage the resulting complexity. There is software (Graphics COPE) specially designed for this purpose. (More information on the software is offered in Resource C.)

Strategic Plans

Strategic plans can vary a great deal in their form and content. The simplest form of strategic plan may be nothing more than an unwritten agreement between key decision makers about the organization's mission and what it should do, given its circumstances. This is the most common form of strategic plan, and it clearly reflects a basic premise of this book—that shared strategic thinking and acting are what count, not strategic plans in and of themselves. As Mintzberg (1994b, p. 252) notes, "Organizations function on the basis of commitment and mind set."

But coordinated action among a variety of organizational actors over time usually requires some kind of reasonably formal plan so that people can keep track of what they should do and why they should do it (Van de Ven and Ferry, 1980). For one thing, people forget, and the plan can help remind them of what has been decided. The plan also provides a baseline for judging strategic performance. And the plan serves a more overtly political purpose: it usually amounts to a "treaty" among key actors, factions, and coalitions. Finally, the plan (perhaps in a summary version) can serve as a communications and public relations document for internal and external audiences.

The simplest form of written strategic plan, perfectly acceptable though somewhat crude, would consist of the final versions of several of the worksheets in Bryson and Alston (1995):

- Mission statement
- Mandates statement (perhaps as an appendix)
- Vision of success, if one has been prepared
- SWOT analysis (perhaps as an appendix)
- Strategic issues (or a set of goals or a scenario outlining the preferred future)
- Strategies—grand; subunit; program, service, product, and business process; and functional

Most organizations will prefer, however, to use the final versions of the worksheets as background material for preparation of a written strategic plan. If this approach is taken, the table of contents might include the following headings (Barry, 1986; Bryson and Alston, 1995):

- Introduction (including purpose, process, and participation)
- Mission statement (including meeting the mandates)
- Mandates statement (perhaps as an appendix)
- Vision of success (if one has been prepared)
- External and internal environmental analysis, including SWOTs (perhaps as an appendix)
- Grand strategy statement
- Issue-specific strategy statements
- Subunit strategy statements (if applicable)
- Program, service, product, or business process plans, including strategy statements, goals, and target markets
- Functional strategy statements
- Implementation plans, including action plans
- Staffing plans, including full-time staff, part-time staff, and volunteers needed
- Financial plans, including operating budgets for each year of the plan plus any necessary capital budgets or fundraising plans
- Monitoring and evaluation plans
- Plans for updating all or parts of the plan

The mission and strategy statements (and the vision of success, if one has been prepared) should in effect constitute an executive summary of the plan. The plan itself need not—and should not—be overly long. If it is, it will be put aside or forgotten by key staff members.

Other sections might be included, perhaps as appendices, in addition to those listed above (Barry, 1986):

- A statement of needs, problems, or goals to be addressed
- A description of the organization's structure, either current, proposed, or both
- Governance procedures (current, proposed, or both)
- Key organization policies (current, proposed, or both)
- Relationships with key stakeholders (current, proposed, or both)
- Assumptions on which the plan is based
- Marketing plans (Stern, 1990)
- Facilities plans
- Contingency plans to be pursued if circumstances change
- Any other sections deemed important

The task of preparing a first draft of the strategic plan should usually be assigned to a key staff person. Once the draft is prepared, key decision makers, including the strategic planning team, the governing board, and possibly several external stakeholders, should review it. Several modifications are likely to be suggested by various stakeholders, and if modifications improve the plan, they should be accepted. After a final review by key decision makers, the revised plan will be ready for formal adoption. After that occurs, the planning team will then be ready to move on to implementation, although many implementing actions may have occurred already as they became obvious and necessary over the course of the planning process.

Plan Adoption

The purpose of Step 7 is to gain an official decision to adopt and proceed with the strategies and plan prepared and informally reviewed in Step 6. For the proposed plan to be adopted, it must address the issues key decision makers think are important with solutions that appear likely to work. Also, the political climate and stakeholder opinion must be favorable, and the barriers to effective action must be down. There must be a "coupling," in other words, of problems, solutions, and politics (Kingdon, 1995).

The planning team should keep Step 6 *conceptually* distinct from Step 7, since the dynamics surrounding the two steps may differ—even though in practice Steps 6 and 7 might merge (for example, when the planning involves small hierarchically organized single-purpose organizations). Step 6 may be quite collegial, as the team engages in dialogue about what might be best for the organization. Step 7, however, can be quite conflictual, particularly when formal adoption must take place in legislative arenas such as city councils, multi-organizational confederations, or the various boards and organizations necessary for effective implementation of community plans. (Readers seeking more detailed advice on this step should see Bryson and Crosby, 1992, pp. 246–280.)

In order to gain the necessary support, key decision makers and important stakeholders must be open to the idea of change, and they must be offered specific inducements in order to gain their support. The arguments and inducements must be geared to these individuals' values, interests, and frames of reference, since they will choose whether or not to support the proposal according to their own judgment. Considerable bargaining and negotiation may be necessary in order to find the right combination of trade-offs and inducements to gain the needed support without also bargaining away key features of the proposed strategies and plans (Susskind and Cruikshank, 1987).

Formal adoption is likely to occur at a "window of opportunity," an occasion when action favoring change is possible. There are three kinds of windows: those opened by the emergence of pressing issues, those opened by important political shifts (new elected or appointed policy makers, new executive directors, changed priorities of funding agencies), and those opened by reaching decision points (times when official bodies are authorized and empowered to act). A major purpose of the initial agreement step was to define the network of stakeholders that is likely to form the basis of a supportive coalition, and to map out likely decision points in advance so that the full-blown coalition and a specific, viable plan would be ready for adoption at a specific time.

Formal adoption of the school district's strategic plan occurred in stages over many months. While there was broad support for most features of the draft plan, which was formally presented in September 1992, there were sharply differing opinions about the desirability of relocating an old high school. The high school was obsolete and did not meet state standards, but it was important symbolically as a focus for much of the community. After much discussion and negotiation over the entire facilities section of the plan, the board finally approved relocation of the old high school to a new facility on a new site. The strategic plan was formally adopted in March 1993, six months after it was presented. Completing this process was often rocky—in sharp contrast to previous steps—except for the final stages of Step 6, when the first-draft strategic plan was formulated for review by the board. The conflicts became clear at that point as did the challenge of resolving them in a way that would preserve a supportive coalition on the board and in the community in favor of change. The difficulties of that challenge carried all the way through Step 7.

Process Guidelines

The following guidelines should be kept in mind as a strategic planning team formulates effective strategies to link the organization with its environment.

1. *Remember that strategic thinking and acting are more important than strategic plans (and any particular approach to formulating them).* The way in which strategies are formulated is less important than how good they are and how well they are implemented. Similarly, whether or not a formal strategic plan is prepared is less important than the effective formulation and implementation of strategies.

2. *Members of the strategic planning team may wish to review Resource D.* It is very important that a variety of creative, even radical, options be considered during the strategy formulation process. The broader the range of alternative strategies the team considers, the more likely they will arrive at supportable, implementable, and effective strategies. Constant awareness of the variety of options available will help ensure that a diverse set of possible strategies are considered before final choices are made. Recall the advice of the late Nobel Prize–winning laureate Linus Pauling: "The best way to have a good idea is to have lots of ideas."

Another way of making this point is to argue that an organization should not engage in strategic planning unless it is willing to consider alternatives that are quite different from "business as usual." If the organization is only interested in minor variations on existing themes, then it should not waste its time on a full-blown strategic planning exercise. Instead, it should concentrate on programming existing strategies (the main focus of Chapter Nine). Or the organization may wish to pursue a strategy of "logical incrementalism," that is, incrementalism organized around a general direction (Quinn, 1980). Or it might wish to give up on strategic planning altogether and pursue traditional incremental decision making, or "muddling through" (Lindblom, 1959), as a way of finding an acceptable fit with its environment.

3. *"Logical incrementalism" can be very effective.* Incrementalism guided by a sense of mission and direction can result in a series of small decisions that can accumulate over time into major changes. Karl Marx is perhaps the progenitor of this line of thought with his observation that changes in degree lead to changes in kind. (Ironically, the collapse of the Soviet Union occurred in just this way.). Indeed, Quinn (1980) argues that most strategic changes in large corporations are in fact small changes that are guided by, and result in, a sense of strategic purpose. And Neustadt (1990, p. 192), in his study of U.S. presidential power, observes that "Details are of the essence in the exercise of power, day by day, and changes of detail foreshadow institutional development; they cumulate and thus suggest the system's future character." In general, realization of a new future is easier if it can be shown to be a continuation of the past and present, even if the new future ultimately is qualitatively different (Weick, 1979; Neustadt and May, 1986).

In effect, there are two strategies that are polar opposites—big wins and small wins (Bryson, 1988a). A big win is "a demonstrable, completed, large-scale victory accomplished in the face of substantial opposition" (Bryson and Crosby, 1992, p. 229), while a small win is "a concrete, completed, implemented outcome of moderate importance" (Weick, 1984, p. 43). The strategic planning process outlined in this book, because it highlights what is fundamental, may tempt organizations to always go for the big win. But the big win strategy may be a mistake. While big-win moves should be considered, the organization should also consider how a whole series of small wins might add up to big wins over time. A small-win strategy reduces risk, eases implementation, breaks projects into doable steps, quickly makes change "real," releases resource flows and human energy, empowers people, encourages participation, boosts people's confidence and commitment, provides immediate rewards, and preserves gains (Weick, 1984; Kouzes and Posner, 1987).

Nonetheless, a big-win strategy may be best when a small-win strategy is unworkable or undesirable for some reason. For example, Britain and France did not first try out a tiny tunnel across the English Channel. Big wins might also be pursued when the time is right—for example, when the need is obvious to a large coalition, the proposed strategy will effectively address the issue, the solution technology is clearly understood and readily available, the resources are available, and there is a clear vision to guide the changes (Bryson and Crosby, 1992,

p. 235). Big wins probably must be controlled by senior decision makers in fairly hierarchical organizations; they may also emerge through the loosely coordinated actions of many people at the operating level (Mintzberg and McHugh, 1985; Mintzberg, 1994b, p. 194).

The public library and Mainline Church basically pursued small-win strategies. Even so, each still encountered significant opposition internally or externally over specific strategy choices. For example, the library has made substantial progress on implementing many of its strategies on a step-by-step basis. The library staff were surprised, however, by the city council's opposition to closing the library's small video-lending service, and they had to keep it open. Mainline Church had achieved most of the goals in its 1990–94 strategic plan by 1993, including altering its Sunday worship schedule to create an education hour for adults and children between the early and late morning services. This relatively small change has been quite successful in increasing participants in Sunday educational programs, but it was also the most conflictual because it pitted older traditionalists against younger families and single people. A serious rift in the congregation was avoided only through considerable pastoral and lay leadership, conversation, kind words, prayer, and faith. The CPI program is moving incrementally into new strategies of greater communication and collaboration with many stakeholders, in part because of budget constraints but also because these changes are challenging the organization's culture. But these incremental changes are likely to cumulate in major change as greater emphasis on communicating with stakeholders and on service innovations results in a rather different program.

The school district decided to pursue a big-win strategy from the outset, and it has achieved significant results. Ultimately, it will get its big win. The final plan, adopted in 1993, included an emphasis on lifelong learning, outcome-based education, a substantially revised curriculum, inclusive and multicultural education, greater use of computer technology, major changes in facilities (including replacing an aged and obsolete high school with a new building on a new site), and changes in governance, including clarifications of board and superintendent roles and a move to site-based management for each school. The sum of these changes will cumulate in a big win. Many of the changes have already occurred, but controversy over relocating the high school and opposition to increased taxes prevented complete implementation of the plan for two years. Finally, after two bond referenda failed, a third was passed in 1994 that provided monies for a new high school and for renovations to other schools. The referendum passed because the board changed its mind in order to accommodate a significant number of voters who wanted the new high school to be built on the symbolically important site of the old high school.

4. *Effective strategy formulation can be top-down or bottom-up.* Indeed, the organizations that are best at strategic planning seem to combine these two approaches into an effective strategic planning system (Lorange and Vancil, 1977; Chakravarthy and Lorange, 1991). Usually some sort of overall strategic guidance is given

at the top, but detailed strategy formulation and implementation typically occur deeper in the organization. Detailed strategies and their implementation may then be reviewed at the top for consistency across strategies and with organizational purposes. Chapter Ten contains more information on strategic planning systems.

5. *Planners should decide whether they will formulate strategies (1) in response to strategic issues identified directly or indirectly, (2) to achieve goals, or (3) to realize a vision of success.* Probably most organizations will choose the direct or indirect approaches, at least at first. Smaller single-function or hierarchically organized organizations, organizations that have engaged in strategic planning for some time, and communities with a significant consensus on values may find the goals or vision of success approach more suitable. Nonprofit organizations are more likely than governments or public agencies to find the goals and vision of success approach useful.

It is important to repeat that the four approaches to strategy formulation are interrelated. For example, an organization can start with the strategic issues approach, and then develop goals based on its strategies. Goals would then represent strategy-specific desired states requiring effective strategy implementation. Mission, goals, and strategies could then be used as the basis for developing a vision of success. Alternatively, an organization may go through several cycles of strategic planning using the direct or goals approaches before it decides to develop a vision of success—if indeed it ever chooses to do so. Or an organization may start with the ideal scenario approach and expand the scenario into a vision of success after it completes the strategy development step. Or the organization may identify strategic issues using the direct or indirect approaches and then develop goals or idealized scenarios to guide strategy development in each issue area.

No matter which approach is chosen, the five-part process outlined in this chapter provides an effective way to formulate strategies, particularly if the snow card technique is employed in each step. The questions will change only slightly for each approach. The strategic planning team may wish to assign different questions to different groups or individuals. If, for example, the team wishes to identify major alternatives and barriers to their achievement, it might ask task forces to develop major proposals and work programs to achieve the alternatives or overcome the barriers.

The ovals process is also an effective way to develop strategies to deal with issues, achieve goals, or realize visions. Again the questions asked will vary slightly depending on the approach taken. The team may wish to develop the broad outlines of a strategy map and then delegate development of detailed strategies and work programs to individuals or task forces. The CPI program's management group took this approach. It developed basic strategic directions using the ovals process but turned over responsibility for detailing strategies to various supporting units and groups. The school district did the same thing. The board, superintendent, and cabinet developed a mission, goals, and strategic issues; they then asked six different task forces to develop strategies to address these items while the board and superintendent dealt with how to improve the governance and administration of the district.

6. *Strategic alternatives should be described in enough detail to permit reasonable judgments about their efficacy and to provide reasonable guidance for their implementation.* Hennepin County, Minnesota (1983), provides a useful example. It typically requires strategy descriptions to include the following information:

- Principal components or features
- Intended results or outcomes
- Implementation timetable
- Organizations and persons responsible for implementation
- Resources required (staff, facilities, equipment, training)
- Costs (start-up, annual operating, capital)
- Estimated savings, if any, over present approaches
- Flexibility or adaptability of strategy
- Effects on other organizations, departments, persons, or communities
- Effects on other strategies
- Rule, policy, or statutory changes required
- Procedures for "debugging" the strategy during implementation (that is, "formative evaluation" plans) and for performing subsequent evaluations to see whether or not the strategy has worked ("summative evaluation" plans) (Scriven, 1967; Bryson and Cullen, 1984)
- Other important features

Financial costs and budgets deserve special attention. Readers are encouraged to look at the section on budgets in Chapter Nine.

7. *Alternative strategies should be evaluated against agreed-upon criteria prior to selection of specific strategies to be implemented.* Those involved in strategy formulation probably should know in advance what criteria will be used to judge alternatives. For example, the Wilder Foundation's principal criteria for evaluating programs (specific strategies) are included in its strategic plan (see Exhibit 7.1). Hennepin County also provides an interesting example. The county's most senior managers typically use the following set of criteria to evaluate strategies prior to adopting them or referring them to the county board for adoption (P. Eckhert, personal communication, 1993).

- Acceptability to key decision makers, stakeholders, and opinion leaders
- Acceptance by the general public
- Client or user impact
- Relevance to the issue
- Consistency with mission, values, philosophy, and culture
- Coordination or integration with other strategies, programs, and activities

- Technical feasibility
- Cost and financing
- Cost effectiveness
- Long-term impact
- Risk assessment
- Staff requirements
- Flexibility or adaptability
- Timing
- Facility requirements
- Training requirements
- Other appropriate criteria

8. *The organization should consider developing a formal strategic plan.* Such a plan may not be necessary, but as the size and complexity of the organization grows, a formal, written strategic plan is likely to become increasingly useful. The strategic planning team should agree on major categories and on general length so that the actual preparer has some guidance. Indeed, a general agreement on the form of the strategic plan should probably be reached during the negotiation of the initial agreement (Step 1) so that key decision makers have some general sense of what the effort is likely to produce, and surprises are minimized.

It is conceivable, of course, that preparation and publication of a formal strategic plan would be politically unwise. Incompatible objectives or warring external stakeholders, for example, might make it difficult to prepare a "rational" and publicly defensible plan. Key decision makers will have to decide whether a formal strategic plan should be prepared, given the circumstances the organization faces.

9. *Even if a formal strategic plan is not prepared, the organization should consider preparing a set of interrelated strategy statements describing a grand strategy; subunit strategies; program, service, product, or business process strategies; and functional strategies.* To the extent they are agreed upon, these statements will provide extremely useful guides for action by organizational members from top to bottom. Again, remember that it may be politically difficult or dangerous to prepare and publicize such statements.

10. *A normative process should be used to review strategy statements and formal strategic plans.* Drafts typically should be reviewed by planning team members, other key decision makers, governing board members, and at least a few selected outside stakeholders. Review meetings themselves need to be structured so that the strengths of the statements or plan are recognized and modifications that would improve on those strengths are identified. Review sessions can be structured around the following agenda (Barry, 1986; Bryson and Crosby, 1992).

1. Present overview of plan.
2. Initiate general discussion of plan and reactions to it.

3. Brainstorm list of plan strengths.
4. Brainstorm list of plan weaknesses.
5. Brainstorm list of modifications that would improve on strengths and minimize or overcome weaknesses.
6. Agree on next steps to complete the plan.

All modifications that actually do improve the statements and plans should be accepted.

11. *It is* very *important to discuss and evaluate strategies in relation to key stakeholders.* Strategies that are unacceptable to key stakeholders will probably have to be rethought. Strategies that do not take stakeholders into consideration are almost certain to fail. Strategists should use techniques such as Eden and Huxham's "Strategic Option Role Playing Exercise" (see Resource C) or Nutt and Backoff's "Evaluating the Stakeholder" matrix (see Resource D) to design winning coalitions for strategy adoption and implementation.

12. *The organization should have budgets and budgeting procedures in place to capitalize on strategic planning and strategic plans.* This may include making sure that monies tied to implementation of strategic plans are flagged so that they always receive special attention and treatment. It also can mean attempting to develop a special contingency fund to allow "bridge" funding, so that implementation of entire strategies or portions of them can begin out of sequence with the normal budgeting process.

Most important, however, is the need to make sure strategic thinking precedes, rather than follows, budgeting. This is the key idea behind "performance budgeting" and "entrepreneurial budgeting" (Halachmi and Boydston, 1991; Osborne and Gaebler, 1992; Cothran, 1993). Unfortunately, the only strategic plans most organizations have are their budgets, and those budgets have typically been formulated without benefit of much strategic thought. Attention to mission, mandates, situational assessments, and strategic issues should precede development of budgets.

13. *The strategy formulation step is likely to proceed in a more iterative fashion than previous steps because of the need to find the best fit between levels of strategies and between elements of different strategies.* Additional time and iterations are likely to be needed if an interorganizational network or community-based strategic planning effort is involved. Strong process guidance and facilitation, along with pressure from key decision makers to proceed, will probably be necessary in order to reach a successful conclusion to this step. Process sponsors and champions, in other words, will be especially needed if this step is to result in effective strategies.

14. *It is important to allow for a period of catharsis as the organization changes.* Strong emotions or tensions are likely to build up as the organization moves to implement new or changed strategies, particularly if these strategies involve fairly drastic changes and challenge the current culture. Indeed, the buildup of emotions and

tensions may prevent successful implementation of the strategies. These emotions and tensions must be recognized, and people must be allowed to vent and deal with them (Dalton, 1970; Bellman, 1990; Spencer and Adams, 1990; Hampden-Turner, 1990; Schein, 1987, 1992). Such emotions and tensions must be a legitimate topic of discussion in planning team meetings. Sessions designed to review draft strategy statements or strategic plans can be used to solicit modifications in the statements or plans to deal with these emotional concerns.

15. *Completion of the strategy development step is likely to be an important decision point.* The decision will be whether to go ahead with strategies or a strategic plan recommended by the planning team. Actually, a number of decision points may result if a formal strategic plan has not been prepared. Proposed strategies to deal with different strategic issues are very likely to be presented to the appropriate decision-making bodies at different times. Thus, there would be an important decision point for each set of strategies developed to deal with each strategic issue.

16. *Key decision makers and planners should think carefully about how the formal adoption process should be managed, particularly if it involves formal arenas.* Formal arenas typically have specific rules and procedures that must be followed. These rules must be attended to carefully so that the plan is not held hostage or overturned by clever opponents. Bargaining and negotiation over the modifications and inducements necessary to gain support and minimize opposition are almost certain to be needed. Any modifications that actually do improve the proposal should be accepted, and agreements reached through bargaining and negotiation obviously should not sacrifice crucial plan components.

17. *Some sense of closure to the strategic planning process should probably be provided at the end of Step 7, or else at the end of Step 6 if no formal plan is prepared.* Formal adoption of a strategic plan provides a natural occasion for developing such a sense of closure. But even without a strategic plan, some sort of ceremony and celebration is helpful to give participants in the process the sense that the strategic planning effort is finished for the present and that the time for sustained implementation is at hand (Bryson, Van de Ven, and Roering, 1987).

18. *If the strategic planning process has been well designed and faithfully followed, but the strategies and plans are nevertheless not adopted, consider the following possibilities:*

- The time is not yet right.
- The draft strategies and plans are inadequate or inappropriate.
- The issues the strategies and plans purport to address simply are not that "real" or pressing.
- The organization (or community) cannot handle the magnitude of the proposed changes, and the changes need to be scaled back.
- The strategies and plans should be taken to some other arena, or the current arena should be redesigned in some way.

Summary

This chapter has discussed strategy formulation and adoption. Strategies are defined as a *pattern* of purposes, policies, programs, actions, decisions, or resource allocations that defines what an organization is, what it does, and why it does it. Strategies can vary by level, function, and time frame; they are the way an organization (or community) relates to its environment.

Two approaches to developing strategies were outlined: the five-part process and the ovals process. Suggestions were offered for the preparation of formal strategic plans. It was again emphasized that strategic thinking and acting are what is important, not any particular approach to strategy formulation or even the preparation of a formal strategic plan. Suggestions also were offered to guide formal adoption of the plan, if necessary or desirable.

CHAPTER EIGHT

ESTABLISHING AN EFFECTIVE ORGANIZATIONAL VISION FOR THE FUTURE

The visionary is the only realist.

FEDERICO FELLINI, FILMMAKER

The purpose of Step 8 in the strategic planning process is to develop a clear and succinct description of what the organization or community should look like after it successfully implements its strategies and achieves its full potential. This description is the organization's vision of success. Typically, this vision is more important as an implementation guide than as a strategy formulation guide. For that reason, the step is listed as optional in Figure 2.1, and it comes after strategy and plan review and adoption. However, Figure 2.1 also indicates that under the right circumstances, visioning might occur at many places throughout the strategic planning process.

While many public and nonprofit organizations have developed clear and useful mission statements in recent years, far fewer have a clear, succinct, and useful vision of success. Part of the reason is that a vision, while it includes mission, goes well beyond it. A mission outlines the organizational purpose while a vision goes on to describe how the organization should look when it is working extremely well in relation to its environment and its key stakeholders. Developing this description is more time consuming than formulating a mission statement (Senge, 1990). It is also more difficult, particularly because most organizations are coalitional (Pfeffer and Salancik, 1978; Pfeffer, 1992), and thus, the vision must usually be a treaty negotiated among rival coalitions.

Other difficulties may hamper constructing a vision of success. People are afraid of how others will respond to their vision. Professionals are highly vested in their jobs, and to have one's vision of excellent organizational performance criticized or rejected can be trying. People may be afraid of that part of themselves that can envision and pursue excellence. First of all, we can be disappointed in our pursuit, which can be painful. Our own competence can be called into question. And second, being true to the vision can be a very demanding discipline, hard work that we may not be willing to shoulder all the time.

Key decision makers must be courageous in order to construct a compelling vision of success. They must envision and listen to their best selves in order to envision success for the organization. And they must be disciplined enough to affirm the vision in the present, to work hard to make it real in the here and now (Lonnie Helgeson, personal communications, 1986, 1994; Terry, 1993).

It may not be possible, therefore, to create an effective and compelling vision of success for the organization. The good news, however, is that although a vision of success may be very helpful, it may not be necessary in order to improve organizational performance. Agreement on strategy is more important that agreement on vision or goals (Bourgeois, 1980a). Simply finding a way to frame and deal with a few of the strategic issues the organization faces often markedly improves organizational effectiveness.

Desired Outcomes and Benefits

While it may not be necessary to have a vision of success in order to improve organizational effectiveness, it is hard to imagine a truly high-performing organization that does not have at least an implicit and widely shared conception of what success looks like and how it might be achieved (Knauft, Berger, and Gray, 1991; Nanus, 1992; Kotter, 1995). Indeed, it is hard to imagine an organization surviving in the long run without some sort of vision to inspire it—hence the merit of Fellini's comment quoted at the beginning of this chapter. Recall as well the famous admonition in Proverbs 29:18: "Where there is no vision, the people perish."

Thus, a vision of success might be advantageous. First, if it is to provide suitable guidance and motivation, it should probably detail the organization's

- Mission
- Basic philosophy, core values, and cultural features
- Goals, if they are established
- Basic strategies
- Performance criteria (perhaps including critical success factors)
- Important decision-making rules
- Ethical standards expected of all employees

The vision should emphasize purposes, behavior, performance criteria, decision rules, and standards that serve the public rather than the organization. The guidance offered should be specific and reasonable. The vision statement should include a promise that the organization will support its members' pursuit of the vision. Further, the vision should clarify the organization's direction and purpose; be relatively future oriented; reflect high ideals and challenging ambitions; and capture the organization's uniqueness and distinctive competence as well as desirable features of its history, culture, and values (Nanus, 1992; Shamir, Arthur, and House, 1994). The vision should also be relatively short and inspiring.

Second, the vision should be widely circulated among organizational members and other key stakeholders after appropriate consultations, reviews, and sign-offs. A vision of success can have little effect if organizational members are kept in the dark about it.

Third, the vision should be used to inform major and minor organizational decisions and actions. Preparing the vision will have been a waste of time if it has no behavioral effect. If, however, copies of the vision are always handy at formal meetings of key decision makers, and especially if performance measurement systems are explicitly attuned to the vision, then the vision can be expected to affect organizational performance.

A number of benefits flow from a clear, succinct, inspiring, and widely shared vision of success:

1. Organizational members are given specific, reasonable, and supportive guidance about what is expected of them and why. They see how they fit into the organization's big picture. Too often, the only guidance for members—other than hearsay—is a job description (which is typically focused on the parts and not the whole). In addition, key decision makers are all too likely to issue conflicting messages to staff members or simply to tell them, "Do your best." A widely accepted vision of success records enough of a consensus on ends and means that it will channel members' efforts in desirable directions while at the same time providing a framework for improvisation and innovation in pursuit of organizational purposes (Taylor, 1984; Osborne and Gaebler, 1992). In this way, the vision serves primarily as an aid to strategy implementation rather than strategy formulation.

2. As noted earlier, conception precedes perception (May, 1969; Schein, 1992). People must have some conception of what success and desirable behavior look like before they can actually see them and thus strive toward achieving them. A vision of success makes it easier for people to discriminate between preferred and undesirable actions and outcomes and thus produce more of what is preferred.

3. The two things that most determine whether or not goals are achieved appear to be the extent to which the goals are specific and reasonable and the extent to which people are supported in their pursuit of the goals (Locke, Shaw, Saari, and Latham, 1981). It seems reasonable to extend the same argument to a vision of success and to claim that the more specific and reasonable the vision and the more organizational members are supported in their pursuit of the vision, the more likely the vision will be realized.

4. If there is agreement on a vision, and if clear guidance and decision-making rules can be derived from it, then the organization will gain an added

increment of power. Less time will be expended on debating what to do, how to do it, and why (Pfeffer and Moore, 1980; Pfeffer, 1992).

5. A vision of success provides a way to claim or affirm the future. If the future is at least in part what we make it, then development of a vision outlines the future we want to have and forces us live it—create it, "real-ize" it—in the present. Thus, one does not predict the future—a hazardous enterprise at best—one *makes* it (Gabor, 1964).

6. A clear yet reasonable vision of success creates a useful tension between the world as it is and the world as we would like it. If goals are to motivate, they must be set high enough to provide a challenge but not so high as to induce paralysis, hopelessness, or too much stress. A well-tuned vision of success can articulate reasonable standards of excellence and motivate the organization's members to pursue them.

7. An inspiring vision of success can supply another source of motivation as well: a calling. If a vision of success becomes a calling, an enormous amount of individual energy, dedication, power, and positive risk taking can be released in pursuit of it. A virtuous calling creates meaning in workers' lives and fuels justifiable pride. Consider, for example, the case of that most remarkable of nonprofit organizations, the Society of Jesus (the Jesuits), founded in 1534 in Paris by Saint Ignatius of Loyola. The organization's vision was first formulated in Ignatius's *Spiritual Exercises* (Guibert, 1964). The worldwide success of order members as missionaries, teachers, scholars, and spiritual directors is a tribute to how much they have been guided by their ideal: to be a disciplined force on behalf of the Roman Catholic Church. The fact that they have succeeded for so long against often incredible odds and trials is in part due to the power of their vision. They clearly have been "called" for a very long time.

8. A well-articulated vision of success will at least help people implicitly recognize barriers to realizing that vision. (In this way a vision acts in much the same way as the first step in the five-part strategy formulation process outlined in Chapter Seven.)

9. A clear vision of success provides an effective substitute for leadership (Kerr and Jermier, 1978; Manz, 1986). People are empowered to lead and manage themselves if they are given clear guidance on the organization's direction and behavioral expectations. More effective decision making will then occur outside the organizational center and below the top of the hierarchy.

10. While constructing a vision of success may be difficult in politicized settings, the task may nonetheless be worth the effort. An agreed-upon vision may contribute to a significant reduction in organizational conflict. A set of overarching goals can help rechannel conflict into useful directions (Filley, 1975; Fisher and Ury, 1981; Terry, 1993).

11. Depending on its content, a vision of success can help the organization stay attuned to its environment and develop its capacity to deal with the almost inevitable crises characteristic of organizational life these days. The vision can

promote the learning and adaptation necessary to avoid catastrophic failure (Mitroff and Pearson, 1993).

12.　To the extent that the vision of success is widely shared, it lends the organization an air of virtue. Although it is not particularly fashionable to talk about virtue, most people wish to act in morally justifiable ways in pursuit of morally justified ends (Frederickson, 1982; Lewis, 1991). A vision of success therefore provides important permission, justification, and legitimation to actions and decisions that further the vision. It also establishes boundaries of permitted behavior, facilitating the self-regulation necessary for any moral community to survive and prosper (Kanter, 1972; Mandelbaum, 1995).

Two Examples

The CPI program's 1994 strategic plan is essentially a vision of success. As a vision, the plan also serves as a very general guide for implementation. Not included in the plan are important decision-making rules and ethical standards, but both of these points are covered in other documents. Also not included are the kinds of *detailed* implementation guidelines that many strategic plans contain, which can be very useful but also make it difficult for strategic plans to serve as visions of success. At fifteen pages, the plan is somewhat lengthy for a vision of success, but its readability is enhanced by thoughtful organization and adroit use of space, graphics, and type. The plan includes an introduction and four major sections.

The first section includes a mission statement, a one-sentence vision statement, a list of the program's core values and stakeholders, and seven program goals in priority order. The mission is as follows:

> The CPI is the primary measure of inflation in the United States. Our mission is to provide a timely, accurate, and objective measure of consumer price changes; to assess their causes; and to cooperate with customers and other key stakeholders to improve our products and their understanding of them.

The vision statement states what the CPI will look like once the program achieves its full potential:

> The CPI will be a premier statistical program that anticipates and strives to meet stakeholders' expectations and continuously improves stakeholders' satisfaction with our products.

In the past twenty years, many federal employees and agencies have become shell-shocked and demoralized. Relentless bureaucrat bashing—or at best lukewarm support—by presidents, members of Congress, and the public; severe budgetary constraints; and mountains of rules and regulations designed more to constrain action than facilitate it have taken their toll. In such circumstances, organizational leaders actively need to help and empower people to work together in a respectful way to pursue the common good. Therefore, the CPI program's statement of core values—the principles by which the program wishes to be guided—is as follows:

> The CPI program's most valuable asset is its dedicated staff. We fully recognize their integrity, industriousness, and professionalism. We operate in an environment that empowers staff to continuously improve our products and make innovations to meet stakeholders' needs. This environment encourages professional growth, teamwork, and problem solving. We want everyone to work in an environment where the focus is *not* on assigning blame but on taking responsibility for solving problems and improving our processes to make them less prone to failure.

The program's goals are listed in priority order, along with an explanation of why they are important and how they fit in with broader Department of Labor initiatives (particularly the Clinton administration's efforts to "reinvent government"). The goals are to

- Provide maximum value to stakeholders
- Produce an accurate, objective measure of consumer price changes
- Develop a customer focus and a proactive relationship with stakeholders
- Produce a timely CPI
- Develop an excellent staff
- Respond to internal users' needs
- Obtain the funding necessary to achieve program goals

The plan's second section outlines the CPI program's major strategies. These are grouped into three categories: strategies for improving products and services, strategies for making the best use of the program's human and financial resources, and strategies for making the best use of technology. Also included is a statement on the organization's commitment to TQM.

The third section covers performance measures by goal. The measures are a blend of objective, subjective, quantitative, and qualitative indicators of program success.

The plan's final section discusses how the upcoming 1998 revision affects the program's goals. The revision (a decennial activity) involves updating market baskets, redesigning data-gathering tools and techniques, and revising price-estimation procedures.

The plan provides much specific and reasonable advice to employees (and other stakeholders) and indicates that the CPI program will support and reward those who act in accordance with the plan. Because much of the program's success depends on the actions and decisions of people in the Bureau of Labor Statistics who are not under the CPI program's control—as well as people in regional CPI program offices and in the field—the importance of wide circulation of this document and agreement on its contents is hard to overstate. It is also important to emphasize that the plan is no mere public relations ploy. Key decision makers and opinion leaders are committed to it. The plan codifies much that the CPI program already does, but it also charts some new agreed-upon directions that are necessary to achieve excellence (in particular, the emphasis on anticipating stakeholders' needs and meeting their expectations, which grew out of the CPI management group's first strategic planning retreat, in November 1992).

As another example, the public library's 1991–93 strategic plan concludes with elements of a vision of success for the year 2000 (see Exhibit 8.1). The library's vision should be read in the light of its mission (also presented in the plan and in Exhibit 4.2). Again, the vision does not cover all the items it might, but it does cover services, technology and automation, personnel, facilities, community input, and funding efforts. (Note that the "Community Demographics" section is more a statement of fact than a vision of success.) The vision also gives staff members and other stakeholders a sense of where the administration thinks the library should be headed in the coming decade.

Process Guidelines

The following guidelines are intended to help a strategic planning team formulate a vision of success.

1. *Remember that in most cases a vision of success is not necessary to improve organizational effectiveness.* Simply developing and implementing strategies to deal with a few important strategic issues can produce marked improvement in the performance of most organizations. An organization therefore should not worry too much if it seems unwise or too difficult to develop a vision of success. Nevertheless, it seems unlikely that an organization can achieve truly superior performance without a widely shared (at least implicitly) vision of success, what theologian Teilhard de Chardin called "a great hope held in common" (quoted in Nanus, 1992, p. 15).

2. *Most organizations should wait until they go through one or more cycles of strategic planning before they try to develop a vision of success.* Most organizations need to develop the habit of thinking about and acting on the truly important aspects of their relationship with their environment before a collective vision of success can emerge. In addition, a consensus on key decisions and an ability to resolve conflicts constructively (both necessary achievements to develop an effective vision of success) are only likely to emerge over more than one cycle of strategic planning.

This guideline may not apply if the organization is already implementing

EXHIBIT 8.1. PUBLIC LIBRARY VISION OF SUCCESS.

Possible/Probable Futures

Projecting current social, educational, and economic trends, the members of the Strategic Planning Committee developed this vision of what the Public Library *might* look like in the year 2000:

Services

- Appropriate materials, services and staffing will address the needs of the increased people of color populations.
- Many of our libraries will have self-service computers with software.
- We will have computer access for searching databases in many of the libraries.
- We will be supporting literacy both in the collection and in programming.
- We will target children's programming to given ages. We will identify elementary and junior high students as a focus group.
- The amount of leisure-time reading materials and popular magazines will be increased to meet the community demand.
- We will have more emphasis on support materials for children through the high school level.
- We will increase cooperation between the schools and public library with some funding coming from schools to support our hours and collection.
- There will be dial-up access 24 hours/day to holdings. There will be the ability to place requests during this transaction.
- There will be telefacsimile service in all agencies.
- There will be more use of the interlibrary loan service.

Technology/Automation

- CD-ROM will be used throughout the system.
- There will be direct-dial access to our catalog of material holdings.
- There will be more PCs available in all agencies.
- Public will have access to information from home and business computers.
- More information will be stored on audio, video, CD-ROM, or other computerized formats.

Personnel

- Greater emphasis will be placed on the staff's need for continuing education.
- The Library will use more highly skilled volunteers, available because of the increased number of highly educated retirees.

Facilities

- More popular access points will be in operation—either storefront or bookmobiles.
- Libraries will be accessible for the disabled.
- The new Merriam Park Branch Library will have been constructed.
- All buildings will have been remodeled and feature appropriate interior layouts.

Community Demographics

- We will continue to have a diverse population using the library.
- There will be more people of color and persons below the poverty line.
- There will be more older adults.

Community Input

- We will actively seek and effectively use input from library support groups and the community in planning and evaluating the Library's service program. Such efforts will hopefully raise the community's awareness of its library system and produce advocates for its support.

Funding

- Administration will play a major role in an ongoing program of fundraising.

effective strategies based on the idealized scenario or goals approach. If there is already enough consensus among key decision makers to make either of these approaches possible, then the organization may also succeed in developing a viable, detailed vision of success before it has completed an entire strategic planning cycle.

3. *A vision of success should include the items listed earlier in this chapter as desired outcomes and benefits.* The vision statement should not be long, preferably no more than ten double-spaced pages.

4. *A vision of success should grow out of past decisions and actions as much as possible.* Past decisions and actions provide a record of pragmatic consensus about what the organization is and should do. Basing a vision on a preexisting consensus avoids unnecessary conflict. Also, the vision should effectively link the organization to its past. Realization of a new future is facilitated if it can be shown to be a continuation of the past and present (Weick, 1979; Hampden-Turner, 1990).

However, a vision of success should not be merely an extension of the present. It should be an affirmation of an ideal and inspirational future. A vision of success should create an image that encourages organizational members to extrapolate backward to the present; this will help them determine which daily actions today can best help the organization achieve success tomorrow.

5. *A vision of success should be inspirational.* It will not move people to excel unless it is. And what inspires people is a clear description of a desirable future backed up by real conviction. An inspirational vision (Kouzes and Posner, 1987, 1993; Nanus, 1992; Shamir, Arthur, and House, 1994)

- Focuses on a better future
- Encourages hopes, dreams, and noble ambitions
- Builds on (or reinterprets) the organization's history and culture to appeal to high ideals and common values
- Clarifies purpose and direction
- States positive outcomes
- Emphasizes the organization's uniqueness and distinctive competence
- Emphasizes the strength of a unified group
- Uses word pictures, images, and metaphors
- Communicates enthusiasm, kindles excitement, and fosters commitment and dedication

Just recall the "I Have A Dream" speech of Martin Luther King, Jr., and you will have a clear example of an inspirational vision of success focused on a better future.

6. *An effective vision of success will embody the appropriate degree of tension to prompt effective organizational change.* On the one hand, too much tension will likely cause paralysis. On the other hand, too little tension will not produce the challenge necessary for outstanding performance. If there is not enough tension, the vision should be recast to raise organizational sights.

7. *A useful way to begin constructing a vision of success is to have planning team members prepare draft visions of success (or at least relatively detailed outlines) individually, using the worksheets in Bryson and Alston (1995).* Team members should then share and discuss their responses with each other. After this discussion, the task of drafting a vision of success should be turned over to an individual, since an inspirational document is rarely written by a committee. The team may find it useful to review the discussion of the vision of success approach to strategic issue identification in Chapter Six, the discussion of visionary leadership in Chapter Eleven, and Resource E before starting the drafts.

Special sessions may be necessary to develop particular elements of the vision of success. For example, the organization's performance criteria or success indicators may not be fully specified. They might be developed out of the organization's mandates, the stakeholder analysis, the SWOT analysis, the strategy statements, or the snow card or ovals mapping activities. Wherever there are gaps in the vision, special sessions may be necessary to fill them.

8. *A normative process should be used to review the vision of success.* Drafts typically are reviewed by planning team members, other key decision makers, governing board members, and at least some selected outside stakeholders. Review meetings need to be structured to ensure that the vision's strengths and any possible improvements are identified and listed. Review sessions can be structured according to the agenda suggested for the review of strategic plans (see Chapter Seven).

9. *Consensus on the vision statement among key decision makers is highly desirable, but it may not be absolutely necessary.* It is rarely possible to achieve complete consensus on anything in an organization, so all that can be realistically hoped for is a fairly widespread general agreement on the substance and style of the vision statement. Actual deep-seated commitment to any vision statement can only emerge slowly over time.

10. *For a vision of success to help guide organizational decisions and actions, it must be widely disseminated and discussed.* The vision statement probably should be published as a booklet and given to every organizational member and to key external stakeholders. Discussion of the statement should be made a part of orientation programs for new employees, and periodically the statement should be discussed in staff meetings.

A vision of success can become a living document only if it is referred to constantly as a basis for determining appropriate organizational decisions and actions. If a vision statement does not regularly inform organizational decision making and actions, then preparation of the statement was probably a waste of time.

Summary

This chapter has discussed developing a vision of success for an organization. A vision of success is defined as a description of what the organization will look like after it successfully implements its strategies and achieves its full potential. A vision statement should include the organization's mission, its basic philosophy and core values, its basic strategies, its performance criteria, its important decision-making rules, and its ethical standards. The statement should emphasize the important social purposes the organization serves and that justify its existence. In addition, the statement should be short and inspirational.

For a vision of success to have a strong effect on organizational decisions and actions, it must be widely disseminated and discussed, and it must be referred to frequently as a means of determining appropriate responses to the various situations that confront the organization. Only if the vision statement is used as a basis for organizational decision making and action will it have been worth the effort of crafting it.

CHAPTER NINE

IMPLEMENTING STRATEGIES AND PLANS SUCCESSFULLY

You give an order around here, and if you can figure out what happens to it after that, you're a better person than I am.

HARRY S TRUMAN

The purpose of the implementation step (Step 9) is to complete the transition from strategic planning to strategic management by incorporating adopted strategies throughout the relevant system. Creating a strategic plan is not enough. Developing effective programs, projects, action plans, budgets, and implementation processes will bring life to the strategies and create real value for the organization (or community) and its stakeholders. Programs, projects, action plans, and budgets are necessary in order to coordinate the activities of the numerous professionals, technicians, and frontline personnel likely to be involved in the process. The implementation process itself should allow for adaptive learning as new information becomes available and circumstances change. Such learning will lead to more effective implementation—to better patterns (strategies) across purposes, policies, programs, actions, decisions, and resource allocations—and to the cognitive and practical basis for emergent strategies and new rounds of strategizing. Recall that *realized* strategies are a blend of what is *intended* with what *emerges* in practice (Mintzberg and Westley, 1992; Mintzberg, 1994a, 1984b).

Desired Outcomes

The most important outcome that leaders, managers, and planners should aim for in this step is real *value added* through goal achievement and increased stakeholder satisfaction. This will be accomplished by achieving a series of more instrumental outcomes. The first of these subordinate outcomes is the reasonably smooth and rapid introduction of the strategies throughout the relevant system. Typically, a broad repertoire of stratagems is necessary to bring all relevant entities onboard or at least to get them to do what needs doing (Chase, 1979; Elmore, 1982; Kaufman, 1986). The second subordinate outcome is the development of a clear understanding by implementers of what needs to be done and when, why, and by whom. Statements of goals and objectives, a vision of success, and educational materials and operational guides can all help.

A third subordinate outcome is the use of a "debugging" process to identify and fix the difficulties that almost inevitably arise as a new solution is put into place. Those concerned with implementation should recall the famed administrative adage known as Murphy's Law: "Anything that can go wrong will go wrong." They should also recall the quip, "Murphy was an optimist"! The earlier steps in the process are designed to ensure, as much as possible, that the adopted strategies and plans do not contain any major flaws. But it is almost inconceivable that some important difficulties will not arise as strategies are put into practice. Key decision makers should pay regular attention to how implementation is proceeding in order to focus attention on any difficulties and how to address them. "Management by wandering around" (Peters and Waterman, 1982) can help in order to gather information and solve difficulties on the spot. "Managing by groping along" can help if it leads to useful adaptive learning (Behn, 1991). Also, as mentioned briefly in Chapter Seven, a conscious formative evaluation process is needed to help implementers identify obstacles and steer over, around, under, or through them to achieve—or if necessary, modify—policy goals during the early stages of implementation (Bryson and Cullen, 1984; Patton, 1986). A good formative evaluation will also provide useful information for new rounds of strategizing.

Fourth, successful implementation will also likely include summative evaluations (Scriven, 1967), to find out if strategic goals have actually been achieved. Summative evaluations often differentiate between outputs and outcomes. Outputs are the actual actions, behaviors, products, services, or other direct consequences produced by the policy changes. Outcomes are the ramifications of those outputs—that is, their larger meanings. In other words, outputs are substantive changes while outcomes include symbolic interpretations. Both are important in determining whether a change has been worth the time and effort required to implement it (Levy, Meltsner, and Wildavsky, 1974; Lynn, 1987).

Summative evaluations may be expensive and time consuming. Further, they are vulnerable to sabotage and to attack on political, technical, legal, or ethical grounds. Nonetheless, without such evaluations, it is very difficult to know whether, and in precisely what ways, things are "better" as a result of implemented changes.

A fifth subordinate desired outcome is the assurance that the important features of the adopted strategies and plans are maintained during implementation. Although the strategies and plans were most likely constructed to address specific issues in specific ways, as situations change and different actors become involved, implementation can become a kind of "moving target" (Wittrock and de Leon, 1986; Calista, 1994). It is possible that mutations developed during the course of implementation can do a better job of addressing the issues than would the original, adopted strategy or plan. In general, however, it is more likely that such distortions will subvert the avowed strategic aims and gut their intent.

A sixth subordinate outcome of successful implementation typically involves the creation of redesigned organizational (or interorganizational or community) settings that will ensure long-lasting changes. These settings are marked by the institutionalization of implicit or explicit principles, norms, rules, decision-making procedures, and incentives; the stabilization of altered patterns of behavior and attitudes; and the continuation or creation of a coalition of implementers, advocates, and supportive interest groups who favor the changes. For example, the school district's move to outcome-based education and site-based management entailed substantial changes to long-established curriculum design procedures and governance processes, respectively.

If the redesign of settings is significant, the result may in fact be a new regime. Regime construction is not easy, and therefore it will not happen unless the changes are clearly seen as "worth it" by relevant implementers. A variety of new or redesigned settings that allow the use of a range of tools, techniques, and positive and negative sanctions or incentives may be necessary in order to steer behaviors and attitudes in desired directions. A vision of success (discussed in Chapter Eight) may be highly desirable to outline what the new regime would look like if the purpose of the changes is realized and the strategies are fully implemented.

The last subordinate desired outcome is the establishment or anticipation of review points during which the strategies may be maintained, succeeded, or terminated. The Strategy Change Cycle is a series of loops, not a straight line. Politics, problems, and desired solutions often change (Kingdon, 1995). There are no once-and-for-all solutions, only temporary victories. Leaders, managers, and planners must be alert to the nature and sources of possible challenges to implemented strategies; they should work to maintain still-desirable strategies, replacing them with better ones when possible or necessary and terminating them when they become completely outmoded.

Benefits

A number of important benefits flow from effective implementation. Obviously, the first is successful goal achievement, in which real issues are addressed smoothly and rapidly. The second benefit is in many ways the reverse of the first—namely, the avoidance of the typical causes of failure. These causes are legion but include the following (Chase, 1979; Wolman, 1981; Elmore, 1982; Morris and Hough, 1986; Goggin, Bowman, Lester, and O'Toole, 1990; Bryson and Bromiley, 1993; Calista, 1994; Kingdon, 1995):

- Resistance based on attitudes and beliefs that are incompatible with desired changes. Sometimes these attitudes and beliefs stem simply from the resisters' not having participated in strategy or plan development.

- Personnel problems such as inadequate numbers, overcommitment to other activities, inadequate orientation or training, poorly designed incentives, or people's uncertainty whether involvement with implementation will help their careers.
- Incentives that are poorly designed to induce desired behavior on the part of implementing organizations or units.
- Implementing organizations or units' preexisting commitment of resources to other priorities and a consequent absence of uncommitted resources to facilitate new activities. In other words, there is little "slack" (Cyert and March, 1963).
- The absence of administrative support services.
- The absence of rules, resources, and settings for identifying and resolving implementation problems.
- The emergence of new political, economic, or administrative priorities.

A third significant benefit is increased support for, and legitimacy of, the leaders and organizations that have successfully advocated and implemented the changes (Bryson and Kelley, 1981; Bartlett and Ghoshal, 1994). Real issues have been identified and effectively addressed—that is what public and nonprofit organizational or community leadership is all about. In addition, leaders who advocate and implement desired changes may well become more secure in their leadership positions. Their formal or informal contracts may be extended. They may receive pay raises or other perks, as well as attractive job offers from elsewhere. Further, since organizations are externally justified by what they do to address basic social or political problems or needs, the advocating organizations should experience enhanced legitimacy and support.

Fourth, individuals involved in effective implementation of desirable changes are likely to experience heightened self-esteem and self-confidence (Dalton, 1970; Schein, 1992). If a person has done a good job of addressing real needs, it is hard for him or her *not* to feel good about it. Effective implementation thus can produce extremely important "psychic income" for those involved. Finally, organizations (or communities) that effectively implement strategies and plans are likely to enhance their capacities for action in the future. They acquire an expanded repertoire of knowledge, experience, tools, and techniques, and therefore they are better positioned to undertake and adapt to future changes.

Programs and Projects

New or revised programs and projects are a component of many strategic change efforts (Koteen, 1989; Normann, 1991; Pettigrew, Ferlie, and McKee, 1992). Many aspects of the decennial revision of the Consumer Price Index are being managed

on a project basis. The school district's moves to outcome-based education and
site-based management are being managed as projects. And many of the public
library's and Mainline Church's change initiatives are programs or projects.
Creation of programs and projects is a way of "chunking" (Peters and Waterman,
1982) changes by breaking them down into smaller pieces designed to address specific issues. Koteen (1989) refers to program and project management as a form
of "bite-sized management" because the creation of programs and projects can
help clarify the overall design of a change initiative, provide a vehicle for obtaining the necessary review and approval, and provide an objective basis for evaluation of progress (pp. 162–163). Programs and projects can also focus attention
on strategic initiatives, facilitate detailed learning, build momentum behind the
changes, provide for increased accountability, and allow for easier termination
of initiatives that turn out be undesirable (Peters and Waterman, 1982; Randolph
and Posner, 1988). Of course, if drawing attention to the changes is unwise for
any reason, a program or project management approach can still be used; but public relations strategy will need to be carefully thought through so as not to arouse
the ire of powerful opponents.

Program and project plans are a version of action plans. Koteen (1989, pp.
163–165) argues that program and project plans should have the following components:

- Definition of purpose
- Calculation of inputs desired
- Definition of outputs to be produced
- Identification of target clientele
- Specification of objectively verifiable indicators
- Indicators of assumptions that are key to the success of the program

The Special Role of Budgets

Budget allocations have crucial, if not overriding, significance for the implementation of strategies and plans. Budgets often represent the most important and
consequential policy statements that governments or nonprofit organizations make.
Not all strategies and plans have budgetary significance, but enough of them do
that public and nonprofit leaders and managers should consider involving themselves deeply in the process of budget making. Doing so is likely to be a particularly effective way to affect the design, adoption, and execution of strategies and
plans (Lynn, 1987, pp. 191–193).

The difficulty in using budgets for planning purposes results partly from the
political context in which budgeting takes place. The hustle, hassle, and uncertainty of politics means that budgeting typically tends to be short-term, incremental, reactive, and oriented toward accountability, rather than long-term,

comprehensive, innovative, proactive, and oriented toward accomplishment of broad purposes, goals, or priorities. The politicized nature of budgeting is likely to be especially pronounced in the public sector, where adopted budgets record the outcomes of a broad-based political struggle among the many claimants on the public purse (Wildavsky, 1984). But the same difficulties emerge (though perhaps in a more muted form and for somewhat different reasons) in the private and nonprofit sectors as well (Mintzberg, 1994b).

Another fundamental reason for the gap between budgeting and planning is that planning for control and planning for action are so fundamentally different, as Mintzberg (1994b, pp. 67–81) argues, that a "great divide" exists between them. In Mintzberg's terminology, performance control consists of two hierarchies, budgets and objectives, while action planning consists of two additional hierarchies, strategies and programs. The research evidence indicates that while it is hard to join together either of the two pairs of hierarchies, it is extremely difficult (and perhaps impossible) to join all four hierarchies together in a completely coherent, reasonable, and workable way. Only capital budgeting seems to be a partial exception to this generalization.

Performance control tends to be "routine in nature, logically carried out on a regular basis, quantitative in approach and largely the concern of the accounting people, easily mapped onto the existing structure, and geared to motivation and control" (p. 78). Further, this control is "after-the-fact. In other words, objectives and budgets are not concerned with predetermining *specific* actions but with controlling overall performance, that is, with the cumulative consequences of many actions. Thus, they have little to do with the formulation of strategy *per se*. Rather, performance control constitutes an *indirect* way to influence the actions taken by an organization" (p. 78).

Conversely, action planning is concerned with "before-the-fact specification of behavior: strategies are supposed to evoke programs that are supposed to prescribe the execution of tangible actions. . . . In contrast with objectives and budgets, strategies and programs tend to be, if not nonquantitative, then at least less so, and more the purview of the line managers, supported perhaps by the planners" (pp. 78–79).

What can be done about the great divide, since both performance control and strategies and programs are important? Several suggestions are possible:

1. Try to have strategic planning precede the budget cycle (Halachmi and Boydston, 1991). Budgeting is more likely to serve overall organizational purposes if environmental assessments, strategic issue identification, and strategy formulation precede rather than follow it. The city of Milwaukee, Wisconsin, provides an excellent example of how this can be done for a large public organization (Anne Spray Kinney, personal communication, 1993; David R. Riemer, personal communications, 1995; City of Milwaukee, 1994).

2. A key way make this happen is to gain control of the "master calendar"

that guides formal organizational planning and budgeting efforts. As Lynn argues, "the master calendar is the public executive's most important device for gaining ascendancy over the process of budget making in the organization . . . [because it] puts public executives in a position to spell out the assumptions, constraints, priorities, and issues they want each subordinate unit to consider in developing its program, budget, and policy proposals. In the process, they can define the roles of the various staff offices . . . and indicate when and how they will make decisions and hear appeals" (1987, pp. 203–205).

3.   Influencing the budget also depends on the personal strategizing of public and nonprofit leaders and managers. Here again Lynn provides a useful insight, when he defines strategy as a "set of value premises that constitute a source of direction or focus for the public executive's decisions and other actions" (1987, p. 139). Thus prior strategic planning efforts can provide many of the premises needed to try to influence budgeting in strategic directions (Halachmi and Boydston, 1991; Bryson and Crosby, 1992, pp. 81–117). And the short-term, incremental nature of budgeting actually can be a source of opportunity rather than constraint for the strategically minded public and nonprofit leader and manager (Lynn, 1987, p. 203; Braybrooke and Lindblom, 1963). The system is a natural setting for organizing a series of small wins informed by a strategic sense of direction.

4.   Pick your budget fights carefully. Given the number of players that budgeting attracts, particularly in the public sector, it is not possible to win every battle. Attention should therefore be focused on those battles that are crucial to moving desired strategies forward. The way the master calendar is organized and attention is focused on budgetary allocations will strongly influence the way potential fights arise, and therefore, leaders and managers should try to influence these as well.

Lynn (1987, pp. 208–209) argues that there are three basic approaches to budgetary allocations. Each has a different effect on the way issues are raised:

- Each budget issue can be treated separately. This means that issues would typically be framed and forwarded by subunits. This approach means that cross-issue or cross-unit comparisons are avoided, and it may be possible to hide particular choices from broad scrutiny. If resolution of the individual issues leads to exceeding the total resources available, then across-the-board cuts or selective comparisons on the margin are possible.
- Particular issues can be selected in advance for detailed consideration during budget preparations. The strategic planning process would be a likely source of strategic issues needing careful review. The typical incremental nature of budgeting might be influenced by the general sense of direction that emerges from addressing these issues.
- Budgetary issues can be examined in light of a comprehensive analytical framework or strategy. Here, the attempt is to influence budgetary allocations based

on a larger strategic vision. This approach is most likely to work when the strategic planning process can be driven by a vision of success, at least in sketch form, and when there is strong leadership in place to follow through with the more detailed vision of success that is likely to result in Step 8.

5. Consider implementing "entrepreneurial budgeting" concepts to advance strategic purposes. A number of governments in various countries around the world are experimenting with reforms that are likely to facilitate implementation of intended strategies, help new strategies emerge via innovation, enhance managerial autonomy along with accountability for results, and promote a new kind of entrepreneurial culture (Osborne and Gaebler, 1992; Cothran, 1993).

Governments using these approaches begin by establishing broad strategic goals and then setting overall expenditure limits along with broad allocations for specific functions such as health, public safety, or roads. Then operating departments are given substantially increased discretion over the use of funds in order to achieve their portion of the strategic goals, "subject to the usual constraints of legality and political prudence" (Cothran, 1993, p. 446). This move decentralizes decisions in a significant way. In a further shift from traditional practice, departments are allowed to keep a significant fraction of the funds left at the end of the fiscal year without having their budget base cut. Cost savings and wise management thus can be rewarded, and the "use it or lose it" phenomenon of foolish buying sprees at the end of the fiscal year is avoided. In a further move to enhance cost savings and wise management, some governments allow individual employees to take as income a fraction of any savings they produce.

The final feature of entrepreneurial budgeting is an emphasis on accountability for results. In return for increased discretion, higher-level decision makers want greater evidence of program achievement and efficiency gains. As Cothran (1993, p. 450) notes, "Often an almost contractual agreement is negotiated between the central budget office and the operating departments in which each department lists and ranks its objectives, specifies indicators for measuring the achievement of those objectives, and quantifies the indicators as much as possible." If objectives are not achieved, serious questioning of managers by policy makers can ensue.

Entrepreneurial budgeting thus involves a blend of centralization *and* decentralization. Control over broad-scale goal setting and monitoring for results is retained by policy makers while managerial discretion over how to achieve the goals is decentralized to operating managers. Authority is delegated without being relinquished; policy makers and managers are each therefore better able—empowered—to do their jobs more effectively (Carver, 1990). In effect, as Cothran (1993, p. 453) observes, "entrepreneurial budgeting, and decentralized management in general, can lead to an expansion of power, rather than a redistribution of power."

The changes that entrepreneurial budgeting are intended to induce are so profound that a shift in organizational culture is likely to result. Indeed, a major reason for moving to entrepreneurial budgeting is to create a culture of entrepreneurship, particularly in government (Osborne and Gaebler, 1992). This change in culture itself needs to be thought about in a strategic fashion (Schein, 1992; Hampden-Turner, 1990).

6. Make sure you have good analysts and wily and seasoned veterans of budgetary politics on your side (Lynn, 1987, p. 207). Budgeting is a complicated game, and having a good team and good coaches can help the leader or manager interested in winning. There is really no substitute for having a savvy insider who can both prepare and critique budgets effectively. But while it is important to have good analysts and advisers, it is also important not to become their captive (Meltsner, 1990). The wise leader or manager will want to make sure that a sense of the organization's desired strategy informs the analysts' and advisers' work.

7. Finally, to the extent that the same people are involved in both strategy formulation and implementation, the action-control gap is likely to be bridged. There are two approaches to doing this—one centralized, the other decentralized (Mintzberg, 1994b, pp. 286–287). In the centralized approach, which is most closely associated with strong entrepreneurial or visionary leaders, the formulater does the implementing. By staying in close contact with the intimate details of implementation, the implementer can continuously evaluate and readjust strategies during implementation. The decentralized approach is more suitable for highly complex situations, where "strategic thinking cannot be concentrated at one center" (pp. 286–287). In this case, the implementers must become the formulaters, as they do when "street-level bureaucrats" determine a public service agency's strategy in practice (Lipsky, 1980). At the extreme, this becomes what Mintzberg (1994b, pp. 287–290) refers to as a "grass-roots model of strategy formation."

Process Guidelines

Successful implementation of strategies and plans depends primarily on the design and use of various "implementation structures" that coordinate and manage implementation activities, along with the continuation or creation of a coalition of committed implementers, advocates, and supportive interest groups (Hjern and Porter, 1981; see also, for example, Goggin, Bowman, Lester, and O'Toole, 1990; Whetten and Bozeman, 1991; Bryson and Crosby, 1992; Calista, 1994). These structures are likely to consist of a variety of formal and informal mechanisms to promote implementation-centered discussion, decision making, problem solving, and conflict management. New attitudes and patterns of behavior must be stabilized and adjusted to new circumstances, particularly through the institutionalization of shared expectations among key actors around a set of implicit or explicit principles, norms, rules, and decision-making procedures; positive and negative sanctions and incentives; and the continuation or creation of a supportive coalition.

The following guidelines should be kept in mind as the adopted strategies or plans move toward implementation.

General Guidance

1. *Consciously and deliberately plan and manage implementation in a strategic way.* The change implementers may be very different from the members of the advocacy coalition that adopted the changes. This is often the case when changes are "imposed" on implementers by legislative or other decision-making bodies. Implementers thus may have little interest in making implementation flow smoothly and effectively (Pressman and Wildavsky, 1973). Further, even if implementers are interested in incorporating adopted changes within their respective systems, any number of things can go wrong. Implementation, therefore, is hardly ever automatic—Harry Truman's discovery quoted at the beginning of the chapter should be kept in mind. Alternatively, consider journalist Robert Sherrill's admonition that "History is one damn thing after another." Or poet William Blake's eloquent, "Help! Help!" The implementation process must therefore be explicitly considered prior to the implementation step as a way of minimizing later implementation difficulties, and it must be continually reconsidered during the implementation step itself.

Change implementers, particularly if they are different from the change formulaters, may wish to view the changes as a mandate (Step 2) and go through the process outlined in Chapter Two to figure out how best to respond to them. This process should include efforts to understand and accommodate the history and inclinations of key implementing individuals and organizations (Neustadt and May, 1986). Programs and projects must be organized carefully in order to effectively implement desired strategies. Budgets will also need to be given careful attention, if they are to help the organization meet its mandates and fulfill its sense of mission. Additional detailed advice can be found in Elmore (1982), Yin (1982), Barry (1986), Friend and Hickling (1987), Rosenhead (1989), Bryant (1989), Bryson and Crosby (1992), and Nutt and Backoff (1992).

The board and cabinet of the school district thought quite strategically about implementation during the strategy and plan formulation, plan adoption, and implementation steps. Of particular concern was how to deal with the inadequacy of the old high school: Should it be remodeled? Should a new "super" high school be built? Should another high school be remodeled and a smaller new high school built? Plan review sessions, for example, focused on where the votes were on the board and what trade-offs might be necessary to achieve a consensus, as well as on how the different proposals would be received in the community. The board was intent on achieving a consensus because board members knew that major changes would be less likely to succeed without unanimous board backing. The search for a board consensus was in turn driven partly by anticipating what the community would support and oppose, an example of what Friedrich (1940) calls "rule by anticipated reactions." Similarly, the CPI program's management group sought to make sure its strategic plan was consistent with broader Bureau of Labor Statistics and Department of Labor initiatives, the public library pursued strategies and implementation plans it thought would gain the support of the mayor and the city council, and Mainline Church pursued its plans in light of anticipated positive and negative stakeholder reactions. Each planning group was willing to provoke negative reactions in pursuit of desirable ends, but each also thought carefully about how to anticipate and accommodate stakeholder concerns constructively, so as not to needlessly undermine the change effort.

2. *Develop implementation strategy documents and action plans to guide implementation and focus attention on necessary decisions, actions, and responsible parties.* Recall that strategies will vary by level. The four basic levels are the organization's or network's grand or umbrella strategy; strategy statements for constituent units; the program, service, product, or business process strategies, designed to coordinate relevant units and activities; and the functional strategies, such as finance, staffing, facilities, information technology, or procurement strategies, also designed to coordinate units and activities. It may not have been possible to work out all of these statements prior to implementation. If not, the implementation step is the time to finish the task, in as much detail as is necessary to focus and channel action without also stifling useful learning.

Strategies may be long term or short term. Strategies provide a framework for tactics—the short-term adaptive actions and reactions used to accomplish fairly limited objectives. Strategies also provide the "continuing basis for ordering these adaptations toward more broadly conceived purposes" (Quinn, 1980, p. 9). (Recall, of course, that tactics can embody emergent strategies as well as implement intended strategies, making it difficult at times to know what the difference is between strategies and tactics; see Mintzberg, 1994b, p. 243.) Action plans are statements about how to implement strategies in the short term (Frame, 1987; Morrisey, Below, and Acomb, 1987; Randolph and Posner, 1988). Typically, action plans cover periods of a year or less. They outline:

- Specific expected results, objectives, and milestones
- Roles and responsibilities of implementation bodies, teams, and individuals
- Specific action steps
- Schedules
- Resource requirements and sources
- A communication process
- A review and monitoring process
- Accountability processes and procedures

Without action planning, intended strategies are likely to remain dreams, not reality. The intentions will be overwhelmed by already-implemented and emergent strategies.

3. *Try for changes that can be easily and rapidly introduced.* Implementers may have little room for maneuvering when it comes to the basic design of the proposed changes and the accompanying implementation process. Nonetheless, they should take advantage of whatever discretion they have to improve the ease and speed with which changes are put into practice, while still maintaining the basic character of the changes. Implementation will flow more smoothly and speedily if the changes (Zaltman, Duncan, and Holbek 1973; Chase, 1979; Wolman, 1981; Mazmanian and Sabatier, 1983; Morris and Hough, 1986; Bryson and Crosby, 1992)

- Are conceptually clear.
- Are based on a well-understood theory of cause-effect relationships.
- Fit with the values of all key implementers.
- Can be demonstrated and made "real" to the bulk of the implementers prior to implementation. (In other words, people should have a chance to see what they are supposed to do before they have to do it.)
- Are relatively simple to grasp in practice, because the changes are not only conceptually clear but are also operationally clear.
- Are administratively simple, requiring minimal bureaucracy and red tape, minimal reorganization of resource allocation patterns, and minimal retraining of staff.
- Allow a period of start-up time in which people can learn about the adopted changes and engage in any necessary retraining, debugging, and development of new norms and operating routines.
- Include adequate attention to payoffs and rewards necessary to gain the wholehearted acceptance of implementers. In other words, have clear incentives favoring implementation by relevant organizations and individuals.

4. *Use a program-and-project management approach wherever possible.* Chunking the changes by breaking them down into clusters, or programs, consisting of specific projects is typically an important means of implementing strategic changes. Utilize standard program and project management techniques to assure the chunks actually add up to useful progress (Koteen, 1989).

5. *Build in enough people, time, attention, money, administrative and support services, and other resources to ensure successful implementation.* If possible, build in considerable redundancy in places important to implementation, so that if something goes wrong—which it no doubt will—there is adequate backup capacity. Almost any difficulty can be handled with enough resources—although these days, budgets are typically exceedingly tight unless money can be freed from other uses. Think about why cars have seat belts and spare tires, why jetliners have copilots, and why bridges are built to handle many times more weight than they are expected to carry: it is to ensure enough built-in capacity to handle almost any unexpected event. Tight resources are an additional reason to pay attention to the earlier steps in the Strategy Change Cycle. In order to garner sufficient resources, the issue must be sufficiently important, the adopted strategies must be likely to produce

desirable results at a reasonable cost, and the supportive coalition should be strong and stable. If these elements are present, the chances of finding or developing the necessary resources for implementation are considerably enhanced. Nonetheless, there may still be resistance from those who must supply the resources, and considerable effort may be needed to overcome that resistance. In almost every case, careful attention will need to be paid to budgeting cycles, processes, and strategies.

Implementation plans should include resources for

- Key personnel
- "Fixers"—people who know how things work and how to fix things when they go wrong (Bardach, 1977)
- Additional staff as needed
- Conversion costs
- Orientation and training costs
- Technical assistance
- Inside and outside consultants
- Adequate incentives to facilitate adoption of the changes by relevant organizations and individuals
- Formative evaluations to facilitate implementation and summative evaluations to determine whether or not the changes produced the desired results
- Unforeseen contingencies

6. *Link new strategic initiatives with ongoing operations in effective ways.* Establishing new units, programs, projects, products, or services with their own organizational structures and funding streams is a typical strategy in the public sector. That way, overt conflicts with ongoing operations can often be minimized. But in an era of resource constraints, new initiatives must often compete directly with, and be merged with, ongoing programs, products, services, and operations. Unfortunately, the implications of a strategic plan for an organization's ongoing operations may be very unclear, particularly in the public sector, where policy-making bodies may impose rather vague mandates on operating agencies. Somehow, new (and often vague) initiatives must be blended with ongoing operations in such a way that internal support is generated from those persons charged with maintaining the organization's ongoing activities. However, the people working in existing operations are likely to feel overworked and undervalued already, and therefore, they will want to know how the changes will help or hurt them. Typically, they must be involved directly in the process of fitting desired strategic changes into the operational details of the organization, both to garner useful information and support and to avoid sabotage.

One effective way to manage the process of blending new and old activities is to involve key decision makers, implementers, and perhaps representatives of external stakeholder groups in evaluating both sets of activities using a common set of criteria (Farnum Alston, personal communication, 1994). At least some of these criteria are likely to have been developed earlier as part of the strategic planning process; they may include client and organizational impacts, stakeholder expectations, resource use, and so on. Once the new and old activities have been so evaluated, it may be possible to figure out how to best fit the new with the old, what part of the new can be ignored, and what part of the old can be dropped. Again, recall that a *realized* strategy will consist of some combination of the strategic plan, ongoing initiatives, and unexpected occurrences that emerge along the way. Worksheets that may help with this process can be found in Bryson and Alston (1995).

7. *Work quickly, to avoid unnecessary or undesirable competition from new priorities.* The economy can always go bad, severely damaging financial support. Those who remember the recessions of the early 1980s and the early 1990s are well aware of this. In addition, tax revolts, tax indexing, and large state and federal deficits have greatly constricted public funds for new initiatives. For these and other reasons, it is wise to build in excess implementation resources, to provide slack. A poverty budget can turn out to be a death warrant. Cheapness should not be a selling point. Instead, program designers should sell cost-effectiveness—that is, the idea that the program delivers great benefits in relation to its costs.

A change in the policy board or administration is also likely to bring a change in funding priorities (Schein, 1992; Kingdon, 1995). New leaders have their own conception of which issues should be addressed and how. For example, the new superintendent of the school district was hired by the board because of his interest in making major changes in many areas. The strategic planning effort was one consequence of the board's hiring him and giving him a mandate to pursue changes.

Further, the anticipation of a new administration often paralyzes any change effort. People want to see what will happen before risking their careers by pushing changes that may not be desired by new leaders. So, once again, leaders and managers must move quickly to implement new strategies and plans before actual or impending change in the economy or the political scene undermines their efforts.

8. *Focus on maintaining or developing a coalition of implementers, advocates, and interest groups who are intent on implementing the changes and are willing to protect them over the long haul.* One of the clear lessons from the past two decades of implementation research is that successful implementation of programs in shared-power situations depends upon developing and maintaining a powerful coalition (Sabatier, 1988; Goggin, Bowman, Lester, and O'Toole, 1990). Coalitions are organized around ideas, interests, and payoffs, so leaders and managers must pay attention to "coaligning" these elements in such a way that strong coalitions are created and maintained (Kotter and Lawrence, 1974). Strong coalitions will result if the people involved see that their interests are served by the new arrangements.

9. *Be sure legislative, executive, and administrative policies and actions facilitate rather than impede implementation.* It is important to maintain a liaison with decision makers

in arenas such as state legislatures, governors' offices, and key administrators' offices if their decisions can affect the implementation effort. Leaders and managers must also pay attention to the development and use by implementers of the supplemental policies, regulations, rules, ordinances, articles, guidelines, and so on that are required for implementation to proceed. Operational details must be worked out, and many of these ancillary materials will need to pass through specific processes before they have the force of law. For example, before implementation regulations can become official at the federal level, they must be developed following the procedures outlined in the Administrative Procedures Act (Shapiro, 1982; Cooper, 1989). States have their own administrative procedures that must be followed. Localities and nonprofit organizations may have analogous routines that must be followed. Change advocates should seek expert advice on how these processes work and should attend to the ways in which supplemental policies are developed. Otherwise, the promise of the previous steps may be lost in practice.

10.   *Think carefully about how residual disputes will be resolved and underlying norms enforced.* This may mean establishing special procedures for settling disputes that arise. It may also mean relying on the courts. It is preferable to rely on "alternative dispute resolution methods" if possible, to keep conflicts out of court and to encourage all-gain solutions that increase the legitimacy and acceptance of the policy, strategy, or plan and the outcomes of conflict management efforts (Fisher and Ury, 1981; Susskind and Cruikshank, 1987; Gray, 1989). It is also important to remember that the court of public opinion is likely to be important in reinforcing the norms supporting the new changes.

11.   *Remember that major changes, and even many minor ones, entail changes in the organization's culture.* Changes in strategy almost inevitably prompt changes in basic assumptions about how to adapt to changes in the internal and external environments. Leaders, managers, and planners should facilitate necessary changes in cultural symbols and artifacts, espoused values, and underlying assumptions, recognizing that it is far easier to change the first two than it is to change the third. Indeed, heavy-handed attempts to change underlying assumptions are more likely to promote resistance and rejection than acceptance (Schein, 1992; Hampden-Turner, 1990; Bryson and Crosby, 1992, pp. 81–117).

12.   *Emphasize learning.* The world does not stop for planning nor once the planning is done. Situations change, and those interested in change must therefore constantly learn and adapt. Formative evaluations can facilitate necessary learning, but learning should also become a habit—part of the culture—if organizations are to remain vital and useful to their key stakeholders (Senge, 1990; Schein, 1992). Said differently, strategies are hardly ever implemented as intended. Adaptive learning is necessary to tailor intended strategies to emergent situations so that appropriate modifications are made and desirable outcomes are produced (Mintzberg, 1994a, 1994b).

13.   *Hang in there!* Successful implementation in complex multi-organizational shared-power settings typically requires large amounts of time, attention, resources,

and effort (Kanter, 1983, 1989; Kingdon, 1995). Also, implementers may need considerable courage to fight resisters. The rewards, however, can be great—namely, effective actions addressing important strategic issues that deeply affect the organization and its stakeholders.

Communication and Education

1. *Invest in communication.* This means paying attention to the design and use of communication networks, including the messages and messengers that compose them (Goggin, Bowman, Lester, and O'Toole, 1990). Particularly when large changes are involved, people must be given an opportunity to develop shared meanings and appreciations that will further the implementation of change goals (Trist, 1983; Sabatier, 1988). These meanings will both guide and flow out of implementation activities (Lynn, 1987). People must *hear* about the proposed changes, preferably many times and across multiple channels so that the messages will sink in. Further, people must be able to *talk* about the changes in order to understand them, fit them into their own interpretive schemes, adapt them to their own circumstances, and explore the implications (Trist, 1983; Johnson and Johnson, 1994). Educational programs, information packets, and guidebooks can help establish a desirable frame of reference and common language for addressing implementation issues. The school district, for example, has sponsored a number of workshops for teachers, administrators, and parents on the meaning of outcome-based education and site-based management, two concepts central to its strategic plan. The district also made it possible for interested stakeholders to attend educational programs on these subjects.

2. *Work to reduce resistance based on divergent attitudes and lack of participation.* Actions likely to reduce resistance among implementers include providing them with orientation sessions, training materials and sessions, problem-solving teams, one-to-one interactions, and technical assistance to support strategy implementation and to overcome obstacles to it. Ceremonies and symbolic rewards are also helpful in reinforcing desired behaviors.

3. *Consider developing a guiding vision of success if one has not been developed already.* Developing a vision of success is an exercise in "rhetorical leadership" (Doig and Hargrove, 1987). Chapter Eight discusses visions of success and offers guidance on how to develop one.

4. *Build in regular attention to appropriate indicators.* This will ensure attention to progress—or lack of progress—in addressing the issues that prompted the strategic planning effort. The CPI program, for example, has developed a list of indicators tied to each of its strategic goals. The school district also looks at key indicators such as student achievement, student enrollment, and financial management on a regular basis, while the public library attends to circulation, financial, and staff-related indicators. Mainstream Church pays particular attention to attendance, financial, and specific program–related indicators.

Personnel

1. *As much as possible, fill leadership and staff positions with highly qualified people committed to the change effort.* As noted, changes do not implement themselves—people make them happen. This is particularly true for major changes. When minor changes are required, systems and structures can often be substitutes for leadership (Kerr and Jermier, 1978; Manz, 1986). But when significant changes are involved, there are no substitutes for leadership, of many kinds. People—intelligent, creative, skilled, experienced, committed people—are necessary to create the new order, culture, systems, and structures that will focus and channel efforts toward effective implementation. In order to attract and retain such people, at least three things are necessary:

- People must be adequately compensated for their work. Fortunately, compensation does not always have to mean money. "Psychic income"—the rewards that come from "doing good" and being part of a new and important adventure—can count as well. Such income is traditionally extremely important in parts of the nonprofit world, and the fact that people are often willing to commit themselves to altruistic pursuits is one of that sector's distinguishing features (Salamon, 1992; Winer and Ray, 1994).
- People must see how their careers can be advanced by involvement in implementation efforts. The most intelligent and able people are likely to take a long view of their careers and will avoid what may be dead-end jobs. Instead, they are likely to choose jobs that can improve their skills, increase their responsibilities, and better their long-term job prospects (Dalton and Thompson, 1986).
- People want to have viable "escape routes" if things go bad or if they want to leave on their own. Many mechanisms can achieve this end—for example, an option of returning to prior jobs, outplacement services, or generous severance packages.

2. *Continue the planning team or establish a new implementation team with a significant membership overlap.* As indicated, successful implementation typically requires careful planning and management. In complex change situations, a team is likely to be necessary to help with this effort. Including some members who were involved in the effort to get strategies and plans adopted helps ensure that important learning from earlier steps is not lost during implementation.

3. *Keep in contact with top administrators during implementation.* This is easy when the change advocates themselves are or become the top administrators. But even if this is not the case, the implementation team may find that administrators are interested in maintaining regular contact with them.

4. *Give special attention to the problem of easing out, working around, or avoiding people who are not likely to help the change effort for whatever reason.* Standard practice in the public sector, of course, is to start a new agency rather than give implemen-

tation responsibilities to an existing agency whose mission, culture, personnel, and history are antagonistic to the intent of the changes. For example, President Lyndon Johnson insisted on a new Office of Economic Opportunity rather than turn over implementation responsibilities for many of his Great Society programs to established agencies such as the Departments of Labor or Health, Education, and Welfare. He remarked at one point, "The best way to kill a new idea is to put it in an old-line agency" (Anderson, 1990, p. 180). Or, as management theorist Frederick Herzberg often says, "It is easier to give birth than to resurrect." But even if a new organization is started, leaders and managers may still be stuck with personnel who are detrimental to implementation. There are several options for dealing with such people. First, help them get jobs for which they are better suited. This may take considerable time initially—establishing people's skills, ascertaining their goals, and writing favorable letters of recommendation—but the resulting increase in the remaining staff's morale and productivity is likely to be worth the effort. Second, award such people merit pay only if they actively implement policy goals. Third, place them in jobs where they cannot damage the change effort. Fourth, buy them off with early retirement or severance packages. And finally, if all else fails, work around them or ignore them.

Direct Versus Staged Implementation

There are two basic approaches to implementation, direct and staged. Direct implementation incorporates changes into all relevant sites essentially simultaneously, while staged implementation incorporates changes sequentially into groups of sites (Bryson and Delbecq, 1979).

1. *Consider direct implementation when the situation is technically and politically simple, immediate action is necessary for system survival in a crisis, or the adopted solutions entail some "lumpiness" that precludes staged implementation.* When situations are simple, direct implementation can work if enough resources are built in to cover costs and to provide sufficient incentives and if resistance to change is low. Therefore, leaders and managers must try to reduce any resistance to change based on divergent attitudes and lack of earlier participation. A crisis can simplify a situation politically in that people become more willing to defer to top leaders and accept centralized decision making (Bryson, 1981; Alterman, 1995). Thus, a crisis often makes direct implementation feasible. However, strategies adopted to address crises must still be technically workable, or they must at least be practical enough so that difficulties can be worked out without weakening people's support for change. Unfortunately, few organizations have a crisis management system in place that is effective enough to respond adequately (Mitroff and Pearson, 1993). Finally, lumpy solutions may demand direct implementation. For example, new buildings, information technology systems, and products or services must often be created all at once rather than piecemeal.

2. *In difficult situations, consider staged implementation.* Staged implementation

presumes that implementation will occur in "waves," in which initial adopters will be followed by later adopters, and finally, even most of the laggards will adopt the changes. The result is the familiar S-shaped curve associated with the adoption of most innovations over time. Early on, there are few adopters, so the area under the curve is small. As time progresses, more and more adoptions occur; the area under the curve grows geometrically, and it begins to assume the S shape. Later, fewer and fewer adoptions occur, partly because there are fewer people, units, or organizations left to adopt the changes and partly because of deep-seated resistance on the part of the laggards. The curve levels off as the top of the S is completed (Rogers, 1982).

The exact nature of the staged process will depend on the difficulties faced. When facing technical difficulties, consider beginning with a pilot project designed to discover or prove cause-effect relationships between particular solutions and particular effects. The more technically difficult the situation is, the more necessary it is to have a pilot project to figure out what techniques do and do not work. Once the technical difficulties are resolved, transfer of the implementation process to the remaining potential implementers can be pursued. For example, pilot tests of new U.S. agricultural products and services occur regularly at agriculture experiment stations that involve universities, the U.S. Department of Agriculture, and often businesses in cooperative partnerships. As another example, the CPI program pilot-tests various computer hardware and software designs and various sampling and measurement procedures before settling on its preferred approach.

When facing political difficulties, consider beginning staged implementation with demonstration projects to make it clear that the proposed solutions can work in the settings the implementers face. Once the applicability of the changes is demonstrated, transfer to remaining implementers can be pursued. Demonstration projects are most likely to work when existing or potential opposition is not well organized; changes can then be put in place before an effective opposition can materialize. When there is organized opposition to the proposed changes, demonstration projects may work as a way of convincing at least some opponents of the merits of the changes and thereby dividing the opposition. When there is a well-organized *and* implacable opposition, direct and massive implementation efforts may be warranted to expand the front and overwhelm opponents, rather than giving them a limited number of smaller targets to oppose (Bryson and Delbecq, 1979). While that may be the best approach, the chances of success in such situations still are not great, given the likely strength of the opponents (Bryson and Bromiley, 1993).

When facing both technical and political difficulties, consider beginning with a pilot project, to be followed by demonstration projects and then transfer to the rest of the implementers. In general, the more difficult the situation, the more important it is to promote education and learning, offer incentives for desired changes, and develop a shared sense of commitment to successful implementation and long-term protection of the changes.

3. *Design pilot projects to be effective.* Consider doing the following:

- Test the scientific validity of the proposed changes, probably by using experimental or quasi-experimental designs. In other words, test whether the proposed changes actually produce the desired effects. The classic source of advice for such testing is Campbell and Stanley (1966).
- Perform the test in a safe and controlled environment that has access to a rich set of resources. The ideal test for causation matches a control group against an experimental group that differs from the control group *only* in that it will experience the policy change, or "treatment," being tested. Only with such controlled trials can plausible rival hypotheses be ruled out.
- Test several possible changes and search for their different strengths and weaknesses.
- Use skilled technical specialists to evaluate cause-effect relationships. If the specialists' credibility is a concern, consider using outside experts, or an inside-outside team whose objectivity will not be questioned.
- Design tests that are concerned with the effectiveness of the changes, not their efficiency. In other words, tests should measure whether the changes produce the desired effects or not, not whether they do so cheaply. Attention should be on both outputs and outcomes.

4. *Design demonstration projects to be effective.* Follow these procedures:

- Test for the applicability of proposed changes to typical implementer settings, probably through the use of quasi-experimental designs. True experiments are rarely possible in the field, but it is still important to have some sort of control group, if possible, in order to determine what works under what circumstances and why. Quasi-experimental designs can make it possible for such learning to occur.
- Test in easy, average, and difficult implementation settings in order to gauge the robustness of the changes and the possibilities for handling a range of implementation difficulties.
- Test several possible changes in order to determine their comparative strengths and weaknesses.
- Use a two-cycle process, in which implementers learn how to work with the changes in the first cycle and the effects of the changes are monitored in the second cycle.
- Include a qualitative evaluation (Patton, 1990), along with quantitative studies, to show different solution strengths and weaknesses. Pay attention to outcomes as well as outputs.
- Remember that what is being tested in the demonstration stage is a process that is already known to work in a technical sense; that is, it can produce the desired effects.
- Assemble a special monitoring team, if necessary, to carry out the monitoring task.
- Provide opportunities for future implementers to witness the demonstrations.

- Develop a media strategy to communicate the desirability of the changes and the best way they might be implemented.

5. *Carefully transfer tested changes to other implementers.* Follow these steps:

- Commit substantial resources to communication tactics, including cycling in observers likely to influence subsequent implementer adoptions and to facilitate word-of-mouth information exchanges.
- Promote the visibility of the demonstration projects.
- Produce, emphasize, and disseminate educational materials and operational guides designed to make adoption and implementation easier.
- Develop credible and easily understood models that show clearly how the desired changes work and how they can be implemented.
- Provide additional resources for technical assistance and problem solving.
- Provide incentives for adopting the changes.
- Be flexible.

6. *Finally, when the implementation process is staged, give special attention to those who will implement changes in the early stages.* In the early stages, when the practical nature of the changes still needs to be worked out, it is important to attract people with enough experience, skill, and desire to make the changes work. People who are likely to do so will have firsthand experience with the issue and the need for an adequate response; above-average ability; and experience with prior major change efforts. Further, later adopters will be watching to see whether or not they wish to embrace the changes or resist them. Therefore, early implementers should be valued and persuasive role models. They are more likely to be effective salespersons for change if they do not mindlessly charge after every new whim and fad that comes over the horizon. Instead, they should be seen as courageous, wise, able, and committed to addressing the issue in a reasonable way. Further, they should be able to describe their experience to effectively educate the next wave of adopters.

Summary

Desired changes are not completed by the adoption of strategies and plans. Without effective implementation, important issues will not be adequately addressed. Implementation therefore should be viewed as a continuation of the Strategy Change Cycle toward its ultimate goal of addressing the issues that prompted change in the first place.

Implementation must be consciously, deliberately, and strategically planned, managed, and budgeted. Further, if major changes are involved, successful implementation typically requires creating a new "regime" to govern decisions and behavior. Elements of the new regime will include new or redesigned settings; implicit or explicit principles, norms, rules, and decision-making procedures; supportive budgets, including both substantive and symbolic incentives promoting the new arrangements; altered patterns of behavior and attitudes; and a supportive coalition composed of implementers, advocates, and interest groups. The new regime may incorporate a widely shared vision of success.

Successful implementation introduces desired changes quickly and smoothly and overcomes the typical causes of implementation failure. It may involve either direct or staged implementation. Direct implementation works best when the time is right, the need is clear to a strong coalition of supporters and implementers, there is a clear connection between critical issues and adopted strategies, the solution technology is clearly understood, adequate resources are available, and there is a clear vision to guide the changes. (These are also the conditions that favor big-win strategies.) Staged implementation is advisable when policy makers, leaders, and managers are faced with technical or political difficulties. It often involves pilot projects, to determine or prove the cause-effect relationship between particular solutions and desired effects, and/or demonstration projects, to show the applicability of adopted solutions to typical implementer settings and to diffuse knowledge to later waves of adopters. Staged implementation involves organizing a series of small wins.

Learning is a major theme underlying successful implementation efforts. It is not possible or desirable to plan everything in advance. People must be given the opportunity to learn new procedures and adapt them to actual situations. More effective implementation is likely to result, and the next round of strategizing is likely to be better informed.

CHAPTER TEN

REASSESSING AND REVISING STRATEGIES AND PLANS

What's past is prologue.

WILLIAM SHAKESPEARE

The Strategy Change Cycle is not over once strategies and plans have been implemented. Ongoing strategic management must ensue to take account of likely changes in circumstances—in part in order to keep desirable strategies vital and in part as a prelude to the next round of strategic planning. Times change, situations change, and coalitions change. Strategies that work must be maintained and protected through vigilance, adaptability, and updated plans. Thus, ironically, changes of some sort are probably in order if you want things to remain the same. But not all strategies continue to work as well as they should. These strategies must be bolstered with additional resources, significantly modified, or terminated. In either case, "What's past is prologue."

Strategies cease to work for four main reasons. First, a basic strategy may be good but may have insufficient resources devoted to its implementation, and therefore insufficient progress is made toward resolving the issue it was meant to resolve. For example, the school district's strategic plan addressed the need to raise enough funds through one or more school bond referenda to enhance existing facilities and build new ones. The first referendum failed in the fall of 1993; the second failed in the spring of 1994. Finally, the third attempt was successful in the summer of 1994. Meanwhile, parts of the strategy were starved for resources, and the facilities segment of the strategic plan had to be revised several times to cope with various exigencies.

Second, problems change, typically prompting a need for new strategies, on the one hand, and making what was once a solution itself a problem, on the other hand. For example, the CPI program's computer systems were a clear advance when they were first installed, but now the systems are getting old, and the main supplier has gone bankrupt. Something will need to be done to upgrade the existing technology and avoid the threat of serious breakdowns.

Third, as substantive problem areas become crowded with various policies and strategies, their interactions can produce results that no one wants and many wish to change. And fourth, the political environment may shift. As strategies become institutionalized, people's attention may shift elsewhere. Or supportive leaders and managers may be replaced by people who are uninterested or even hostile to the strategy, and they may change elements of it or appoint other people who undermine it. Or people may reinterpret history—"play tricks on the dead," to use historian Charles Beard's phrase—ignoring the facts to support their own positions. For example, in the national health care reform efforts of the early years of the Clinton administration, any proposals to develop a national health service for the United States were labeled "socialized medicine"—like the British system, for example—and we all "know" socialism "doesn't work." Meanwhile, the British allocate only 6 percent of their GDP for health care and cover everyone, while the United States allocates over 12 percent of its GDP to health care and leaves out almost forty million people. Furthermore, population-level outcome statistics for both countries are fairly similar and, in many cases, better in Britain than in the United States. My own conclusion, based on having used the British system as a patient and on having been a management consultant to it for almost a decade, is that we should be cautious about letting ideologically loaded labels get in the way of the facts. For any of these four reasons, therefore, policy and strategy can become their own cause—the proximate reason for the initiation of a new round of strategy change (Wildavsky, 1979).

Desired Outcomes and Benefits

The purpose of this phase of the Strategy Change Cycle is to review implemented policies, strategies, plans, programs, and projects and to decide on a future course of action. Desired outcomes include maintenance of good strategies, modifications of less successful ones through appropriate reforms or plan revisions; and elimination of undesirable strategies. A further desired outcome is the mobilization of energy and enthusiasm to address the next important strategic issue that comes along.

Several benefits flow from successful action in this phase. First is the assurance that institutionalized capabilities remain responsive to important substantive and symbolic issues. Organizations often become stuck in permanent patterns of response to "old" issues. When the issues change, the institutions often do not, and therefore they become a problem themselves (Wilson, 1989; Schön, 1971). A sort of goal displacement occurs, in which the institutions cease to be a means to an end and instead become an end in themselves (Merton, 1940; Schön, 1971). Ensuring that organizations remain responsive to real issues and problems takes effort. Periodic studies, reports, conferences, hearings, fact-finding missions, and on-site observations and discussions with stakeholders are necessary to stay in touch with the "real world" (Mintzberg, 1973, 1994b).

A second important benefit is the resolution of residual issues that occurs during sustained implementation. Even if implemented strategies remain generally responsive to the issues that originally prompted them, inevitably there will be a host of specific difficulties that must be addressed if the strategies are to be really effective. Attention and appropriate action over the long haul are necessary to ensure that strategies in practice remain as good as they were in concept.

A third substantial benefit is the development of the energy, will, and ideas for significant reform of existing strategies. Minor difficulties can be addressed through existing administrative mechanisms such as regular staff meetings, "management by exception" routines, administrative law courts, periodic strategy review and modification exercises, and routine access channels to key decision makers for advocates and advocacy groups. Major change, however, will not occur without development of a substantial coalition in favor of it. And such a coalition will not develop unless there are real issues to be addressed and the energy, will, and ideas for doing so can be harnessed. This is the step, therefore, in which the beginnings of such a coalition are likely to emerge; in other words, this "end" to the Strategy Change Cycle is often the "beginning" of the next Strategy Change Cycle.

Finally, this step should result in the continuous weeding, pruning, and shaping of crowded strategy areas. While there may be an appropriate "micrologic" to individual strategy elements, elements piled upon elements often creates a kind of unintended and unwanted "macrononsense" (see also Peters and Waterman, 1982; Wildavsky, 1979). Complaints about excessive bureaucracy and red tape often have their source in the foolishness that results from the interaction of rules that make sense individually but not collectively (Barzelay, 1992). Public and nonprofit leaders and managers must discover how to talk about the "system-as-a-whole" in order to figure out what should stay, what should be dropped, and what should be added (Schön, 1971; Cleveland, 1985; Senge, 1990).

Two Brief Examples

The public library and Mainline Church provide brief examples of how things can change over time. The library's 1989–91 strategic plan focused attention on its most important strategic issues and outlined actions to address them. The issues were:

- Mission
- Workload
- Funding

The plan also focused attention on a less important set of issues, referred to as "ongoing strategic issues":

- Automation issues
- Central library issues
- Branch library issues
- Staff issues
- "Other" issues

The library's 1991–93 strategic plan identified a somewhat different set of issues:

- Given the library's sense of its mission and role in the community (addressed as part of the previous cycle's mission analysis), identify and define the services the library will offer.
- Improve library facilities.
- Increase library funding.
- Increase the efficiency of library operations.

The first issue, services, takes the earlier mission question further, asking what services the library should offer in the new time frame (in which staff are short-handed and feeling very overworked). Facilities and finance issues are part of both plans, but the specific issues addressed and the actions outlined are different. Finally, the efficiency issue is similar in some ways to the workload and automation issues of the previous plan, but mostly it is different, emphasizing utilization of new information technologies and collaboration with other libraries and organizations in the region. The two plans thus identify a changing agenda of strategic issues, in which some topics remain constant, but the specifics addressed beneath them change as the situation changes.

The library has engaged in a further round of strategic planning, with a new strategic plan completed near the end of 1994. Many of the issue headings were the same, but again, the specifics differed as the library tried to respond to its mandates, sense of mission, and the changing environment.

Mainline Church's 1990–94 "long-range plan" was organized around vision statements on each of the following topics: worship, nurture (including Christian education), outreach, ministry of caring, evangelism, stewardship, the environment, and communications. Specific goals and actions were included for each vision area. Most of the actions were accomplished well before the end of the planning period.

The process clearly was successful in the sense that a number of specific actions were taken that were informed by the church's mission statement and organized around a general sense of direction—a vision—in each area. The process was less successful in that the vision statements did not result in focusing attention on some of the key issues the church faced in such areas as membership, fundraising, and setting priorities for programs. In the past, the church had always been wealthy enough to do almost whatever its members wanted. But that no longer was the case; now the church either had to raise more money, get better at setting priorities, or both.

The main champion behind the effort (who as an elder of the church was also a sponsor) wanted to push ahead and have the church address these issues. In addition, he thought the church should think carefully about how its next five-year plan should be prepared. Finally, he wanted the church to think about how it wanted to look in the year 2000, as a prelude to hiring a successor to its senior pastor. The retirement of this popular, inspiring, and effective leader was bound to be a moment of historic importance for the church (not least because—following national patterns—most of the rest of the clergy could be expected to move elsewhere within a year of the successor's appointment). Clearly, some advance strategic thinking by the church's formal decision makers and informal opinion leaders was necessary to help them find the right successor.

The champion convinced the church to begin a new process, called "Vision for 2000," to study the 1990–94 plan, look at a 1991 membership study, examine a number of national trends affecting churches, and then identify a set of strategic issues to be addressed. A Vision 2000 planning team was organized. Team members focused on six strategic issues and how to address them: membership, stewardship, program priorities, facilities, capital funds, and leadership development. The plan they prepared was formally adopted by the church's main governing board in May 1992, shortly before the senior pastor retired.

Many of the vision themes from the old plan are clearly echoed in the new plan, but the vision statements in the new plan are organized around the strategic issues noted above. Strategies are then articulated to achieve the vision. In other words, something of a reversal in the approach to the planning process occurred. In the previous plan, strategic issue identification occurred implicitly, via the framing of a vision. As a result, some important issues were ignored or glossed over, but they did not go away. In the new plan, issues were identified first, then vision statements were developed to guide strategy development. The new plan therefore contributes some needed attention to fundamental concerns that were not addressed directly in the previous plan.

Mainline Church's experience is a good example of how organizations learn as they go. The first plan reaffirmed the church's mission (with some minor revisions), resulted in important actions, built an expectation that there would be effective planning, established a number of useful relationships among key individuals and decision-making bodies, and led to the realization that some key issues had not been addressed adequately. The second plan identified these issues clearly and identified strategies likely to address them effectively. It also made the transition to having a new senior pastor easier in three ways:

- It made issuing a "call" for a new pastor easier because the church had a clearer idea of what it wanted to be.
- It provided guidance for the interim pastor (required as a result of the national church policy that says a call for a new pastor cannot go out until the previous pastor has retired).
- It provided direction for the new pastor, hired at the end of 1993. It provided a sense of continuity with the past along with a sense of vision for the future.

Strategic Planning Systems

Strategic planning systems are organizational mechanisms or arrangements for strategically managing the implementation of agreed-upon strategies. These systems, in other words, are themselves a kind of organizational (or interorganizational) strategy for implementing policies and plans. The systems also typically embody procedures and occasions for routinely reassessing those strategies. There appear to be five main types of systems, although any strategic planning system in practice will probably be a hybrid of the five types. These "types" therefore refer to dominant tendencies:

- Layered or stacked units of management model
- Strategic issues management model
- Contract model
- Portfolio management model
- Goal or benchmark model

Before describing each approach, I must express the ambivalence I feel about attempts to institutionalize strategic planning and management. While it often is important to create and maintain a strategic planning system, it also is important to guard against the tendency such systems have of driving out wise strategic thought and action—precisely those features that strategic planning (at its best) promotes. In practice, the systems often become excessively formal and bureaucratic, calendar-driven (as opposed to issue-driven), numbers oriented, captured by inappropriate forecasts, and conservative. The reader is therefore advised to recall my admonition in Chapter Two: whenever any strategic planning system (or strategic planning process) threatens to drive out wise strategic thought and action, you should scrap the system (or process) and get back to promoting effective strategic thought and action.

It is also important to realize that each system embodies a set of arrangements that empowers particular actors and makes particular kinds of issues more likely to be addressed and particular strategies more likely to be pushed.

Layered or Stacked Units of Management Model

The purpose of this approach is to link inside and outside environments in effective ways through development and implementation of an integrated set of strategies across levels and functions. Figure 2.2 outlines a possible two-cycle layered or stacked strategic planning system. It represents the classic private-sector corporate-style "top-down, bottom-up" strategic planning process. In the first cycle, there is a bottom-up development of strategic plans within a framework of goals, objectives, and other guidance established at the top; this is followed by reviews and reconciliations at each succeeding level. In the second cycle, operating plans are developed to implement the strategic plans. In each cycle, efforts are made to relate levels, functions, and inside and outside environments in effective ways. The process is repeated each year, within the general framework established by the organization's grand or umbrella strategies. Every three to five years, these overarching strategies are reviewed and modified based on experience, changing conditions, and the emergence of new strategies that were not necessarily planned in advance.

Many companies, such as 3M (Tita and Allio, 1984), have developed such a system and are able to produce sometimes stunning results in terms of sales, profits, and growth. Public and nonprofit organizations also have used variants of this approach to their advantage (Boschken, 1988a; Bryson, King, Roering, and Van de Ven, 1986). Nevertheless, it is precisely this sort of system that is most prone to drive out strategic thought and action when it is underpinned by a belief that the future can actually be predicted accurately—a belief detached from the messiness of operational reality (Frederickson, 1984; Frederickson and Mitchell, 1984; Roberts, 1993; Mintzberg, 1994b; Roberts and Wargo, 1994). Such systems are very likely to be blindsided by unpredictable events, with the result that existing strategies and plans become ineffective. The systems therefore must be used with extreme caution, since they can take on a life of their own, promote incremental change when major change might be needed, and serve only the interests of the planners who staff them and the leaders and managers who wish to resist—not promote—major change.

Strategic Issues Management Model

Strategic issues management systems are the most common form of institutionalized strategic planning and management in public and nonprofit organizations. These systems do not attempt to integrate strategies across levels and functions to the same extent as layered or stacked units of management approaches. The reason is that the issues are likely to be on different time frames, to involve different constituencies and politics, and to not need to be considered in the light of all other issues.

Strategic issues management systems, including Hennepin County's approach, were discussed briefly in Chapter Two (Eckhert, Haines, Delmont, and Pflaum, 1988, 1992, 1993). In the Hennepin County system (see Figure 10.1), strategic guidance is issued at the top, and units further down are asked to identify issues they think are strategic. Leaders and managers at the top then select which issues they wish to have addressed, perhaps reframing the issues before passing them on to units or task forces. Task forces then present strategic alternatives to leaders and managers, who select which ones to pursue. Strategies are then implemented in the next phase. Each issue is managed relatively separately, although it is necessary to make sure that choices in one issue area do not cause trouble in other issue areas.

While many public and nonprofit organizations have several task forces in operation at any one time, fewer go the next step, which is to design and use a strategic issues management system. They do not establish an overall framework of organizational goals or policy objectives; nor do they seek out issues to address or make sure that their various issues-management activities add up to increased organizational effectiveness. To make this model work, organizational leaders and managers should consider taking this next step, keeping in mind that the resulting centralization of certain key decisions at the top is likely to draw the attention and resistance of those who do not want to see power concentrated in that way or who dislike the resulting decisions.

Contract Model

The contract model is becoming an increasingly popular approach to institutionalizing strategic planning and management (see Figure 10.2). It is the basic model for organizing the National Health Service in the United Kingdom, where area boards assess health needs for their geographical area and then contract with health care units they directly control as well as independent health care trusts (similar to public nonprofit corporations in the United States), group medical practices, and various nonprofit and voluntary organizations for delivery of desired services. The contracting organizations may be inside or outside the area (Pettigrew, Ferlie, and McKee, 1992). The contract model is also employed for much of the planning and delivery of many publicly financed social services in the United States, via either public or nonprofit service providers (Milward, Provan, and Else 1993). The model is also used to institutionalize strategic planning and management in school districts utilizing site-based management.

In this model, there is a "center" that establishes strategic objectives for the jurisdiction or organization as a whole, negotiates contracts with individual units of management, monitors performance, and ensures the integrity of the system. The contract between the center and a unit outlines the unit's expected performance, defines its resources, lists other support the unit can expect from the center, and describes a review and renegotiation sequence. Within the framework and legal strictures of the contract, general managers of individual units and their

FIGURE 10.1 STRATEGIC ISSUES MANAGEMENT MODEL, HENNEPIN COUNTY.

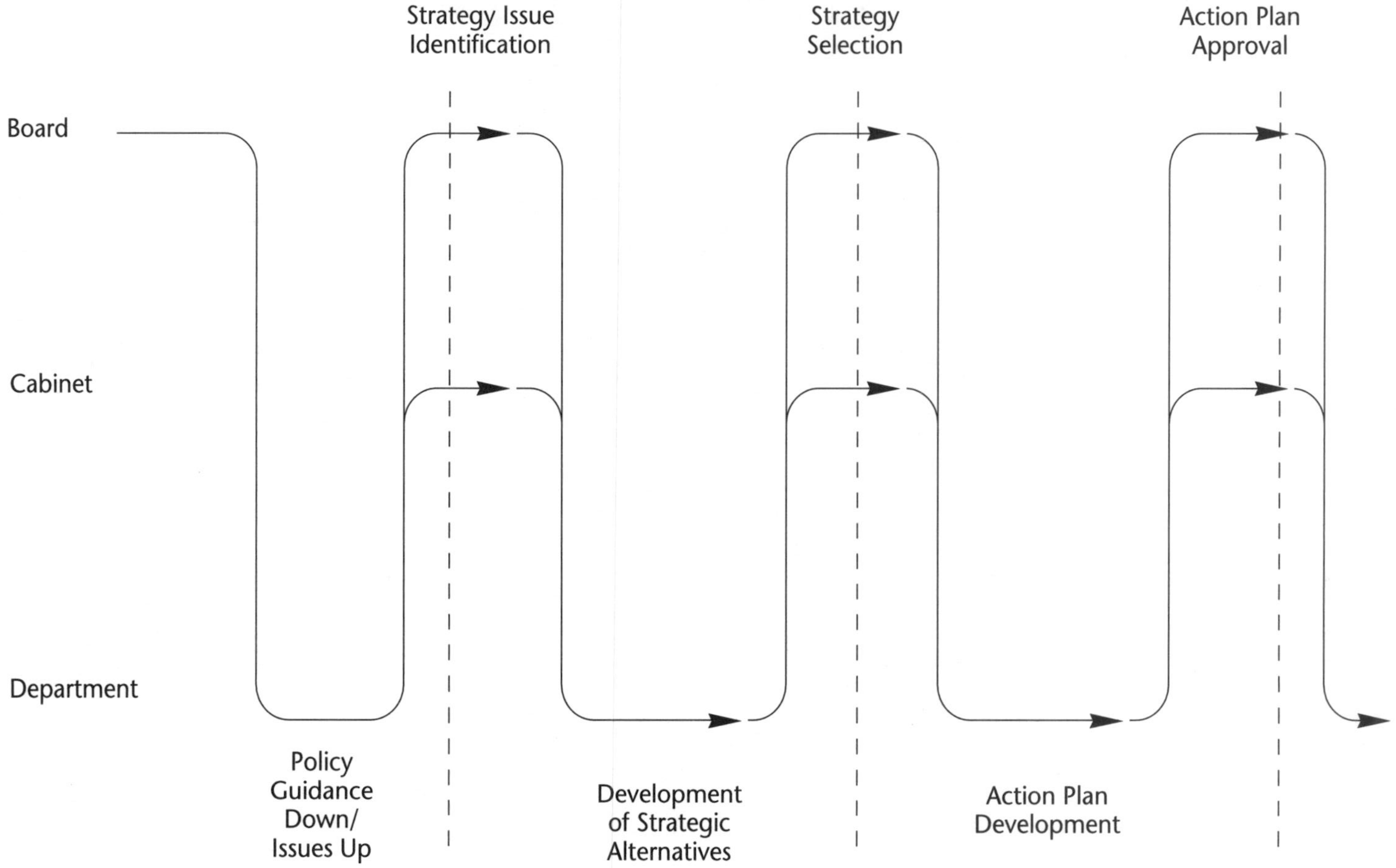

FIGURE 10.2. PURCHASER-PROVIDER CONTRACT MODEL.

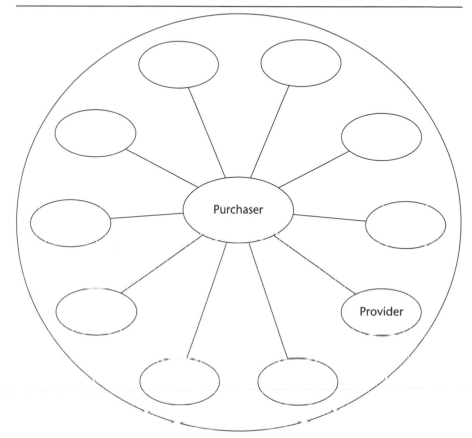

staffs are free to do whatever they think is necessary or desirable to ensure adequate performance. This approach allows both the center and the individual units to focus on what is important for them—both are empowered to do their jobs better. In such a system, there would be a strategic plan for the center and one for each of the units. Key system concerns would include the content and approach embodied in the center's plan, the center's difficulties in acquiring adequate information, and the difficulties the center might have in exercising control in the face of a large number of contractors.

Portfolio Management Model

In this approach, entities of various sorts (programs, projects, products, services, or providers) are arrayed along dimensions of strategic importance. The dimensions usually describe the attractiveness or desirability of the entity (from high to low) and the capability of the organization or community to deliver what is needed.

Figure 10.3 shows one of the portfolio models used to develop the three-year market strategy for the Royal Hospitals Trust in Belfast, Northern Ireland. The Royal is a self-governing trust that is part of the National Health Service system and must compete for the business it receives. The portfolio outlines the Royal's services in terms of desired market share for the three years beginning in 1993 in the Belfast (Eastern Health and Social Services Board, EHSSB) region. The Royal has or seeks a monopoly or near-monopoly in some services, such as neurosurgery and neurology (upper right quadrant of the matrix). It faces much more competition for the delivery of other services (the lower left corner). The Royal therefore has to have different strategies to manage the competitive services than it does for the services in which is has a stronger market position.

As this example shows, portfolio methods are quite flexible in that dimensions of interest may be arrayed against one another and the entities mapped onto the resulting matrix. Portfolio methods can also be used at the suborganizational and supraorganizational levels to assess options against strategically important factors (Sorkin, Ferris, and Hudak, 1984; Bryson, Freeman, and Roering, 1986; Bryson and Roering, 1987; Nutt and Backoff, 1992). Unfortunately, few public and nonprofit organizations or communities utilize portfolio models in a formal way, even though many probably use portfolio methods in an informal way. The problem, of course, with using the models in a formal way is that they create comparisons that may be troubling for politically powerful actors.

Goal or Benchmark Model

In general, this approach is also much looser than the layered or stacked units of management model. Goal or benchmark models are generally applied at the community, regional, or state levels. They are designed to gain reasonable agreement on overarching goals or indicators (benchmarks) toward which relatively independent groups, units, or organizations might then direct their energies. Consensual agreement on goals and indicators thus provides a weak surrogate for the corporate control exercised in layered models. Nonetheless, when agreement can be reached and support for implementation generated, the models can work reasonably well. Besides, in the fragmented, shared-power environments in which most public problems occur, the approach may be the only viable approach. For example, most community strategic plans are implemented via goal or benchmark models. Large numbers of leaders and citizens are typically involved in the process of goal-setting and strategy development. Then action plans outline what each organization might do to help implement the strategies and achieve the goals on a voluntary basis.

The Oregon Benchmarks Program and the Minnesota Milestones Program are state-level examples (National Governors Association, 1993; Oregon Progress Board, 1994). In the Oregon program, a statewide inclusive effort was undertaken to develop a set of goals and indicators that most Oregonians would support. State

FIGURE 10.3. PORTFOLIO MODEL, ROYAL HOSPITALS TRUST.

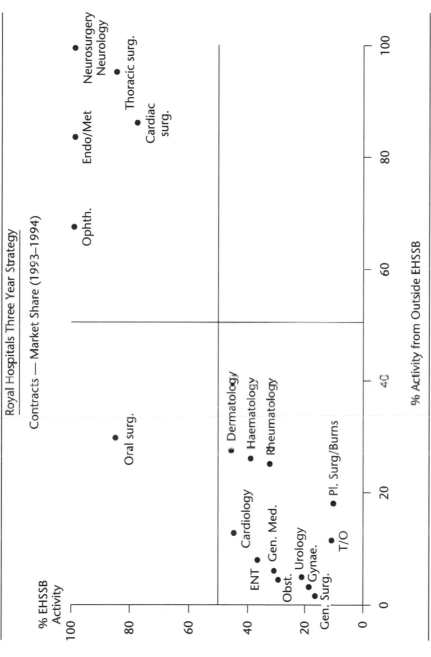

Royal Hospitals Three Year Strategy

Contracts — Market Share (1993–1994)

Reprinted with the permission of the Royal Hospitals.

agencies are expected by the governor and legislature to gear their plans and budget requests against the indicators. This feature is the "tightest" part of the system. Cities, counties, communities, and others throughout the state are also encouraged to do their part. The success of the system depends on broad-based, bipartisan political support. The Minnesota program is similar, but it has less support in the legislature and outside the state government.

While there are five general types of strategic planning systems, any actual system is likely to be a hybrid of all five types. For example, in the school district some issues, such as overall staffing and finance, are handled in a layered or stacked way. Others, such as how to manage various types of curriculum reform, are handled on an issue-by-issue basis. Site-based management of individual schools fits the contract model—there is a contract between the district office and individual schools that outlines performance expectations; resource allocations; basic rules, regulations, and procedures; and a review schedule. Within the envelope provided by the contract, individual schools have considerable freedom to manage their own affairs. Community education staff utilize an informal portfolio approach to assess what their program offerings should be, based on their desirability and the ability of the district to deliver. And finally, the school board establishes an overall set of goals toward which everyone is expected to contribute.

Process Guidelines

The following guidelines should be kept in mind as leaders and managers review implemented strategies and ponder what to do about them. General guidelines are presented first, and then specific suggestions are offered for strategy maintenance, succession, and termination (for additional details, see Hogwood and Peters, 1983).

General Guidelines

1.   *Stay focused on what is important.* Pay attention to the organization's mission and mandates and the social needs and political problems that justify its existence. Pay attention to the fundamental challenges—strategic issues—that the organization faces as it tries to meet its mandate and pursue its mission. Never let the organization and its strategies or plans become ends in themselves. Instead, leaders and managers should focus on key stakeholders and their own ideals and how best to serve them.

2.   *Focus on signs or indicators of success and failure.* Attention should be paid to changes in the signs or indicators that were used to argue for strategy changes in the first place, to new indicators that are important to key stakeholders and that shed light on implementation effectiveness, and to results of any summative evaluations. To the extent that any or all of these indicators provide valid signs of

strategic progress or failure, they can provide support for deciding to maintain, reform, or terminate a strategy or plan.

3. *Review the issue framings used to guide strategy formulation in the first place.* Are they still accurate and useful interpretations of reality? Have they led to constructive issue strategies and plans, or have they suggested new strategies and plans? Or has something changed about the reality—political, economic, social, technological, internal, external, or otherwise—that has turned these issue framings into distortions that suggest unhelpful strategies and plans?

4. *Use existing review opportunities or create new ones.* Periodic policy-reauthorization sessions, strategic issue identification exercises, and annual budget review periods provide regular review opportunities. Election campaigns and changes in top political or executive leadership provide predictable occasions for strategy reviews in public organizations. Similarly, board turnover or new executive appointments in nonprofit organizations provide occasions for review. (For example, the impending retirement of Mainline Church's senior pastor in part prompted the "Vision for 2000" exercise discussed above.)

However, leaders and managers can create strategy review opportunities almost anytime they wish. Conferences, hearings, study sessions or commissions, media events, investigative reporting, discussion groups, and so on can be arranged whenever leaders and managers wish to promote discussion and critique strategies.

5. *Create a review group.* The composition of this review group may vary considerably, depending on the nature of the review. Legislation and policies requiring scheduled reviews may specify a particular group—for example, a legislative committee, city council, or nonprofit board of directors. Often, however, flexibility is possible in choosing participants, and it is often wise to include outsiders who do not have a vested interest in the status quo. They can be counted on to focus on important issues and offer constructive suggestions for change.

6. *Challenge institutional and organizational rules that favor undesirable inertia.* Institutions have an uncanny ability to take on a life of their own, making constructive change extremely difficult (Kouzes and Posner, 1987; Wilson, 1989; Osborne and Gaebler, 1992; Barzelay, 1992). There are many political routines that challenge anything new, but rarely subject what is already in place to a searching critique (Sharkansky, 1970). These routines and other rules—embedded in the design and use of existing forums, arenas, and courts—often make present arrangements the taken-for-granted "way things are." They can make a different future unlikely. If the future is what we want it to be, these rules must be confronted and set aside when the need arises (Mangham, 1986). For example, the decision of the school district's board and superintendent to engage in strategic planning was a signal to key stakeholders and the community that many of the existing rules and routines would be examined and innovative strategies explored.

7. *Remember that organizations usually have greater staying power than their strategies (Hogwood and Peters, 1983).* Typically, therefore, it is easier to change the strategies than the organizations. And typically, it is more productive to call into question or

attack the strategies than the organizations. In other words, it is likely to be more effective to praise the intentions and goodwill of an organization while attacking its strategies than to attack its motives and goodwill directly. Further, from a strategic standpoint, it is often wise to figure out whether problems can be solved with existing organizational or network strategies, since strategies may be created or changed more easily than organizations and networks. Moreover, it is wise to figure out how existing organizations and their adherents might benefit from possible changes in strategy so that allies can be created rather than opponents (Neustadt and May, 1986). Sometimes, this simply means organizing support for new units or programs within existing organizations. But given the distressing inertia of many organizations—particularly public ones—change advocates may ultimately conclude that new organizations and networks are required to solve important issues. Community planning efforts, for example, often involve developing at least partially new networks to frame and address key issues (Kemp, 1993).

8. *Finally, stay fresh—keep from going stale!* Build energy and enthusiasm for continuing good strategies and addressing new strategic issues. Issues will not be formulated and addressed effectively unless leaders and managers take responsibility for doing so. To paraphrase Edmund Burke, all that is necessary for the powers of evil to triumph is for good people to do nothing.

Strategy Maintenance

1. *To maintain existing strategies, seek little change in current organizational (interorganizational or community) arrangements.* Any significant change is likely to undermine the regime established in the previous phase. It is important, however, to find occasions to recall the mission or vision that originally inspired people to seek new strategies or validated the results of previous strategy formulation efforts.

2. *To maintain or marginally modify existing strategies, rely on implementers and focused input from consumers and involve supportive advocates.* Broader involvement of elites and the public is likely to raise issues and conflicts that may require more fundamental policy changes (Hogwood and Peters, 1983). The public library, for example, employed an extensive patron survey and several focus groups to evaluate its existing services and to identify possible new services. The Friends of the Public Library and one other nonprofit organization were kept fully informed. Both of these groups contained a number of community notables but no one likely to propose radical and damaging changes. The mayor and council were also kept informed, but they were also unlikely to propose damaging changes, given the broad support the library has in the community.

Strategy Change or Succession

1. *To facilitate a move to new strategies, significantly alter existing arrangements.* A new set of issues, decisions, conflicts, and policy preferences are then likely to emerge. For

example, opponents of the school district's strategic planning process campaigned successfully to unseat the board president in the 1992 election. He had been a strong advocate of capping the teachers' benefit plan as a way of freeing resources for new strategic initiatives. There was concern on the part of the remaining board members and the superintendent that the two new board members—both of whom had teacher support—would seek to scuttle the process. Fortunately, both turned out to be supporters of the process and were part of the unanimous vote in favor of the plan. The critics outside the board, however, did not give up. As the questions of relocating the old high school and financing new facilities festered, two new members of the board were elected in 1994. They, too, have turned out to be supportive of the plan, which attests to its reasonableness.

2. *Create occasions to challenge existing meanings and estrange people from them and to create new meanings and facilitate their enactment.* Leaders and managers may wish to estrange people from the missions, mandates, policies, and strategies that support the organizational status quo (Mangham, 1986). New ways of interpreting reality can supply the seed from which a different configuration of policies, plans, programs, projects, products, services, or resource allocations can grow. For example, a strategy reassessment may imply that a different set of external or internal stakeholders, value judgments, signs or indicators, or comparisons is relevant. Change advocates may articulate a new or revised vision that inspires action. Leaders and managers must estrange people from existing meanings, because "estrangement creates a circumstance in which *givenness* becomes *possibility*" (Mangham, 1986, p. 144). Often the estrangement will occur as a result of altering the way issues are formulated so that they highlight certain features of the internal and external environments and not others. For example, the first strategic planning retreat of the CPI program's management group featured a stakeholder analysis. The emphasis on stakeholders and their satisfaction led to a reframing of the situation the CPI faced. This ultimately resulted in a modification of the program's mission and development of new strategies designed to produce value added for stakeholders.

Even when change advocates are successful in challenging existing strategies on intellectual grounds, they should not expect new strategies to be adopted without a change in the political circumstances surrounding the strategy—particularly in public organizations. As Kingdon (1995) notes, these changes may arise from public opinion swings, election results, administrative changes, ideological or partisan redistribution in legislative bodies, and interest group pressure. Before new strategies can be adopted, key decision makers must be receptive—and political changes may be necessary before this is likely to occur.

Major change may also depend on a successful search for important ideas. For example, the school district had to find out what outcome-based education and site-based management means for it. The definitions and approaches it decides on must not only address the educational issues the district faces, they must also be politically salable. The district has relied on several workshops for staff and community members to explore these topics.

3.   *Strategy succession may be more difficult than adoption of the initial strategy was because earlier strategies already exist and are likely to have a coalition of supporters already in place.* Hogwood and Peters (1983) add that the concessions and compromises embedded in the existing strategy are likely to prevent major reforms and that reformers are likely to be disappointed with the gains achieved in relation to their efforts. The extreme difficulty the school district has faced in implementing key components of its plan, especially those related to facilities, is an example.

4.   *Remember that both implementers and beneficiaries of existing policies are more likely to be concerned with strategy implementation details than with policy innovation* (Hogwood and Peters, 1983; Delbecq, 1977). Policies themselves are often more symbolic than real. What counts is how they are implemented—what they mean in practice. That is where the real action is for implementers and beneficiaries. There is good news and bad news here. The good news for change advocates is that if the issues they are tackling stem mainly from existing policies, policy changes may be adopted before implementers and beneficiaries of the status quo know what is happening. The bad news is implementers and beneficiaries may be able to kill any policy they do not like during implementation. More good news for change advocates is that if the problem is not caused by existing policy, only policy implementers may need to be convinced of the virtues of the changes. The bad news is they may not be convinced. The school district's principals and teachers pay careful attention to the implementation details of outcome-based education and site-based management. Their support has to be nurtured every step of the way since they can successfully torpedo almost any major change.

5.   *To make major strategy changes, rely on key decision makers along with policy implementers and beneficiaries.* In all likelihood, to make substantial changes leaders and managers will need the support of a different coalition from the one that adopted and implemented the existing strategies. A new constellation of ideas, stakeholder interests, and agreements will need to be worked out (Hogwood and Peters, 1983; Sabatier, 1988, 1991). For example, the school district relied on a relatively stable board, an incumbent superintendent and assistant superintendent, and the support of most of the staff and a substantial fraction of the community to formulate and implement its reform agenda. The group wishing to overturn the coalition in support of the plan included some politically active teachers, a group of residents and businesspeople unwilling to pay higher taxes for new facilities, and a group with emotional attachments to the old high school. The opponents made a concerted effort to replace plan supporters on the board with opponents. The opponents had to be kept at bay so the board, implementers, and beneficiaries could successfully implement the plan.

6.   *To achieve strategy succession, consider a move to either "split" or "consolidate" aspects of the strategy.* For example, the public library tried to divest itself of ("split off") its videotape loan service in its first strategic plan. Much to the library staff's surprise, the city council did not agree; however, the library was able to gain some increased resources in exchange for keeping the program. Reframing the way is-

sues and strategies are viewed can facilitate policy splitting or consolidation. Reframing can either combine issues, leading to policy consolidation, or separate issues, leading to policy splitting. Moreover, key stakeholders will favor consolidation or splitting if it is in their interest. Splitting or consolidation can also resolve political conflicts by separating or combining budgetary allocations and, depending on the circumstances, reinforcing or relaxing jurisdictional requirements. For example, the school district's move to site-based budgeting will sharpen some conflicts between the district and individual schools, particularly those conflicts related to the fairness of allocations across the district; however, it will relieve district management of other conflicts, particularly those involving allocations within schools. Conflicts over ideas are less easily resolved. Good analysis may help, but there may be strong coalitions in place that no amount of analysis will convince to reassess their positions (Lynn, 1987; Sabatier, 1988; Benveniste, 1989; Anderson, 1990).

7. *Consider building a new system without dismantling the old system.* The result will be parallel, redundant, or competing systems, but often there are overall net social gains through better market segmentation and the benefits of competition (Bendor, 1985). For example, as also mentioned in Chapter Nine, Lyndon Johnson championed the creation of the Office of Economic Opportunity to oversee many of his programs, which he thought would be eclipsed or destroyed if they were housed in the Departments of Labor or Health, Education, and Welfare. He did not wipe out Labor or HEW; he simply left them to their historic tasks and created a new organization to fill in important gaps in those tasks.

Strategy Termination

1. *Think of strategy termination as an extreme version of strategy change.* Many of the guidelines outlined under "Strategy Change or Succession" are applicable to strategy termination as well. A new coalition organized around new ideas, stakeholder interests, and agreements is likely to be necessary. Given the probable resistance of current implementers and beneficiaries, leadership will be a crucial component of all strategy termination efforts. A fundamental leadership task will be to estrange important stakeholders from strategies to be terminated (Mangham, 1986).

2. *Engage in cutback management when programs need to be eliminated or severely reduced.* A substantial literature has developed on how to manage cutbacks in general, although this literature is less helpful when it comes to specifics (Mercer, 1992). Behn (1983), for example, argues that there are two stages to cutback efforts in public organizations. In the first stage, the organization borrows against the future to cover the gap between current revenues and needed expenditures. Yet if revenues are not increased in the future, this tactic merely makes the adjustments to retrenchment worse by postponing the second stage, or "day of reckoning,"

when major cuts and redesigns are made. Behn lists the following basic tasks of cutback management:

- Decide what to cut.
- Maintain morale.
- Attract and keep quality people (this may be particularly difficult when people think the ship is sinking).
- Develop the support of key constituencies and decision makers, including legislators, if necessary, in the public sector.
- Create opportunities for innovation.
- Avoid mistakes.

These are difficult tasks that are unlikely to be executed without effective leaders and managers. According to Behn, leaders and managers must

- Explain the reality.
- Take a long-term view.
- Develop new strategies for their organizations.
- Develop measures of performance in order to know which units to cut and which to reward.
- Create incentives for cooperation.
- Be compassionate.

The school district followed these guidelines when it had to develop a plan to emerge from "statutory operating debt." The superintendent was hired partly to get the district out of its financial troubles and partly to get it moving again in desirable new directions. The district did get its financial house in order, but it ran into difficulties when it sought to relocate an old, but symbolically important, high school (a kind of cutback and reallocation) as well as remodel existing facilities and build new ones with the aid of a major proposed bond referendum. The political opposition to the relocation and to two successive bond referenda was strong. But the board and superintendent mostly maintained their course, and eventually they succeeded as students and parents experienced continuing difficulties with the inadequate facilities and as the board agreed to place the new school on the old site. Now that a bond referendum has finally been passed, the district should be able to address most of its facilities problems and diminish the pain of the outmoded high school's demolition. Behn's guidelines are therefore useful, but obviously, they are no panacea or quick fix.

Summary

In the last step in the Strategy Change Cycle, leaders, managers, and other stakeholders review strategies that have resulted from previous steps or emerged along the way, to determine whether they should be maintained, significantly altered, or terminated. This chapter has discussed why strategies cease to work and has outlined the benefits of moving successfully through this review step. Chief among those benefits are assurance that the new strategy remains responsive to important issues, resolution of residual implementation difficulties, generation of needed energy for strategy renewal, and pruning of areas that are overcrowded with bits and pieces of assorted strategies.

In this step leaders and managers should focus on the issues that prompted the strategy under review, and decide whether those issues are still relevant. They should rely on indicators of strategy success or failure to help them decide whether strategies should be maintained, reformed, or terminated. If the strategies have not been effective or the situation has changed, it may be necessary to identify new strategic issues and modify or eliminate particular strategies. Whatever the cause of this changed approach, it may also be necessary to revise the understandings that underlie the adopted strategies. Leaders and managers also must recognize that working with existing organizational structures, rather than trying to change or replace them, may be very productive at this point. A review group and review opportunities must be established and institutional inertia must be overcome, however, in order to review and perhaps modify existing strategies.

The design and use of forums, arenas, and so on in this step will vary depending on whether the new strategy is to be maintained, reformed, or terminated. In order to maintain and incrementally improve the strategy, leaders and managers should seek little change in the existing settings. They may be able to involve mainly implementers and beneficiaries in the strategy review. If significant change is needed, the design and use of the pertinent forums, arenas, and such will have to be significantly altered. Leaders and managers will have to create or redesign forums to allow challenges to existing meanings and enactment of new meanings. Once again, implementers and beneficiaries are the most likely participants in the review, although some key decision makers and probably a new supportive coalition will have to be enlisted as well.

Possible approaches to strategy succession involve splitting or consolidating strategy elements or developing parallel systems. Strategy termination is an extreme version of strategy succession. Leaders and managers will need to employ cutback management techniques to minimize the resulting pain and dislocation. Finally, leaders and managers should renew their own energy for working on the important issues their organizations or communities face.

PART THREE

MANAGING THE PROCESS AND GETTING STARTED WITH STRATEGIC PLANNING

Strategic planning is in no way a substitute for leadership. Nor does strategic planning implement itself. It is simply a set of concepts, procedures, and tools designed to help an organization's (or community's) leaders, managers, planners, and staff think and act strategically. People who want to use strategic planning must attend to a wide range of leadership concerns. This section addresses these needs.

Chapter Eleven addresses the leadership tasks in making strategic planning work. They include the need to understand the context; understand the people involved; sponsor and champion the process; foster collective leadership; design and use formal and informal settings

for discussion, decision making, and conflict management; and put it all together over the course of a strategic planning process. Many different people will need to lead and follow at different times to accomplish these tasks. When strategic planning does work, it is a collective achievement.

In Chapter Twelve, the four major examples of strategic planning used throughout this book—the school district, the public library, the CPI program, and Mainline Church—are summarized and discussed. Then a number of process guidelines are presented to help organizations get started with their own strategic planning process.◆

CHAPTER ELEVEN

LEADERSHIP ROLES IN MAKING STRATEGIC PLANNING WORK

JOHN M. BRYSON AND BARBARA C. CROSBY

Leaders perform political, spiritual, and intellectual functions as well as managerial and group-maintenance tasks. These range from providing vision and strategies for change, to mobilizing a constituency, to facilitating group decisions or creating coalitions.

CHARLOTTE BUNCH, *PASSIONATE POLITICS*

As has been pointed out before, strategic planning is *not* a substitute for effective leadership. There is *no* substitute for effective leadership when it comes to planning. Instead, strategic planning is simply a set of concepts, procedures, and tools designed to help leaders, managers, and others think and act strategically on behalf of their organizations and their organizations' stakeholders. At its best, strategic planning helps leaders pursue virtuous ends in desirable ways so that the common good is advanced. At its worst, strategic planning drives out strategic thought and action, makes it more difficult for leaders to do their job, and keeps organizations from meeting their mandates and fulfilling their missions. Whether strategic planning helps or hurts depends on how leaders use it—or misuse it.

In each of the cases detailed in this book, leaders, managers, and others had the ability to think and act strategically. They used strategic planning to tap this ability, canvassing diverse views, building coalitions and commitment, and identifying and addressing key organizational issues to enhance organizational performance in the eyes of key stakeholders. Without effective leadership focused on both content *and* process concerns, strategic planning simply would not have happened.

So what is leadership? We are particularly taken by Barbara Crosby's definition: "Public leadership is the inspiration and mobilization of others to undertake collective action in pursuit of the common good" (Bryson and Crosby, 1992, p. 31). Crosby's definition makes it clear that *leadership* and *leaders* are not the same thing. Effective leadership is a collective enterprise, involving many people playing different roles at different times. Many people of the type described by Charlotte Bunch in the chapter-opening quotation will be needed, and indeed these same people will be leaders and followers at different times over the course of a Strategy Change Cycle.

The following interconnected leadership tasks are important if strategic planning and implementation are to be effective:

- Understanding the context
- Understanding the people involved, including oneself
- Sponsoring the process
- Championing the process
- Facilitating the process
- Fostering collective leadership
- Using dialogue and discussion to create a meaningful process, clarify mandates, articulate mission, identify strategic issues, develop effective strategies, and possibly develop a vision of success
- Making and implementing decisions in arenas
- Enforcing rules, settling disputes, and managing residual conflicts
- Putting it all together

Understanding the Context

Leaders need an appreciation of social, political, and economic history; at the same time, they must avoid being captured by that history (Burns, 1978; Neustadt and May, 1986; Hunt, 1991). They must see history as the interplay of continuity (stability) and change, and they must recognize how best to balance these forces in a given context. They also must have an intimate knowledge of their organization in order to make sense of it in relation to the broader context (Mintzberg, 1994a). This understanding and knowledge are important elements in a leader's capacity for recognizing emergent strategies, understanding how strategic planning might help an organization, tailoring the process to an organization's specific circumstances, negotiating initial agreements, framing issues effectively, developing viable strategies for addressing issues, and getting those strategies adopted and implemented. The leaders in each of our four cases were very attentive to their organization's internal and external contexts (including the historical backdrop behind their organization's founding and growth) and the possibilities for change those contexts presented.

External and internal environmental assessments, stakeholder analyses, and special studies are all designed to attune strategic planning participants to important specifics of the organization's context. But those explorations typically occur *after* the process has started. Leaders need some understanding of the context *before* the process begins, too, so they can make the best use of the process to take advantage of the world and the organization as they both are in order to make both better. It is therefore very important for leaders to stay in touch with both through personal contacts and observation, broad reading, continuing education, and reflection.

Leaders should be especially attentive to the possibilities for dramatic strategic change. Organizational strategies typically remain stable over long periods and then suddenly change all at once in response to cumulative changes in the organization's environment (Gersick, 1991; Land and Jarman, 1992; Mintzberg, 1994b, p. 75; Kingdon, 1995). Leaders need to be in touch with the possibilities for significant change in order to know whether strategic planning should be used to help formulate major intended strategy changes or should be primarily a tool for programming improvements in stable strategies. Without some intuitive sense of whether big or small changes are in the cards, strategic planning might be used quite inappropriately. Hopes for big changes might be raised when such changes are not possible, or time might be wasted in reprogramming strategies that ought to be drastically changed.

Understanding the People Involved (Including Oneself)

Leaders should have a reasonable understanding of the people who are or should be involved in strategic planning and implementation, including themselves. Leaders should develop an appreciation of the rich diversity of these people, as well as their commonality. This is the heart of leadership. Understanding oneself and others is particularly important for developing the strength of character and insight that invigorates leadership and increases the chances that strategic planning and implementation will help the organization. Such strength enables people to focus on what matters to them, balance competing demands, develop spiritual depth, maintain a sense of humor, and find the courage to take risks, explore difficult issues and new strategies, and pursue what might be unpopular causes—activities that, in turn, reinforce strength of character.

Useful approaches to understanding oneself and others range from formal assessments to deep study and reflection and informal storytelling. Effective strategic thinking and acting seem to depend a great deal on intuition, creativity, and pattern recognition—none of which can be programmed, although they may be recognized, facilitated, and encouraged (Mintzberg, 1994b). Knowing people well, relying on the recommendations of trusted colleagues, and betting on people's ability based on their past performance thus may be about the only ways of finding people who are effective strategists.

Sponsoring the Process

Process sponsors are typically top positional leaders. They have enough prestige, power, and authority to commit the organization to strategic planning and to hold people accountable. They are not necessarily involved in the day-to-day details of making strategic planning work—the champions do that—but they do set the stage for success and pay careful attention to progress. They have a vested interest in a successful outcome. They also typically are important sources of knowledge about key strategic issues and effective strategies for addressing them. The information they have about the organization and its environment is invaluable. They are likely to be especially knowledgeable about how to fit the process to key decision points, so that dialogue and discussion can inform decisions in the relevant arenas.

Leaders interested in sponsoring a strategic planning process should consider the following guidelines.

1. *Articulate the purpose and importance of the strategic planning effort.* Many participants will need some convincing about why the organization should undertake a strategic planning effort. Leaders can start by outlining their view of the organization's past, present, and future. The discussion is likely to focus on core organizational missions and competencies, key changes in the environment, significant strategic issues that the organization faces or will face, possible actions the organization will need to consider, and the likely consequences of failure to engage in strategic planning. Based on this sketch, leaders should outline in general how they want the organization to engage in strategic planning and what they hope the outcomes and benefits of the process will be. These leaders will demonstrate a concern both for the content and process of strategic planning.

2. *Commit the necessary resources—time, money, energy, legitimacy—to the effort.* A crucial way of making the process real is by allocating resources to it. Nothing else demonstrates leaders' seriousness (or lack of it) about strategic planning more than the level of resources they allocate to the effort.

3. *Emphasize at the beginning and at critical points that action and change will result.* This is another crucial way of making the process real for participants and getting them to take it seriously. If they see that strategic planning is real and will have tangible consequences, they will invest the necessary effort in the process.

4. *Encourage and reward creative thinking, constructive debate, and multiple sources of input and insight.* It is important for sponsors to emphasize the importance of creativity and constructive debate and the value of strategically significant ideas (no matter what their origin). It is also important for them to reward those who deliver what the leaders say they value. Otherwise, the leaders will be viewed as hypocrites, and important sources of new ideas and information will be cut off. The school district's final strategic plan included virtually all of the recommendations of the task forces charged with addressing the district's strategic issues. The district's culture of participative decision making was thereby enhanced, the plan

was strengthened, and the superintendent and board gained credibility as leaders who meant what they said about valuing inclusion and empowerment.

Encouraging constructive debate also means anticipating where conflicts might develop and thinking about how those conflicts might be productively addressed. In particular, leaders must think about which conflicts can be addressed in accordance with the existing rules of the game and which can be managed only if the rules are changed. The school district's board and superintendent, for example, decided that they had to change the rules of the game regarding employees' (especially teachers') pay and benefits if the district was to have the money necessary to pay for important educational reforms. One of the first steps in the district's strategic change process was to negotiate a cap on the district's pay and benefit package in order to free up additional monies for reforms the teachers said they supported.

5. *Be aware of the possible need for outside consultants.* Outside consultants may be needed to help design the process, facilitate aspects of it, do various studies, or perform other tasks. It is a sign of strength to ask for help when you need it. Enough money must be budgeted to pay for any consultants you may need.

6. *Be willing to exercise power and authority to keep the process on track.* Strategic planning is inherently prone to breaking down (Bryson and Roering, 1988, 1989). For one thing, effective strategic planning is not part of the daily routine. As March and Simon (1958, p. 185) point out, there is a sort of "Gresham's Law of Planning" at work in organizations: "Daily routine drives out planning."

Another danger is that people are likely to fight or flee whenever they are asked to deal with tough issues such as failing strategies, serious conflicts, or significant changes. Sponsors have a key role to play in keeping the process going over the rough spots. How these difficulties are handled will say a lot about the character of leaders and of organizations. Challenges are an opportunity to demonstrate courage, to forge character, and to end up with a more effective organization to boot (Selznick, 1957; Csikszentmihalyi, 1990; Terry, 1993). Wise dispute-resolution and conflict-management strategies are called for, and they may need to be backed up by sufficient power and authority to make them work well.

Championing the Process

The champions are the people who have primary responsibility for managing the strategic planning process day to day. They are the ones who keep track of progress and pay attention to all the details. They model the kind of behavior they hope to get from the other participants: reasoned, diligent, committed, enthusiastic, good-spirited pursuit of the common good. They are the cheerleaders who, along with the sponsors, keep the process on track and push, encourage, and cajole the strategic planning team and other key participants through any difficult spots.

Sometimes the sponsors and champions are the same people, but usually they are not.

Champions should keep the following guidelines in mind:

1. *Keep strategic planning high on people's agendas.* Daily routine can easily drive out attention to strategic planning. Blocking out time in people's appointment books is one way to gather participants together and focus their attention. Another is to call on sponsors to periodically emphasize the importance of the process. Yet another is to publish updates on the process in special memoranda or regular newsletters. Yet another is to circulate "think pieces"—special reports, relevant audiotapes, and so on—that encourage strategic thought and action. By whatever means, people will need to be reminded and shown on a regular basis that something good will come from the planning process.

2. *Attend to the process without promoting specific solutions.* Champions are far more likely to gain people's participation and constructive involvement if they are seen as advocates for the process rather than for specific solutions. If the champions are seen as committed partisans of specific solutions, then other participants may boycott or torpedo the process rather than seek to find mutually agreeable strategies to address key issues.

3. *Think about what has to come together (people, tasks, information, reports) at or before key decision points.* When it comes to strategy formulation and strategic planning, time is not linear; instead, it is junctural. The best champions think like theater directors, orchestrators, choreographers, or playwrights. They think about stage setting, themes, acts and scenes, actors and audiences, and how to get the right people with the right information on stage *at the right time*—and then get them off.

4. *Organize the time, space, materials, and participation needed for the process to succeed.* Without attention to the details of the process, its benefits simply will not be achieved. The "trivialities" of the process matter a great deal—they are not trivial at all (Huxham, 1990). Effective champions, therefore, arrange the retreats, book the rooms, make sure any necessary supplies and equipment are handy, send out the meeting notices, distribute the briefing papers and minutes, oversee the production details of draft and final plans, and keep track of the work program.

5. *Pay attention to the language used to describe strategic planning and implementation.* One function of strategic planning is to provide a vocabulary and format to allow people to share views about what is fundamental for the organization (Mintzberg, 1994b, p. 352). At various points in the process, participants are therefore likely to wonder about the meaning of particular planning concepts and how they relate to various matters of concern. An introduction to strategic planning, commonly in a retreat setting, is often a useful way to begin developing a common vocabulary. As the process proceeds further, discussion will almost invariably return to the meaning of planning concepts (mission, vision, goals, issues, strategies) and how they relate to the issues at hand. Champions should be prepared to discuss similarities and differences between various concepts and how they do or

do not relate to substantive concerns. The specific vocabulary group members use does not matter as much as their developing a shared understanding of what things mean.

6. *Keep pushing the process along.* Successful strategic planning processes can vary in length from a few weeks or months to two or more years (Bryson and Roering, 1988, 1989). Some processes must fail one or more times before they succeed. Some never succeed. Part of the role of champions is to keep pushing until the process does succeed—or until it is clear that it will fail and there is no point to continuing. At the same time, it is important to remember that strategic planning is likely to "feel like a failure in the middle," as Kanter (1983) has said of innovations. Champions keep pushing to help the strategic planning team and the organization move through the failure stage toward obtaining success. Champions also need to know when it is time to quit pushing, at least for a while, and when it is time to quit altogether.

Facilitating the Process

Process facilitators are often helpful in moving a strategic planning process along, because of their group-process skills, the attention they can give to structuring and managing group interactions, and the likelihood that they have no stake in the substantive outcomes of the process—particularly if they are outsiders (Schwarz, 1994). The presence of a facilitator means that champions can be free to participate in substantive discussions without having to worry too much about managing group processes.

A skilled facilitator can also help build up the level of trust in a group and the interpersonal skills and conflict management abilities of its members. Building trust is important, because often the members of a strategic planning team come from different parts of the organization and have never worked together before, let alone on fundamental strategic questions facing the organization.

Skilled facilitation usually depends on establishing a successful partnership among facilitators, sponsors, and champions. For facilitators to do their work well, they must learn a great deal very quickly about the organization and its politics, issues, culture, and secrets. They must quickly gain the trust of the sponsors and champions, learn the lay of the land, and demonstrate their ability to further the strategic planning effort. But they can do none of those things unless the sponsors and champions put a great deal into the relationship as well. The sponsors, champions, and facilitators usually form the core group that moves the process forward with the help of the strategic planning team (Friend and Hickling, 1987; Bellman, 1990; Bentley, 1994; Schwarz, 1994; Bryson, Ackermann, Eden, and Finn, forthcoming).

Facilitators should come to any strategic planning process with a well-developed set of group-process skills (Schein, 1988; Johnson and Johnson, 1994;

Bentley, 1994; Schwarz, 1994), along with those skills especially applicable to planning for public and nonprofit organizations (Friend and Hickling, 1987; Rosenhead, 1989; Nutt and Backoff, 1992). Equipped with these skills, they should then consider these guidelines.

1. *Know the strategic planning process, and explain how it works at the beginning and at many points along the way.* Participants will often be engaged in other important work for the organization at the same time that they are learning the strategic planning process. The fact that so much will be new to people means that they can easily get lost. Facilitators play a key role in explaining to people where they are, where they can head, and how they might get there.

2. *Tailor the process to the organization and to the groups involved.* There is general agreement in the literature that planning processes must be fitted to the unique circumstances in which organizations and groups find themselves (Bryson and Delbecq, 1979; Christensen, 1985; Bryson, Bromiley, and Jung, 1990; Bryson and Bromiley, 1993; Sager, 1994; Mintzberg, 1994b; Roberts and Wargo, 1994). Facilitators, along with sponsors and champions, are the ones who are in the best position to design the process so that it fits the organization, its circumstances, and the participants. Facilitators must pay careful attention both to the *tasks* of strategic planning and to the social and emotional *maintenance* of the groups and teams involved in the process. Both content and process are crucial to effective group functioning and, indeed, are the basic elements of effective team leadership (Johnson and Johnson, 1994).

3. *Convey a sense of humor and enthusiasm for the process and help groups get unstuck.* Sponsors and champions can express humor and enthusiasm for the process but not the way a facilitator can. Strategic planning can be alternately tension-ridden and tedious. Good facilitators can help to manage the tension and relieve the tedium. Facilitators can also help groups confront the difficulties that arise over the course of a strategic planning process. By helping groups reframe their situations imaginatively, invent new options, channel conflict constructively, and tap hidden sources of courage, hope, and optimism, facilitators can provide important resources to help groups move forward (Von Oech, 1983; Simon, 1988; Seligman, 1991; Buzan, 1993; Terry, 1993; Morgan, 1993; Bentley, 1994; Schwarz, 1994).

4. *Press groups toward taking action and assigning responsibility for specific actions.* Part of keeping the process moving is making sure that action is taken in a timely way. Partly, this is a matter of keeping people's interest, enthusiasm, and commitment up. If the whole process is devoted entirely to talking with no acting, people will quickly quit participating. It is also partly a matter of recognizing that not all of the thinking has to take place before any of the acting can occur. Whenever useful and wise actions become apparent—as a result of attention to mission and mandates, stakeholder analyses, SWOT analyses, strategic issue identification, and various strategizing efforts—they should be taken, as long as they do not jeopardize possible choices that decision makers might want to make in the future. In

part, it is a matter of recognizing that there are limits to thinking things out in advance. Often, people can only know what they think by acting first, and often, important strategies can only emerge by taking small steps and using adaptive learning to figure things out as one goes along (Weick, 1979; Mintzberg, 1994a, 1994b).

By pushing people toward action, the facilitator always runs the danger of inducing premature closure. People may act on what is immediately at hand without thinking creatively about other options (or simply waiting until the time is right). A good facilitator will have a well-developed intuitive sense about when to push for action and when to hold back. He or she will also be good at probing people and groups about the merits of options and the advisability of taking specific actions.

5. *Congratulate people whenever possible.* In our experience, most people in most organizations suffer from chronic—and sometimes acute—positive reinforcement deprivation. People respond very favorably to kind words and praise from people who are important to them. Indeed, many excellently managed organizations are known for the praise and emotional support they give their employees (Peters and Waterman, 1982; Kanter, 1983, 1989). Facilitators are in an especially good position to congratulate people and to say good things about them in a genuine, natural way.

Fostering Collective Leadership

When strategic planning for public organizations is successful, it is a collective achievement. Many people contribute to its success, sometimes by leading, other times by following. Collective leadership may be fostered through the following approaches.

1. *Rely on teams.* The team is the basic vehicle for furthering strategic planning. Champions, in particular, will find that much of their time will be focused on making sure strategic planning teams or task forces perform well and make effective contributions. There are two reasons why teams are so important. The first is that no one person can have all the relevant quantitative and qualitative information, so forming a team is one way to increase the information available for strategic planning. The second reason is political. To be viable, strategic planning and strategies need support at many points throughout the organization and from external stakeholders. A strategic plan and intended strategies need the support of a critical coalition when they are adopted and during implementation. A wisely constructed strategic planning team can provide the initial basis for such a coalition, and team members can do much of the work leading to forming the necessary coalition.

Team leaders naturally must focus on accomplishing team goals or tasks, but they must also attend to individual team members' needs and consciously promote group cohesion (Johnson and Johnson, 1994). Team leadership involves the right balance of direction, mentoring, and facilitation—what Schaef (1985, p. 128) describes as "[enabling] others to make their contributions while simultaneously making one's own." Team leaders will benefit from

- Communicating effectively
- Balancing unity and diversity
- Defining team roles, goals, and norms
- Establishing an atmosphere of trust
- Fostering group creativity and sound decision making
- Obtaining necessary resources
- Tailoring direction and support to team members to fit their competence and commitment
- Rewarding achievement and overcoming adversity

2. *Focus on network and coalition development.* Coalitions are basically organized around ideas and interests that foster the notion that people can achieve together what they cannot achieve separately. The way issues, goals, or visions—and strategies for achieving them—are framed will structure how stakeholders interpret their interests, how they assess the costs and benefits of joining a coalition, and the form and content of winning and losing arguments. Therefore, leaders must articulate the view of the world that lies behind the way issues, goals, visions, and strategies are framed in such a way as to draw significant support from key stakeholders. The worldview that leaders should seek is one that will call up widely shared notions of what constitutes the public interest and the common good (Stone, 1988; Kidder, 1994; Lappé and Du Bois, 1994).

A strategic plan's or strategy's political acceptability increases as the benefits to key stakeholders of adopting and implementing it increase and the costs diminish. As Light (1991) notes in relation to presidential agenda setting, it is primarily the issues with the greatest potential benefit for key stakeholders that get on the agenda, while the ones that are the least costly for those stakeholders receive prime consideration. Moreover, any proposal likely to be adopted and implemented will be a carefully tailored response to specific circumstances rather than an off-the-shelf solution imported from somewhere else (Nutt, 1992; Kingdon, 1995).

It is very important to keep in mind that typically every member of a winning coalition will not agree on every specific aspect of a plan or set of strategies, and that this is okay. It is also important to keep in mind that coalition development depends on following many of the same guidelines that help develop effective teams. In particular, coalitions are probably more likely to be formed if the diversity of coalition members and their various ideas and special gifts are valued. Acquiring the necessary resources is also vital to coalition development, and the coalition itself can become a major source of resources afterward. Rewarding and celebrating collective achievements and sharing credit for them broadly are also likely to help.

In a broader sense, public and nonprofit leaders should work to build a sense of community—that is, a sense of relationship, mutual empowerment, and common purpose—within and beyond their organizations. This is desirable because so many of the problems that public and nonprofit organizations are called upon to address require multi-organizational (or community) responses. Although a "community" is often defined in terms of location, it can also be what Heifetz and Sinder (1988) and others have called a community of interest, an interorganizational network that often transcends geographical and political boundaries and is designed to address transorganizational problems (Trist, 1983). Leaders contribute to community building by facilitating communal definition and resolution of issues, fostering democratic leader-follower relations (Kahn, 1982; Boyte, 1989), providing resources, and using their knowledge of group process to help people work together. Most importantly, as Palmer (1990, p. 138) suggests, leaders build community by "making space for other people to act."

3. *Establish specific mechanisms for sharing power, responsibility, and accountability.* Authority is not usually shared by policy-making bodies or chief executives—it often cannot be, by law—but that does not mean that power, responsibility, and accountability cannot be shared. Doing so can foster participation, trigger information and resource flows, and help build commitment to plans and strategies and their implementation. The use of strategic planning teams, strategic issue task forces, and implementation teams are typical vehicles for sharing power. Action plans should indicate any shared responsibilities. Credit is something else that should be broadly shared.

Using Dialogue and Discussion to Create a Meaningful Process

Creating and communicating meaning is the work of visionary leaders. Sometimes, visionary leadership results in a vision of success for the organization; in the present discussion, visioning covers a broader range of purposes and is meant more as a verb than a noun. Leaders become visionary when they play a vital role in interpreting current reality, fostering a collective group mission, articulating desirable strategies, and shaping a collective sense—perhaps a vision—of the future (Doig and Hargrove, 1987; Denhardt, 1993). Furthermore, visionary leaders must understand important aspects of their own and others' internal worlds, and they must also grasp the meaning of related external worlds. As truth tellers and direction givers, they help people make sense of experience—they offer guidance for coping with the present and the future by helping answer these questions: What's going on here? Where are we heading? How will things look when we get there? They frame and shape the perceived context for action (Smircich and Morgan, 1989), and they "manage" important stakeholders' perceptions of the organization, its strategies, and their effects (Lynn, 1987; Neustadt, 1990). In order to foster change, particularly major change, leaders should adhere to the following guidelines in creating and communicating new meanings.

1. *Understand the design and use of forums.* Forums are the basic settings we humans use to create shared meaning through dialogue and discussion (Bryson and Crosby, 1992). Much of the work of strategic planning takes place in forums, where fairly free-flowing consideration of ideas and views can take place before proposals are developed for adoption and action in decision-making arenas. The tasks of sponsoring, championing, and facilitating strategic planning are primarily performed in forums. Retreats, team meetings, task force meetings, focus groups, newsletters, and the strategic plans themselves—when used as educational devices—are all examples of forums. These forums can be used to help develop a shared understanding about what the organization is, what it does or should do, and why.

2. *Seize opportunities to provide interpretation and give direction in difficult and uncertain situations.* Leadership opportunities expand in times of difficulty, confusion, and crisis, when old approaches clearly are not working and people are searching for meaningful accounts of what has happened and what can be done about it (Boal and Bryson, 1987a; Kouzes and Posner, 1987; Schein, 1992). Turning dangers, threats, and crises into manageable challenges is an important task for visionary leaders (Dutton and Jackson, 1987; Jackson and Dutton, 1988; Dutton and Ashford, 1993). Doing so not only promotes optimism and hardiness but is also most likely to free up the necessary thinking, resources, and energy to successfully confront challenges. The school district's superintendent used a financial crisis to mobilize action not only to address that particular issue but also to pursue the more inspiring goals of educational reform and "preparing students for the next century." Impending massive staff burnout in part triggered the public library's strategic planning effort. Financial shortfalls and concerns about declining membership at Mainline Church were used by the sponsors and champions to involve many people in the strategic planning effort.

3. *Reveal and name real needs and real conditions.* New meaning unfolds as leaders encourage people to see the "real" situation and its portents. They find and communicate ways to align experience and feelings about a situation with behaviors that have consequences people care about (Boal and Bryson, 1987a; Neustadt, 1990).

To illuminate "real" conditions, leaders may use intuition or integrative thinking (Cleveland, 1985; Quinn, 1988; Mintzberg, 1994b). Either they formally or informally scan their environment to discern the patterns emerging from local conditions, or they accept the patterns and issues identified by others, such as pollsters or planners. Simply articulating these patterns publicly and convincingly can be an act of revelation. However, leaders cannot just delineate emerging patterns and issues; they must also explain them (Neustadt, 1990). They must relate what they see to their knowledge of societal systems (Maccoby, 1983) and to people's experience (Boal and Bryson, 1987a). Going further, leaders alert followers to the need for action by "uncovering and exploiting of contradictions in values and between values and practice" (Burns, 1978, p. 43).

4. *Help followers frame and reframe issues and strategies.* In revealing and explaining real conditions, leaders lay the groundwork for framing and reframing the issues facing the organization and the strategies for addressing them (Stone, 1988; Bolman and Deal, 1991; Morgan, 1993). The *framing* process consists of naming and explaining the issue, opening the door to alternative ways of addressing it, and suggesting outcomes. The *reframing* process involves breaking with old ways of viewing an issue or strategy and developing a new appreciation of it (Mangham, 1986).

5. *Offer compelling visions of the future.* Leaders convey their visions through stories rooted in shared history yet focused on the future. These stories link people's experience of the present (cognitions), what they might do about the situation (behaviors), and what they might expect to happen as a result (consequences). In other words, the stories help people grasp desirable and potentially real futures (Brickman, 1978; Boal and Bryson, 1987a). Effective stories are rich with metaphors that make sense of people's experience, are comprehensive yet open-ended, and impel people toward union or common ground (Terry, 1993). Finally, leaders transmit their own belief in their visionary stories through vivid, energetic, optimistic language (Kouzes and Posner, 1987; Shamir, Arthur, and House, 1994).

6. *Champion new and improved ideas for addressing strategic issues.* Championing ideas for addressing issues is different from championing the process of strategic planning, but it is nonetheless important. Astute leaders gather ideas from many sources (Burns, 1978; Neustadt, 1990). They foster an atmosphere in which innovative approaches flourish (Kouzes and Posner, 1987; Heifetz and Sinder, 1988). The best political leaders, says Burns (1978), provide intellectual leadership by sorting out large public issues and combining analytical ideas, data, and moral reasoning to clarify needed action. Acting in the mode of Schön's (1983) "reflective practitioner," these leaders champion "improved" ideas, ones that have emerged from practice and been refined by critical reflection. Mintzberg (1994a, 1994b) argues strongly that strategic planners typically help leaders when they are "finders" of strategies, "analysts" searching for good information and options, or "catalysts" of strategizing efforts by others rather than "strategists" themselves.

7. *Detail actions and expected consequences.* Often, actions and consequences are an integral part of leaders' visions—or organizational missions and strategies—and become more detailed as implementation proceeds (Mintzberg and Westley, 1992). Crises, however, can necessitate reversing this sequence. When old behaviors are not working and disaster is imminent, followers may wish leaders to prescribe new behaviors and may be willing to try those behaviors without a clear vision of the outcome for the organization or for specific strategies. To sustain a leader-follower relationship founded on crisis, however, leaders must soon link the recommended course of action to a "higher purpose" (Boal and Bryson, 1987a,

p. 17; Alterman, 1995), such as a shared sense of mission. Providing evidence of causal links between the new behaviors and desired outcomes is also critical.

Making and Implementing Decisions in Arenas

Public and nonprofit leaders are also required to be political leaders—partly because all organizations have their political aspects (Pfeffer, 1992; Peters, 1995) and partly because public and nonprofit organizations are involved in politicized decision making much of the time. As political leaders, leaders ultimately fail or succeed through their impact on decision making and implementation. The key to success, and the heart of political leadership, is understanding how intergroup power relationships shape decision making and implementation outcomes. Particularly important is understanding how to affect outcomes by having some things never come up for a decision. Specifically, political leaders should consider the following guidelines.

1.   *Understand the design and use of arenas.* Political leaders must be skilled in designing and using formal and informal arenas, the basic settings for decision making (Bryson and Crosby, 1992). In the public sector, these arenas may be legislative, executive, or administrative. For nonprofit organizations, they will include the board and management. For interorganizational networks and communities, there will be many relevant arenas. It is in arenas that the products of forums—such as strategic plans and important aspects of strategies—are either adopted as is, altered, or rejected.

A major issue in any strategic planning process is how to sequence the move from planning forums—particularly planning team meetings that include key decision makers—to decision-making arenas. A large fraction of the necessary strategic thinking will occur as part of the dialogue and discussion in forums. Once viable proposals have been worked out, they then can move to arenas for any necessary revisions and for adoption and implementation—or else rejection. At a minimum, managing the transition from forums to arenas depends on figuring out when key decision points will occur. The planning process can then be designed to fit those points in such a way that decisions in arenas can be influenced constructively by the work done in forums.

A further issue is how to handle any residual conflicts or disputes that may arise during implementation. The decisions made in arenas usually cannot—and should not try to—cover all of the details and difficulties that may come up during implementation. Some advance thinking, therefore, is almost always in order about how these residual or subsidiary conflicts might be handled constructively.

2.   *Mediate and shape conflicts within and among stakeholders.* Conflict (or at least the existence of recognizable differences) is necessary if people are to be offered real choices in arenas (Burns, 1978) and if decision makers are to understand

the choices and their consequences (Janis, 1989). Further, political leaders must possess transactional skills for dealing with followers, other leaders, and various key stakeholders with conflicting agendas. To forge winning coalitions, leaders must bargain and negotiate, inventing options for mutual gain so that they can trade things of value for support.

3. *Understand the dynamics of political influence and how to target resources appropriately.* The first requirement for influencing political decision making may be knowing whom to influence. Who controls the agenda of the relevant decision-making bodies, whether city councils, boards of directors, or some other group? Who chairs the group and any relevant committees? The next requirement is knowing how to influence. What forms of information delivery, lobbying, vote trading, arm-twisting, and so on are acceptable? Should change advocates try to change the composition of the decision-making bodies? Given the available time, energy, and resources, how might they best be spent (Coplin and O'Leary, 1976; Kaufman, 1986; Benveniste, 1989)? Basically, political leaders manipulate the costs and benefits of actions so that supporters are more motivated to act in desired directions and opponents are less motivated to resist (Kaufman, 1986; Baron, 1987).

Outcomes in arenas can be dramatically affected by influencing the agenda of what comes up for decision and what does not, thereby becoming a "nondecision" (Bachrach and Baratz, 1963; Bryson and Crosby, 1992). Decision outcomes can also be affected by "strategic voting," in which participants use their knowledge of voting rules and manipulation of their voting right to steer outcomes in directions they favor. Reshaping the way issues are viewed can also have dramatic effects on how people vote (Riker, 1986).

4. *Build winning, sustainable coalitions.* For strategic planning to be effective, a coalition of support must be built for the process and its outcomes. There must be a coalition in place that is strong enough to adopt intended strategies and to defend them during implementation. Building winning coalitions can be pretty gritty work. As Riker (1986, p. 52) notes, "Politics is winning and losing, which depend, mostly, on how large and strong one side is relative to the other. The actions of politics consist in making agreements to join people in alliances and coalitions— hardly the stuff to release readers' adrenaline as do seductions, quarrels, or chases." Finding ideas (visions, goals, strategies) that people can support and that further their interests is a large part of the process, but so is making deals in which something is traded in exchange for that support.

5. *Avoid bureaucratic imprisonment.* Political leaders in government, particularly, may find their ability to make and implement needed decisions is severely constrained by the bureaucracies in which they serve. Those bureaucracies usually have intricate institutionalized rules and procedures and entrenched personnel that hamper any kind of change. Leaders committed to change must continually challenge the rules or else find their way around them, including appealing over the heads of resistant bureaucrats to high-level decision makers or to key external stakeholders (Burns, 1978; Lynn, 1987; Kouzes and Posner, 1987).

Enforcing Norms, Settling Disputes, and Managing Residual Conflicts

Leaders are always called upon to be ethical—not least when they are handling conflicts. Disputes and residual conflicts are likely to arise during the implementation of strategies. The decisions made in arenas are unlikely to cover all of the details and difficulties that may come up when implementing strategies. These residual or subsidiary conflicts must be handled constructively, either in other arenas or through the use of formal or informal courts, both to address the difficulty at hand *and* to reinforce or change important norms governing the organization. The following skills are vital to exercising ethical leadership.

1. *Understand the design and use of formal and informal courts.* Courts operate whenever two actors having a conflict rely on a third party (leader, manager, facilitator, mediator, arbitrator, judge) to help them address it. Managing conflict and settling disputes not only takes care of the issue at hand, it also reinforces the important societal or organizational norms used to handle it. Leaders must be skilled in the design and use of formal and informal courts, which are the settings for enforcing ethical principles, constitutions, and laws and for managing residual conflicts and settling disputes (Bryson and Crosby, 1992). Formal courts theoretically provide the ultimate social sanctions for conduct mandated or promoted through formal policy-making arenas, but in practice the informal "court of public opinion" can be even more powerful.

2. *Foster organizational integrity and educate others about ethics, constitutions, laws, and norms.* In nurturing public and nonprofit organizations that contribute to the common good, leaders must adopt practices and systems that provide what Wallace and White (1988) call "organizational integrity." Such leaders make a public commitment to ethical principles and then act on them. They involve the organization's stakeholders in ethical analysis and decision making, inculcate a sense of personal responsibility in followers, and reward ethical behavior.

3. *Apply constitutions, laws, and norms to specific cases.* Constitutions, such as the U.S. Constitution, are usually broad frameworks establishing basic organizational purposes, structures, and procedures. Laws, while much more narrowly drawn, still typically apply to broad classes of people or actions; moreover, they may emerge from the legislative process with purposeful omissions and generalities that were necessary to obtain enough votes for passage (Posner, 1985). Therefore, both constitutions and laws require authoritative interpretation as they are applied to specific cases. In the U.S. judicial system, judges, jurors, and attorneys, and even interest groups filing amicus curiae briefs, all contribute to that authoritative interpretation. Outside of formal courts, leaders typically must apply norms rather than laws.

4. *Adapt constitutions, laws, and norms to changing times.* Judicial principles endure even as the conditions that prompted them and the people who created them

change dramatically. Sometimes, public leaders are able to reshape the law to current needs in legislative, executive, or administrative arenas; often, however, as Neely (1981) suggests, leaders must ask formal courts to mandate a change because vested interests hold sway over the executive and legislative branches.

5. *Resolve conflicts among constitutions, laws, and norms.* Ethical leaders working through the courts must find legitimate bases for deciding among conflicting principles. This may mean relying on judicial enforcement or on reconciliation of constitutions, laws, and norms. Conflict management and dispute resolution methods typically emphasize the desirability of finding principles or norms that all can support as legitimate bases for settling disputes (Filley, 1975; Fisher and Ury, 1981; Susskind and Cruikshank, 1987). Obviously, these principles and norms should be applied in such a way that the public interest is served and the common good advanced.

One of the best tests for discerning the public interest or common good is respect for future generations, which, as Lewis (1991, p. 47) points out, typically requires an understanding of the context and "accommodating rather than spurning the important values, principles, and interests at stake." Another test is empathy, which calls upon public and nonprofit leaders to act as stewards of the "vulnerable, dependent, and politically inarticulate, those mostly likely to be overlooked in formulations of the public interest" (Lewis, 1991, p. 47; Block, 1993).

Summary

The tasks of leadership for strategic planning are complex and many. Unless the organization is very small, no single person or group can perform them all. Effective strategic planning is a collective phenomenon, typically involving sponsors, champions, facilitators, teams, task forces, and others in various ways at various times. Over the course of a Strategy Change Cycle, leaders of many different kinds must put together the elements we have described in such a way that organizational effectiveness is enhanced—thereby making some important part of the world outside the organization noticeably better.

CHAPTER TWELVE

GETTING STARTED WITH STRATEGIC PLANNING

With hope it is, hope that can never die,
Effort, and expectation, and desire,
And something evermore about to be.

WILLIAM WORDSWORTH, *THE PRELUDE*

The preceding chapters have presented an overview of strategic planning, an introduction to the Strategy Change Cycle, detailed guidance on working through the process, and a discussion of the leadership roles in strategic planning. This chapter presents a number of guidelines on how public and nonprofit organizations and communities interested in strategic planning might proceed.

The Four Examples Revisited

How have our four examples—three public organizations and one nonprofit— fared with strategic planning? Each has achieved notable successes, and each also has encountered challenges to its ability to think and act strategically. A number of lessons can be drawn from each organization's experience. The lessons have been discussed before, but they become more concrete in relation to specific cases.

School District

The school district passed an extremely ambitious strategic plan about two years after the process began. The plan included changes in curriculum, governance, facilities, community education, technology, and other areas. The plan has been virtually completely implemented. Board and administration responsibilities have been sorted out, and site-based management is now well on its way to full implementation. Outcome-based education continues to evolve in useful ways. Some areas of the plan, such as those dealing with technology, needed further explication; those plans have now been developed and are being implemented. Community education plans have also been finalized. The financing plans and facilities plans needed more work, since a proposal to relocate a symbolically important but outmoded high school to a new building in a different community provoked such intense opposition that two bond referenda designed to raise money for the change failed. Finally, the decision was made to locate the new high school on the site of the old high school; as a result, a third bond referendum passed. Now the district is in a position to complete site clearance and begin construction before the end of 1995. The bond referendum also provided monies to implement the completed technology plan.

Financing for most of the plan (other than the technology and building changes) was made possible in part by capping teachers' and other employees' health benefits in contract renegotiations, and in part by increasing enrollment in the district, a change that brought in more state resources. The health plan is still one of the most generous in the state, but the cap reduces the rate of increase by placing employees in a managed care program. Health benefits costs are now stable rather than increasing at a rate of 20 percent a year. Thus, while renegotiating the benefits package slowed down the strategic planning process, it was critical to the ultimate success of the plan.

The school district case is clearly a strategic planning success story. The board mapped out its mission, goals, and key issue areas, charged task forces of insiders and outsiders to develop strategies to address them, adopted a strategic plan that incorporated almost all of the recommendations, and then worked hard—not without conflict on the board and in the community—to implement them. Now the goals and objectives of the strategic plan are close to being fully achieved.

Implementing the plan has not been without cost, however. Two board presidents lost their seats because of their commitment to the process. The first was out front in the move to cap the benefits package and lost the subsequent election. The second was simply unwilling to compromise much and lost against a forceful foe. Other board members burned out from the stresses and strains of "staying the course" and getting the bond referendum passed. By the time of the November 1994 election, only three of the original seven board members were still on the board, and one of these decided against running again. The superintendent is still in place and still a steadfast advocate of the plan (although he was clearly willing to make the necessary compromises to get its main components implemented). All these advocates, both the ones who are still with the process and those who were forced to leave, were inspired by a hope of "something evermore about to be" and had the courage to pursue it. William Wordsworth would be proud of them. So would Maya Angelou, who says, "Courage is the most important virtue, because without courage you can't have the other virtues."

The superintendent and the board, however, also see a pressing need to heal the divisions on the board and in the community that were opened by the facilities issue and the first two bond referenda. The time is right for a new though scaled-down round of strategic planning to deal with these divisions and with some other issues left over from the process, as well as additional issues now emerging on the horizon.

The lessons from the school district's experience seem clear. First, unless the top decision makers are fully committed to strategic planning, it is unlikely to succeed in the organization as a whole. This is particularly true when major changes—big wins—are planned. The board presidents, a solid majority of the board, and the superintendent stayed committed to the process and the resulting plan. Again, there simply is no substitute for that kind of leadership. Second, one of the biggest innovations that strategic planning promotes is the habit of focusing key decision makers' attention on what is truly important. The process helped the board and staff identify the key issues, figure out what to do about them, and follow through. There is no substitute for that kind of dialogue and deliberation. Third, if strategic planning is to be really effective in an organization that has a governing board, the board itself must understand and "own" the process (Eadie and Kethley, 1994). Fourth, the board must understand what it means to be an effective policy-making body and must act the part (Houle, 1989; Carver, 1990). The school district's board initiated the process in part to help it become a better policy-making body. One reason to engage in a new, scaled-down version of strategic planning at this point is to educate a board composed mostly of new members about how to be an effective policy-making body. Fifth, strategic planning is an iterative process that can lead to surprising understandings—and to new and more effective rounds of strategic thought and action. The school district's board and administration underestimated the symbolic importance of the old high school; instead, they thought the cost of relocating the school was the main issue. They were wrong, in part because they were incorrectly counseled by the marketing consultants hired to explore district opinion on the matter. It turned out that money was not the issue, location was. After the board changed its mind and decided to use the old site, the bond referendum to finance a new high school building passed easily.

Sixth, staff must be assigned to work on what is truly important. The plan's contents would not have been implemented had the superintendent and staff not followed through. Here is a place where process champions are again critical. The most important champion in this case was the assistant superintendent. She diligently and faithfully followed through and made sure that what was necessary occurred—no matter how overworked, tired, or frustrated she became. Strong overall citizen support also helped, although there was considerable citizen opposition to the facilities part of the original plan. Widespread citizen support was especially welcomed by the superintendent and assistant superintendent when they needed extra encouragement. The strategic planning consultants also provided support, encouragement, and needed insight at key points. And facilitators were often used to help various task forces and focus groups work through difficult issues.

Seventh, if strategic planning discussions precede budgeting and bond referenda, budgets may be prepared and reviewed in light of their consequences for the organization as a whole. Referenda are more likely to be passed, even in an antitax era. A persuasive case must be made in order to get citizen support.

Eighth, advocates of strategic planning and plans must be prepared for disruptions, delays, and unexpected events, because they are almost bound to happen. The slowdown as a result of the teacher contract renegotiations is an example, as is the disruption caused by turnover on the board. Both slowed the process, but each was probably necessary before ultimate success could be achieved.

Ninth, strategic planning by itself is not enough. The key decision makers in the system (in this case the board members and superintendent) must be willing to take effective political action to promote strategic thought and action. As a consequence, some decision makers may need to be "sacrificed" in order to get the changes introduced. Some of the turnover on the board resulted from members' willingness to make personal sacrifices in order to benefit the district as a whole. These board members had the courage and integrity to stand their ground and take the consequences. Hope and courage are necessary civic virtues, though they are not without cost. Public leaders must be willing to pay the price when necessary.

Public Library

The public library used strategic planning to continue its tradition of excellent public service. At the time its 1989–91 strategic plan was formulated, the library was receiving patron satisfaction ratings of 93 to 94 percent. But resource constraints have since forced the library to engage in a kind of continuous quality improvement in order to maintain its ratings in the face of increased demands and fewer resources. Strategic plan updates have been used to guide these efforts.

Many of the lessons from the school district case apply to the public library (and the other cases) as well. Rather than repeat them, however, I will focus on two particularly significant ones. First, leadership counts (Behn, 1991). The library's top administrators are deeply committed, thoughtful, service-oriented professionals. They are committed to providing a quality service. They understand how to be effective sponsors and champions and know when to involve consultants and facilitators. And they are shrewd about building support on the city council and in the community for any necessary changes. They have relied on a supportive nonprofit organization (the Friends) to help with building public support; a special fund administered by a foundation provides staff development resources not available through the city government. They have also relied on their well-developed political instincts.

Second, it is hard to engage in a process of continuous quality improvement without a dedicated staff. The library's administrators are very attentive to staff needs. Indeed, it was their concern about staff burnout that prompted the first strategic planning exercise, and issues related to staff well-being have been a part of each subsequent plan.

Consumer Price Index Program

The CPI program adopted its strategic plan in June 1994. The plan (covered in Chapter Eight) provides guidance for the program's efforts at employing TQM and "reinventing government," upgrading its technology, managing the decennial revision, and other activities. These efforts are well under way.

One of the interesting things about this example is that when the plan was first adopted, few of the members of the management group thought there was anything new in it. But when the first retreat was held, the group discovered that two rather radical shifts in thinking were called for: the program needed to have much more communication with various stakeholders and to provide value added to various stakeholders through innovative uses of technology, data, and services. By forcing the management group to talk through these changes, the process facilitated an important shift in thinking, to the point that some things that once were only pipe dreams became givens (Mangham, 1986; Isabella, 1990). Here is an example—and a lesson—that fits de Gues's observation (1988, p. 71) that "the real purpose of strategic planning is not to make plans but to change the mental models decision makers carry in their heads." Recall Mintzberg's observation (1994b, p. 252), noted earlier, that "organizations function on the basis of commitment and mindset." Strategic planning can help alter the premises and binding choices that govern behavior.

The CPI program's experience also strongly emphasizes a lesson about the importance of forums in any strategic planning process that bridges organizational boundaries. As a matrix organization, the CPI program necessarily relies on discussion and dialogue to figure out what it should be doing and how. This discussion and dialogue allowed the members of the management group to challenge the existing strategies. The conversation had to occur both within the management group and also within the divisions the managers came from. A lot of talk occurred, and sometimes it seemed to group members to be going nowhere. But eventually, the dialogue resulted in a plan people could commit to, one that would guide subsequent actions including budget requests.

Of all the cases, the CPI program's experience most strongly illustrates a lesson about the need to fit strategic planning to other ongoing processes in an organization. The process had to be compatible with the Labor Department's TQM efforts, the Clinton administration's "reinventing government" efforts, and the federal rules, regulations, and guidelines governing budgeting, personnel, and contracting procedures. If the planning effort had not been meshed with these other activities, it would have been useless.

Finally, strategic planning can help organizations cope with a variety of unexpected situations. For example, the program's management group was surprised when initial stakeholder and SWOT analyses indicated that the program really needed to change its strategies to emphasize communication with key stakeholder groups and the addition of various valued-added services. The more significant surprise management group members had to address, however, was that the decennial revision would have to be partially financed initially out of existing budget allocations instead of through the usual multimillion-dollar supplemental appropriation. This information would have been very hard to handle under ordinary circumstances, but because of the group's ongoing discussions, group members were able to absorb the shock and quickly move on to figuring out how to start the revision and achieve critical objectives without the additional money. They even concluded that there was a benefit to the situation, in that they decided the strategic plan and revision were not separate processes but could and should be merged. In other words, the strategic planning process conditioned the group to think and act strategically—to find opportunities in threats and strengths in weaknesses.

Mainline Church

The church had implemented almost all of its 1990–94 strategic plan well before 1994. It then began a new process, called "Vision for 2000," to address issues not covered in the plan and to promote the habit of strategic thinking and acting on the part of the church's leadership. The *Vision for 2000* report was approved in May 1992. Implementation efforts have been proceeding apace, but perhaps most importantly, the report helped the church prepare the "call" for a new senior pastor—and helped him accept the call. It was clear to him that the church knew where it wanted to go, and that he wanted to participate in the journey. He became senior pastor in January 1994. The process and plan thus helped the church manage a very important and potentially difficult transition (one that it has had to make only once every couple of decades). The fact that the church managed this transition relatively smoothly is a tribute to the consensus the process helped achieve and to the attractiveness of the result.

There are some additional lessons, not tied to any of these cases in particular, that should also be emphasized. First, operational details can overwhelm strategic planning efforts. Even though each organization was successful at strategic planning, it still took each one a fairly long time to get through the process. Often attention to day-to-day routines simply drove out attention to long-term planning. It takes a real commitment to find the time to attend to fundamental analysis and planning on a regular basis. This may well be the most important discipline strategic planning promotes. Without it, strategic thinking and acting among groups of senior decision makers are not likely to occur. Strategic planning cannot be simply an add-on to already overworked leaders, managers, and staff.

Second, quicker really can be better. If threats are serious and imminent— bankruptcy, for example—a lengthy and elaborate strategic planning process can doom the organization to an early death. Third, simpler can be better, too. Focusing on the most critical issues in a direct and timely way and developing effective strategies to address them may be all that is needed. Such a process will not be "data heavy," although some key quantitative and qualitative data are likely to be necessary. Instead, it will be heavy on strategic thinking and acting. Finally, if there is no real reason to plan strategically—no major threats or important opportunities—then perhaps strategic planning is a waste of time. "Muddling through" may work acceptably until more formal strategic planning does become necessary.

Getting Started

These four cases, plus the others cited in this book, indicate that strategic planning can help public and nonprofit organizations and communities fulfill their missions and satisfy their key stakeholders more effectively. These cases also indicate that a number of difficulties and challenges must be overcome if strategic planning is to fulfill its promise. Let me conclude with some advice about how to get started with strategic planning (see also Bryson, 1991).

1. *Start where you and the other people who might be involved in or affected by the process currently are.* This is one of the most important principles for organizing collective action (Kahn, 1982). You can always undertake strategic planning for that part of the organization that you control. Whatever you are in charge of—a unit, department, division, or a whole organization—you can always start there. But wherever you start, you must also keep in mind where the participants currently are. Other involved or affected parties are likely to need some education concerning the purposes, processes, and products of strategic planning. If they are important for the formulation or implementation of strategies, you will have to bring them along so that they can be effective supporters and implementers.

2. *You need a compelling reason to undertake strategic planning.* Otherwise, the process is not likely to be worth the effort or to reach a satisfactory conclusion. The obverse of this lesson is that people can create an infinite number of reasons *not* to engage in strategic planning, even when it would be the best thing for the organization or community; such "reasons" may be nothing more than excuses.

There are many compelling reasons to engage in strategic planning. The organization or community may be performing well, but key decision makers may be fully aware of important strategic issues that must be addressed if the organization is to continue to do well. That was the case with the CPI program, arguably the best such program in the world, and with the public library, which had a demonstrated high level of patron satisfaction. Another reason is that the organization may feel threatened by the emergence of strong rivals. That was also the case with the CPI program, which faced severe competition for resources as a consequence of strong pressures to cut the federal deficit. The public library also faced competition for revenues from rivals, notably the police and fire departments. The school district faced the prospect of competition as a result of the state's open educational enrollment legislation. And Mainline Church faced competition from everything in a secular society that might draw people away from voluntary participation in the organization.

Another reason is that the organization may be confronting a real turning point in its history—a point that might lead to success or deterioration. Recall that organizational strategies are usually fairly stable for rather long periods of time during which strategic planning is usually more concerned with programming strategy implementation than with formulating whole new strategies. (The public library's efforts, for example, have been focused mostly on making marginal improvements in existing strategies, although efforts at utilizing new computer and telecommunications technologies may ultimately prove revolutionary.) But then, after long periods of stability, come significant shifts—either as a result of changes in the environment or of new leadership. At such times strategic planning is much more concerned with enhancing strategy formulation (Gersick, 1991; Jarman and Land, 1992; Mintzberg and Westley, 1992; Mintzberg, 1994a, 1994b). That was the case with Mainline Church, whose process champion said that the organization would in the future become either "older and smaller" or "younger and bigger"—either it would alter its strategies or it would wither and die. In response to major environmental changes, the school district's plan embodied significant changes in many areas (curriculum, facilities, governance) that cumulatively amounted to a "quantum" change (Miller and Friesen, 1984). The CPI program's strategic plan also involved major shifts for the organization in terms of communication strategy and service offerings. While the organization could draw on precedents for such changes, the scale of change envisaged amounted, in effect, to a change in the previous identity of the organization. It will still be arguably the best such organization in the world, but it will be different because the environment will be different.

Yet another reason is that the organization may feel the need for strategic planning but not engage in the process until ordered to do so by top-level decision makers. That was not the case with any of the four organizations highlighted in this book, but it can happen; indeed, recent federal legislation and many states now require certain organizations to engage in strategic planning. But whatever the compelling reason, organizational or community members—especially key decision makers—must see some important benefits to be derived from strategic planning, or they will not be active supporters and participants. And if they do not support and participate, the process is bound to fail.

3. *There is no substitute for leadership.* The concepts, procedures, and tools that strategic planning comprises cannot think by themselves. Nor can they inspire and mobilize others to act on behalf of what is best for an organization or community. Only concerned and committed people—leaders and followers—can do that. Broad-based collective leadership spread throughout an organization is

necessary to ensure that it fulfills its mission and mandates and meets the expectations of its key stakeholders. And when the organization succeeds, it is a collective accomplishment.

Two leadership roles are especially important to the success of any strategic planning effort. Unless the process is *sponsored* (ultimately, if not initially) by important and powerful leaders and decision makers, it is likely to fail. Only key decision makers who are also effective leaders will be able to motivate and guide their organizations through a successful strategic thinking and acting process. Leadership from the key decision makers is absolutely necessary if the organization itself must be changed as a result of strategic planning.

A strategic planning process also will not succeed unless it is *championed* by someone. This person should believe in the process and see his or her role as promoting effective thinking, deciding, and acting on the part of key decision makers. A process champion does not have a preconceived set of answers to the important issues the organization faces, but he or she pushes a process that is likely to produce effective answers. It certainly helps if the process champion is near the top of the organizational hierarchy. (That was the case in all four of our example organizations.) But it does not hurt to have champions from other levels as well. Indeed, the process is likely to be more effective if more than one champion is involved.

A third leadership role—*facilitating*—can also be very important, though I would not place it in the same category as the first two. Facilitation is a special skill and can be very important at particular points, especially during design of the process and as groups of participants learn how to work together effectively (Schwarz, 1994).

4.   *Tailor the process to the organization or community and its unique situation.* Strategic planning efforts must clearly fit the situation at hand, even if their ultimate aim is to change that situation (Mintzberg, 1994b). The roles the official planners play in that process will also depend on the specific situation. In most cases involving strategic planning across units or levels within an organization or for a community, planners will need to facilitate strategic thought and action by key decision makers. In other situations, planners will also be called upon to serve as technical experts.

Another key situational factor concerns the presence or absence of formal and informal forums (for discussion), arenas (for decision making and implementation), and courts (for managing residual conflicts and enforcing underlying norms). These are the settings within which strategic planning and implementation will occur, and their design and use are very important to the success of the process. If it is clear that key strategic issues bridge organizational boundaries, then it is probably necessary to create forums that also bridge these boundaries. Forums might include strategic planning teams, task forces, or discussion groups. Similarly, if implementation will require coordinated action across boundaries, some sort of arena-like mechanism to manage the process across those boundaries may be necessary. Appropriate mechanisms might include a policy board, cabinet, interagency coordinating council, project management group, or community leadership council. Courtlike vehicles to manage residual conflicts are also likely to be needed. Referral procedures, alternative dispute-resolution mechanisms, administrative tribunals, and access to formal courts may also be needed.

The strategic plans themselves must also be tailored to fit the situation. It may be important, for example, not to prepare a written strategic plan. Indeed, some of the best strategic "plans" I have seen were unwritten agreements among key decision makers about what was important and what actions they would take. In other cases, plans will consist of informal letters, memoranda of agreement, issue-specific strategy documents, or full-blown glossy publications intended for public consumption. It all depends on the purposes to be served by the plan.

A final area of needed situational sensitivity concerns the evaluative criteria used to assess strategies and plans. Viable strategies and plans need to be politically acceptable, technically workable, and legally and ethically justifiable—a severe test, given the many stakeholders who are likely to be involved or affected. Finding strategies that can satisfy many stakeholders means that leaders, managers, and planners need to be willing to construct and consider arguments geared to many different evaluative criteria.

5. *The biggest innovation in strategic planning is having key decision makers talk with one another about what is truly important for the organization or community as a whole.* A strategic planning process is merely a way of helping key decision makers think and act strategically. The process can in no way substitute for the presence, participation, support, and commitment of key decision makers to raise and resolve the critical issues facing the organization or community. Initiation and institutionalization of the process, however, can provide the occasions, settings, and justification for gathering key decision makers together to think and act strategically on behalf of the organization or community. In all too many organizations and communities, such occasions, settings, and justifications do not exist. Organizational and community performance and stakeholder satisfaction suffer accordingly.

6. *The resource most needed to undertake strategic planning is not money but the attention and commitment of key decision makers.* Strategic planning is not expensive in dollar terms, but it is expensive when it comes to the resource that is typically most scarce—the attention and commitment of key decision makers. For organizations, strategic planning may involve having key decision makers spend up to 10 percent of their ordinary work time working together to identify and address fundamental policy questions. That may not seem like much. Indeed, one might argue that decision makers unwilling to devote up to 10 percent of their work time to what is truly important for the organization are either incompetent or disloyal and ought to be fired! But realistically, for a variety of reasons it is hard to persuade key decision makers to commit more than 10 percent of their time to strategic planning.

The reasons include the fact that the urgent often drives out the important and what is routine drives out what is nonroutine. Beyond that, since major strategy changes are relatively rare, many decision makers realize that strategic planning usually focuses on strategy implementation rather than strategy formulation. Thus, strategic planning may seem redundant to them, repeating what they are already doing, or it may appear less glamorous and important than its sponsors and champions think. In addition, decision makers may be justifiably concerned that strategic planning could drive out strategic thought and action or may unreasonably or unwisely limit their own discretion. Or they may simply be afraid of the consequences, conflictual or otherwise, that may result from focusing on particular strategic issues. For whatever reason, it is simply hard to get much attention for the process in many situations. And it may be even more difficult to get substantial blocks of time from community leaders for community strategic planning.

Strategic planning processes are also quite likely to be thrown off track by various disruptions and delays. Processes in which I have been involved have been thrown off course by elections, promotions, crises, scandals, deaths and life-threatening illnesses, pregnancies, horrible public gaffes, and chance events both favorable and unfavorable of numerous sorts. Such eventualities are normal, and sponsors and champions should expect them. Also, strong sponsors and champions are necessary to keep key decision makers focused on what is important, so wise strategic thought and action are not lost in the disruptions and delays.

Given the difficulties of getting key decision makers' attention, an effective strategic planning process is therefore likely to be one that is fairly simple ("simpler is better") and quick ("quicker is better"), and it should always be treated in a special and sensitive way so that key decision makers will give it the time and attention it needs when it needs them. In addition, it is important that sponsors and champions think of *junctures* as a key temporal metric. Time in strategic planning is generally not linear (*chronos*) or characterized by peaks or optimal experiences (*kyros*). Instead, it is junctural: key people must come together at the right time and with the right information in order to discuss what is important and do something effective about it (Albert, 1995). The ability to think juncturally, to think about timing, is a special skill that must be cultivated (particularly by sponsors and champions) if the strategic planning process is to be successful (Bryson and Roering, 1988, 1989).

7. *Remember that the biggest payoffs from strategic planning may come in surprising ways or from surprising sources.* For example, Hennepin County, Minnesota, found that organizational development, team building, and heightened morale throughout the organization were among the greatest benefits derived from its strategic planning process (Eckhert, Haines, Delmont, and Pflaum, 1988). The CPI program discovered that it needed to communicate far more effectively with stakeholders and to promote quite innovative approaches to creating value added for key stakeholders. People in the school district discovered that, much to their dismay, they

needed to confront the teachers' union about pay, benefits, and work rules if the district's goals were to be achieved. The public library found that—in opposition to the prevailing professional culture—it was going to have to stop trying to be all things to all patrons, and focus instead on particular roles aimed at certain categories of patrons. Mainline Church found out some very surprising things about its demographics and governance processes as part of its strategic planning efforts—for example, it discovered that it had an aging congregation but many young families with children, fewer big donors than in the past, and too many committees. The church also found that by altering its strategies it could maintain itself in the face of opposing national and metropolitan trends.

There is no telling what will happen as a result of the strategic planning process. But the organization or community that is open to surprises may create and take advantage of its own opportunities. As Louis Pasteur said, "Chance favors the prepared mind."

8. *Outside consultation and facilitation can help.* Often organizations and communities need some consultation, facilitation, and education from outsiders to help with the design and management of the strategic planning process. The CPI program, the school district, the public library, and Mainline Church all relied on outside help of various kinds at various points in the strategic planning process. If help is needed, try to get it.

9. *If the going gets tough, keep in mind the potential benefits of the process.* Recall that strategic planning can help organizations and communities in a number of ways. For example, strategic planning can help organizations and communities

- Think strategically and develop effective strategies
- Clarify future direction
- Establish priorities
- Make today's decisions in light of their future consequences
- Develop a coherent and defensible basis for decision making
- Exercise maximum discretion in the areas under organizational control
- Make decisions across levels and functions
- Solve major organizational problems
- Improve organizational performance
- Deal effectively with rapidly changing circumstances
- Build teamwork and expertise

But it may not be easy to achieve these benefits. The faith of process sponsors and champions can often be sorely tried, particularly if the organization or community is engaged in strategic planning for the first time. For example, the process seems particularly prone to disintegration in the middle—the strategic issue identification and strategy development steps. And the big payoffs may take a long time to achieve. For instance, it may take several years to know if some important strategy has worked or not. In the meantime, therefore, try to label as much as possible that comes out of the process a success—count every small win and work hard to improve the process along the way.

In order to maintain enthusiasm for its planning process while it waited for successes tied directly to implemented strategies to appear, Hennepin County emphasized—even celebrated—the achievements and benefits of the process as they occurred (Eckhert, Haines, Delmont, and Pflaum, 1988, 1992, 1993). Achievements were highlighted at special meetings of all three hundred managers, in newsletters, in glossy brochures, at special meetings of the county board, and even in a theater pantomime show. Achievements included forming a cabinet of top administrators, developing strategic planning educational materials and guidebooks, identifying thirty-two strategic issues, developing alternative strategies to deal with specific issues, and creating innovative strategies. Thus, the process was managed so that it was "successful" long before any actual strategies were implemented.

It is also useful for sponsors and champions to do what they can to maintain an optimistic stance toward the world—to see difficulties as specific rather than pervasive, temporary rather than permanent, and as things that can be changed (Seligman, 1991). They should do what they can to build their own and others' "psychological hardiness," through building commitment to the organization's mission, building a sense of control over the organization's future, and seeing difficulties as manageable challenges (Kouzes and Posner, 1987).

Sponsors and champions should also be realistic—at least with themselves—about what strategic planning can achieve. They might keep in mind, for example, Sigmund Freud's observation that "the purpose of analysis is to replace neurosis with ordinary unhappiness." Strategic planning will not lead to perfection, but it can result in useful, implementable strategies for addressing a few key issues—and that is something worth pursuing. By organizing hope, strategic planning can make the courageous organization's hopes reasonable.

10.   *Lastly, keep in mind that strategic planning is not right for every organization or community.* In the following situations, strategic planning perhaps should not be undertaken (Barry, 1986):

- The roof has fallen.
- The organization or community lacks the necessary skills, resources, or commitment of key decision makers to produce a good plan.
- The costs outweigh benefits.
- The organization or community prefers to rely on the vision, intuition, and skill of extremely gifted leaders.
- Incremental adjustments or muddling through in the absence of a guiding vision, set of strategies, or plan are the only processes that will work.
- Implementation of strategic plans is extremely unlikely.

However, while there may be *reasons* not to undertake strategic planning, those reasons can all too easily become *excuses* for not paying attention to what is really important for the organization or community. An organization or community that gives in to excuses has suffered a failure of hope and courage. Wordsworth reminds us that "our destiny, our being's heart and home" are with hope, effort, expectation, and desire. And Maya Angelou reminds us that only courage will get us there.

Strategic planning can help public and nonprofit organizations to fulfill their missions and communities to serve important purposes. And it can help both to satisfy their key stakeholders. But it will only work if people want it to work. This book was written to help all those who want their organizations and communities to survive, prosper, and serve noble purposes. I hope it will prompt more than a few of these organizational and community citizens to proceed with strategic planning because then significant change can occur. As Margaret Mead said, "Never doubt that a small group of thoughtful, committed citizens can save the world; indeed, it is the only thing that ever has."

RESOURCES

Five resources are included here. The first (Resource A) presents an ongoing approach for identifying external threats and opportunities. The second (Resource B) offers advanced concepts for identifying strategic issues, and the third (Resource C) describes how to use the "oval mapping process" to identify strategic issues and formulate effective strategies. The fourth (Resource D) presents advanced concepts for strategy formulation and implementation. The final resource (Resource E) presents advanced concepts for establishing an effective organizational vision for the future.◆

RESOURCE A

AN ONGOING APPROACH FOR IDENTIFYING EXTERNAL THREATS AND OPPORTUNITIES

Public and nonprofit organizations should consider establishing a regular external scanning operation so that they can routinely monitor the external environment for opportunities and threats. If the external scanning function is *not* routine, almost certainly the organization will be in a reactive rather than anticipatory position. Important opportunities will be missed, and threats will not be recognized until it is too late or until many important strategic options have been foreclosed.

A Three-Part Model for External Scanning

Pflaum and Delmont (1987) have proposed an inexpensive, pragmatic, and effective model for public and nonprofit organizations to use in external scanning. They argue that external scanning consists basically of three steps.

1. Identifying key issues and trends that pose actual or potential threats or opportunities
2. Analyzing and interpreting these issues and trends
3. Creating information that is useful for decision making

The three steps will be discussed in order.

Deciding on Purposes, Participants, and Time

The reasons for scanning should be clarified at the outset.

- To provide information on emerging issues and trends
- To develop networks and partnerships among scanners and their organizations
- To educate the participants about the scanning function and about specific issues and trends
- To provide useful information for strategic planning

An organization interested in strategic planning should probably engage in regular external scanning for all four of these purposes.

Pflaum and Delmont argue that scanning is most cost effective if it is undertaken by a group or network of organizational insiders interested in scanning and willing to devote part of group members' time to the effort. The group should be coordinated by a lead person. Outside consultants might be used as needed. The efforts of the insiders may be enhanced if they are part of a network of scanners in other organizations.

Time commitments are important to the success of scanning. If volunteers are to be involved, the organization must try to keep time demands to a minimum. Pflaum and Delmont propose three options for meetings: annual or quarterly meetings lasting half a day to a full day, monthly sessions lasting two to three hours, and meetings twice a month lasting two hours. In addition to meetings, time must be spent reading and preparing short scanning reports, possibly on a one-page scanning form. How much time should be spent on reading will vary. Most professionals spend a portion of their time reading anyway, so scanning may not involve any additional reading time—though the reading itself may be redirected to agreed-upon categories: periodicals, newsletters, and so on.

Identifying Key Issues

Once purposes, participants, and time commitments are clarified, the next step is to carry out major scanning activities. Pflaum and Delmont identify the following activities:

1. Select issues and trends categories (political, economic, social, educational, and technological).
2. Identify appropriate sources (professional journals, newsletters, conference proceedings, and key informants).
3. Understand issues cycles (see Resource B).
4. Ask key questions (Is the issue or trend new? Does it come from a surprising source? Does it contradict prevailing wisdom? Is there a pattern to the issue or trend?).

5. Develop a simple record-keeping system (simple one-page scanning report forms or more elaborate computerized key word systems).

Analyzing the Issues

Analysis and interpretation of the strategic importance of issues and trends can be accomplished by a number of techniques, but the simplest and best is group discussion. There simply is no substitute for the collective wisdom likely to emerge from a probing discussion of an issue or trend by an experienced and heterogeneous group of people.

Additional techniques—the simpler the better—may be used to inform judgments about the meaning and implications of particular issues and trends. Brainstorming (Johnson and Johnson, 1994), the nominal group technique (Delbecq, Van de Ven, and Gustafson, 1975), the snow card technique (discussed in Chapter Five), and the oval mapping process (discussed in Resource C) are simple yet effective techniques that can be used with groups. Brainstorming is good for creating ideas, the nominal group technique can help create and rank ideas, snow cards are effective for creating and synthesizing ideas into categories, and the oval mapping process can be used to structure issue areas.

Scenarios (Schwartz, 1991) are also relatively simple to construct and can be used to present an array of options for discussion. Scenarios are stories that pose alternative futures for the organization, based on assumptions about current trends and events. Usually a best-case scenario, a worst-case scenario, and a scenario somewhere in between are developed to map out the range of possible futures the organization might face, the threats and opportunities each future might pose, and what the "critical success factors" might be in addressing those futures (Leidecker and Bruno, 1984). Schwartz (1991, pp. 226–234) and Nanus (1992, pp. 203–217) describe simple yet effective processes for developing scenarios and drawing out their strategic implications.

Another useful technique is the "impact network" (Pflaum and Delmont, 1987). Impact networks are constructed by brainstorming secondary or tertiary impacts, trends, or events that might follow from some primary impact, trend, or event. And a final simple technique is an impact/probability matrix (Pflaum and Delmont, 1987). This matrix has two dimensions: the likely impact of an issue, trend, or event (high, medium, or low) and the likelihood that it will occur (high, medium, or low). Issues, trends, or events are mapped onto the matrix so that planners may judge which ones they should most closely monitor and which ones they should make contingency plans for. Additional techniques can be found in Nutt (1989) and Nutt and Backoff (1992).

The final step in the analysis and interpretation process is to decide what to do next. A possible next step might be to decide which issues and trends to monitor more closely, which to act upon or refer to appropriate decision makers for consideration, and which to drop.

Creating Information for Decision Making

The reporting and referral process produces information that is useful for decision making. Several approaches might be used to produce such information. Planners might prepare brief issue or trend summaries, often called "scans," which can condense onto a single page the essence of an issue or trend. Three- to five-page policy papers might be developed to explore specific issues or trends in further depth. Comprehensive environmental scans covering a range of issues and trends might be put together. Seminars or forums on specific issues or trends might be organized for particular stakeholder groups. Finally, a regular newsletter might cover a changing selection of issues and trends.

The basic idea is that for environmental scanning to be useful, it must become a regular and expected part of several persons' jobs, it must not place excessive demands on their time, and it must produce useful information for decision making. When information produced by environmental scanning is coupled with information produced on an organization's actual or potential clients, customers, and payers and on its competitors and collaborators, the organization is in a good position to identify external opportunities and threats in a timely way.

ADVANCED CONCEPTS FOR IDENTIFYING STRATEGIC ISSUES

Strategic issues are the fundamental policy questions or challenges that affect an organization's (or community's) mandates, mission, and values; product or service level and mix; clients, users, or payers, or costs, financing, management, or organizational design. Basically, strategic issues emerge from the way organizations choose to—or are forced to—relate to their internal and external environments. The issues define the choices the organization faces over exactly what its "fit" with its environment will be.

This section will concentrate on several sources of what might be termed "generic" strategic issues for governments and, to a lesser extent, nonprofit organizations. The purpose of the section is to provide readers with a better understanding of what strategic issues are and where to look for them.

Strategic issues can be expected to emerge from public and nonprofit sector environments, issue cycles and agendas, the nature of public policies, and the use of the various tools such as environmental scanning and SWOT analyses that help identify issues. Each of these sources will be discussed.

Public and Nonprofit Sector Environments

An appreciation of the important differences between the public, nonprofit, and private sectors must lie behind any appropriate application of strategic planning to public and nonprofit purposes (Ring and Perry, 1985; Nutt and Backoff, 1992, pp. 22–54, 1993). As a starting point, it is worth noting why we have public and nonprofit organizations in the first place. Like most market-based societies, we in the United States basically rely on markets to handle most exchanges of goods and services. We also rely on markets to make many of our most important societal decisions (what most people's jobs are, how much they earn, where they live) *as a by-product of market operations* (Lindblom, 1977). As a consequence, a major fraction of the government's attention is devoted to controlling the activities of the marketplace and correcting its failures. Indeed, the primary rationale for government intervention in society is to provide for what markets either cannot do, will not do, or do badly (Moore, 1978). The nonprofit sector, then, occupies a space in between the public and private sectors, serving some public purpose or contributing to the public good (which justifies its nonprofit status) while being institutionally separate from government. The nonprofit sector is thus in a position to help address market failures *and* government failures while also providing an independent institutional base in support of solidarity, joint action, pluralism, and freedom (Salamon, 1992, pp. 6–11).

The interactions of public organizations with nonprofit and for-profit organizations may generate strategic issues. Particularly important in this regard is the power of public bodies to regulate or otherwise influence the activities of private sector bodies and the concomitant efforts by private sector bodies to influence public policies and actions. Thus, strategic issues for governments include if, when, and how to intervene in market operations. In the relatively recent past, if government determined that a market was failing in some fashion, the normal response would have been to replace the market with a public bureaucracy (Schultze, 1977). Now the trend is to rely on less drastic interventions involving marketlike public policy tools such as vouchers, taxes, subsidies, insurance schemes, and contracts with public, private, or nonprofit organizations to provide services; but the strategic issues over if, when, and how to correct market failures still remain (Savas, 1982; Bryson and Ring, 1990). Raising and resolving these issues is likely to involve attempts to gain political influence by actors from all three sectors (Nutt and Backoff, 1992, 1993).

The fact that the United States is characterized by a federal system of government (the formal sharing of power by state and local governments through dual sovereignty) as well as extensive intergovernmental relations (Agranoff, 1989) is also significant. Strategic issues of several kinds might be expected to emerge from such a system of government (Ring, 1988). Some issues might be expected to emerge at the boundaries between lateral governments. For example, how will the legislators in one state react to changes in the tourism promotion plans of a neighboring state? Other issues might be expected to emerge around issues of coordination, responsibility, and shared resources for program operations and outcomes across vertical levels of government. These issues are typical of many health, education, and social service programs that are initiated, regulated, and funded at levels other than the one that implements them. Still other issues might emerge, involving policy or program focus, responsibility, effort, and financing in situations where no one appears to be "in charge" (Cleveland, 1973).

There are additional differences between the public, nonprofit, and private sectors. First, the ill-defined nature of much public policy creates conflict over public organizational goals or purposes as well as difficulties for those in public, nonprofit, and private sectors who are charged with implementing the policies. Implementers often must do without clear guidance (Ring and Perry, 1985), even as they are constrained by public mandates that sharply limit their autonomy and flexibility. In other words, performance expectations in the public sector are often vague and in constant flux, while in the private sector they tend to be much clearer and more stable. Nonprofit organizations often find themselves somewhere in between the extremes (Nutt and Backoff, 1992, 1993).

Public and nonprofit organizations typically serve a more diverse group of stakeholders than do private organizations. As a result, it often is more difficult for them to identify strategic issues and develop the strategies to deal with them. The artificial time constraints in the public sector—particularly those imposed by periodic elections—can create strategic issues such as the need for elected officials to demonstrate tangible accomplishments in a restricted time frame. Shaky coalitions usually characterize political decision making in the public sector. As a result, the creation and maintenance of coalitions may itself become a strategic issue. Nonprofit (and private) organizations dependent on governmental decision making and financing can find themselves whipped about by these shaky coalitions (Ring and Perry, 1985).

Typically, there is more extensive public scrutiny of the public sector than of either the nonprofit or private sectors. The nonprofit sector, however, typically faces more scrutiny than the private sector—as, for example, when nonprofit organizations depend on public funding or must be reviewed by external professional or accrediting bodies.

Finally, the incentives available to influence individuals in the three sectors differ. In the public sector, the incentives involve the call to public service, job security, power, recognition, and specific roles and tasks. In the nonprofit sector, the incentives can be the same, but more often, strong professional norms feature prominently (as they do, for example, in health, social welfare, and educational institutions). Financial incentives predominate in the private sector (Nutt and Backoff, 1992, 1993).

Issue Cycles

Issue cycles are another source of strategic issues (Renfro, 1993). Schön (1971) has pointed out that there is a life-cycle to issues and to the attention they receive from organizations and the public. The cycle begins with public awareness that a problem exists. The awareness may be prompted in a number of different ways, including the basic frameworks and myths people use to make sense of the world (their "interpretive schemes"; Schutz, 1967), the categories that people use to partition experience and data (health, education, housing, employment), value judgments, warning signals from key indicators, troubling comparisons (with other jurisdictions, organizations, nations), triggering events such as crises, and feedback (from citizens, customers, consultants, reports, information systems) (Bryson and Crosby, 1992, pp. 161–169; Kingdon, 1995). Solutions to the problem are then articulated, and networks or coalitions of public, nonprofit, and private actors are organized to advocate the different solutions. A political debate ensues, and a solution is adopted and legitimized. The solution is then institutionalized and, eventually, taken for granted. Finally, as the problems change, the institution—and the policy solution it symbolizes—decays and becomes outmoded.

Strategic issues might emerge for a public or nonprofit organization at any point in the cycle (Bryson, Van de Ven, and Roering, 1987). Issues might concern, for example, how to widen the appreciation of a problem, which solutions to advocate, how to gain adoption of favored solutions, how to institutionalize solutions, and how to dismantle outmoded regimes.

Strategic planning can be seen as a way to pay routine attention to ideas relevant to policy formation so that the organization can take action early in the cycle, when it may have a greater impact on the way events unfold. If an organization is to act quickly, however, it must have an effective environmental scanning system that focuses organizational attention on the strategic significance of problematic situations or events, new environmental trends, or emerging opportunities. Strategic planning also may help organizations realize when the time has come to change solutions and the organizations designed to implement them. To repeat a point from an earlier chapter, public and nonprofit organizations must always be seen as a means to an end—as a solution to a problem—not as an end in themselves.

Agendas

Cobb and Elder (1983) identify two types of public agendas: systemic and institutional. The systemic agenda "consists of all issues that are commonly perceived by members of the political community as meriting public attention and as involving matters within the legitimate jurisdiction of existing governmental authority." The institutional agenda is "that set of items explicitly up for active and serious consideration of authoritative decision makers" (p. 85). Items on either agenda may be potentially strategic for a public organization, but they only become so when fundamental policy choices for the organization are involved.

The important point is that governmental decision making is "governed by" agendas, often quite formal ones like the legislative agenda of a governing body, and that there are some issues that are seen as legitimately within the purview of government and others that are not. If an issue requires formal action, typically the choices must be placed on the organization's agenda, and the issue itself must, of course, be seen as within the legitimate purview of government. Similarly, action can be avoided on an issue if it is kept off the institutional or systemic agendas.

Cobb and Elder argue that whether or not an issue appears on the institutional agenda depends upon relationships among three sets of factors: triggering devices, initiators, and gatekeepers. Triggering devices include natural catastrophes, human disturbances (such as riots or assassinations), technological changes, actual imbalances or biases in resource allocations, and ecological changes. Initiators find the issues they wish to pursue in the effects of the triggering devices. Whether or not the initiators are able to place the issue on the institutional agenda depends primarily on their access to institutional gatekeepers, that is, key decision makers such as executives or legislators. The strategic planning process can be used to routinize attention to triggering devices and to involve initiators and gatekeepers directly in the process so that the organization has a clear link to the institutional agenda.

It is worth noting that nonprofit organizations are also governed at least in part by agendas and that many of the factors that help place an issue on a government's agenda also affect placement of an issue on a nonprofit organization's agenda.

Public Policies

Public policies may be both the source of strategic issues and the strategies used to resolve them. Types of public policies and how they might be implemented, therefore, are of special concern. We will deal with policy types first because the kind of policy involved is likely to influence how the issues are framed, what solutions are proposed, and how implementable those solutions are.

Lowi (1966) has argued that there are three basic categories of policy: distributive, regulatory, and redistributive. Distributive policies produce tangible results, such as those resulting from traditional "pork barrel" politics; most public land and resource policies; rivers and harbors legislation; research and development contracts; defense procurement programs; and labor, business, and agricultural "clientele" services. They are in effect "patronage" policies—almost not policies at all but simply the aggregated effects of numerous highly individualized decisions. The policies benefit many individuals or organizations, and they result from an accumulation of diverse interests in a "log-rolling" fashion. Winners and losers never need to come into direct contact with one another. Decisions usually are made by legislative committees or public agencies in which the power structure consists of stable, nonconflicting elites along with associated support groups. The policies are then implemented by an agency, typically a primary functional unit (or "bureau").

Regulatory policies control the activities of specified populations and how various resources can be used. They therefore cannot be disaggregated to the level of individuals or specific organizations the way distributive policies can, because implementation must be through application of a general rule and with reference to the broader standards of law. Regulatory policies thus can only be disaggregated down to "sector" levels, such as, for example, all bus companies, or food preparation facilities, or households of a certain kind. It is fairly clear who is helped and hurt by the regulatory decisions, at least in the short run. The policies are the outcome of a struggle among competing groups, or coalitions, with something to gain or lose from regulatory decisions. This is the classic "pluralist," or group struggle, form of decision making (Dahl, 1984). The coalitions are usually unstable, meaning that many regulatory decisions are made on the floor of legislative bodies and not in committee. Once decisions are made, implementation is usually delegated to an appropriate agency.

Redistributive policies involve shifting benefits away from one group toward another (as occurred, for example, in the shifting of federal spending in relative terms away from defense and toward social programs in the 1960s, and later, under the Reagan administration, back in the other direction). Redistributive policies thus are like regulatory policies in their impact, except that they affect a much broader proportion of the population (entire social classes). Issues involving redistribution therefore activate special interests roughly along class lines; those interests are expressed by "peak associations" such as the U.S. Chamber of Commerce and the National Association of Manufacturers. The competing coalitions involve elites and counterelites and are usually quite stable. Key decisions are typically made within the peak associations and the executive branch. Implementation occurs toward the top of some major agency; that is, above the bureau level. Implementation of federal tax reforms, for example, is the responsibility of the Internal Revenue Service as a whole.

In framing and resolving strategic issues, planners should take account of the different actors, power structures, dynamics, decisional loci, and implementation vehicles typically involved in each policy type. Planners should also realize that policy types can overlap in a given strategic issue. Other useful policy typologies are offered by Wilson (1986) and Waste (1989).

A number of authors have explored public policy implementation in detail (Pressman and Wildavsky, 1973; Van Meter and Van Horn, 1977; Bardach, 1977; Mazmanian and Sabatier, 1983; Goggin, Bowman, Lester, and O'Toole, 1990; Bryson and Crosby, 1992). Their research indicates that policy implementation can be problematic, giving rise to a number of strategic issues (Ring, 1988).

Mazmanian and Sabatier (1983), for example, offer a model of the policy implementation proccss that indicates three specific sources of strategic issues: the tractability of the problem, the statute or other policy vehicle used to structure the course of implementation, and nonstatutory variables that may affect the course of implementation. The tractability of the problem will determine whether or not measurable progress can be made in addressing the issue and, therefore, whether or not key stakeholders can be satisfied in the long run. Tractability decreases with increases in technical difficulties, size and diversity of target groups, and behavioral change requirements.

Mazmanian and Sabatier argue that there are seven features of statutes or other policy vehicles used to structure implementation that may affect implementation success. Each feature, in fact, might produce strategic issues or choices. First, are the policy objectives clear and consistent? Second, has an adequate causal theory been incorporated into the statute? Third, what allocation of resources is involved? Fourth, what degree of hierarchical integration within and among competing institutions is needed to achieve the policy objectives? Fifth, what decision rules will be used? Sixth, how will implementation officials and staff be recruited? And finally, how much formal access will outsiders have to the implementation process?

The third element of the model is a set of nonstatutory variables that may affect the course of implementation. These include general socioeconomic and technological conditions, the extent of public support, attitudes and resources of constituent groups, support from sovereigns, and the commitment and leadership skill of implementing officials.

Mazmanian and Sabatier's model provides a useful checklist of areas in which strategic issues may emerge. This checklist offers guidance on how to design public policies so that implementation difficulties may be avoided in the first place. Since the factors included in the model probably affect the implementation of programs, projects, products, or services, the checklist is also useful in identifying strategic issues emerging from those other implementation efforts. Similarly, the model helps planners avoid difficulties in implementing programs, projects, products, or services.

Tools

The final generic source of strategic issues to be discussed concerns the tools that might be used to identify issues. Different tools can be expected to uncover different kinds of issues, so one should not expect any single tool to uncover all of the potentially fundamental issues facing an organization. The tools that will be discussed briefly in this section include stakeholder analyses, environmental scanning, competitive and collaborative analyses, portfolio methods, scenarios, and SWOT analyses. Each of these tools is relatively simple in concept and use. The reader interested in other, typically more complicated tools should consult Friend and Hickling (1987); Rosenhead (1989); Nutt (1989, 1992); Nutt and Backoff (1992); and Buzan (1993).

Stakeholder analyses are likely to uncover issues related to the satisfaction of key stakeholders and to areas in which stakeholders' criteria for evaluating organizational performance are either complementary, in conflict, or nonexistent. Environmental scanning will detect issues, trends, and events in the categories in which searches occur. Competitive analysis will focus attention on the forces affecting the level of returns in specific industries and on specific firms within those industries. Collaborative analysis will help identify costs and benefits of possible collaborations.

Portfolio methods will array entities of some sort against dimensions thought to be of strategic importance. Potential strategic issues will concern what to do about the resulting array. For example, Ring (1988) presents a useful portfolio model that arrays the tractability of an issue against likely stakeholder support for addressing it. Issues that the organization can do something about and that have high stakeholder support are "sitting ducks." Issues that stakeholders want to have addressed but that are relatively intractable are "angry tigers" (because whatever the organization does is not likely to work, which will make stakeholders mad). Issues that are tractable but do not generate stakeholder support are "dark horses." Finally, issues that are not tractable and are not on the public agenda are "sleeping dogs," and public and nonprofit organizations might be wise to let them lie.

Scenarios present alternative pictures of possible futures. Strategic issues are likely to emerge as a result of the distance or tension between where the organization is now and what the scenario describes as a likely or possible future.

Stakeholder analyses, environmental scanning, competitive analysis, portfolio methods, and scenarios can each lead into more formal SWOT analyses. The snow card technique is a particularly inexpensive and effective way to uncover SWOTs. The strategic issues identified as a result of a SWOT analysis will concern how to take advantage of the organization's strengths and opportunities while minimizing or overcoming its weaknesses and threats.

Not all of these tools need to be used as part of every strategic planning effort, but at a minimum, stakeholder and SWOT analyses should be undertaken. Neither analysis has to take much time, and yet each is likely to have a profound effect on which strategic issues are identified and how they are framed.

RESOURCE C

USING THE "OVAL MAPPING PROCESS" TO IDENTIFY STRATEGIC ISSUES AND FORMULATE EFFECTIVE STRATEGIES

JOHN M. BRYSON, FRAN ACKERMANN, COLIN EDEN, AND CHARLES B. FINN

Many effective idea-producing techniques, such as brainstorming (Johnson and Johnson, 1994) and the nominal group technique (Delbecq, Van de Ven, and Gustafson, 1975), can produce lots of ideas but do not identify relationships between them for purposes of carrying the discussion further. The snow card technique (see Chapter Five) gives some structure to brainstormed ideas by grouping them into categories that can then be organized into logical, priority, or temporal order. "Mind mapping" (Buzan, 1993) does much the same thing. But often, along with categorization, the relationships between ideas within or across categories need to be further clarified. Thus, a process is needed to capture and "map" these relationships. The resulting map, or "directed graph" (Eden, Jones, and Sims, 1983), consists of concepts (phrased as actions) recorded on oval-shaped pieces of paper and linked by arrows indicating the cause-effect or influence relationships between them—such as A may cause or influence B, which in turn may cause or influence C, and so on. In other words, the action A is expected to lead to outcome B, while B in turn is expected to lead to outcome C. These maps can consist of hundreds of interconnected relationships, showing different areas of interest and their relationships to one another.

The "oval mapping process," which uses this mapping technique, was developed and refined over a number of years by Colin Eden and a large number of associates (Eden, Jones, and Sims, 1983; Eden and Huxham, 1988; Eden, Ackermann, and Cropper, 1992; Ackermann, 1993; Bryson and Finn, 1995). Ackermann (1993), in particular, is a key source of material for this resource. The process was developed as part of an approach to strategic management called Strategic Options Development and Analysis (SODA) (Eden, 1989), which has strongly influenced my own approach to strategic planning (outlined in Chapter Two).

The process can be used with individuals or with groups of up to twelve members (seven is optimal). In groups larger than twelve, participants can be lost in the crowd and feel they are not part of the group. More than twelve people can be involved, however, through the use of subgroups. Dividing the team into subgroups can produce different interpretations of an issue area, along with subsequent insights gained from comparing and contrasting these interpretations. Subgroups can all be assigned the same question or issue, or each can consider a different aspect of an issue. Subgroups may be homogeneous, representing a single class of stakeholder or organizational level, or heterogeneous, representing diverse interests. The simplicity of the basic process means it can be adapted to a number of uses, including stakeholder analyses, scenario development, strategic issue identification, strategy development, and clarifying the meaning of symbolically or substantively important concepts. Several of these applications are discussed below.

Purpose, Desired Outcomes, and Benefits

The purpose of the oval mapping process is to make sense of an area of concern by capturing and structuring the ideas that compose it. The meaning of any particular idea consists of its context—that is, the ideas that influence it ("arrows in") and the ideas that flow from it as consequences or outcomes ("arrows out"). Comparing and contrasting ideas and elaborating their connections establishes a rich context that makes understanding easier (Kelly, 1963; Schein, 1992). As ideas are explored, different interpretations are identified, leading to a more complete picture. The most important desired outcome of the oval mapping process is thus increased understanding of an important problem or issue area.

For example, the school district's board and cabinet mapped relationships between ideas in order to identify strategic issues and develop strategies to address them (Bryson and Finn, 1995). The resulting map included over 850 ideas that captured much of the board's thinking about the district's mission, goals, and strategic issues. One set of strategic issues that emerged centered around how and why "to manage the integration and inclusion of all populations effectively." The board was asked these questions: "How can we effectively manage the integration and inclusion of all populations?" And, "Why would we want to do so—that is, what should our goals be?" The group's initial thoughts are presented in Figures C.1 and C.2. (Each concept on the map received a unique number so it could be entered into a computer program [discussed below]; these numbers are noted in the figures.) Figure C.1 answers the "how" question and indicates various actions that might be taken to lead to effective integration and inclusion of all populations (concept 193). These actions include, for example, "Promote multicultural education" (106), "Redefine the way curriculum is developed" (214), "Use new

FIGURE C.1. RELATIONSHIP MAP: HOW TO MANAGE INTEGRATION AND INCLUSION OF ALL POPULATIONS EFFECTIVELY.

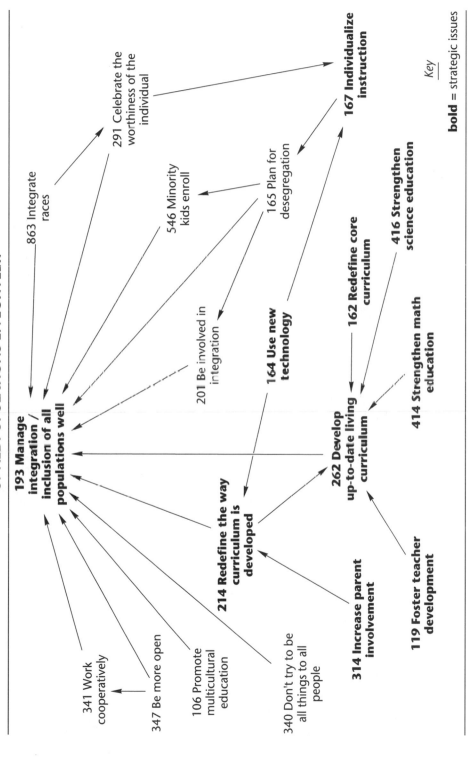

Source: Bryson and Finn, 1995, p. 270. Used by permission of Jossey-Bass Inc., Publishers.

technology" (164), "Individualize instruction" (167), and "Plan for desegregation" (165). Figure C.2 answers the "why" question, indicating the various consequences—leading to goals, values, and beliefs—that might follow from managing integration and inclusion well. These include "Prepare students to function successfully in a diverse society" (66), "Ensure that all kids have equality of opportunity" (270), "Teach morality in schools" (31), and "Develop good linkages with other organizations" (107).

A significant insight that emerged from the board's discussion of the map in Figure C.1 was that effective management of integration and inclusion is part and parcel of—not isolated from—a number of other issues that the board initially had thought were far more important. These subissues included "Redefine way curriculum is developed" (214), "Develop up-to-date living curriculum" (262), "Increase parent involvement" (314), "Use new technology" (164), "Individualize instruction" (167), and so on. The centrality of the integration and inclusion issue was further highlighted by its close connection to the board's higher-order goals for the district (Figure C.2), including "Prepare learners for next century" (3), "Provide educational services to meet community needs" (34), and, as already noted, "Prepare students to function successfully in a diverse society" (66).

There are a number of important benefits to using the oval mapping process, including its capacity to enhance reasoning ability, improve dialogue, manage complexity, and build teamwork within the group. Other benefits are as follows:

1. The process is easy to understand, teach, and use, and thus, complex maps can be developed relatively quickly. Mapping typically is a very efficient use of a group's time.

2. Structuring action-outcome relationships helps people figure out what they can do about an area of concern. This makes the process very useful to leaders and managers, who typically have an action orientation and often are uncomfortable with vague abstractions. It also promotes understanding through working out what is necessary to make something happen.

3. The process promotes a fuller understanding of an area of concern and thereby helps ensure that any actions taken are constructive rather than shortsighted, foolish, or downright damaging.

4. Much of this fuller understanding comes from the inclusion of many people's views. The process helps to create a *shared* view of the area of concern and what might be done about it. Thus, it promotes intra- and interorganizational, as well as intra- and interdisciplinary, understanding and creativity (de Bono, 1970; Van Oech, 1983; Johnson and Johnson, 1994). In most cases, the shared view represents a "reconstrual" of reality (Kelly, 1963); that is, participants see the world differently than they did before they came together—not as a result of arguments but through the way statements come to be linked together. For example, prior to developing its map, the school district did not realize to what ex-

FIGURE C.2. RELATIONSHIP MAP: PURPOSES OR CONSEQUENCES OF EFFECTIVELY MANAGING INTEGRA- TION AND INCLUSION OF ALL POPULATIONS.

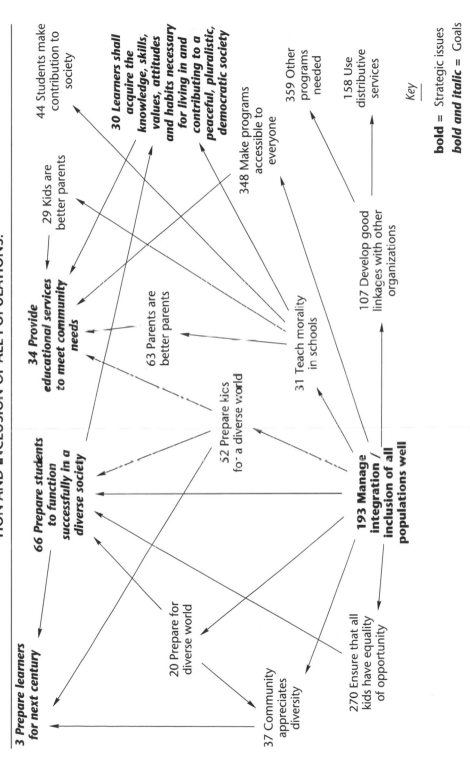

Source: Bryson and Finn, 1995, p. 269. Used by permission of Jossey-Bass Inc., Publishers.

tent "managing the inclusion of diverse populations" was linked to its other activities or how central the issue was to the district's mission.

5.   The process is highly participative and attends to the social aspects of group work. This promotes the participants' understanding of each other's roles. It also means the process can build cohesion and generate commitment to, and ownership of, subsequent actions. The process thus is an effective team-building tool (Ackermann, 1993).

6.   The process creates a forum for discussion and dialogue around important areas of concern—a fundamental feature of effective strategic planning and a crucial precursor to taking effective action (Bryson and Crosby, 1989, 1992).

7.   The process typically results in the creation of a tangible product, usually a map, that provides a record of the participants' merged contributions. To the extent that the map represents a shared and agreed-upon view, it serves as a "transitional object" (de Gues, 1988), or bridge, to the next step in the strategic planning process (Eden, 1989; Bryson and Finn, 1995). The map and the shared understanding of what it means can strongly influence mission formation, strategy development, and implementation.

8.   The process and the maps that result provide a useful way of managing complexity (Eden, 1989). The maps can incorporate broad and abstract statements of desired states (goals) as well as clusters of more specific options (issues) and agreed-upon portfolios of actions (strategies and work programs). The general form of a map is presented in Figure C.3. Goals are at the top, issues are below goals, options for achieving issues are below issues, and statements of fact or assertions are at the bottom. Typically, a workshop process is used to convert a draft map to an agreed-upon set of goals, strategies, actions, and assertions.

9.   Finally, the process enhances group productivity. Everyone can both "speak" (write on ovals), and "listen" (read ovals) in a full and broad context, rather than having to hear one person's views at a time and in sequence. Further, participants can come and go without negatively affecting the process in a significant way.

Process Guidelines

Persons wishing to use the process may find the following guidelines useful.

Equipment Needs

A large, smooth, unbroken wall space is needed for each map that will be constructed. The wall space should be approximately twelve to fifteen feet wide and six to eight feet high. It is often difficult to find suitable wall space without some

FIGURE C.3. GENERAL SHAPE OF AN ACTION-ORIENTED STRATEGY MAP.

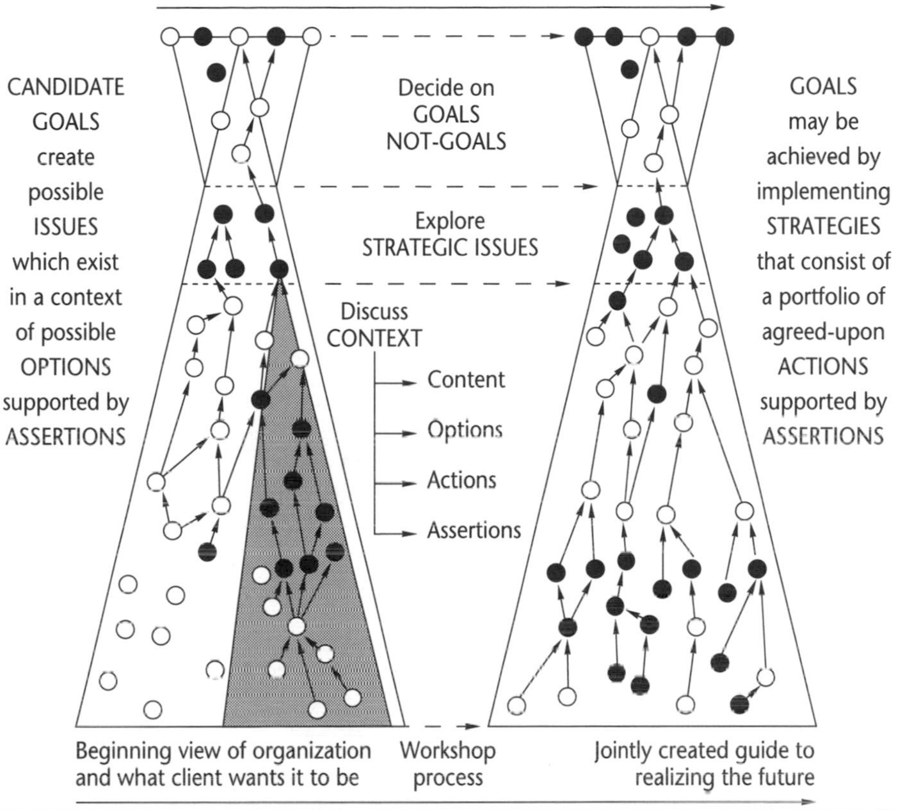

CANDIDATE
GOALS
create
possible
ISSUES
which exist
in a context
of possible
OPTIONS
supported by
ASSERTIONS

Decide on
GOALS
NOT-GOALS

Explore
STRATEGIC ISSUES

Discuss
CONTEXT

➤ Content

➤ Options

➤ Actions

➤ Assertions

GOALS
may be
achieved by
implementing
STRATEGIES
that consist of
a portfolio of
agreed-upon
ACTIONS
supported by
ASSERTIONS

Beginning view of organization
and what client wants it to be

Workshop
process

Jointly created guide to
realizing the future

Copyright Fran Ackerman, 1989; Real-izations, Inc., 1995. Reprinted with permission.

advance reconnaissance. This space will be papered-over with flip chart sheets in two or three rows, one above the other. Each row should be four to six flip chart sheets wide, depending on how many ideas are likely to be included on the map. The sheets should be hung with masking tape or self-adhesive putty so that they overlap each other by about an inch. When all the sheets are hung, the seams should be taped with masking tape so that the map can be taken off the wall in one piece when completed, and easily transported. It is also advisable to photograph the map before taking it down; each photograph should be of a single flip chart sheet. If the map does not need to be transported, it can be constructed on a large whiteboard (although it may be difficult to find one large enough), using whiteboard markers to indicate links among ideas.

It helps if the room is spacious and well lit, with easily accessible refreshments and rest rooms. In addition, the following materials and equipment will prove useful:

- *A full flip chart pad.* Remember, each map will need eight to eighteen sheets, so do not get caught short.
- *Masking tape or self-adhesive putty, such as Blu-Tack.* This is used to affix the flip chart sheets to the walls. Architect's drafting tape usually does not work as well because it is not as sticky.
- *A stack of ovals.* Cut out or have made oval-shaped pieces of paper for use in the exercise, approximately seven and one-half inches long and four and one-half inches wide. Typically, they are the same weight as construction paper. A template is provided in Exhibit C.1. Ovals should be yellow or some other light color so that they contrast with the background of the flip chart sheets yet allow any writing on them to be read easily. Twenty to thirty ovals per participant should be sufficient. (Alternatively, half-sheets of paper, 3-inch by 5-inch cards, or large self-stick notes can be used. The difficulty with these alternatives, however, is that they usually result in rows and columns rather than the full and creative use of the map's two dimensions.)
- *A bullet-tipped marking pen for each participant.* Bullet-tipped marking pens may be harder to find, but they are easier to use than chisel-point pens, and the results are more legible. The pens should all be the same color—usually black—to promote anonymity and to contrast with the color of the ovals. Some additional marking pens in different colors should be available to highlight particular features of the map (links, titles, key observations) during group discussions. Do not use regular ballpoint pens, as the resulting writing will likely be impossible to read from a distance.
- *Self-adhesive putty (such as Blu-Tack) for attaching the ovals to the flip chart sheets.* You need only a small amount of putty to attach an oval. Larger amounts are a waste and also make it harder to move the ovals around. Alternatively, have participants attach a tape roll to the back of each oval. A tape roll is made of tape rolled sticky side out. Drafting tape is better than masking tape for this purpose, since masking tape is too sticky and will likely tear the flip chart sheets if you try to move ovals around.
- *A sharpened, soft lead pencil with attached eraser for each participant.* These will be used for tentatively linking ovals and for making notes on the map.
- *Large erasers for use with lead pencils.* These will be used for large erasing jobs.
- *Self-adhesive dots in various colors to identify the nature of particular ovals or clusters of ovals and for straw polls.* Have on hand packets of at least one hundred red, purple, blue, green, and orange dots, three-quarters of an inch in diameter. (Larger dots cover too much space, particularly when used for straw polling, while smaller dots are harder to see.)
- *Suitable refreshments.* Have a supply of coffee, tea, soft drinks, mineral water, fresh fruit, nuts, cookies, and pastry, if possible.
- *A fully automatic camera.* This is to photograph the final map and the group as the process proceeds. The photographs can be used to remind participants of what happened and to indicate to others the nature of the process.

EXHIBIT C.1. TEMPLATE FOR AN OVAL.

Preparing a Starter Question

Have a "starter" question (or set of questions) already written out and clearly visible to participants. *Starting with the "right" question is very important* since it will have a dramatic impact on the answers. The question should be reasonably broad without being ambiguous. It should not be so narrow as to invite only yes or no answers. The planning team probably will need to devote considerable time to developing and pilot-testing the starter question(s), including consulting with key informants. Consider: "What should we do in the next three to five years?"

Introducing the Process

Participants will want information about the purpose of the session and the process to be used. For presentation purposes, let us assume that the purpose of the session is to develop a sense of the strategic issues that face the organization and the possible strategies that might address them.

1. Introduce the session by saying that the purpose is to gather opinions about the issues the organization faces and what might be done about them. All of the information created will be used to inform the strategic planning process. Be as specific as you can be about what will happen to the information and how it will be used; typically, this means that the information will influence decisions rather than creating them directly.

2. All views must be written down on ovals, or else they will get lost. This is an important opportunity for participants to have a significant influence on the identification of issues and development of strategies. Note that the process will result in a very efficient use of participants' time since they can all "speak" simultaneously by writing on their ovals—thus increasing each person's "air time"—and "listen" simultaneously when reading them.

3. Ideas should be expressed in action terms, preferably starting with a verb such as *do, buy, get, formulate, implement, achieve,* or some other imperative.

4. The process does not necessarily seek consensus or attempt to resolve conflict. Instead, the purpose is to clarify and understand how individuals and the group view the organization and its environment. If there are disagreements, it is important to clarify the rationales behind them and record them on separate ovals. It is *not* acceptable to remove other participants' ovals, to edit them without the participants' consent, or to disparage any ovals or their authors.

For example, in one recent exercise designed to address the needs of students with disabilities, one group thought an oval labeled "Have inclusive educational environment" meant having blind and hearing-impaired children in regular classrooms with sighted and hearing students. Another group thought it meant having separate schools for blind and hearing-impaired children so that they could experience being in a majority. Each view was placed on a separate oval and had an arrow going into the "Have inclusive educational environment" oval.

5.   Put ideas up on the wall as soon as they have been written down, rather than allowing participants to hoard them, so that others may see the ideas and build ("piggyback" or "hitchhike") on them.

6.   Either the facilitator or the participants themselves should sort the ovals into clusters that make sense. Clusters should be organized according to common themes or subjects. The advantage of using a facilitator is that all participants can observe and join in the discussion of where each idea belongs. A shared understanding of what all the ideas are may therefore emerge more quickly than if participants work in subgroups of two or three. If a facilitator does do the sorting, however, all participants should be encouraged to offer advice on where ovals should go. If participants do not know where they should go, the ovals should be placed to one side, to be revisited by the group after all the clusters have been examined or else sorted by the facilitator into the appropriate clusters as they become apparent. (Often, some combination of small-group and large-group work is desirable. For example, small groups may do the initial clustering, and then a facilitator may help the large group make sense of the initial clusters and do any regrouping that is necessary.)

7.   Keep the wording of ideas to around eight to ten words. This will help ensure that there is only one idea per oval, as well as make it easier for participants to read each other's ideas. Also, the facilitator should encourage participants to lengthen shorter answers so that their meaning is more clear.

Facilitating the Process

1.   Some participants may grasp the process quickly, start writing and displaying their ideas, and actively participate in structuring clusters of ideas. Others may take longer before they feel comfortable with the process and actively engage in it. It usually takes no more than twenty minutes to half an hour for everyone to be onboard.

2.   Ideas are first sorted into clusters that make sense. The next step in structuring the clusters involves placing ideas that are more general, abstract, or goal-oriented near the top of clusters. Ideas that are more concrete, specific, and detailed are placed toward the bottom. Also, assertions or statements of fact ("Our budget will be cut 10 percent"; "Client numbers are growing 20 percent per year"; "The executive director will retire in one year") are placed toward the bottom.

3.   Encourage participants to elaborate on the ideas and emergent issue clusters by asking questions. Say, for example, "I do not really understand this, could you say more?" or, "How would you make this happen?" or, "What would you hope to get out of doing this?" Questions also prompt other participants to add alternative perspectives as they discover that their interpretation is different from the proponent's.

4.   Make sure that ideas are worded in the imperative to suggest an action orientation.

5.   Each oval should contain only one idea. If an oval contains more than one, have participants make separate ovals for each idea. If an oval contains more than twelve words, it usually means there are two separate ideas presented.

6.   Keep encouraging people to write their ideas down, especially those participants who are less dominant. One way to do this is to write a person's ideas on ovals as he or she is speaking and then place them on the wall, to give the person confidence that his or her ideas are worth including. Groups that are discussing or debating ideas can be encouraged to capture their views on ovals and attach them to the wall.

7.   It can be helpful to number each oval as it is put up to help participants locate ideas on the wall. Numbering also helps if computer support is used (see below).

Further Structuring the Clusters

1.   Tentatively title the clusters. Once fairly stable clusters appear and the number of new ideas diminishes, review each cluster and give it a name that describes the theme or subject of the ovals inside it. Write the name, phrased in action terms ("Get our finances sorted out"; "Improve board-staff relations") on a new oval and place it at the top of the cluster. The cluster label will typically be the name of a potential strategic issue—indicated by the content of the cluster—while all of the ovals beneath it will consist of options for addressing it.

2.   With the help of participants, pencil in links within clusters and across clusters. Arrows *to* an idea indicate causes, influencers, or something that has to happen first (the rules do not need to be absolutely precise). Arrows *from* an idea indicate effects, outcomes, or consequences. Using a pencil is a good idea, because the placement of arrows can change based on discussion. Use an eraser to get rid of unwanted arrows. The placement of arrows shows participants which clusters or ideas are more important or "busy," with greater numbers of cross-links to other clusters or ideas.

3.   Decide whether the idea on an oval is an issue label, possible option, assertion, assumption, or statement of fact. Assertions, assumptions, and statements of fact are not directly actionable (except that they may call for further research), so they should be placed at the bottom of clusters. Typically, they provide premises for subsequent strings of possible actions. For example, if "The executive director will retire in one year" (a statement of fact), then a search committee may need to be established, the job description reviewed, and a choice made about whether to search for a replacement outside the organization as well as inside. Assertions or statements of fact may also lead to research (to find out whether they are true), or they may be converted into options by highlighting any implied actions.

Options are those ideas that contribute to achieving the purpose of a cluster (as indicated by the cluster's title). They are actionable ("Produce staff phone directory"; "Conduct focus groups"; "Use a telephone bank for fundraising") rather than being assertions or statements of fact.

Issues, the label for a cluster of options, are more complex. They are usually the most superordinate oval, although discussion may indicate that some other existing oval or a new one may better capture the essence of the issue. Issues usually are broad based, long term, and highly consequential in terms of associated threats or opportunities, effects on stakeholders, resource use, or irreversibility of possible strategies to address them. Issues may be identified by marking the relevant oval with an asterisk or colored stick-on dot.

4.   Once ovals are arranged hierarchically as issues, options, and assertions, decide on the relative importance of the different issues. (This step may come after the following step if that change in order is thought desirable.) Colored stick-on dots may be used to graphically indicate the group's views of the issues' relative importance. For example, give each participant five dots and ask him or her to place a single dot on each of the five most important issues. Alternatively, participants might be allowed to put more than one dot on an issue label to provide a measure of intensity of feeling. It may also be helpful to straw poll participants directly on the relative *unimportance* of the issues.

Often it is important to know which issues participants think are most important in the short term and which are most important in the long term. Dots of one color can be used to identify important short-term issues, and another color can be used for long-term issues.

5.   Identify goals by asking "So what?" questions about the issue clusters. In other words, query participants about what they would hope to achieve ("arrows out") by addressing the issues. Usually this line of questioning (or "laddering"; see Eden, Jones, and Sims, 1979) leads participants to additional issues or options before the set of goals is fully specified. Possible goals include those ideas that are obviously good things in their own right and do not seem to need any further elaboration. Typically, they are morally virtuous and upright and tap the deepest values and most worthy aspirations of the organization's culture. For example, pursuing this line of questioning led the school district's board to the goals outlined in Figure C.2 (ideas 3, 66, 34, and 30). Goals may be identified with a new color stick-on dot or self-stick notes to highlight their significance. Again, strawpolling procedures may be useful to indicate what participants believe are the most important goals.

Formulating and understanding a goal system includes identifying linkages among goals, issue labels, and options that compose issues. When working in a large group divided into subgroups, it is often useful to have subgroups switch the map they are working on after strategic issues have been identified— that is, groups should try to figure out the goal system implied by some other group's strategic issues. This procedure can open groups up to one another's thinking, promote creativity, and lead to a convergence across groups on goals, issues, options, and assertions.

The most superordinate goals in a strategy map usually outline the organization's mission. If there is little connection between these goals and the organization's existing mission statement, then determining the organization's mission is probably a strategic issue.

6.   Decide on actions for the immediate future to address the issues and achieve the goals. The group should review the options (and their resource implications) and indicate which are already being done and which new ones should be pursued over the course of the next six months to a year. Those options that help address more than one issue ("potent" options) are particularly desirable ones to choose. A straw-polling exercise—typically using green dots for "Go"—may be used to pool participants' opinions about which items should be included in the action set. The group may wish to place two dots on items it wishes to take responsibility for itself and single dots on items it wishes to delegate to others outside the group. Once actions to address an issue have been chosen, the broad outlines of a strategy should be reasonably clear from looking at the map. The action set also typically comprises the basic tasks to be performed, which are included in a work program that names the responsible parties, reporting dates, resources needed, and expected products or outcomes (see Chapter Nine).

7.   Provide closure to the session. It is possible to get many groups of five to approximately thirty participants (in several subgroups) through the process of constructing a draft map (including identifying goals, strategic issues, options, assertions, and actions) in a retreat setting over the course of one long day—or as part of a two- or three-day retreat that includes other activities, such as stakeholder analyses and SWOT analyses. At the end of the mapping exercise, some sort of closure is desirable, usually in the form of a review of what the group has done, what understandings or agreements have been reached, and a statement of what the next steps in the strategic planning process will be. For example, individuals or task forces may be assigned specific action items or the task of developing the issues further and recommending strategies for dealing with them.

Recording the Work of the Map Construction Session

There are several ways to record the group's work.

1.   The map can simply be taken off the wall and saved. Before doing so, however, it is advisable to run long strips of transparent tape across all of the ovals so that they do not come loose. The saved map can be posted wherever convenient so that its contents can be recorded in outline form, or for use as a focus of follow-up sessions.

2.   Contents of the map may be recorded on a computer as the group discusses them, either in map form using a software program especially designed for the purpose (such as Graphics COPE; see p. 275), or in outline form.

3.   The map may also be photographed. A standard fully automatic 35-millimeter camera with built-in flash can be used to photograph each flip chart sheet

separately. As long as participants have written legibly on their ovals, the map's contents can be read from the photographs. Photographs provide a useful backup copy in case the map itself gets lost. They can also be a reminder to participants of what the day was like and can help nonparticipants understand how the process progressed. The photographs can be mounted on standard sheets of paper (four to a page), inserted into transparent holders, and put into a three-ring binder, along with a title page, date, and list of those who attended. Alternatively, there are photocopying machines that can copy full flip chart sheets, reducing them to a smaller size if desired.

Useful Variations on the Mapping Process

The mapping process is very flexible and can be used in various ways over the course of a strategic planning process. For example, Chapters Two and Six discussed the indirect approach to identifying strategic issues. In that approach, options are invented to make or keep stakeholders happy, build on strengths, take advantage of opportunities, and minimize or overcome weaknesses and threats and to capture action-oriented features of mission and mandates, existing strategies, and background studies or reports. These options (assertions, issues, and goals) are then arranged into clusters in an effort to find issues that emerge indirectly via the options. The mapping process obviously can be used to provide additional structure to the issues and options and to clarify the goal system that might be pursued by addressing them. This was the approach used by the CPI program management group to identify strategic issues. The importance of the issues that emerged regarding stakeholders, including the need to communicate better with them and to enhance their satisfaction with the CPI program's products and operations, led to new goals that ultimately resulted in changing the CPI program's mission.

Stakeholder Analyses

Mapping may be used to develop a more integrated picture of an organization's stakeholders and how they relate to each other and the organization. For example, the planning team might try to articulate each stakeholder's goal system. This might be done by first asking what criteria the stakeholder might use to judge the organization's performance, or what the stakeholder's expectations are of the organization (see Chapter Four). The team members can then extrapolate the implied goals from these criteria or expectations, and postulate any other goals they think the stakeholder might have.

The team can then expand the map for each stakeholder by placing the team's own organization's goals on the map and indicating what the stakeholder does or can do to affect achievement of the organization's goals. Next the team members can identify what their own organization does or can do to meet the stakeholder's criteria or expectations. The pattern of influences and outcomes can then be explored and elaborated. The resulting map should help the team become clear about what the organization wants or needs from the stakeholder, what the stakeholder can do to give or withhold it (and why), and what the organization can do, if anything, about it.

These maps should help highlight potential strategic issues and the elements of useful strategies. They also can be used for role-plays within the strategic planning team, aimed at developing strategic options that are most likely to address stakeholder interests effectively, build a supportive coalition, and ensure effective implementation. To conduct a role-play, each member of the planning team should play the role of a different stakeholder. With the stakeholder's map as a guide, each team member should answer two questions about any strategic option (or portfolio of options) from the stakeholder's point of view: How would I react to this option? and, What could be done that would increase my satisfaction? Modifications should be placed on ovals and linked to, or substituted for, the focal option. Strategic options may thus be modified through a series of role-plays in such a way that stakeholder support and satisfaction can be increased and implementation success made far more likely (Eden and Huxham, 1988; Huxham and Eden, 1990).

The maps are also helpful in clarifying areas of potential collaboration with different stakeholders. In particular, the maps can highlight any potential "collaborative advantages," which occur when it is clear that two or more stakeholders can achieve desirable outcomes jointly that they cannot achieve alone (Huxham, 1993).

Unpacking Loaded Concepts

Often, strategic planning is temporarily stymied by the need to deal with issues that carry extraordinary emotional freight for various stakeholders. The need to address issues of gender, race, disability, or political ideology, for example, has given headaches (sometimes heartaches) to teams with which we have worked. The issues are highly emotive because of the negative consequences people have already suffered or think they might suffer depending on how issues are resolved (Ortony, Clore, and Collins, 1990; Kaufman, 1992). Reasonable dialogue becomes difficult or impossible under ordinary circumstances.

For example, in 1993, a large group of seventy stakeholder representatives working under the auspices of the U.S. Department of Education was interested in developing a national agenda for better addressing the needs of students with disabilities. The group was stymied by a lack of consensus about what "inclusive" education meant for students with disabilities. The emotional temperature was high, and many people were willing to accuse others of pretty awful things. There was a certain humorous irony in the situation, in that what *divided* people was *in-*

clusion, but few present saw anything at all funny about it. Group members imagined the worst about each other, partly because in the absence of real dialogue no one really knew what others thought, and therefore many were prone to stereotype, project, and rationalize in inaccurate and unhelpful ways. Eventually, the group was unwilling to proceed further until the facilitators helped them deal directly with this issue of inclusion. In response, the facilitators invented a variant of the mapping process employing the following guidelines:

1.   Write the "loaded concept" on an oval and place it in the middle of a wall covered with flip chart paper. In the case of the educational group, the loaded concept was "inclusive education for students with disabilities."

2.   Have participants seat themselves in a semicircle in front of the wall.

3.   Ask each person to take out a sheet of scratch paper and draw a line down the middle, dividing it into two columns of equal size. Label the left column "How?" and the right column "Why?" Then have each person individually and silently brainstorm as many answers to the two questions as possible. In the case of the educational group, this meant brainstorming as many possible *means* to achieving inclusive education as each person could imagine ("How?") and as many possible *ends* (outcomes, consequences, goals) of inclusive education as they could imagine ("Why?").

4.   Have each person select a specified number of the most important means and an equivalent number of the most important ends and write each one on a separate oval. In the educational case, participants were asked to select one item from each list, since there were seventy people in the group and their selecting a greater number would have drawn the process out too much and probably have generated redundant ideas.

5.   Cluster the "means" ovals below the loaded concept and cluster the "ends" ovals above. Structure can be added if necessary to indicate how the various ideas within and across clusters are related.

6.   Lead participants in a conversation about the resulting clusters. Add ovals, linkages, and clusters as necessary. As the precise nature of the disagreements becomes more clear, people are better able to discuss them, including inventing additional options or goals along the way. Keep asking "how" and "why" questions to help clarify people's reasoning and to keep them from coming to blows over particular options. In other words, help people to be reason-*able.* Record key points right on the flip chart–papered wall or on a separate flip chart.

In most cases, the major disagreements will be over means and not ends. The map will make this graphically clear. When people realize that they actually *share* some important goals, they are far more likely to engage in constructive dialogue about how to achieve them (Filley, 1975; Fisher and Ury, 1981; Susskind and Cruikshank, 1987; Johnson and Johnson, 1994; Terry, 1993). They also are less likely to stereotype, project, and rationalize in destructive ways (Fisher and Brown, 1988). In the educational group, many participants were surprised to find out that the entire group really did share most of the goals but differed on the far more numerous means. Heightened respect emerged, along with a less tense atmosphere and a commitment to solving problems. After a number of months, the project resulted in a valuable report and a new sense of direction for the future (U.S. Department of Education, 1994).

Scenario Construction

The mapping process can also be used to develop the elements of scenario story lines. The main benefit of constructing scenarios is to promote learning by the planning team; sensitize team members to plausible, though perhaps unlikely, futures; and develop strategies better able to handle most eventualities (de Gues, 1988; Schwartz, 1991). The following guidelines may be used:

1.   Prepare a set of ovals for each team member, containing the organization's mission, mandates, and existing goal system stated in action terms. The writing on these ovals should be in a different color than the one participants use to create additional ovals.

2.   Have the planning team consider the three *external* assessment categories outlined in Chapter Five: forces and trends (political, economic, social, technological); stakeholders who control key resources (clients, customers, payers, members of nonprofit organizations, regulators); and competitors, collaborators, and competitive and collaborative forces and advantages. Each person should then take three sheets of scratch paper, one for each category, and brainstorm as many trends or events as he or she can imagine happening in each category. The team members should also consider trends and events that might affect the *internal* assessment categories as well—resources, present strategy, and performance. By looking externally and internally, the organization and all of its stakeholders are likely to be considered.

3.   Each participant should place ten to twenty brainstormed entries onto ovals, one entry per oval. Each oval should indicate the source of the idea (forces and trends; resource controllers; competitors, collaborators, and competitive or collaborative forces or advantages; resources; present strategies; performance).

4.   The facilitator should merge the participant-created ovals into a single set and shuffle them. Each participant (or small group) should be given up to twenty ovals. The participants should then be asked to arrange their ovals into a map on a flip chart sheet–covered wall in a way that indicates a plausible (though not necessarily likely) set of influence relationships and that connects them positively or negatively to the ovals indicating the organization's mission, mandates, and goals. Any extra ovals should be added as necessary. In other words, each participant should construct a "story" that links the ovals together and indicates influence chains that would either help or hinder achievement of the organization's goals.

5.   The team should then review each story and answer the following questions:

- What threats or opportunities are highlighted?
- Which stakeholders are affected by this story, and would they be happy or unhappy if it happened?
- What strengths or weaknesses might we draw on to deal with this scenario?
- In the case of threatening scenarios, what could we do, if anything, to keep this story from happening?
- If we cannot do anything to stop it, what should we do to defend against it? Or is there any way to turn it into an opportunity?
- What can we do, if anything, to make sure desirable stories happen?

The answers to these questions should be recorded. If the team uses the indirect approach to strategic issue identification, many of the answers can be placed on ovals and used to construct issue clusters. Similarly, if the team develops a strategy map, many of the ovals can be included on the map.

Computer Support

Computer support becomes increasingly helpful as the number of ideas to be mapped, managed, and analyzed increases. Graphics COPE, developed by Colin Eden and associates, is an extremely powerful and useful software program designed to help record, manage, and analyze maps. The software can handle maps containing more than two thousand concepts and their associated links. The concepts and links are stored in a central database and can be displayed in a similar format to maps on walls. The software operates in a Windows environment and can draw on Windows for program management, color graphics, printing, and data storage and transfer.

In North America, information about this software can be obtained from John M. Bryson and Charles B. Finn, Real-izations, Inc., 2709 Silver Lane, St. Anthony Village, Minneapolis, MN 55421. Elsewhere, interested parties should contact Graphics COPE Marketing Manager, Department of Management Science, Strathclyde Business School, University of Strathclyde, Graham Hills Building, 40 George Street, Glasgow G1 1BA, United Kingdom.

ADVANCED CONCEPTS FOR STRATEGY FORMULATION AND IMPLEMENTATION

A number of different concepts may prove useful to the strategic planning team members as they formulate strategies for the organization or community. Several are presented in this section, including Osborne and Gaebler's distinction (1992) between "steering" and "rowing"; typologies of strategies developed by Miles and Snow (1978), Boschken (1988a, 1988b), Nutt and Backoff (1992, 1995), Wechsler and Backoff (1987), Rubin (1988), Nutt (1984a), Barry (1986), and Porter (1980); the implementation approaches of Nutt and Backoff (1992) and Mazmanian and Sabatier (1983); and Elmore's idea (1982) of forward mapping and backward mapping.

First, however, it is worth noting briefly the various ways in which the term *strategy* is used. My own definition emphasizes that a strategy is a *pattern*. Mintzberg (1994a, pp. 23–29), however, points out various other meanings that people often have in mind when they use the word. Many people equate a strategy with a *plan*—a direction, guide, or course of action for the future. Others, notably Porter (1980, 1985), think of strategy as the organization's *position* in the marketplace, which is determined by its providing particular products or services. And still others think of strategy as an organization's *perspective*, or particular way of doing things. Finally, Nutt and Backoff (1992, pp. 62–63) point out that strategy can also be a *ploy*, or a way of outwitting an opponent.

Concepts Related to Organizational Role

Three concepts—Osborne and Gaebler's distinction between steering and rowing, and Miles and Snow's and Nutt and Backoff's typologies of strategy types—relate primarily to the organization's conceptualization of its role. Osborne and Gaebler's best-selling book, *Reinventing Government* (1992), has popularized a set of ideas first articulated by Kolderie (1986) and later featured prominently in the report of the National Performance Review chaired by Vice President Al Gore (1993). Osborne and Gaebler argue that government needs to concentrate more on *steering*—setting policy, delivering funds to operational bodies (public, nonprofit, private), and evaluating performance—and concentrate less on *rowing*—actually producing or delivering the service. By concentrating on the steering functions, governments *cause* things to happen but do not *do* them themselves. Osborne and Gaebler believe that effective steering requires leaders and managers to look at the universe of issues, develop appropriate policies and incentives, and balance competing demands for resources. Once steerers have decided what they want, they can shop around for the most effective and efficient service providers. Steering allows the use of competition to promote efficiency, preserves flexibility to respond to changing circumstances, and promotes accountability of producers (the service delivers) to purchasers (the steering organization or customers generally). The success of the approach clearly depends on the presence of strong and competent public leadership and management, effective strategic planning, adequate funding, a healthy civic infrastructure, useful models to follow, and the existence of desirable and viable alternatives (public, nonprofit, or private) to produce what is desired by the steerers.

Education offers a particularly interesting example of the importance of the steering-rowing (or provision-production) distinction (Bryson and Ring, 1990). State governments typically require compulsory education for all children under the age of sixteen and agree to provide the money for the education. These are steering functions. That education is then typically produced in publicly owned, operated, controlled, and financed schools. These are rowing functions. Parents and students usually have little choice about which schools children attend and what is taught there (although parents with enough money can send their children to private or nonprofit schools). Government, in other words, has a monopoly on the production of public education and dictates where, when, and under what conditions it will be received.

Various educational voucher schemes have been advanced to break this government monopoly, expand parental (and student) choice, and force schools to improve their performance. In simplest terms, these schemes would give the parents of school-age children vouchers to be used in the schools of their choice to pay for their children's education. Vouchers would allow a choice of programs within the schools and, under some schemes, would even be good for use in for-profit or nonprofit—not just public schools. What the educational voucher schemes are about, therefore, is *not* whether public education will be *provided* (because the compulsory education laws and voucher monies ensure that it will). Instead, they are about breaking up the government's monopoly control over the *production* of education (Kolderie, 1986). Vouchers would allow parents (and perhaps students) far greater choice over what education will be produced and by whom, how, when, and where.

Miles and Snow (1978) offered a different way of thinking about the role of an organization (not just of government). They were concerned primarily with private sector organizations, but Boschken (1988a, 1988b), in a study of West Coast port authorities, has demonstrated the applicability of their typology to public sector enterprises.

Miles and Snow developed a strategic behavior typology. Along half of the scale are proactive behavior types, the "prospector" and the "analyzer." The prospector actively scans the environment for opportunities and develops a wide range of relations with external actors. The prospector is also an active innovator. The analyzer, while also proactive, is not as active a scanner and innovator as the prospector. Instead, the analyzer watches the prospector and adopts or adapts his or her innovations after they have proved their effectiveness. While prospectors are more concerned with strategic effectiveness than with operational efficiency, the analyzers show a balanced concern for both.

On the other side of Miles and Snow's scale are two reactive strategic behavior types, the "defender" and the "reactor." These two types resist change, protect against any infringement of their "turf," and actively scan the environment for threats—while they often overlook opportunities. The difference between the two is that the defender at least has a consistent strategy while the reactor does not. The reactor just responds to events inconsistently and with little or no vision of the future.

Boschken found in a paired-comparison test of six West Coast port authorities that the prospectors and analyzers consistently outperformed the defenders and reactors. One is reminded of the old adage that "the best defense is a good offense." Ironically, because of their reactive strategic behavior, the defenders and reactors faced losing precisely what they sought to preserve.

Boschken found a number of additional factors that correlated with high performance. The prospectors and analyzers tended to emphasize strategic effectiveness while the defenders and reactors highlighted operational efficiency. The leaders of the prospectors and analyzers played a catalytic, proactive role. While turnover was low among their chief administrative officers (CAOs), prospectors and analyzers also tended to have a larger number of civil service–exempt staff than did defenders and reactors. In contrast, the leaders of the defenders and reactors took a more "political" role (in the negative sense) or even relied on cronyism. Turnover among CAOs tended to be higher. Similarly, port authority commission members who were prospectors and analyzers had a higher average tenure than commission members who were defenders and reactors.

Prospectors and analyzers rely much more on mutual exchange in their involvements with other governments while defenders and reactors rely more on power struggles or submission. The organizational skills and responsibilities of the prospectors and analyzers—particularly their strategic planning capacities and functions—were oriented much more toward active harbor development than were those of the defenders and analyzers. Within their strategic planning functions, prospectors and analyzers relied much more on matrix (or dual-authority) relations than did defenders and reactors, who relied more on a uniform hierarchical command structure. Finally, prospectors and analyzers tended to be much more autonomous organizations, requiring fewer political approvals by other officials or bodies than their worse-performing rivals required.

Nutt and Backoff (1992) offer another useful typology, explicitly for both public and nonprofit organizations. They first posit two dimensions, one consisting of the volatility in needs (low to high) that create pressures for action and the second consisting of the responsiveness to legitimate authorities that is required to meet those needs (low to high). At one extreme, the organization can respond by avoiding doing anything about the needs, while at the other extreme, it can engage actively in collaborations with others to meet the needs. When the two dimensions are dichotomized, a set of stances toward the world is created. Low demand and low responsiveness result in a "bureaucratic" posture. Low demand and high responsiveness lead to an "accommodator" role. High demand and low responsiveness imply that the organization has a "director" stance, in which it basically controls the agenda for action. Finally, high demand and high responsiveness lead either to a "compromiser" role, in which various differences are split, or, preferably, to a "mutualist" role, in which major efforts are made to find "all gain" solutions.

A Potpourri of Strategies

This section presents the strategy typologies developed by Wechsler and Backoff (1987), Rubin (1988), Nutt (1984a), Barry (1986), and Porter (1980). Each provides a useful way to think about alternative strategies.

Wechsler and Backoff (1987) identified three strategy "patterns" in their study of several Ohio state agencies. The patterns are labeled "developmental," "political," and "protective." They bear some resemblance to Miles and Snow's role types. The advantage of Wechsler and Backoff's typology is that it graphically points out the interaction between an agency's understanding of its environment and its efforts to make strategy. Decision makers and planners rarely can do all they wish to do strategically, but with careful thought and effective action, they can achieve as much as their situations allow—and in some cases, can change their situations.

A developmental strategy attempts to improve the organization's status, capacity, resources, and influence. It also seeks to create a new and better future for the organization. Formal planning systems can play an important role in guiding the deployment of existing resources to build capacity. The organization must have support from the external environment for a developmental strategy to work.

Political strategies come in two types. The first is a response to changing environmental conditions and seeks to accommodate the balance of power among external stakeholders. This strategy is not totally reactive, as the organization's key decision makers can still exercise some control over the organization's direction. The second type of political strategy involves seeing the organization as one of the "spoils" of partisan political contests. Organizational positions, structure, policy, and program changes are viewed as rewards for individual supporters and important constituencies. This type of strategy occurs most frequently after changes in governmental regimes.

Protective strategies are formulated by organizations with limited capacities in response to a hostile or threatening environment. This type of strategy attempts to maintain the organizational status quo while accommodating strong external pressures. It is the most reactive of the set, as decisions are made and actions taken in response to external stakeholders and actions may actually be dictated by external actors. Indeed, insiders may be led to question the skill and commitment of the organization's leaders.

Rubin (1988) has developed a typology of public sector strategies based on whether the time horizon is short or long and whether the change involves reaction to a disruptive present or the fashioning of a future that will be quite different from the past. Rubin's typology is reprinted in Figure D.1.

In Rubin's typology, "sagas" are patterns of actions taken over the long term to reestablish a set of core values, goals, or institutions that have been lost or are in danger of being lost due to environmental changes or the inadequacies of institutional or managerial capacities. The idea is not to reestablish the past but to regain the lost qualities of the past through strategic responses to new or changed circumstances. The saga thus is the organizational analogue of Homer's great literary saga *The Odyssey,* which recounts the hero's efforts to return to Greece after the Trojan War. Rubin identifies three kinds of sagalike strategies: (1) restorative, aimed at restoring lost qualities through the design of new policies and reorientation of institutional agendas; (2) reformative, designed to change governmental policies and procedures so they reflect an appreciation of an earlier era; and (3) conservatory, predicated on the preservation of values, institutions, or goals that appear to be threatened by major environmental changes.

"Quests" are like sagas in that the time frame is long term. But they differ from sagas in that the pattern of action is not aimed at the restoration, appreciation, or preservation of a venerable past but at the creation of a new and differ-

FIGURE D.1. RUBIN'S TYPOLOGY OF PUBLIC SECTOR STRATEGIES.

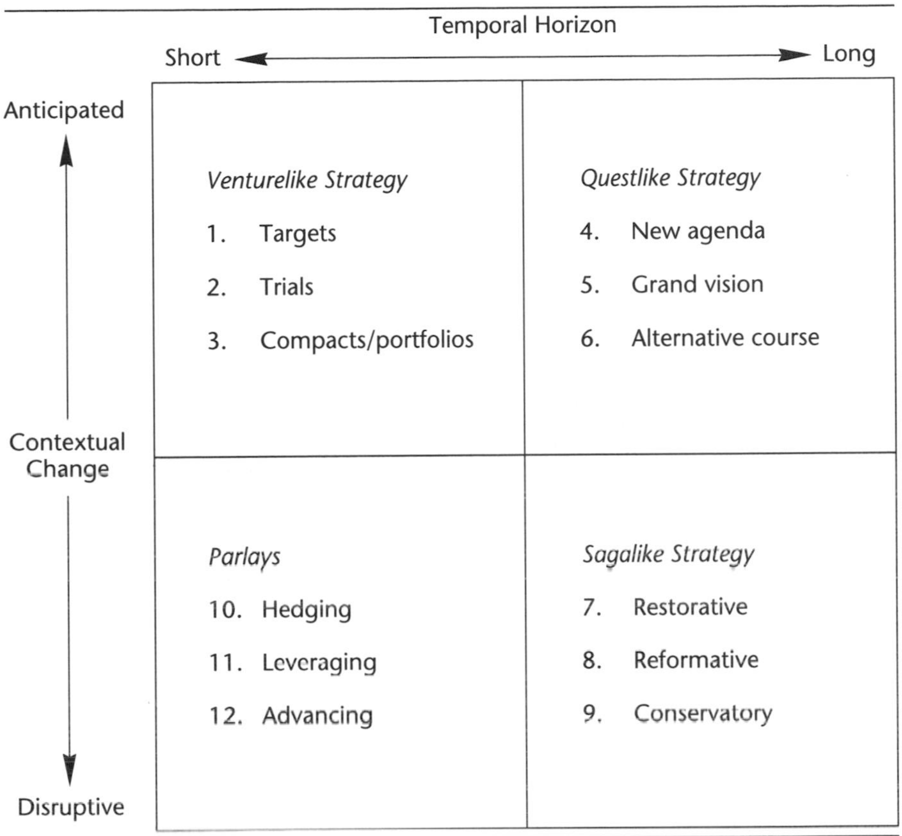

Temporal Horizon

Short ←————————————————————→ Long

Anticipated	Venturelike Strategy	Questlike Strategy
	1. Targets	4. New agenda
	2. Trials	5. Grand vision
	3. Compacts/portfolios	6. Alternative course
Contextual Change	Parlays	Sagalike Strategy
	10. Hedging	7. Restorative
	11. Leveraging	8. Reformative
	12. Advancing	9. Conservatory
Disruptive		

Source: Rubin, 1988, p. 93.

ent future. Rubin identifies three questlike strategies: (1) the new agenda of long-term goals or objectives often associated with newly elected or appointed officials; (2) the grand vision for an organization, city, region, or state; and (3) the alternative course of action, formulated as a direct but long-term response to an anticipated conflict or crisis.

"Ventures" are similar to quests except that the time frame is short term. The associated strategies are (1) targets that focus efforts to take advantage of a short-term opportunity or overcome a current strategic issue or threat; (2) trials, or short-term experiments designed to deal with issues; and (3) compacts, or short-term agreements among departments or organizations to deal with difficulties or opportunities that require joint action.

Lastly, "parlays" are deliberate efforts to maneuver toward a preferred position while overcoming or mitigating unacceptable levels of risk. These actions are typically taken in the face of immediate difficulties that prevent the formulation of a longer-term strategy. The idea is to "parlay" what one has into a winning

hand. Three kinds of strategies that fit this circumstance are (1) hedging, or coun-
terbalancing risks; (2) leveraging, or engaging in strategic negotiation in areas or
subjects of less interest in order to gain leverage in areas or subjects of high interest; and (3) advancing, or making a short-term response to an immediate situation, a response that may advance one's long-term interest even though the
advance is not part of a clearly articulated long-term strategy.

The special virtue of Rubin's typology is that it allows strategists to incorporate both time *and* situations into their deliberations. Drawing a distinction between long- and short-term strategies is quite conventional, but Rubin's is the only
typology that links temporal horizons with different kinds of contextual change.

Nutt (1984a) proposes eight archetypal strategies for public and nonprofit organizations, based on whether some combination of three criteria used to judge
the strategies is essential to the strategy's success. The three criteria are quality, acceptance, or innovation. The virtue of a criteria-based approach is that some lines
of strategy development can be ruled out because they do not meet the criteria.
In addition, the team gains a better idea of what kinds of planning methods might
prove most useful.

Barry (1986) has catalogued a number of strategies commonly pursued by
nonprofit organizations: (1) Large nonprofits often choose growth and diversifi-
cation of funding sources as a way of gaining control over their environments.
(2) Nonprofits may choose to "team up" with other nonprofits through mergers,
consolidations, joint programming, joint ventures, or shared services. (3) Organizations may choose to "downsize" or "rightsize" through a reduction in the scope
or scale of their services to fit financial or other constraints. (4) Nonprofits may
choose to specialize or focus their activities so that they only do what they can
do well within a particular market niche. (5) "Piggybacking" can be an effective
strategy—that is, income earned in one sphere of activity can offset declining revenue in other areas or subsidize particularly desirable activities. (6) Nonprofits can
seek contracts for service from governments or other organizations, a practice particularly common in the health and social service field. (7) Nonprofits can choose
to upgrade and "professionalize" their staff capabilities. (8) Nonprofits can take
the opposite tack and "deprofessionalize," organizing services provided through
mutual help, community-based social support systems, client-to-client methods,
or volunteers. (9) Finally, a nonprofit can choose to go out of business if the organization is no longer viable or if its mission has been fulfilled.

Porter (1980) provides a final set of strategy concepts useful for service or product management. He introduces the notion that in *competitive* situations organizations can pursue three generic strategies (positions). They can choose
"differentiation"—the creation of something that is perceived in the marketplace
to be unique. They can choose "cost leadership"—production of the lowest-cost
products or services. Or they can choose to "focus"—to aim at a particular customer group, segment of the product or service line, or geographic market. Porter
argues that these strategies are mutually exclusive; an organization cannot pursue

more than one of these strategies at the same time for the same product or service and still succeed against savvy competitors.

Portfolio Approaches

The adaptability of portfolio approaches to strategic purposes is discussed in Chapter Ten and Resource B. A portfolio approach allows planners to measure strategies against dimensions deemed to be of strategic importance. In Chapter Ten, a portfolio used by the Royal Hospitals in Northern Ireland is presented, outlining their preferred service strategies. San Luis Obispo, California, presents another example of the portfolio approach to evaluating strategic options (Sorkin, Ferris, and Hudak, 1984, p. 9). The decision matrix (or portfolio) in Figure D.2 was prepared as part of the city's strategic planning effort. The matrix was used

FIGURE D.2. DECISION MATRIX FOR DEVELOPMENTAL STRATEGIES, SAN LUIS OBISPO, CALIFORNIA.

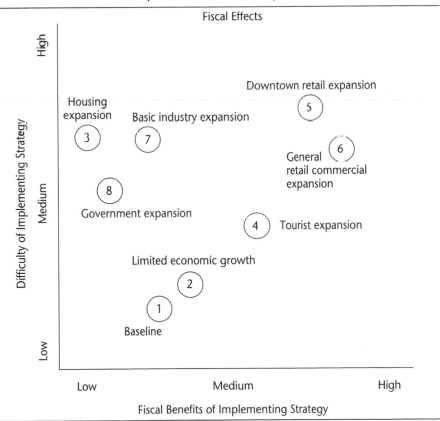

Source: Sorkin, Ferris, and Hudak, 1984, p. 9.

to evaluate the fiscal effects of the strategies against their ease of implementation. On the one hand, according to the matrix, housing expansion is a poor strategic choice because fiscal benefits are low and implementation difficulties are high. On the other hand, tourist expansion may be a fairly good strategy because fiscal benefits are fairly high and implementation difficulties may not be too hard to overcome. Unfortunately for the city, no strategies fall into the lower right-hand corner, in which fiscal benefits are high and implementation difficulties are low.

Implementation Approaches

A number of authors have offered advice on formulating strategies with implementation in mind. This section discusses the ideas of Nutt and Backoff (1992) and Mazmanian and Sabatier (1983).

Nutt and Backoff, drawing on the work of Freeman (1984), argue that different strategies will be needed for different organizational stakeholders, depending on the importance of the stakeholders and their position with respect to any given course of action. Nutt and Backoff propose using the two-by-two ma-

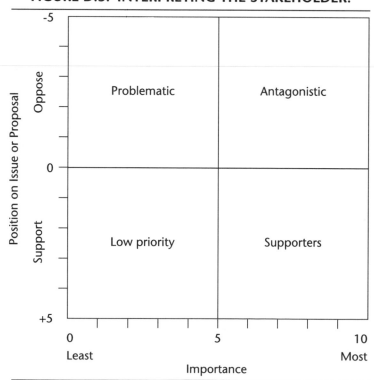

FIGURE D.3. INTERPRETING THE STAKEHOLDER.

Source: Adapted from Nutt and Backoff, 1992, p. 198.

trix reproduced in slightly modified form in Figure D.3. One dimension represents the stakeholder's importance to the organization, particularly in relation to the proposed course of action. The other dimension indicates whether the stakeholder supports or opposes the proposed course of action. For a given proposed course of action, the strategic planning team locates stakeholders on the matrix in order to determine (1) whether a winning coalition is possible, (2) the likely size of the opposition coalition, and (3) the neutral or "swing" stakeholders who might be targeted for special lobbying and influence efforts. Nutt and Backoff go on to propose a set of tactics to deal with the different categories of stakeholders.

Potentially "antagonistic" stakeholders are those who would oppose the proposed course of action but are very important to the organization. Possible tactics to deal with this group include the following:

1. Identify potential coalitions by determining neutral actors in the problematic and low-priority categories who are closely aligned or related to the antagonistic stakeholders.
2. Take steps to block formation of coalitions among antagonistic and neutral stakeholders.
3. Prevent antagonistic stakeholders from undermining the support of supporters.
4. Determine which antagonistic supporters must be surprised (kept in the dark) to delay or prevent the mobilization of their opposition.
5. Anticipate the nature of antagonists' opposition and develop counterarguments in advance.
6. Engage selected antagonists in negotiations to determine and perhaps adopt changes in the proposed course of action that would change antagonists into neutrals or even supporters.

Potential "supporters" are stakeholders who are very important to the organization and who support the proposed course of action. They are managed quite differently. Potential tactics to use with them include the following:

1. Provide information to reinforce their beliefs.
2. Co-opt their support by involving them in some or all of the strategic planning team's deliberations.
3. Ask supportive stakeholders to sell the strategy to those who are neutral.
4. Invite some potential supporters who are at present neutral to react to proposed strategies so that changes can be incorporated to turn potential support into actual support.

"Problematic" stakeholders are those who oppose the proposed course of action and are relatively unimportant to the organization. These stakeholders present fewer problems than antagonists but important precautions should be taken nonetheless to prevent problematics from becoming antagonists. Possible tactics include the following:

1. Prepare defensive tactics to be used if a coalition formed of problematic stake-holders and antagonists becomes possible or likely or if a problematic appears likely to take a public position in opposition to the strategy.
2. Moderately problematic stakeholders can be targeted for education or lobbying efforts.
3. Redefine the strategy to assuage the concerns of strongly negative stakeholders.

Finally, there are "low-priority" stakeholders, who are relatively unimportant to the organization but do support the proposed course of action. Possible tactics for use with this group include the following:

1. Use low-cost education with those stakeholders who almost fall into the high-importance category.
2. Find ways to promote involvement of low-priority stakeholders with supporters to expand the size of the coalition in support of the proposed strategy.

Obviously, many more tactics might be developed to use with each group of stakeholders. The main importance of Nutt and Backoff's scheme, however, is that it prompts strategists to think of the implementation (indeed, the formulation) of any strategy in the stakeholder's terms. Nutt and Backoff's scheme can be used in concert with the role-play exercise discussed in Resource C.

Mazmanian and Sabatier (1983, pp. 41–42) also provide valuable advice on how to implement strategies, particularly statutes or other policy decisions. Their model was outlined in Resource B. They argue that six conditions are sufficient for effective implementation of a policy decision that represents a substantial departure from the status quo. Achievement of the goals of the policy will occur if

1. The enabling legislation or other legal directive outlines clear and consistent policy objectives or criteria for resolving goal conflicts.
2. The legislation incorporates a sound theory of what is needed for achievement of the policy objective and gives implementing officials sufficient jurisdiction over target groups and other factors that are likely to affect achievement of the goals.
3. The legislation structures the implementation process to favor successful implementation (for example, by providing supportive and capable agencies, supportive decision rules, and adequate resources).
4. Key officials possess the necessary managerial and political skills and are committed to achieving the goals.
5. A coalition of key supporters (including important legislators or chief executives) actively supports the implementation process, and the courts are either supportive or neutral.
6. New priorities or conflicting policies do not emerge and underlying social conditions do not change to weaken the policy's political support or underlying causal theory.

"Forward Mapping" and "Backward Mapping"

There are two contrasting approaches to implementation planning, labeled "forward mapping" and "backward mapping" by Elmore (1982). Forward mapping is the rational planning model described in Chapter One. It is also compatible with the goals and vision of success, or idealized scenario, approaches to strategic issue identification outlined in Chapter Six. A forward mapping process "begins at the top of the process, with as clear a statement as possible of the policy maker's intent, and proceeds through a sequence of increasingly more specific steps to define what is expected of implementers at each level. At the bottom of the process, one states, again with as much precision as possible, what a satisfactory outcome would be, measured in terms of the ordinal statement of intent" (p. 19).

There is a sound logic to forward mapping, and certainly, there are situations in which it makes sense. However, the major difficulty with it is "its implicit and unquestioned assumption that *policymakers control the organizational, political, and technological processes that affect implementation*" (p. 20). Clear lines of hierarchical authority and accountability are assumed. Forward mapping is thus problematic in many organizations—and certainly in multiorganizational networks or communities—where leaders and managers have only influence, not control, over the various implementation processes. In such situations, much of what happens during implementation "cannot be explained by the intentions and directions of policymakers" (p. 20) because it has very little to do with their intentions and a great deal to do with the implementers' intentions and incentives.

An alternative approach is backward mapping, which begins not at the "top" of an implementation process but with a statement of the specific behavior, at the lowest level of the implementation process ("street level"), that generates the need for policy (p. 21). The direct and indirect approaches to strategic issue identification outlined in Chapter Six may facilitate preparation of this statement, which is focused on specific behavior on the ground that merits new strategies or plans. Next, planners formulate an objective, consisting of possible organizational actions at the lowest level that are likely to result in desired changes in behavior, or effects, that would minimize the problem. A careful strategy development process should underpin preparation of such an objective. Once the objective is formulated, planners go backward up the actual or possible structure of implementers or implementing agencies and ask two questions at each level: What is the ability of this unit to affect the behavior that is the target of policy changes? What rules and resources does this unit need to create the desired effect?

Once these questions are answered, the final stage in the exercise is the formulation of a set of policies and strategies that direct or provide the necessary rules and resources to the units that are likely to have the greatest effects. Further, the exercise must involve explicit consideration of the settings that are likely to produce and protect desired changes. The source of the greatest effect, in other words, will be actors in settings—particularly those closest to the actual behaviors that create the issues that should be addressed—so those settings, and the kind of behavior leaders seek to influence within them, must be given careful thought. Effective backward mapping can be seen in the public library case, in which numerous focus groups of stakeholders were organized to explore how they felt about the library and what they would like to see in the way of changes. Many of their suggestions became statements of lower-level objectives, which the planners sought strategies or actions to achieve. In addition, the strategic planning team included several representatives of the frontline staff, whose needs for reduced stress and workloads were part of what drove the planning process in the first place. Here, too, many of the suggestions of these staff members became lower-level objectives.

Backward mapping, like forward mapping, is concerned with what policy makers can do to produce desirable change. Backward mapping, however, does not assume that policy makers are the most important influence on the behavior of implementers or on the subjects of implementation. Nor does it assume that the appropriate measure of success is the policy makers' intentions; rather, it assumes that the appropriate measure is a reasonable estimate of what can be done in shared-power situations to influence change. The evaluation of policy makers', leaders', and managers' actions is thus less idealistic and more realistic. The logic of backward mapping—of "turning implementation on its head" (Lipsky, 1980)—should be kept in mind during the earlier strategic-issue identification and strategy-development steps. If it is not, and only forward mapping is used, the policies and strategies that are developed and adopted are less likely to alter behavior on the ground in directions that effectively address the real social problems or political needs the organization faces.

It must be emphasized, however, that forward mapping and backward mapping are not antithetical. Indeed, planners should use both. Once they have worked backward, revealing the desired behavior at the lowest level and the chains of influence that may produce that behavior, the results of the analysis can be written up in a "forward" fashion, as if they had followed that model. This allows them to recheck and elaborate the reasoning behind implementation plans as they travel back down the influence chains. Both approaches have something to offer and should be considered by change advocates as they attempt to design, facilitate, and institutionalize lasting policy changes (Goggin, Bowman, Lester, and O'Toole, 1990). Furthermore, the bottom-up approach may be helpful even when the policies to be implemented were developed in an exclusively forward (or otherwise impractical) way. Even in these situations, there is often enough flexibility available to implementers to justify a backward mapping exercise designed to reveal practical ways to bring about change.

The oval mapping process (described in Resource C), designed to map influence relations, is an effective way to combine the two approaches. The process was used by the CPI program's management group to develop its goals and strategies. Some goals were already mandated, and the team had to map forward to develop its strategies and action programs. Other actions were suggested as a result of using the indirect approach to strategic issue identification, in which options for action were invented to address specific stakeholder concerns on the ground or to build on strengths, take advantage of opportunities, and minimize or overcome weaknesses and threats. Clusters of these options led the team to realize that it needed to map backward and create at least two new goals: one aimed at providing value added to stakeholders and the other aimed at educating them about the CPI program's products and services.

ADVANCED CONCEPTS FOR ESTABLISHING AN EFFECTIVE ORGANIZATIONAL VISION FOR THE FUTURE

Several approaches appear useful to organizations interested in constructing a vision of success. In Chapter Six, I described two approaches. One involved writing a fictional newspaper story set five years in the future that describes what the organization looks like once it has realized its vision. The other involved capturing what the organization is moving "from" and "to." In Chapter Eight, I offered examples of visions of success and general advice for preparing one. (Bryson and Alston [1995] contains vision of success worksheets that the strategic planning team might find useful.)

This section discusses three additional approaches that can help public and nonprofit organizations envision success. They involve use of (1) key success indicators, or critical success factors, and core competencies; (2) excellence criteria or characteristics, as developed by Peters and Waterman in their book *In Search of Excellence* (1982) and adapted for use in the public sector; and (3) the principles for "reinventing government" from Osborne and Gaebler (1992).

Key Success Indicators and Core Competencies

The idea of key success indicators has been articulated by Peter Drucker (1973, pp. 552, 572–591) and related specifically to planning by several authors, including Jenster (1987) and Leidecker and Bruno (1984), although these authors call them "critical success factors." Key success indicators are the ones against which an organization must demonstrate at least adequate performance if it is to survive and prosper. They are likely to be a distillation of two sets of criteria: those used by key stakeholders to judge organizational performance and those that emerge from an understanding of how the organization works as a system in relation to its external environment (Senge, 1990; Mintzberg, 1994b, pp. 36–37).

The indicators can be expected to be different for different organizations. For a private, for-profit organization, key indicators might include profit rate, return on investment, market share, and customer satisfaction measures. Key success indicators for a public or nonprofit organization are likely to be more numerous and perhaps inherently more ambiguous than those for a private for-profit organization (Nutt and Backoff, 1992, 1993). Nonetheless, it is important to be clear about the indicators if performance against them is to be measured, appreciated, and rewarded. The CPI program's strategic plan, discussed in Chapter Eight, is basically a vision of success that in part outlines the measures against which the program will judge itself in each goal area. The indicators are a mixture of quantitative and qualitative, objective and subjective measures. Not all may be "critical," but the CPI program clearly thinks it wants to do well against them as a set.

Three possible techniques for developing key success indicators have been discussed in earlier chapters and in Resource C. One is the stakeholder analysis discussed in Chapter Four. A stakeholder analysis asks organizational members to specify the organization's key stakeholders and the criteria that the stakeholders use to judge organizational performance. By scrutinizing the list of stakeholder criteria, planners can develop candidates for a parsimonious list of success indicators. Another useful method involves using the snow card technique (see Chapter Five) to develop a set of key success indicators (probably after the snow card technique has been used to identify opportunities and threats). The question put before strategic planning team members would be simply, "What are the key success indicators for our organization?"

A third useful tool is the oval mapping process discussed in Resource C. In general, discussing a full-blown strategy map should reveal to a planning team many possible indicators that can provide evidence of goal achievement and mission fulfillment. Oval mapping can also be used to focus specifically on identifying key success indicators. A separate "key success indicators" map might be prepared for each organizational (or community) goal in the overall strategy map. To prepare an indicators map, one of the goals (or mission elements) should be placed in the middle of a flip chart sheet–covered wall. Planning team members should then be asked *how* they would know progress was being made toward achieving the goal. Each idea should be placed on a separate oval and clustered with other ovals according to common themes or subjects below the goal. Additional structuring among clusters of ovals and across ovals may be necessary to figure out how the ovals relate to one another. When maps have been constructed for each of the goals, they may be related to one another and discussed, as an aid to identifying a very limited set of key success indicators.

Core competencies, too, might be emphasized in a vision of success. For example, the CPI program's skills at data collection and statistics are emphasized in its plan. Three possible approaches to the identification of core competencies have been discussed in earlier chapters and in Resource C. The first is the snow card technique, which might be used to answer the question, What are our core competencies?—probably after the technique has been used to identify strengths and weaknesses. The second is the Organizational Highs, Lows, and Themes exercise presented in Chapter Five. Qualitative insights about what caused the highs and lows can help clarify core competencies. And finally, the oval mapping process can be used. A full-blown strategy map should help the team better understand the areas in which the organization has notable competencies.

Excellence Criteria

Peters and Waterman (1982) developed eight interrelated criteria that seem to characterize successfully managed "excellent" companies. Their research was not particularly scientific, but the criteria do make sense as ideals to pursue for many public and nonprofit organizations. The criteria probably need some modification in order to be applied to general-purpose governments, however, and those modifications will be discussed later. Here are the eight criteria as they were formulated for businesses:

1. A bias for action. Companies that meet this criterion quickly identify problems, find answers, and implement them. Their motto is "Do it, fix it, try it."
2. Close to the customer. Excellent organizations spend a great deal of time and effort listening closely to what their customers want, and then strive to meet those needs in a way that emphasizes quality, reliability, and service.
3. Autonomy and entrepreneurship. Excellent companies promote innovation and risk taking. The motto here comes from the 3M corporation: "Never kill a good idea."
4. Productivity through people. People are viewed by excellent companies as a valuable resource—indeed, their most valuable resource.
5. Hands-on, value-driven. Excellent companies all have a clearly articulated philosophy and set of key values, and their executives and employees behave in accord with them. People are deeply involved; they *live* the business.
6. Stick to the knitting. The excellent companies do not move far from the businesses they know how to run. They have core businesses that *remain* the core; they do not pursue ideas or acquisitions that are at odds with those businesses.
7. Simple form, lean staff. Structural forms are kept simple, and corporate staffs are kept relatively small.
8. Simultaneous loose-tight properties. Excellent companies have some core values to which they cleave almost fanatically, but at the same time, they promote decentralization and autonomy in decision making and action as long as they are in accord with the core values.

It is easy to see how these criteria might apply to many single-function public authorities and to many nonprofit organizations. For example, the Amherst H. Wilder Foundation, discussed in Chapters Four and Seven, is probably characterized by these eight criteria (Bryson, King, Roering, and Van de Ven, 1986), as are many other excellently led and managed nonprofit organizations (Knauft, Berger, and Gray, 1991).

As noted above, however, adaptations or modifications of some criteria are probably necessary before they can be applied to general purpose governments. Sipel (1984) recommends specific changes in order to apply the criteria to local government. The recommended changes are listed in Table E.1. Like Peters and Waterman's criteria, these criteria have been the subject of little research, either individually or as a set. Nonetheless, since the criteria appeal to common sense, they are worth a second look by key decision makers.

Actually, the changes suggested are remarkably few: excellent local governments are *action oriented*, even though quick action may be difficult in the public sector due to statutory limitations, unwillingness to take risks, and limited resources. Excellent local governments are *close to their citizens* (not just their customers), even though there are numerous stakeholders in the public sector and public-sector organizations in many cases hold monopoly positions. Outstanding local governments also promote *autonomy and entrepreneurship*, even though the public sector is notorious for risk avoidance and for lack of a market orientation. An *employee orientation* characterizes excellent local governments, even though taxpayers may see people-oriented programs as a waste of money.

Excellent local governments have a commitment to *values*, particularly a commitment to superior public service. Excellent local governments are committed to *mission, goals, and competence* (the stick-to-the-knitting criterion), even though it is hard in the public sector to determine these things. The seventh criterion of local government excellence is *structure*, which combines two of the Peters and Waterman criteria, "simple form" and "simultaneous loose-tight properties." Creating simple structures that correspond to an organization's guiding values is often difficult in the public sector because structures may be prescribed by law, but excellent local governments find a way to design and implement such structures.

The last criterion of local government excellence is a new one, *political relationships*. Excellent political relationships entail positive, open, respectful relationships among elected officials and management staff, effective dealings with the internal and external organizational environment, and reasonable political stability. Supportive and effective political relationships are often hard to achieve in the public sector because of great turnover among elected officials and political appointees and because of the hostility that can develop between elected officials and management staff. But excellent local governments find effective methods of handling these problems.

Whether the criteria apply at the state and federal levels is an open question. It would appear, however, that they at least would apply to major departments,

TABLE E.1. "EXCELLENCE" CRITERIA COMPARISON.

Local government excellence criteria	Peters and Waterman criteria	Criteria differences	Public sector special conditions making "excellence" attainment difficult
1. Action orientation	A bias for action	None	Laws making it difficult for local government to act quickly Low inclination to take risks Limited resources
2. Closeness to citizens	Close to the customer	Customer becomes citizen	Multiplicity of public sector "publics" Captive consumers
3. Autonomy and entrepreneurship	Autonomy and entrepreneurship	None	Reluctance by local government to "market" or take risks
4. Employee orientation	Productivity through people	None	People-oriented programs sometimes perceived as a waste of taxpayers' money
5. Values	Hands-on, value driven	None	Traditional values that are hard to change
6. Mission, goals, and competence	Stick to the knitting	Expansion to include mission and goals	Difficulty of determining mission and goals Difficulty of measuring results
7. Structure	Simple form, lean staff	Combination of "simple form" and loose-tight properties	Some local governments with complex structures written into basic law
8. Political relationships	Simultaneous loose-tight properties	New local government criterion	Frequent changes in key actors Perceptions that roles of policy makers and administrators are different and/or conflicting

Source: Sipel, 1984, p. 4. Reprinted by permission from "Putting *In Search of Excellence* to Work in Local Government," an article by George A. Sipel, as it appeared in the April 1984 issue of *Public Management Magazine.* © 1987, The International City Management Association, Washington, D.C.

even if they might be impossible to apply practically across the whole of a government.

Reinventing Government Principles

Osborne and Gaebler offer ten "principles" for reinventing government and making it more "entrepreneurial." The principles serve as a guide to moving government away from a bureaucratic model toward what Osborne and Gaebler believe will be a more responsive, citizen-friendly, efficient, and better approach. Their approach is not grounded very well in theory, not totally coherent intellectually, and not well tested. To their credit, the authors say they are presenting a framework, not a fully articulated and tested theory. As long as the principles are taken with a grain of salt, they merit careful consideration. Osborne and Gaebler believe governments should be

- *Catalytic.* They should focus on steering rather than rowing. Government should decide what should be done but does not have to do it itself.
- *Community-owned.* The programs that work best are the ones that are community owned, capacity building, and empowering rather than delivered by bureaucracies to clients.
- *Competitive.* Competition is to be preferred to monopoly provision of service since competition is more likely to lead to better, more innovative, and less expensive service.
- *Mission-driven.* Government should be animated by mission and vision rather than driven by rules.
- *Results-oriented.* Funding should be based on outcomes, not inputs.
- *Customer-driven.* Government should meet the needs of the customer and citizen, not the bureaucracy.
- *Enterprising.* Entrepreneurship and earning money should be rewarded more than spending money.
- *Anticipatory.* The focus of attention should be on preventing rather than curing problems.
- *Decentralized.* Participation and teamwork should be emphasized more than hierarchy.
- *Market oriented.* Governments should think creatively about how to use markets to achieve public purposes.

It is also worth noting that Osborne and Gaebler argue that *wholesale* reinvention is not likely to occur without a crisis, supportive and continuous leadership, a healthy civic infrastructure, shared vision and goals, trust, outside resources, and models to follow. And finally, without careful strategic maintenance of government's capacities for the both steering *and* the rowing that may be necessary, government can become what Milward, Provan, and Else (1993) call a "hollow state," incapable of either steering or rowing. Milward, Provan, and Else have studied in detail the very system of contracting for health and social services in Arizona that Osborne and Gaebler laud. In the area of mental health services, Milward, Provan, and Else found a system that has serious gaps and is almost completely unaccountable to anyone other than the private and nonprofit professionals who run it. Obviously, reinventing government is a useful framework of concepts but no panacea for what ails us as a nation.

REFERENCES

Ackermann, F. "Strategic Direction Through Burning Issues: Using SODA as a Strategic Decision Support System." *OR Insight,* 1992, *5*(3), 24–28.

Ackermann, F. "Using Dominos—For Problem Structuring." Working paper. Glasgow, Scotland: University of Strathclyde, Department of Management Science, 1993.

Agor, W. H. (ed). *Intuition in Organizations: Leading and Managing Productively.* Newbury Park, Calif.: Sage, 1989.

Agranoff, R. "Managing Intergovernmental Processes." In J. L. Perry (ed.), *Handbook of Public Administration.* San Francisco: Jossey-Bass, 1989.

Albert, S. "Towards a Theory of Timing: An Archival Study of Timing Decisions in the Persian Gulf War." In L. Cummings and B. Staw (eds.), *Research in Organizational Behavior,* 1995, *17,* 1–70.

Alterman, R. "Can Planning Help in Time of Crisis? Planners' Responses to Israel's Recent Wave of Mass Immigration." *Journal of the American Planning Association,* 1995, *61*(2), 156–177.

Anderson, J. E. *Public Policymaking.* Boston: Houghton Mifflin, 1990.

Ansoff, I. "Strategic Issue Management." *Strategic Management Journal,* 1980, *1*(2), 131–148.

Bachrach, P., and Baratz, M. S. "Decisions and Non-Decisions: An Analytical Framework." *American Political Science Review,* 1963, *57,* 632–642.

Barber, B. *Strong Democracy: Participatory Politics for a New Age.* Berkeley: University of California Press, 1984.

Bardach, E. *The Implementation Game.* Cambridge, Mass.: MIT Press, 1977.

Baron, D. P. *An Introduction to Political Analysis for Business.* Stanford, Calif.: Graduate School of Business, Stanford University, 1987.

Barry, B. W. *Strategic Planning Workbook for Nonprofit Organizations.* St. Paul, Minn.: Amherst H. Wilder Foundation, 1986.

Bartlett, C. A., and Ghoshal, S. "Changing the Role of Top Management: Beyond Strategy to Purpose." *Harvard Business Review,* Nov./Dec. 1994, pp. 79–88.

Bartunek, J., and Moch, M. "First-Order, Second-Order, and Third-Order Change and

Organizational Development Interventions: A Cognitive Approach." *Journal of Applied Behavioral Science,* 1987, *23*(4), 483–500.

Barzelay, M. *Breaking Through Bureaucracy: A New Vision for Managing in Government.* Berkeley: University of California Press, 1992.

Behn, R. D. "The Fundamentals of Cutback Management." In R. J. Zeckhauser and D. Leebaert (eds.), *What Role for Government?* Durham, N.C.: Duke University Press Policy Studies, 1983.

Behn, R. D. *Leadership Counts.* Cambridge, Mass.: Harvard University Press, 1991.

Bellman, G. M. *The Consultant's Calling: Bringing Who You Are to What You Do.* San Francisco: Jossey-Bass, 1990.

Bendor, J. B. *Parallel Systems: Redundancy in Government.* Berkeley: University of California Press, 1985.

Bentley, T. *Facilitation: Providing Opportunities for Learning.* New York: McGraw-Hill, 1994.

Benveniste, G. *The Politics of Expertise.* Berkeley, Calif.: Glendessary Press, 1972.

Benveniste, G. *Mastering the Politics of Planning: Crafting Credible Plans and Policies That Make a Difference.* San Francisco: Jossey-Bass, 1989.

Berger, P. L., and Luckmann, T. *The Social Construction of Reality.* New York: Doubleday Anchor Books, 1967.

Berry, F. S., and Wechsler, B. "State Agencies' Experience with Strategic Planning: Findings from a National Survey." *Public Administration Review,* 1995, *55*(2), pp. 159–168.

Block, P. *The Empowered Manager: Positive Political Skills at Work.* San Francisco: Jossey-Bass, 1987.

Block, P. *Stewardship.* San Francisco: Berrett-Koehler, 1993.

Boal, K. B., and Bryson, J. M. "Charismatic Leadership: A Phenomenological and Structural Approach." In J. G. Hunt, B. R. Balinga, H. P. Dachler, and C. A. Schriescheim (eds.), *Emerging Leadership Vistas.* Elmsford, N.Y.: Pergamon Press, 1987a.

Boal, K. B., and Bryson, J. M. "Representation, Testing and Policy Implications of Planning Processes." *Strategic Management Journal,* 1987b, *8,* 211–231.

Bolan, R. S. "Generalist with a Specialty—Still Valid? Educating the Planner: An Expert on Experts." In *Planning 1971: Selected Papers from the ASPO National Conference.* Chicago: American Society of Planning Officials, 1971.

Bolman, L. G., and Deal, T. E. *Reframing Organizations: Artistry, Choice, and Leadership.* San Francisco: Jossey-Bass, 1991.

Boschken, H. L. *Strategic Design and Organizational Change.* London: University of Alabama Press, 1988a.

Boschken, H. L. "Turbulent Transition and Organizational Change: Relating Policy Outcomes to Strategic Administrative Capacities." *Policy Studies Review,* 1988b, *7*(3), 477–499.

Boschken, H. L. "Analyzing Performance Skewness in Public Agencies: The Case of Urban Mass Transit." *Journal of Public Administration Research and Theory,* 1992, *2*(3), 265–288.

Boschken, H. L. "Organizational Performance and Multiple Constituencies." *Public Administration Review,* 1994, *54,* 308–312.

Bourgeois, L. J., III. "Performance and Consensus." *Strategic Management Journal,* 1980a, *1,* pp. 227–248.

Bourgeois, L. J., III. "Strategy and Environment: A Conceptual Integration." *Academy of Management Review,* 1980b, *5,* 25–39.

Boyte, H. C. *Commonwealth: A Return to Citizen Politics.* New York: Free Press, 1989.

Bozeman, B., and Straussman, J. D. *Public Management Strategies: Guidelines for Managerial Effectiveness.* San Francisco: Jossey-Bass, 1990.

Bracker, J. "The Historical Development of the Strategic Management Concept." *Academy of Management Review,* 1980, *5,* 219–224.

Braybrooke, D., and Lindblom, C. E. *A Strategy of Decision: Policy Evaluation as a Social Process.* New York: Free Press, 1963.

Brickman, P. "Is It Real?" In J. H. Harvey, W. Ickes, and R. F. Kidd (eds.), *New Directions in Attributional Research,* Vol. 2. Hillsdale, N.J.: Erlbaum, 1978.

Bromiley, P., and Marcus, A. "Deadlines, Routines, and Change." *Policy Sciences,* 1987, 20, pp. 85–103.

Bryant, J. *Problem Management.* Chichester, England: Wiley, 1989.

Bryson, J. M. "A Perspective on Planning and Crises in the Public Sector." *Strategic Management Journal,* 1981, *2,* 181–196.

Bryson, J. M. "Strategic Planning: Big Wins and Small Wins." *Public Money and Management,* 1988a, *8*(3), 11–15.

Bryson, J. M. *Strategic Planning for Public and Nonprofit Organizations: A Guide to Strengthening and Sustaining Organizational Achievement.* San Francisco: Jossey-Bass, 1988b.

Bryson, J. M. "Know Thy Stakeholders." *Government Executive,* 1990, *22*(4), 46.

Bryson, J. M. *Getting Started with Strategic Planning.* San Francisco: Jossey-Bass, 1991. Audiotape.

Bryson, J. M. "Strategic Planning and Action Planning for Nonprofit Organizations." In R. D. Herman and Associates, *The Jossey-Bass Handbook of Nonprofit Leadership and Management.* San Francisco: Jossey-Bass, 1994.

Bryson, J. M. "Approaches to Strategic Planning." In J. Shafritz (ed.), *International Encyclopedia of Public Policy Analysis and Management.* New York: Marcel Dekker, forthcoming.

Bryson, J. M., Ackermann, F., Eden, C., and Finn, C. B. "Critical Incidents and Emergent Issues in Managing Large-Scale Change Efforts." In D. Kettl and H. B. Milward (eds.), *The State of Public Management.* Baltimore, Md.: Johns Hopkins University Press, forthcoming.

Bryson, J. M., and Alston, F. K. *Creating and Implementing Your Strategic Plan: A Workbook for Public and Nonprofit Organizations.* San Francisco: Jossey-Bass, 1995.

Bryson, J. M., and Bromiley, P. "Critical Factors Affecting the Planning and Implementation of Major Projects." *Strategic Management Journal,* 1993, *14,* 319–337.

Bryson, J. M., Bromiley, P., Jung, Y. S. "Influences of Context and Process on Project Planning Success." *Journal of Planning Education and Research,* 1990, *9*(3), 183–195.

Bryson, J. M., and Crosby, B. C. "The Design and Use of Strategic Planning Arenas." *Planning Outlook,* 1989, *32*(1), 5–13.

Bryson, J. M., and Crosby, B. C. *Leadership for the Common Good: Tackling Public Problems in a Shared Power World.* San Francisco: Jossey-Bass, 1992.

Bryson, J. M., and Cullen, J. W. "A Contingent Approach to Strategy and Tactics in Formative and Summative Evaluations." *Evaluation and Program Planning,* 1984, *7,* 267–290.

Bryson, J. M., and Delbecq, A. L. "A Contingent Approach to Strategy and Tactics in Project Planning." *Journal of the American Planning Association,* 1979, *45*(2), 167–179.

Bryson, J. M., and Delbecq, A. L. "A Contingent Program Planning Model." Working paper. Minneapolis: Hubert H. Humphrey Institute of Public Affairs, University of Minnesota, 1981.

Bryson, J. M., and Einsweiler, R. C. "Editors' Introduction to the Strategic Planning Symposium." *Journal of the American Planning Association,* 1987, *53,* 6–8.

Bryson, J. M., and Einsweiler, R. C. (eds.). *Strategic Planning—Threats and Opportunities for Planners.* Chicago: Planners Press, 1988.

Bryson, J. M., and Einsweiler, R. C. (eds.). *Shared Power: What Is It? How Does It Work? How Can We Make It Work Better?* Lanham, Md.: University Press of America, 1991.

Bryson, J. M., and Finn, C. B. "Development and Use of Strategy Maps to Enhance Organizational Performance." In A. Halachmi and G. Bouckaert (eds.), *The Challenge of Management in a Changing World.* San Francisco: Jossey-Bass, 1995.

Bryson, J. M., Freeman, R. E., and Roering, W. D. "Strategic Planning in the Public Sector:

Approaches and Directions." In B. Checkoway (ed.), *Strategic Perspectives on Planning Practice*. Lexington, Mass.: Lexington Books, 1986.

Bryson, J. M., and Kelley, G. "Leadership, Politics, and the Functioning of Complex Organizational and Interorganizational Networks." In A. Neghandi, G. Englund, and B. Wilpert (eds.), *The Functioning of Complex Organizations*. Cambridge, Mass.: Oelgeschlager, Gunn, and Hain, 1981.

Bryson, J. M., King, P. J., Roering, W. D., and Van de Ven, A. H. "Strategic Management at the Amherst H. Wilder Foundation." *Journal of Management Case Studies*, 1986, *2*, 118–138.

Bryson, J. M., and Ring, P. S. "A Transaction-Based Approach to Policy Intervention." *Policy Sciences*, 1990, *23*, 205–229.

Bryson, J. M., and Roering, W. D. "Applying Private Sector Strategic Planning to the Public Sector." *Journal of the American Planning Association*, 1987, *53*, 9–22.

Bryson, J. M., and Roering, W. D. "Initiation of Strategic Planning by Governments." *Public Administration Review*, 1988, *48*, 995–1004.

Bryson, J. M., and Roering, W. D. "Mobilizing Innovation Efforts: The Case of Government Strategic Planning." In A. Van de Ven, H. Angle, and M. S. Poole (eds.), *Research on the Management of Innovation*. New York: Harper Business, 1989.

Bryson, J. M., and Roering, W. D. "Understanding Options for Strategic Planning." In J. Perry (ed.), *Handbook of Public Administration*. San Francisco: Jossey-Bass, forthcoming.

Bryson, J. M., Van de Ven, A. H., and Roering, W. D. "Strategic Planning and the Revitalization of the Public Service." In R. Denhardt and E. Jennings (eds.), *Toward a New Public Service*. Columbia, Mo.: Extension Publications, University of Missouri, 1987.

Burns, J. M. *Leadership*. New York: HarperCollins, 1978.

Burns, L. E. *Busy Bodies*. New York: Norton, 1993.

Buzan, T., with Buzan, B. *The Mind Map Book: Radiant Thinking: The Major Evolution in Human Thought*. London: BBC Books, 1993.

Calista, D. J. "Policy Implementation." In S. Nagel (ed.) *Encyclopedia of Policy Studies*. New York: Marcel Dekker, 1994, pp. 117–155.

Campbell, D. T., and Stanley, J. C. *Experimental and Quasi-Experimental Designs for Research*. Skokie, Ill.: Rand McNally, 1966.

Carver, J. *Boards That Make a Difference: A New Design for Leadership in Nonprofit and Public Organizations*. San Francisco: Jossey-Bass, 1990.

Chakravarthy, B., and Lorange, P. *Managing the Strategy Process: A Framework for the Multi-Business Firm*. Englewood Cliffs, N.J.: Prentice-Hall, 1991.

Chase, G. "Implementing a Human Services Program: How Hard Will It Be?" *Public Policy*, 1979, *27*(4), 385–435.

Christensen, K. S. "Coping with Uncertainty in Planning." *Journal of the American Planning Association*, 1985, *51*(1), 63–73.

City of Milwaukee, Wisconsin. *1995 Proposed Plan and Executive Budget Summary*. Milwaukee, Wis.: City of Milwaukee, Department of Administration, Budget and Management Division, 1994.

Cleveland, H. *The Future Executive*. New York: HarperCollins, 1973.

Cleveland, H. *The Knowledge Executive*. New York: Dutton, 1985.

Cleveland, H. *Birth of a New World: An Open Moment for International Leadership*. San Francisco: Jossey-Bass, 1993.

Cobb, R. W., and Elder, C. D. *Participants in American Politics: The Dynamics of Agenda Building*. (2nd ed.) Baltimore, Md.: Johns Hopkins University Press, 1983.

Cohen, S., and Brand, R. *Total Quality Management in Government: A Practical Guide for the Real World*. San Francisco: Jossey-Bass, 1993.

Cohen, M. D., March, J. G., and Olsen, J. P. "A Garbage Can Model of Organizational Choice." *Administrative Science Quarterly*, 1972, *17*, 1–25.

Cooper, P. J. "Legal Tools for Accomplishing Administrative Responsibilities." In J. L. Perry (ed.), *Handbook of Public Administration*. San Francisco: Jossey-Bass, 1989.

Coplin, W. D., and O'Leary, M. K. *Everyman's Prince: A Guide to Understanding Your Political Problems*. Boston: PWS, 1976.

Cornish, E. *The 1990s and Beyond*. Bethesda, Md.: World Future Society, 1990.

Cothran, D. A. "Entrepreneurial Budgeting: An Emerging Reform?" *Public Administration Review*, 1993, *53*(5), 445–454.

Crow, M., and Bozeman, B. "Strategic Public Management." In J. M. Bryson and R. C. Einsweiler (eds.), *Strategic Planning—Threats and Opportunities for Planners*. Chicago: Planners Press, 1988.

Csikszentmihalyi, M. *Flow: The Psychology of Optimal Experience*. New York: HarperCollins, 1990.

Cyert, R. M., and March, J. G. *A Behavioral Theory of the Firm*. Englewood Cliffs, N.J.: Prentice-Hall, 1963.

Dahl, R. A. *Modern Political Analysis*. Englewood Cliffs, N.J.: Prentice-Hall, 1984.

Dalton, G. W. "Influence and Organizational Change." In G. Dalton, P. Lawrence, and L. Greiner (eds.), *Organization Change and Development*. Homewood, Ill.: Richard D. Irwin, 1970.

Dalton, G. W., and Thompson, P. H. *Novations: Strategies for Career Management*. Glenview, Ill.: Scott, Foresman, 1986.

Davis, S. M., and Lawrence, P. R. *Matrix*. Reading, Mass.: Addison-Wesley, 1977.

de Bono, E. *Lateral Thinking*. New York: HarperCollins, 1970.

de Gues, A. P. "Planning as Learning." *Harvard Business Review*, Mar./Apr. 1988, pp. 70–74.

Delbecq, A. L. "Negotiating Mandates Which Increase the Acceptance of Evaluation Findings Concerning Demonstration Findings in Human Services." Paper presented at the annual conference of the Academy of Management, Orlando, Fla., 1977.

Delbecq, A. L., and Filley, A. *Program and Project Management in a Matrix Organization*. Graduate School of Business Monograph No. 9. Madison: University of Wisconsin, 1974.

Delbecq, A. L., Van de Ven, A. H., and Gustafson, D. *Group Techniques for Program Planning*. Glenview, Ill.: Scott-Foresman, 1975.

Denhardt, R. B. *The Pursuit of Significance: Strategies for Managerial Success in Public Organizations*. Belmont, Calif.: Wadsworth, 1993.

Doig, J. W., and Hargrove, E. C. (eds.), *Leadership and Innovation: A Biographical Perspective on Entrepreneurs in Government*. Baltimore, Md.: Johns Hopkins University Press, 1987.

Drucker, P. F. *Management: Tasks, Responsibilities, Practices*. New York: HarperCollins, 1973.

The Peter F. Drucker Foundation for Nonprofit Management. *The Drucker Foundation Self-Assessment Tool for Nonprofit Organizations*. San Francisco: Jossey-Bass, 1993.

Dutton, J. E., and Ashford, S. J. "Selling Issues to Top Management." *Academy of Management Review*, 1993, *18*(3), 397–428.

Dutton, J. E., and Dukerich, J. "Keeping One Eye on the Mirror: The Role of Image and Identity in Organizational Adaptation." *Academy of Management Journal*, 1991, *34*, 517–554.

Dutton, J. E., and Jackson, S. E. "Categorizing Strategic Issues: Links to Organizational Action." *Academy of Management Review*, 1987, *12*(1), 76–90.

Eadie, D. C. *Boards That Work: A Practical Guide for Building Effective Association Boards*. Washington, D.C.: American Society of Association Executives, 1994.

Eadie, D. C., and Kethley, A. J. "7 Keys to a Successful Board-Staff Retreat." *Nonprofit World*, 1994, *12*(6), 23–28.

Eadie, D. C., and Steinbacher, R. "Strategic Agenda Management: A Marriage of Organizational Development and Strategic Planning." *Public Administration Review*, 1985, *45*, 424–430.

Eckhert, P., Haines, K., Delmont, T., and Pflaum, A. "Strategic Planning in Hennepin County, Minnesota: An Issues Management Approach." In J. M. Bryson and R. C. Einsweiler (eds.), *Strategic Planning—Threats and Opportunities for Planners.* Chicago: Planners Press, 1988. Also found in R. L. Kemp (ed.), *Strategic Planning for Local Government: A Casebook.* Chicago: Planners Press, 1992; also found in R. L. Kemp (ed.), *Strategic Planning for Local Government.* Jefferson, N.C.: McFarland, 1993.

Edelman, M. *The Symbolic Uses of Politics.* Urbana: University of Illinois Press, 1964.

Edelman, M. *Politics as Symbolic Action.* New York: Academic Press, 1971.

Edelman, M. *Political Language.* New York: Academic Press, 1977.

Eden, C. "Using Cognitive Mapping for Strategic Options Development and Analysis (SODA)." In J. Rosenhead (ed.), *Rational Analysis for a Problematic World.* New York: Wiley, 1989.

Eden, C., Ackermann, F., and Cropper, S. "The Analysis of Cause Maps." *Journal of Management Studies,* 1992, *29*(3), 309–324.

Eden, C., and Huxham, C. "Action-Oriented Strategic Management." *Journal of the Operational Research Society,* 1988, *39*(10), 889–899.

Eden, C., Jones, S., and Sims, D. *Thinking in Organizations.* London: Macmillan, 1979.

Eden, C., Jones, S., and Sims, D. *Messing About in Problems.* Oxford: Pergamon Press, 1983.

Eden, C., and Sims, D. "On the Nature of Problems in Consulting Practice." *Omega,* 1978, *7*(2), 119–127.

Elmore, R. F. "Backward Mapping: Implementation Research and Policy Decisions." In W. Williams (ed.), *Studying Implementation.* Chatham, N.J.: Chatham House, 1982.

Emmert, M. A., Crow, M., and Shangraw, R. F., Jr. "Public Management in the Future: Post-Orthodoxy and Organization Design." In B. Bozeman (ed.), *Public Management: The State of the Art.* San Francisco: Jossey-Bass, 1993.

Etzioni, A. *The Spirit of Community.* New York: Crown, 1993.

Fesler, J., and Kettl, D. *The Politics of the Administrative Process.* (2nd ed.) Chatham, N.J.: Chatham House, 1994.

Filley, A. *Interpersonal Conflict Resolution.* Glenview, Ill.: Scott, Foresman, 1975.

Finn, C. B. "Utilizing Stakeholder Strategies to Ensure Positive Outcomes in Collaborative Processes." Prepublication draft. Minneapolis, Minn.: Hubert H. Humphrey Institute of Public Affairs, University of Minnesota, 1995.

Fischer, F., and Forester, J. (eds.). *The Argumentative Turn in Policy Analysis and Planning.* Durham, N.C.: Duke University Press, 1993.

Fisher, R., and Brown, S. *Getting Together: Building a Relationship That Gets to Yes.* Boston: Houghton Mifflin, 1988.

Fisher, R., and Ury, W. *Getting to Yes: Negotiating Agreement Without Giving In.* New York: Penguin, 1981.

Flynn, N. "Performance Measurement in Public Sector Services." *Policy and Politics,* 1986, *3,* 389–909.

Flynn, N. *Public Sector Management.* (2nd ed.) New York: Harvester Wheatsheaf, 1993.

Frame, J. D. *Managing Projects in Organizations: How to Make the Best Use of Time, Techniques, and People.* San Francisco: Jossey-Bass, 1987.

Fredrickson, J. G. "The Recovery of Civism in Public Administration." *Public Administration Review,* 1982, *42,* 501–508.

Frederickson, J. W. "The Comprehensiveness of Strategic Decision Processes." *Academy of Management Journal,* 1984, *27*(2), 445–466.

Frederickson, J. W., and Mitchell, R. R. "Strategic Decision Processes: Comprehensiveness and Performance in an Industry with an Unstable Environment." *Academy of Management Journal,* 1984, *27*(2), 399–423.

Freedman, N., and Van Ham, K. "Strategic Planning in Philips." In B. Taylor and D. Hussey (eds.), *The Realities of Planning.* Oxford: Pergamon Press, 1982.

Freeman, R. E. *Strategic Management: A Stakeholder Approach.* Boston: Pitman, 1984.

Friedrich, C. J. "Public Policy and the Nature of Administrative Responsibility." *Public Policy,* 1940, *1,* 3–24.

Friend, J., and Hickling, A. *Planning Under Pressure: The Strategic Choice Approach.* Oxford: Pergamon Press, 1987.

Gabor, D. *Inventing the Future.* New York: Knopf, 1964.

Gersick, C. "Revolutionary Change Theories: A Multilevel Exploration of the Punctuated Equilibrium Paradigm." *Academy of Management Review,* 1991, *16,* 10–36.

Goggin, M. L., Bowman, A. O., Lester, J. P., and O'Toole, L. J., Jr. *Implementation Theory and Practice: Toward a Third Generation.* Glenview, Ill.: Scott, Foresman, 1990.

Gore, A. *The Gore Report on Reinventing Government.* New York: Times Books, 1993.

Gray, B. *Collaborating: Finding Common Ground for Multiparty Problems.* San Francisco: Jossey-Bass, 1989.

Greenblat, C., and Duke, R. *Principles and Practices of Gaming Simulation.* Newbury Park, Calif.: Sage, 1981.

Guibert, J. de. *The Jesuits: Their Spiritual Doctrine and Practice: A Historical Study* (W. J. Young, trans., G. E. Gauss, ed.). Chicago: Institute of Jesuit Sources, 1964.

Halachmi, A., and Boydston, R. "Strategic Management with Annual and Multi-Year Operating Budgets." *Public Budgeting and Financial Management,* 1991, *3*(2), 293–316.

Hall, P. *Great Planning Disasters.* Berkeley: University of California Press, 1980.

Hammer, M., and Champy, J. *Reengineering the Corporation.* New York: Harper Business, 1993.

Hampden-Turner, C. *Corporate Culture.* Hutchinson, England: Economist Books, 1990.

Healey, P. "A Planner's Day: Knowledge and Action in Communicative Practice." *Journal of the American Planning Association,* 1992a, *58*(1), 9–20.

Healey, P. "Planning Through Debate: The Communicative Turn in Planning Theory." *Town Planning Review,* 1992b, *63*(2), 143–162.

Heifetz, R. A., and Sinder, R. M. "Political Leadership: Managing the Public's Problem Solving." In R. B. Reich (ed.), *The Power of Public Ideas.* New York: Harper Business, 1988.

Hennepin County, Minnesota. *Strategic Planning Manual.* Minneapolis, Minn.: Hennepin County Office of Planning and Development, 1983.

Hennepin County, Minnesota. *Hennepin County Strategic Plan 1995.* Minneapolis, Minn.: County Administrator, Hennepin County (A-2303 Government Center, Minneapolis, MN 55487), 1995.

Herman, R. D., and Associates. *The Jossey-Bass Handbook of Nonprofit Leadership and Management.* San Francisco: Jossey-Bass, 1994.

Herson, L.J.R. *The Politics of Ideas.* Prospect Heights, Ill.: Waveland Press, 1984.

Hjern, B., and Porter, D. O. "Implementation Structures: A New Unit of Administrative Analysis." *Organization Studies,* 1981, *2*(3), 211–227.

Hogwood, B., and Peters, B. G. *Policy Dynamics.* New York: St. Martin's Press, 1983.

Houle, C. O. *Governing Boards: Their Nature and Nurture.* San Francisco: Jossey Bass, 1989.

Howe, E. "Role Choices of Urban Planners." *Journal of the American Planning Association,* 1980, *46,* 398–409.

Howe, E., and Kaufman, J. "The Ethics of Contemporary American Planners." *Journal of the American Planning Association,* 1979, *45,* 243–255.

Hunt, H. G. *Leadership: A New Synthesis.* Newbury Park, Calif.: Sage, 1991.

Huxham, C. "Our Trivialities in Process." In C. Eden and J. Radford (eds.), *Tackling Strategic Problems: The Role of Group Decision Support.* Newbury Park, Calif.: Sage, 1990.

Huxham, C. "Pursuing Collaborative Advantage." *Journal of the Operational Research Society,* 1993, *44*(6), 599–611.

Huxham, C., and Eden, C. "Gaming, Competitor Analysis and Strategic Management." In C. Eden and J. Radford (eds.), *Tackling Strategic Problems: The Role of Group Decision Support.* Newbury Park, Calif.: Sage, 1990.

Innes, J. E. "Planning Through Consensus Building: A New View of the Comprehensive Planning Ideal." Working Paper 626. Berkeley: Institute of Urban and Regional Development, University of California, 1994.

Isabella, L. A. "Evolving Interpretations as a Change Unfolds: How Managers Construe Key Organizational Events." *Academy of Management Journal*, 1990, *33*(1), 7–41.

Isenberg, D. J. "How Senior Managers Think." *Harvard Business Review,* Nov./Dec. 1984, pp. 81–90.

Jackson, P. M., and Palmer, B. *Performance Measurement: A Management Guide.* Leicester, England: The Management Centre, University of Leicester, 1992.

Jackson, S. E., and Dutton, J. E. "Discerning Threats and Opportunities." *Administrative Science Quarterly,* 1988, *33,* 370–387.

Janis, I. L. *Crucial Decisions: Leadership in Policymaking and Crisis Management.* New York: Free Press, 1989.

Jenster, P. "Using Critical Success Factors in Planning." *Long Range Planning,* 1987, *20*(4), 102–110.

Johnson, D. W., and Johnson, F. P. *Joining Together: Group Theory and Group Skills* (5th ed.). Englewood Cliffs, N.J.: Prentice-Hall, 1994.

Kahn, S. *Organizing.* New York: McGraw-Hill, 1982.

Kanter, R. M. *Commitment and Community: Communes and Utopias in Sociological Perspective.* Cambridge, Mass.: Harvard University Press, 1972.

Kanter, R. M. *The Changemasters.* New York: Simon & Schuster, 1983.

Kanter, R. M. *When Giants Learn to Dance.* New York: Touchstone, 1989.

Karpik, L. "Technological Capitalism." In S. Clegg and D. Dunkerley (eds.), *Critical Issues in Organizations.* New York: Routledge & Kegan Paul, 1977.

Kaufman, G. *Shame: The Power of Caring.* Rochester, Vt.: Schenkman Books, 1992.

Kaufman, H. *Are Government Organizations Immortal?* Washington, D.C.: Brookings Institution, 1976.

Kaufman, J. L. "Making Planners More Effective Strategists." In B. Checkoway (ed.), *Strategic Perspectives on Planning Practice.* Lexington, Mass.: Lexington Books, 1986.

Kelly, G. *A Theory of Personality.* New York: Norton, 1963.

Kemp, R. L. *Strategic Planning for Local Government.* Jefferson, N.C.: McFarland, 1993.

Kennedy, P. M. *The Rise and Fall of the Great Powers.* New York: Vintage Books, 1987.

Kennedy, P. M. *Preparing for the Twenty-First Century.* New York: Random House, 1993.

Kerr, S., and Jermier, J. "Substitutes for Leadership: Their Meaning and Measurement." *Organizational Behavior and Human Performance,* 1978, *22,* 375–403.

Kidder, R. W. *Shared Values for a Troubled World: Conversations with Men and Women of Conscience.* San Francisco: Jossey-Bass, 1994.

King, J., and Johnson, D. A. "The Oak Ridge, Tennessee, Experience." In J. M. Bryson and R. C. Einsweiler (eds.), *Strategic Planning—Threats and Opportunities for Planners.* Chicago: Planners Press, 1988.

Kingdon, J. R. *Agendas, Alternatives, and Public Policies.* (Rev. ed.) Boston: Little, Brown, 1995.

Knauft, E. B., Berger, R. A., Gray, S. T. *Profiles of Excellence: Achieving Success in the Nonprofit Sector.* San Francisco: Jossey-Bass, 1991.

Kolderie, T. "Two Different Concepts of Privatization." *Public Administration Review,* 1986, *46,* 285–291.

Koteen, J. *Strategic Management in Public and Nonprofit Organizations.* New York: Praeger, 1989.

Kotler, P. *Marketing Management.* Englewood Cliffs, N.J.: Prentice-Hall, 1976.

Kotter, J. P. "Leading Change: Why Transformation Efforts Fail." *Harvard Business Review,* Mar./Apr. 1995, pp. 59–67.

Kotter, J. P., and Lawrence, P. *Mayors in Action.* New York: Wiley, 1974.

Kouzes, J. M., and Posner, B. Z. *The Leadership Challenge: How to Get Extraordinary Things Done in Organizations.* San Francisco: Jossey-Bass, 1987.

Kouzes, J. M., and Posner, B. Z. *Credibility: How Leaders Gain and Lose It, Why People Demand It.* San Francisco: Jossey-Bass, 1993.

Krasner, S. D. "Structural Causes and Regime Consequences: Regimes as Intervening Variables." In S. D. Krasner (ed.), *International Regimes.* Ithaca, N.Y.: Cornell University Press, 1983.

Kubler-Ross, E. *On Death and Dying.* New York: Macmillan, 1969.

Land, G., and Jarman, B. *Breaking Point and Beyond.* New York: Harper Business, 1992.

Lappé, F. M., and Du Bois, P. M. *The Quickening of America: Rebuilding Our Nation, Remaking Our Lives.* San Francisco: Jossey-Bass, 1994.

Least Heat-Moon, W. *Blue Highways: A Journey into America.* Boston: Houghton Mifflin, 1982.

Leidecker, J. K., and Bruno, A. V. "Identifying and Using Critical Success Factors." *Long Range Planning,* 1984, *17*(1), 23–32.

Levine, C. "More on Cutback Management: Hard Questions for Hard Times." *Public Administration Review,* 1979, *39,* 179–183.

Levitt, T. "Marketing Myopia." Harvard Business Review, 1960, *38*(4), 45–56.

Levy, F., Meltsner, A., and Wildavsky, A. *Urban Outcomes.* Berkeley: University of California Press, 1974.

Lewis, C. W. *The Ethics Challenge in Public Service: A Problem-Solving Guide.* San Francisco: Jossey-Bass, 1991.

Light, P. C. *The President's Agenda.* Baltimore, Md.: Johns Hopkins University Press, 1991.

Lindblom, C. E. "The Science of Muddling Through." *Public Administration Review,* 1959, *19,* 79–88.

Lindblom, C. E. *The Intelligence of Democracy.* New York: Free Press, 1965.

Lindblom, C. E. *Politics and Markets.* New York: Free Press, 1977.

Lindblom, C. E. *The Policy-Making Process.* (2nd ed.) Englewood Cliffs, N.J.: Prentice-Hall, 1980.

Linden, R. M. *Seamless Government: A Practical Guide to Re-Engineering in the Public Sector.* San Francisco: Jossey-Bass, 1994.

Linneman, R. E., and Klein, H. E. "The Use of Multiple Scenarios by U.S. Industrial Companies: A Comparison Study, 1977–1981." *Long Range Planning,* 1983, *16*(6), 94–101.

Lipsky, M. *Street-Level Bureaucracy: Dilemmas of the Individual in Public Services.* New York: Russell Sage Foundation, 1980.

Locke, E. A., Shaw, K. N., Saari, L. M., and Latham, G. P. "Goal Setting and Task Performance: 1969–1980." *Psychological Bulletin,* 1981, *90,* 125–152.

Lorange, P., and Vancil, R. F. *Strategic Planning Systems.* Englewood Cliffs, N.J.: Prentice-Hall, 1977.

Lowi, T. J. "Distribution, Regulation, Redistribution: The Functions of Government." In R. B. Ripley (ed.), *Public Policies and Their Politics: Techniques of Government Control.* New York: Norton, 1966.

Luke, J. S. , and Caiden, G. E. "Coping with Global Interdependence." In J. L. Perry (ed.) *Handbook of Public Administration.* San Francisco: Jossey-Bass, 1989, pp. 83–93.

Luke, J. "Managing Interconnectedness: The Challenge of Shared Power." In J. M. Bryson and R. C. Einsweiler (eds.), *Shared Power: What Is It? How Does It Work? How Can We Make It Work Better?* Lanham, Md.: University Press of America, 1991, pp. 25–50.

Luttwak, E. *The Grand Strategy of the Roman Empire.* Baltimore, Md.: Johns Hopkins University Press, 1977.

Lynn, L. E., Jr. *Managing Public Policy.* Boston: Little, Brown, 1987.

Maccoby, M. *The Leader.* New York: Ballantine, 1983.

McGowan, R. P., and Stevens, J. M. "Local Government Initiatives in a Climate of Uncertainty." *Public Administration Review,* 1983, *43*(2), 127–136.

Maidique, M. A. "Entrepreneurs, Champions and Technological Innovation." *Sloan Management Review,* 1980, *21,* 58–76.

Maier, M. *"We Have to Make a Management Decision": Morton-Thiokol and the NASA Space Shuttle 'Challenger' Disaster.* Binghamton: State University of New York at Binghamton, School of Education and Human Development, 1992.

Mandelbaum, S. J. *Open Moral Communities.* Berkeley: University of California Press, 1995.

Mangham, I. L. *Power and Performance in Organizations.* Oxford: Basil Blackwell, 1986.

Mangham, I. L., and Overington, M. *Organization as Theatre: A Social Psychology of Dramatic Appearances.* New York: Wiley, 1987.

Manz, C. C. "Self-Leadership: Toward an Expanded Theory of Self-Influence Processes in Organizations." *Academy of Management Review,* 1986, *11,* 585–600.

March, J. G., and Olsen, J. P. *Rediscovering Institutions: The Organizational Basis of Politics.* New York: Free Press, 1989.

March, J. G., and Simon, H. A. *Organizations.* New York: Wiley, 1958.

May, R. *Love and Will.* New York: Norton, 1969.

Mazmanian, D. A., and Sabatier, P. A. *Implementation and Public Policy.* Glenview, Ill.: Scott, Foresman, 1983.

Meltsner, A. J. *Rules for Rulers: The Politics of Advice.* Philadelphia: Temple University Press, 1990.

Mercer, J. L. *Strategic Planning for Public Managers.* Westport, Conn.: Quorum, 1991.

Mercer, J. L. *Public Management in Lean Years: Operating in a Cutback Management Environment.* Westport, Conn.: Quorum, 1992.

Merton, R. K. "Bureaucratic Structures and Personality." *Journal of Social Forces,* 1940, *17,* 560–568.

Miles, R. E., and Snow, C. *Organizational Strategy, Structure, and Process.* New York: McGraw-Hill, 1978.

Miller, D., and Friesen, P. H. *Organizations: A Quantum View.* Englewood Cliffs, N.J.: Prentice-Hall, 1984.

Milward, H. B., Provan, K. G., and Else, B. A. "What Does the 'Hollow State' Look Like?" In Bozeman, B. (ed.), *Public Management: The State of the Art.* San Francisco: Jossey-Bass, 1993.

Mintzberg, H. *The Nature of Managerial Work.* New York: HarperCollins, 1973.

Mintzberg, H. *Power In and Around Organizations.* Englewood Cliffs, N.J.: Prentice-Hall, 1983.

Mintzberg, H., and McHugh, A. "Strategy Formation in an Adhocracy." Administrative Science Quarterly, 1985, *30,* 160–197.

Mintzberg, H. "Crafting Strategy." *Harvard Business Review,* July/Aug. 1987, pp. 66–75.

Mintzberg, H. "The Fall and Rise of Strategic Planning." *Harvard Business Review,* 1994a, Jan./Feb., pp. 107–114.

Mintzberg, H. *The Rise and Fall of Strategic Planning.* New York: Free Press, 1994b.

Mintzberg, H., and Waters, J. A. "Of Strategies, Deliberate and Emergent." *Strategic Management Journal,* 1985, *6*(3), 257–272.

Mintzberg, H., and Westley, F. "Cycles of Organizational Change." *Strategic Management Journal,* 1992, *13,* 39–59.

Mitroff, I. I. "Systemic Problem Solving." In M. W. McCall, Jr., and M. M. Lombardo (eds.), *Leadership: Where Else Can We Go?* Durham, N.C.: Duke University Press, 1978.

Mitroff, I. I., and Pearson, C. M. *Crisis Management: A Diagnostic Guide for Improving Your Organization's Crisis-Preparedness.* San Francisco: Jossey-Bass, 1993.

Montanari, J. R., and Bracker, J. S. "The Strategic Management Process." *Strategic Management Journal,* 1986, *7*(3), 251–265.

Moore, T. "Why Allow Planners to Do What They Do?" *Journal of the American Planning Association,* 1978, *44,* 387–398.

Moore, T. *Care of the Soul.* New York: HarperCollins, 1992.

Morgan, G. *Images of Organization.* Newbury Park, Calif.: Sage, 1986.

Morgan, G. *Imaginization: The Art of Creative Management.* Newbury Park, Calif.: Sage, 1993.

Morris, P., and Hough, G. *Preconditions of Success and Failure in Major Projects.* Major Projects Association Technical Paper No. 3. Oxford: Templeton College, Oxford University, 1986.

Morrisey, G. L., Below, P. J., and Acomb, B. L. *The Executive Guide to Operational Planning.* San Francisco: Jossey-Bass, 1987.

National Governors Association. *An Action Agenda to Redesign State Government.* Washington, D.C.: National Governors Association, 1993.

Naisbitt, J., and Aburdene, P. *Megatrends 2000.* New York: Avon Books, 1990.

Nanus, B. *Visionary Leadership: Creating a Compelling Sense of Direction for Your Organization.* San Francisco: Jossey-Bass, 1992.

Neely, R. *How the Courts Govern America.* New Haven, Conn.: Yale University Press, 1981.

Neustadt, R. E. *Presidential Power and the Modern Presidents.* New York: Free Press, 1990.

Neustadt, R. E., and May, E. R. *Thinking in Time: The Uses of History for Decision Makers.* New York: Free Press, 1986.

Normann, R. *Service Management: Strategy and Leadership in Service Businesses.* (2nd ed.) New York: Wiley, 1991.

Nutt, P. C. "A Strategic Planning Network for Non-Profit Organizations." *Strategic Management Journal,* 1984a, *5,* 57–75.

Nutt, P.C. "Types of Organizational Decision Processes." *Administrative Science Quarterly,* 1984b, *29,* 414–450.

Nutt, P. C. *Making Tough Decisions: Tactics for Improving Managerial Decision Making.* San Francisco: Jossey-Bass, 1989.

Nutt, P. C. *Managing Planned Change.* New York: Macmillan, 1992.

Nutt, P. C., and Backoff, R. W. *Strategic Management for Public and Third Sector Organizations: A Handbook for Leaders.* San Francisco: Jossey-Bass, 1992.

Nutt, P. C., and Backoff, R. W. "Organizational Publicness and Its Implications for Strategic Management." *Journal of Public Administration Research and Theory,* 1993, *3*(2), 209–231.

Nutt, P. C., and Backoff, R. W. "Strategy for Public and Third Sector Organizations," *Journal of Public Administration Research and Theory,* 1995, *5*(2), 189–211.

Olsen, J. B., and Eadie, D. C. *The Game Plan: Governance with Foresight.* Washington, D.C.: Council of State Planning Agencies, 1982.

Oregon Progress Board. *Oregon Benchmarks, Standards for Measuring Statewide Progress and Institutional Performance.* Salem, Ore.: Oregon Progress Board, 1994.

Ortony, A., Clore, G. L., and Collins, A. *The Cognitive Structure of Emotions.* Cambridge, England: Cambridge University Press, 1990.

Osborne, D., and Gaebler, T. *Reinventing Government.* Reading, Mass.: Addison-Wesley, 1992.

Ouchi, W. *Theory Z: How Many American Businesses Can Meet the Japanese Challenge.* Reading, Mass.: Addison-Wesley, 1981.

Palmer, P. J. *The Active Life: A Spirituality of Work, Creativity, and Courage.* New York: Harper-Collins, 1990.

Panetta, L. "Government Performance and Results Act of 1993." Memorandum for the Heads of Executive Departments and Agencies, M-94–2. Washington, D.C.: Executive Office of the President/Office of Management and Budget, Oct. 8, 1993.

Parkinson, C. N. *Parkinson's Law and Other Studies in Administration.* Boston: Houghton Mifflin, 1957.

Patton, M. Q. *Utilization-Focused Evaluation.* (2nd ed.) Newbury Park, Calif.: Sage, 1986.

Patton, M. Q. *Creative Evaluation and Research Methods.* Newbury Park, Calif.: Sage, 1990.

Peters, G. *The Politics of Bureaucracy.* (4th ed.) White Plains, N.Y.: Longman, 1995.

Peters, T. J., and Waterman, R. H., Jr. *In Search of Excellence: Lessons from America's Best-Run Companies.* New York: HarperCollins, 1982.

Pettigrew, A., Ferlie, E., and McKee, L. *Shaping Strategic Change*. Newbury Park, Calif.: Sage, 1992.

Pfeffer, J. *Power in Organizations*. Boston: Pitman, 1981.

Pfeffer, J. *Managing with Power: Politics and Influence in Organizations*. Boston: Harvard Business School Press, 1992.

Pfeffer, J., and Moore, W. "Power in University Budgeting: A Replication and Extension." *Administrative Science Quarterly*, 1980, *25*, 637–653.

Pfeffer, J., and Salancik, R. *The External Control of Organizations: A Resource Dependence Perspective*. New York: HarperCollins, 1978.

Pflaum, A., and Delmont, T. "External Scanning: A Tool for Planners." *Journal of the American Planning Association*, 1987, *53*(1), 56–67.

Popcorn, F. *The Popcorn Report*. New York: HarperCollins, 1992.

Porter, M. *Competitive Strategy*. New York: Free Press, 1980.

Porter, M. *Competitive Advantage*. New York: Free Press, 1985.

Posner, R. A. *The Federal Courts: Crisis and Reform*. Cambridge, Mass.: Harvard University Press, 1985.

Prahalad, C. K., and Hamel, G. "The Core Competencies of the Corporation." *Harvard Business Review*, May/June 1990, pp. 79–91.

Pressman, J., and Wildavsky, A. *Implementation*. Berkeley: University of California Press, 1973.

Quinn, J. B. *Strategies for Change: Logical Incrementalism*. Homewood, Ill.: Richard D. Irwin, 1980.

Quinn, R. E. *Beyond Rational Management: Mastering the Paradoxes and Competing Demands of High Performance*. San Francisco: Jossey-Bass, 1988.

Radin, B. A. "Managing Across Boundaries: The Monday Management Group of the National Initiative on Rural Development." A paper presented at the National Public Management Research Conference, Robert M. LaFollette Institute of Public Affairs, University of Wisconsin, Madison, Sept. 30–Oct. 2, 1993.

Rainey, H. G. *Understanding and Managing Public Organizations*. San Francisco: Jossey-Bass, 1991.

Randolph, W. A., and Posner, B. Z. *Effective Project Planning and Management: Getting the Job Done*. Englewood Cliffs, N.J.: Prentice-Hall, 1988.

Renfro, W. L. *Issues Management in Strategic Planning*. Westport, Conn.: Quorum, 1993.

Rider, R. W. "Making Strategic Planning Work in Local Government." *Long Range Planning*, 1983, *16*(3), 73–81.

Riker, W. H. *The Art of Political Manipulation* New Haven, Conn.: Yale University Press, 1986.

Ring, P. S. "Strategic Issues: What Are They and from Where Do They Come?" In J. M. Bryson and R. C. Einsweiler (eds.), *Strategic Planning—Threats and Opportunities for Planners*. Chicago: Planners Press, 1988.

Ring, P. S., and Perry, J. L. "Strategic Management in Public and Private Organizations: Implications of Distinctive Contexts and Constraints." *Academy of Management Review*, 1985, *10*, 276–286.

Roberts, N. "Limitations of Strategic Action in Bureaus." In B. Bozeman (ed.), *Public Management: The State of the Art*. San Francisco: Jossey-Bass, 1993.

Roberts, N., and Wargo, L. "The Dilemma of Planning in Large-Scale Public Organizations: The Case of the United States Navy." *Journal of Public Administration Research and Theory*, 1994, *4*, 469–491.

Rogers, E. *Diffusion of Innovations*. (3d ed.) New York: Free Press, 1982.

Romzek, B. S., and Dubnick, M. J. "Accountability in the Public Sector: Lessons from the Challenger Tragedy." *Public Administration Review*, 1987, *47*(3), 227–238.

Rosenhead, J. (ed.). *Rational Analysis for a Problematic World*. New York: Wiley, 1989.

Rubin, M. S. "Sagas, Ventures, Quests, and Parlays: A Typology of Strategies in the Public

Sector." In J. M. Bryson and R. C. Einsweiler (eds.), *Strategic Planning—Threats and Opportunities for Planners.* Chicago: Planners Press, 1988.

Rushdie, S. *Midnight's Children.* London: Jonathan Cape/Picador, 1981.

Sabatier, P. A. "An Advocacy Coalition Framework of Policy Change and the Role of Policy-Oriented Learning Therein." *Policy Sciences,* 1988, *21,* 129–168.

Sabatier, P. A. "Toward Better Theories of the Policy Process." *PS: Political Science and Politics,* 1991, *24*(2), 144–156.

Sager, T. *Communicative Planning Theory,* Aldershot, England: Avebury, 1994.

Salamon, L. M. *America's Nonprofit Sector: A Primer.* New York: Foundation Center, 1992.

Savas, E. S. *Privatizing the Public Sector.* Chatham, N.J.: Chatham House, 1982.

Schaef, A. W. *Women's Reality.* San Francisco: Harper San Francisco, 1985.

Schein, E. H. *Process Consultation: Lessons for Managers and Consultants,* Vol. 2. Reading, Mass.: Addison-Wesley, 1987.

Schein, E. H. *Process Consultation: Its Role in Organization Development,* Vol 1. (2d. ed.) Reading, Mass: Addison-Wesley Publishing Co., 1988.

Schein, E. H. *Organizational Culture and Leadership.* (2nd ed.) San Francisco: Jossey-Bass, 1992.

Schenkat, R. *Quality Connections.* Alexandria, Va.: Association for Supervision and Curriculum Development, 1993.

Schlesinger, A. M., Jr. *The Cycles of American History.* Boston: Houghton Mifflin, 1986.

Schön, D. A. *Beyond the Stable State.* London: Temple Smith, 1971.

Schön, D. A. *The Reflective Practitioner.* New York: Basic Books, 1983.

Schultze, C. "The Public Use of Private Interest." *Harpers,* 1977, *254,* 43–62.

Schutz, A. *The Phenomenology of the Social World.* Evanston, Ill.: Northwestern University Press, 1967.

Schwartz, P. *The Art of the Long View.* New York: Doubleday, 1991.

Schwarz, R. M. *The Skilled Facilitator: Practical Wisdom for Developing Effective Groups.* San Francisco: Jossey-Bass, 1994.

Scriven, M. S. "The Methodology of Evaluation." In R. E. Stake (ed.), *Curriculum Evaluation.* Vol. 1: *AERA Monograph Series on Curriculum Evaluation.* Skokie, Ill.: Rand McNally, 1967.

Seligman, M.E.P. *Learned Optimism.* New York: Knopf, 1991.

Selznick, P. *Leadership in Administration.* Berkeley. University of California Press, 1957.

Senge, P. M. *The Fifth Discipline: The Art and Practice of the Learning Organization.* New York: Doubleday, 1990.

Shamir, B., Arthur, M., and House, R. "The Rhetoric of Charismatic Leadership: A Theoretical Extension, a Case Study, and Implications for Research." *The Leadership Quarterly,* 1994, *5*(1), 25–42.

Shapiro, M. "On Predicting the Future of Administrative Law." *Regulation,* 1982, *6*(3), 18–25.

Sharkansky, I. *The Routines of Politics.* New York: Van Nostrand Reinhold, 1970.

Simon, S. B. *Getting Unstuck: Breaking Through Your Barriers to Change.* New York: Warner, 1988.

Sipel, G. A. "Putting *In Search of Excellence* to Work in Local Government." *Public Management Magazine,* 1984, *66*(4), 2–5.

Smircich, L., and Morgan, G. "Leadership: The Management of Meaning." *Journal of Applied Behavioral Science,* 1989, *18,* 257–273.

Sorkin, D. L., Ferris, N. B., and Hudak, J. *Strategies for Cities and Counties: A Strategic Planning Guide.* Washington, D.C.: Public Technology, 1984.

Spencer, L. *Winning Through Participation.* Dubuque, Iowa: Kendall/Hunt, 1989.

Spencer, S. A., and Adams, J. D. *Life Changes: Growing Through Personal Transitions.* San Luis Obispo, Calif.: Impact, 1990.

Stalk, G., Evans, P., and Shulman, L. E. "Competing on Capabilities: The New Rules of Corporate Strategy." *Harvard Business Review,* Mar./Apr. 1992, pp. 57–69.

Steiner, G. A. *Strategic Planning: What Every Manager Must Know.* New York: Free Press, 1979.

Stern, G. J. *Marketing Workbook For Nonprofit Organizations.* St. Paul, Minn.: Amherst H. Wilder Foundation, 1990.

Stone, D. A. *Policy Paradox and Political Reason.* Glenview, Ill.: Scott, Foresman, 1988.

Sun Tzu. *The Art of War* (T. Cleary, trans.). Boston: Shambhala, 1991.

Susskind, L., and Cruikshank, J. *Breaking the Impasse.* New York: Basic Books, 1987.

Taylor, B. "Strategic Planning: Which Style Do You Need?" *Long Range Planning,* 1984, *17,* 51–62.

Terry, R. W. *Authentic Leadership: Courage in Action.* San Francisco: Jossey-Bass, 1993.

Thompson, F., and Jones, L. R. *Reinventing the Pentagon: How the New Public Management Can Bring Institutional Renewal.* San Francisco: Jossey-Bass, 1994.

Thompson, J. D. *Organizations in Action.* New York: McGraw-Hill, 1967.

Tita, M. A., and Allio, R. J. "3M's Strategy System: Planning in an Innovative Organization." *Planning Review,* Sept. 1984, pp. 10–15.

Trist, E. "Referent Organizations and the Development of Inter-Organizational Domains." *Human Relations,* 1983, *36*(3), 269–284.

Tuchman, B. *The March of Folly: From Troy to Vietnam.* New York: Knopf, 1984.

U.S. Department of Education. *The National Agenda for Achieving Better Results for Children and Youth with Disabilities.* Washington, D.C.: Office of Special Education and Rehabilitative Services, U.S. Department of Education, 1994.

United Way of America. *What Lies Ahead: Countdown to the 21st Century.* Alexandria, Va.: The United Way of America's Strategic Institute, 1989. (Reprinted as "Nine Forces Reshaping America," *The Futurist,* July/Aug. 1990, pp. 9–16.)

Ury, W. L., Brett, J. M., and Goldberg, S. B. *Getting Disputes Resolved: Designing Systems to Cut the Costs of Conflict.* San Francisco: Jossey-Bass, 1988.

Van de Ven, A. H., and Ferry, D. L. *Measuring and Assessing Organizations.* New York: Wiley, 1980.

Van Meter, D. S., and Van Horn, C. "The Policy Implementation Process: A Conceptual Framework." *Administration and Society,* 1975, *6,* 445–488.

Verba, S., and Nie, N. H. *Participation in America: Political Democracy and Social Equality.* New York: HarperCollins, 1972.

Von Oech, R. *A Whack on the Side of the Head: How to Unlock Your Mind for Innovation.* New York: Basic Books, 1983.

Wallace, D., and White, J. B. "Building Integrity in Organizations." *New Management,* Summer 1988, *6*(1), 30–35.

Warren, R. B., and Warren, D. I. *The Neighborhood Organizer's Handbook.* South Bend, Ind.: University of Notre Dame Press, 1977.

Waste, R. J. *The Ecology of City Policymaking.* New York: Oxford University Press, 1989.

Watzlawick, P., Weakland, J., and Fisch, R. *Change, Principles of Problem Formation and Problem Resolution.* New York: Norton, 1974.

Wechsler, B., and Backoff, R. W. Dynamics of Strategy Formulation in Public Agencies." *Journal of the American Planning Association,* 1987, *53,* 34–43.

Weick, K. *The Social Psychology of Organizing.* (2nd ed.) Reading, Mass.: Addison-Wesley, 1979.

Weick, K. "Small Wins: Redefining the Scale of Social Problems." *American Psychologist,* 1984, *39*(1), 40–43.

Wetherbe, J. C. *Systems Analysis and Design: Traditional, Structured, and Advanced Concepts and Techniques.* (2nd ed.) St. Paul, Minn.: West, 1984.

Whetten, D. A., and Bozeman, B. "Policy Coordination and Interorganizational Relations." In J. M. Bryson and R. C. Einsweiler (eds.), *Shared Power: What Is It? How Does It Work? How Can We Make It Work Better?* Lanham, Md.: University Press of America, 1991.

Wholey, J. S., and Hatry, H. P. "The Case for Performance Monitoring." *Public Administration Review,* 1992, *52*(6), 604–610.

Widener, R., and others. *Divided Cities in the Global Economy: Human Strategies.* Columbia, S.C.: PASRAS Fund, 1992.

Wildavsky, A. *Speaking Truth to Power.* Boston: Little, Brown, 1979.

Wildavsky, A. *The Politics of the Budgetary Process.* (4th ed.) Boston: Little, Brown, 1984.

Amherst H. Wilder Foundation. *Strategic Plan.* St. Paul, Minn.: Amherst H. Wilder Foundation, 1993.

Wilson, J. Q. "Innovation in Organizations: Notes Toward a Theory." In J. D. Thompson (ed.), *Approaches to Organizational Design.* Pittsburgh, Pa.: University of Pittsburgh Press, 1967.

Wilson, J. Q. *American Government: Institutions and Policies.* Lexington, Mass.: Heath, 1986.

Wilson, J. Q. *Bureaucracy.* New York: Basic Books, 1989.

Winer, M., and Ray, K. *Collaboration Handbook.* St. Paul, Minn.: Amherst H. Wilder Foundation, 1994.

Wittrock, B., and de Leon, P. "Policy as a Moving Target: A Call for Conceptual Realism." *Policy Studies Review,* 1986, *6*(1), 44–60.

Wolman, H. "The Determinants of Program Success and Failure." *Journal of Public Policy,* 1981, *1*(4), 433–464.

Yin, R. K. "Life Histories of Innovations: How New Practices Become Routinized." *Public Administration Review,* Jan./Feb. 1982, pp. 21–28.

Zaltman, G., Duncan, R., and Holbek, J. *Innovations and Organizations.* New York: Wiley/Interscience, 1973.

NAME INDEX

A

Aburdene, P., 87
Ackerman, D., 02, 05
Ackermann, F., 22, 34, 55, 104, 217, 257–275
Acomb, B. L., 140, 176
Adams, J. D., 107, 137, 153
Agor, W. H., 114
Agranoff, R., 250
Albers, A., 130, 131
Albert, S., 50, 238
Allio, R. J., 40, 194
Alston, F. K., 44, 57, 80, 114, 143, 144, 164, 178, 179, 290
Alterman, R., 183, 223–224
Anderson, J. E., 183, 205
Angelou, M., 229, 241
Ansoff, I., 30
Armknecht, P., 16
Arthur, M., 157, 163
Ashford, S. J., 31, 222

B

Bachrach, P., 225
Backoff, R. W., 3, 6, 7, 23, 28, 47, 52, 74, 86, 94, 96, 104, 105–106, 110, 118, 122, 131, 152, 175, 198, 218, 247, 249, 250, 251, 255, 276, 277, 279, 284–286, 291
Baratz, M. S., 225
Barber, B., 89
Bardach, E., 178, 254
Baron, D. P., 225

Barry, B. W., 6, 7, 111, 118, 144, 151, 175, 240, 276, 279, 282
Bartlett, C. A., 68, 169
Bartunek, J., 31
Barzclay, M., 27, 190, 201
Beard, C., 189
Behn, R. D., 53, 78, 167, 205, 206, 231
Bellman, G. M., 98, 153, 217
Below, P. J., 140, 176
Bendor, J. B., 205
Bentley, T., 217–218
Benveniste, G., 13, 49, 53, 68, 205, 225
Berger, P. L., 113
Berger, R. A., 156, 293
Berra, Y. 67, 87
Berry, F. S., 7
Blake, W., 140, 175
Block, P., 53, 227
Boal, K. B., 66, 106, 137, 222, 223
Bolan, R. S., 42
Bolman, L. G., 223
Boschken, H. L., 27, 70, 194, 276, 278
Bourgeois, L. J., III, 156
Bowman, A. O., 23, 168, 174, 179, 181, 254, 288
Boydston, R., 152, 171, 172
Boyte, H. C., 89, 221
Bozeman, B., 40, 52, 174
Bracker, J. S., 5, 132
Brand, R., 27, 53, 73
Braybrooke, D., 9, 89, 172
Brett, J. M., 51, 69
Brickman, P., 106, 223

Bromiley, P., 50, 67, 77, 105, 168, 184, 218
Brown, S., 273
Bruno, A. V., 29, 84, 247, 290
Bryant, J., 175
Bryson, J. M., 4, 6, 13, 16, 19, 22, 23, 31, 34, 35, 37, 42, 44, 49, 50, 51, 55, 57, 62, 63, 66, 67, 71, 74, 77, 80, 83, 88, 92, 105, 106, 111, 113, 114, 122, 127, 137, 143, 144, 145, 147–148, 150, 151, 153, 164, 167, 168, 169, 172, 174, 175, 177, 179, 180, 183, 184, 194, 198, 212, 215, 217, 218, 222, 223–224, 225, 226, 234, 238, 250, 252, 254, 258, 262, 275, 277, 290, 293
Bunch, C., 211, 212
Burke, E., 202
Burns, J. M., 64, 68, 89, 212, 223, 224, 225
Buzan, T., 218, 255, 257

C

Calista, D. J., 167, 168, 174
Campbell, D. T., 185
Carver, J., 61, 89, 173, 230
Chakravarthy, B., 148
Champy, J., 27, 73, 88, 132
Chase, G., 167, 168, 176
Christensen, K. S., 38, 218
Cleveland, H., 3, 9, 50, 88, 190, 222, 250
Clore, G. L., 97–98, 105, 272
Cobb, R. W., 252, 253

313

SUBJECT INDEX